D1489176

Women returning to work : an evaluation
of policies and programs in five
countries / edited by Alice M.
Yohalem ; foreword by Eli Ginzberg.
-- Montclair, N.J. : Allanheld,
Osmun, c1980.
xii, 292 p. ; 24 cm. -- (Conservation
of human resources series ; 12)
(LandMark studies)

WOMEN RETURNING TO WORK
Policies and Progress in Five Countries

Reports by researchers in France, Sweden, West Germany, the United Kingdom and the United States analyze recent reentry trends according to population characteristics, reasons for exit from and return to work, and incentives and disincentives to return. Institutional programs to facilitate reentry are evaluated and means of increasing their scope and effectiveness are suggested. The need for assistance to women returning to work is examined in the wider context of the need to provide general full employment.

Conservation of Human Resources Series: 12

OTHER VOLUMES IN THE
Conservation of Human Resources Series

WOMEN RETURNING TO WORK

Policies and Progress in Five Countries

Edited by
ALICE M. YOHALEM

Foreword by Eli Ginzberg

LandMark Studies   **ALLANHELD, OSMUN** Montclair

ALLANHELD, OSMUN & CO. PUBLISHERS, INC.
Montclair, New Jersey

Published in the United States of America in 1980
by Allanheld, Osmun & Co. Publishers, Inc.
19 Brunswick Road, Montclair, New Jersey 07042

Library of Congress Cataloging in Publication Data

Main entry under title:

Women returning to work.

(Conservation of human resources series ; 12)
      Includes bibliographies.
      1. Women—Employment—Case studies.   2.   Labor
mobility—Case studies.   I.   Yohalem, Alice M.
II.   Series.
HD6053.W64   331.4   79-55819
ISBN 0-916672-51-4

Printed in the United States of America

Contents

Tables and Figures

Figures

Contributors

Alice M. Yohalem is Senior Research Associate, Conservation of Human Resources, Columbia University. Her research interests have been primarily concerned with the social and economic status of women and ethnic minorities, and with health policy. Publications related to the subject of this inquiry include *Life Styles of Educated Women* (1966), *Educated American Women: Self-Portraits* (1966), *Corporate Lib: Women's Challenge to Management* (1973), and *The Careers of Professional Women: Commitment and Conflict* (1979).

Eli Ginzberg is Director of the Conservation of Human Resources Project at Columbia University, where he is Hepburn Professor Emeritus of Economics. He is also Chairman of the National Commission for Employment Policy. Dr. Ginzberg is the author or coauthor of and the contributor to numerous books dealing with various aspects of human resources. Of particular relevance to the present work are *Womanpower* (1957), *Work in the Lives of Married Women* (1958), *Life Styles of Educated Women* (1966), *Educated Women: Self-Portraits* (1966), *Career Guidance* (1971), *The Manpower Connection: Education and Work* (1975), and *Good Jobs, Bad Jobs, No Jobs* (1979).

Geneviève Gontier is a research technician at Centre d'Études de L'Emploi. Recent publications include "Les Désirs de Travail des Femmes Mariées," *Population* (1969); La Carrière Universitaire des Étudiants, *No. Spécial 1970 de Population*, "L'Attitude des Familles d'Agriculteurs Devant la Migration Professionnelle," *No. Spécial 1971 de Population; and "Les Ouvriers Vieillissants de la Région Parisienne," Cahier No. 17 du C.E.E.* (1978). She is presently engaged in a study entitled "Études sur la Diversification de l'Emploi Féminin en France: Les femmes formées à des métiers traditionnellement masculins."

Christina Jonung is a researcher at the Department of Economics at the University of Lund. Her research interest has focused on the labor market situation of women, and she has published several articles in Swedish on the subject. Her publications in English are "Sexual Equality in the Swedish Labor Market," *The Monthly Labor Review* (October 1978); and "Policies of Positive Discrimination in Scandinavia in Respect to Women's Employment," *Research Series of the International Institute for Labor Studies* (1979). She participated in the German Marshall Fund project on women and social security and wrote the Swedish commentary (*Working Paper 5069-01,* The Urban Institute).

Annie Labourie-Racape is Director of Research at the Centre d'Études de l'Emploi. Among her recent publications are "La Structure de l'Emploi Féminin Dans Trois Zones: La Rochelle, Limoges et Montlucon" (1971); "Formations, Emplois et Carrieres des Femmes en France," *Séminaire International Sur l'Emploi Féminin*—O.I.T., Turin (1974); "Activité Feminin et Structure des Emplois," *Cahier no. 6 du C.E.E.* (1974); and "Activité Féminine: Enquête sur la Discontinuite de la Vie Professionnelle," *Cahier No. 11 du C.E.E.* (1977). She is currently engaged in "Recherches sur les Carrières Féminines dans la Banque en France, au Royaume Uni et aux État-Unis" in collaboration with the London School of Economics, and "Études sur la Diversification de l'Emploi Feminin en France: les femmes formées à des métiers traditionellement masculins."

Monika Langkau-Herrmann is a research worker in the Research Institute of the Friedrich-Ebert-Stiftung. She is a graduate in sociology and her dissertation was entitled "Differences in the Reaction of Female and Male Workers to Working Conditions." She is primarily involved in labor market research, especially problems of the integration of women in the labor market, urban and regional science, and investment decisions of enterprises.

Jochem Langkau is Division Head in the Research Institute of the Friedrich-Ebert-Stiftung. He is responsible for labor market research and sectorial and regional economic policy. His research interests include labor market studies and predictions, social policy, regional science, regional economic policy and foreign workers in the Federal Republic of Germany.

Sheila Rothwell researched and lectured in industrial relations and personnel management at the London School of Economics before becoming Assistant Secretary (Negotiations) of the National Union of Bank Employees. She joined the Equal Opportunities Commission when it was set up in 1976 and became Assistant Chief Executive. She has recently joined the Henley Administrative Staff College, as Inbucon Fellow, where she is involved in management teaching and research in the Centre for Employment Policy Studies. Publications have included "Recent Trends in Collective Bargaining in the U.K.," *International Labour Review*, (1972); and contributions to the Report of the House of Lords Select Committee on the Anti-Discrimination Bill (1973), for which she acted as Research Secretary; E.E.C. Report on Employment of Women in U.K. (1975), "Health and Safety: Should We Distinguish Between Men and Women?", *E.O.C. Report.*

Bodil Thordarsson is a member of the faculty of the Department of Economics at the University of Lund. Her main area of teaching has been labor market issues and policies. Her present research concerns labor-managed firms.

Preface

This study grows out of the interest of the German Marshall Fund of the United States in sponsoring policy research concerned with the changing role of women in advanced industrial nations. Dr. Harvey Brooks, the former chairman of the board, and Robert Gerald Livingston, president of the Fund, played important roles both in eliciting the participation of the Conservation of Human Resources Project, Columbia University, in this inquiry and in helping to shape and support it.

The Conservation Project's positive response grew out of its long-term interest and involvement in delineating the enlarged role of women in the United States labor force, an interest which began when I prepared planning papers for the Executive Office of the President that pointed up the potentially critical role of women in the mobilization of the economy in World War II. Since then, we have undertaken research into the changing relationship between women and work in each of the postwar decades. The most recent effort was Alice Yohalem's study, *The Careers of Professional Women: Commitment and Conflict*, published in 1979.

Plans for comparative studies by several contributors will succeed or flounder on the selection of collaborators. We were fortunate in receiving the assistance of Beatrice Reubens, Graham Reid, and Isabel Sawhill and the staff of the German Marshall Fund, in identifying possible collaborators in each selected nation and in helping us to persuade them to participate in this joint effort.

The effective starting date of the project was April 1978. In May of that year, the participants met for two days in Paris to review and discuss all facets of the inquiry. At that time, it was the unanimous opinion that the term "mature" women in the original title should be discarded since it implied sole attention to reentrants in their middle or later years, an investigation which seemed too narrow in view of the increasing numbers of younger women who were reentering the work force.

If it is to succeed, a cross-national study must contain an appropriate balance between common coverage of the key themes and consideration of each country's unique history and development. In the present inquiry, the collaborators agreed that each of the reports would include the following elements: the dimensions of the outflow of women workers from the labor force and of women's reentry and delayed entry to work; the special problems encountered by different groups of reentrants; programmatic responses to these problems, both specifically and within the framework of national manpower policy; and recommendations aimed at facilitating reentry. Each contributor was free to handle the subject in the manner that best fit into her or his analytic framework and that would optimize the extant statistical data.

The editors persuaded their European collaborators that the joint undertaking would be much stronger if, in addition to the statistical and institutional analyses, a limited number of interviews were conducted in each country to deepen the understanding of how different groups of women dealt with the problem of reentry. Some quotations and summaries of interview findings are included in the report.

Marion Bieber, the German Marshall Fund's representative in Paris, assumed the task of arranging the Paris meeting of the study participants, and Christina Graf served as project officer. We are deeply indebted to both for their assistance at various stages of the inquiry.

I would like to make clear the heavy involvement of my colleague Alice Yohalem. While I was engaged at every stage of the undertaking, it was Ms. Yohalem who was responsible, on a day-to-day basis, for keeping the inquiry on the tracks.

Last but not least, I wish to express my appreciation to the participants in this study for their interesting and comprehensive reports, which I believe make valuable contributions to the understanding of a serious and widespread problem and offer many sensible recommendations for solutions.

Eli Ginzberg, Director
Conservation of Human Resources

Columbia University
July 1979

1

Foreword

by ELI GINZBERG

INTRODUCTION

To resolve analogous problems, cross-national social research can facilitate the analysis of approaches followed by selected countries. Its principal aim is to provide information which will enable nations that currently or potentially face similar problems to judge the applicability of alternative resolutions to the challenges which they face. The problem on which this study is focused has arisen as the result of the increasing propensity of adult women to reenter or belatedly enter the labor force, a phenomenon common to the countries under scrutiny—the Federal Republic of Germany, France, Sweden, the United Kingdom, the United States—as well as to virtually all other advanced industrial nations. This alteration in female behavior has added a new component to the employment problems of these nations, and the difficulties encountered by adult women in obtaining jobs after periods of nonwork activity have provoked demands for policies and programs to aid and abet their reentry. The ways in which each of these countries has responded to pressures for assistance to reentrants is the central theme of this inquiry.

The entry of long-time homemakers to the labor force has been the major element in the transformation of the labor forces of industrialized countries since World War II. Modifications in women's expectations which de-emphasize the centrality of their family role point to profound and probably irreversible changes in social structures and in the functional assignments of men and women.

1

In the past, female labor force participation generally peaked at ages 20 to 24 years, followed by a progressive decline as marriage and childbirth depleted the ranks of women workers. In recent years, however, the pattern of participation in most developed countries has assumed a new shape as increasing numbers of older married women have entered or reentered the labor force. In most countries, instead of a one-time peak following school completion, there is a second, lower peak at ages 35 to 40, or thereabout. In Sweden, the female participation rate at ages 35 to 44 is even higher than their 20- to 24-year level; and in the United States, the characteristic M-shaped curve has flattened due to reduced withdrawal in the twenties and a plateau in work participation among women between the ages of 25 and 44.

At the same time that women's work activity has been rising, that of men has been steadily decreasing due to declining participation of the young, resulting from lengthened schooling, and of the older group, because of early retirement. Hence, the traditional gap between male and female labor force participation rates has been narrowing in many developed countries.

While the proportion of older married women in paid employment varies considerably in developed countries, the trend to higher participation is sufficiently pervasive to reflect underlying influences that transcend national boundaries. In each of the countries in this survey, efforts have been made to respond to the changed work aspirations of adult women, although more recently some of these efforts have been directed to slowing their entrance into the labor force. The several approaches reviewed in these reports illuminate the pressures and conflicts that have arisen in the wake of the attempts of mature women to develop a new role for themselves in the world of work and the impediments that they are likely to encounter in realizing this goal.

INFLUENCES ON REENTRY

The recent change in the role of work in the life cycle of women has multiple roots. The most common explanation is financial need, a powerful but not inclusive theory, for it fails to account for the fact that numbers of adult women have always needed additional income but were unable to satisfy this need through gainful employment. The preconditions for expanded reentry are to be found in changes in the labor market, in the larger society, and in women's own lives. Apart from idiosyncratic factors, the following elements have stimulated reentry to a greater or lesser degree in each of the countries included in this study. Shortages of young female entrants during the first two postwar decades created job opportunities for middle-aged married women that had not previously existed. The accelerated growth of the service sector resulted in an expansion of public and private jobs in such traditional female occupations as clerical work, retail sales, personal services, education and health care. Early marriage and early family formation reduced the pool of single women, the conventional source of supply for female jobs, and opened opportunities for middle-aged women. Only in Germany did the rise in adult female work rates fail to match the sharp decline of teenage female workers, because employment in the service sector has grown relatively slowly, about 17 percentage points below that of the United States, which has the highest rate of service employment (66 percent) among these five countries.

The shrinkage of the agricultural sector accompanied by a growth of urban agglomerations placed more women within reach of newly expanding employment opportunities. The United Kingdom and the United States have the lowest proportion of employment in agriculture (under 4 percent), but all five countries have experienced marked declines in the proportion of farm workers.

A substantial proportion of new opportunities for women consist of part-time jobs developed in part to attract married women into the labor market while allowing them time to meet their homemaking responsibilities. The increased availability of labor-saving appliances in the household lightened their housekeeping burdens. Moreover, fewer children, born in the early years of marriage, shortened the years mothers allocated to child care and facilitated women's early reentry to the labor market.

More women became heads of household because of increased marital disruptions and births out-of-wedlock and, as a consequence, had to assume the primary burden of family support. Recently, inflationary trends have led more and more wives to seek employment in order to supplement their husbands' earnings and thus help to maintain their families' standard of living. While married women tend to slow their labor force entry during recessions because of decreased job opportunities, a longer period of economic slackness intensifies pressures upon wives to obtain employment.

The lengthening of the years of women's schooling and their increased acquisition of specialized training have enhanced their potential earnings, thereby encouraging them to maximize their time in the labor force. Furthermore, the elongation of education has reduced the participation of young females in the labor force, thus expanding the demand for older women.

Such factors as increased societal sensitivity to sex discrimination in employment and the changing attitudes toward women's roles have also contributed to the greater participation of women in paid employment, but the stimulus has been mutual. Probably increased educational attainment has been the key factor since it has raised the career expectations of women, particularly those best able to articulate and publicize grievances about barriers and inequalities that continue to confront them.

In certain countries, expanded work activity among mature women can be traced to the greatly accelerated demand for workers during World War II. In other nations, the sharp postwar declines in the agricultural sector, a concomitant of expanding industrial development, initially acted to depress adult women's employment by precipitating the exit of many from unpaid family work without opening new opportunities due to their lack of qualifications or their distance from the expanding job centers. In these situations, reentry did not make much headway until further urbanization, relocation and rising living standards began to reshape women's aspirations, competencies and opportunities.

The checkered history of reentry in different nations suggests that structural alterations in each nation's economy were the root cause of women's changed work patterns. While altered personal circumstances undoubtedly encouraged women's affirmative response to increased job opportunities, absent demand, the number of mature reentrants would not have reached its current dimensions. Beyond poverty, a person's *need* to work is subjective, strongly influenced by living standards and personal qualifications; over the last generation, women's felt need to work has grown due to their increased desire for consumption goods and their higher level of education and skill. The rapid growth of the service sector was fortuitous, inasmuch as it offered many of them the opportunity to realize their expectations.

The receptivity of the labor market to adult women was the magnet for reentry, and they were attracted despite the mediocre nature of available jobs in terms of wages and benefits. At first, pressures for assistance in reentry were minimal because most women had no particular difficulty in finding a job, if not suitable employment. As time went on, however, it became clear that many reentrants were encountering problems that either discouraged them from job search or blocked their access to satisfactory jobs.

REENTRY PROBLEMS

Most middle-aged women who had worked briefly, if at all, before exiting from the labor force withdrew voluntarily at the time of their marriage or some time prior to the birth of their first child. That was the established pattern. Few women who were financially able to leave their jobs did so reluctantly. More relaxed attitudes which do not censure young mothers from continuing to work have developed in the wake of the feminist revolution, but they are too recent to have had much effect on the older generation. Reluctance to interrupt one's work and career for any length of time, however, is probably a major cause of decreased family size, since most women suspect that pursuing a career is not compatible with raising large families.

The persistence of financial disincentives and inadequate support systems for married women workers reflects the almost universal attitude toward culturally appropriate behavior, which views child-raising as a mother's first duty. Tax provisions often penalize families with working wives; child care facilities give preference to women in financial distress; and family allowances seek to tilt the incentive structure in favor of child rearing. At this time, the foregoing conventional biases are in subtle and often overt conflict with the new aspirations and desires of married women to remain in or return to work in their twenties or early thirties.

Governments have been slow to recognize this heightened interest of many women to return to work early, and even slower to revise their policies to facilitate this goal. This is not due so much to a lack of recognition of the change but to a reluctance to acknowledge it (because of the soft economy), reinforced by the strength of tradition. Except in Sweden, there is no national consensus about the desirability of assisting women to enjoy broadened options with respect to work. Consequently, tax, social security, and child care measures that would facilitate women's reentry have not been substantially adjusted. Equal employment opportunity laws, by themselves, are not directly responsive to this problem. Equal treatment in the labor market is not enough; equal access is the key.

In each of the five countries, the majority of women who enter or reenter the labor force after a period devoted to childrearing are able to do so without formal assistance. This has enabled policy-makers to underestimate the realities of the situation facing many potential reentrants. Women who are able to make their own way into the labor market comprise two groups: those whose skills, even if somewhat dulled, are in demand; and those who take low-paying jobs because they need the money and cannot afford an extended search. The first group, if they make a connection, are likely to do fairly well, but many of them could profit from a period of retraining and informed job search. Those forced to accept what is immediately available are likely to be caught in a situation where their potential is underutilized. The situation of the second group of reentrants is more serious, since these women tend to be among the least skilled and most needy returnees. The opportunity for subsidized training and other support services in place of immediate placement holds promise of providing many of them with eventual access to better jobs, of increasing their productivity, and of improving the possibility of a permanent attachment to work.

Part-time jobs, held out of necessity not desire, represent one form of underemployment. In Sweden, for example, female participation is so high that the current focus is upon improving the relatively inferior status of women who are in the market by expediting their transition from part- to full-time work. In all countries, part-time jobs rarely provide the income, fringe benefits and nonpecuniary advantages of full-time employment.

The availability of part-time jobs, however, is often crucial to the reentry decision and to maintaining continuity in work experience. The growth of part-time job opportunities has been a major factor in the parallel growth of the female labor force in all these countries except France, where the relative sparsity of part-time work has served to deter reentry. For women who do not have to provide sole or substantial family support, part-time work can be a satisfactory resolution to the dilemma of combining home and work responsibilities.

But such a solution runs afoul of the promotion of equal employment opportunities because part-time jobs, disproportionately filled by women, perpetrate the myth that women's labor force participation is peripheral and spurs occupational segregation. Yet, efforts to limit part-time jobs are bound to increase women's exits from the labor force and prolong their period of nonwork. A solution posed in the German report is to promote the introduction of more part-time jobs and/or an overall shortening of the workweek to enable both men and women better to meet their family and work commitments. In the long run, greater flexibility in work time might not only provide additional occupational choices for women but also contribute to ensuring tautness in future labor supplies. Since women do not appear to be responding to incentives to increase family size, their acceptance as a stable component of the regular labor force can simultaneously contribute to equal opportunity and to an adequate labor supply.

Nevertheless, as long as the better jobs are full-time jobs, many reentrants will view part-time employment as a temporary expedient. Thus, the better prepared they are at the time of initial reentry, the easier it will be for them to make an eventual transition to full-time work.

Regardless of the apparent ease with which most reentrants have been able to reattach themselves to the labor force, there is evidence that this group may represent the tip of the iceberg. Every country can point not only to unemployed reentrants but to sizable pools of women who are out of the labor force because they have been unable to find jobs or because they do not believe that their job search will be successful. Sweden's aggressive full employment policies are designed to minimize the number of discouraged workers, but in the other countries where unemployment has been rising steeply, any activation of the female reserve has been resisted because of the further disequilibrium that it would cause in the labor market. Since helping women who want and need assistance in order to prepare for a resumption or late entry into employment would stimulate their inflow, policymakers faced with rising unemployment have shown preference for other groups, such as regularly attached males. For example, the requirement of a period of unemployment prior to admission to training programs effectively debars potential reentrants who, by definition, are out of the labor force. Furthermore, constraints on public expenditures have restricted the number of persons accepted into employment programs, so that only a portion of those eligible are actually served. In many cases, only those reentrants who are heads of households are assisted.

In Sweden, this limitation does not apply since this nation's employment policies have been designed to eliminate the concept of the secondary worker. In that country, disincentives to work are principally confined to single mothers and wives in low-income families whose prospective earnings may not compensate them for lost benefits, day care costs, and time that they could put to alternative use. Conversely, in some countries, such as the United States, public policy is directed to "forcing" women on welfare to enter or reenter the labor force.

The availability of adequate support systems and the elimination of financial deterrents to work are of equal concern to the young woman, who is attempting to maintain her ties to work, as well as to older women, who are planning to return to work or belatedly to enter the labor market. Most problems that set reentrants and delayed entrants apart from women with continuous work histories stem from their absence from the labor force. When the considerations that originally motivated women to opt for homemaking rather than gainful employment change, i.e., their children are older, many may encounter special difficulties upon seeking to enter or reenter the work force.

The difficulties involve evaluating their job readiness, orientation to the work world, preparation for employment, and job placement. While most prospective entrants to the labor force require information, skill evaluation, and job search assistance, extended absence from the labor force and prolonged disuse of job-connected skills place many reentrants in particularly disadvantaged positions. Additionally, they are often psychologically unprepared to assume a work role because of uncertainty about their reception in the work force, their unfamiliarity with the workplace, and their anxiety about being able to combine work and family responsibilities. Hence, their principal need is for specialized counseling to provide them with an accurate evaluation of their job potential, psychological support for their work decision, and assistance in negotiating the training structure and the labor market.

Because of universal inadequacies of data collection, it has not been possible to arrive at authoritative estimates of the numbers of women who reenter the labor force after a lengthy separation, nor of the proportion who have been assisted in making the transition from home to market. While large numbers of reentrants, as noted above, have made the shift without the intervention of third parties, this does not necessarily argue for a do-it-yourself approach. Some are too timid to try; others try and fail; still others settle for work below their capacity and potential.

THE CLIMATE FOR INTERVENTION

The attitudes and behavior of such key groups as employers, trade unions, government, and social welfare organizations in facilitating adult women's entry or reentry to the labor force are affected by their preconceptions about which groups should receive priority assistance and by the general conditions of the labor market.

In advanced industrial countries, the prime work force consists of adult males between the ages of 20 and 55. When the labor market weakens and members of this group work on reduced schedules, are placed on furlough, or are provided with relief work or income transfers, employers, trade unions and government authorities focus their efforts on returning these men as quickly as possible to full-time employment. Also singled out for priority assistance are youth, males primarily, who have reached working age. Young persons customarily have higher rates of unemployment than adult workers, and all of the countries in the study have recently experienced a rise in teenage unemployment. In the United States and increasingly in the United Kingdom, minority youth are a major problem; on the continent all unemployed youth are viewed as a threat to social stability.

The recent acceleration of inflationary pressures has led to budgetary stringencies that have set rigid limits on new public expenditures for job training, job creation, and related social services (such as the expansion of child care facilities). Males generally have preference for available training and retraining opportunities, and ceilings or reductions have been placed on social welfare expenditures that might facilitate the reentry of women. Hence, the environment at the beginning of the 1980s is no longer as receptive to encouraging a large-scale inflow of mature women into the labor force as in the 1960s.

In some countries, there has been a growing concern, about sharp declines in birth rates. Accordingly, governments are experimenting with neo-natal policies which, if successful, would be a deterrent to women's resumption of work. It would be naive to underestimate the extent to which the machinery of the labor market and new concerns about a declining population have had an adverse effect upon the movement to enlarge the scope of women's rights and options. Conservatives may have stilled their misgivings in the face of unmet requirements for female labor and the desire of families for more income and a higher standard of living, but now that the advanced economies are experiencing difficulties in providing regular employment for male heads of household and for young men entering the work force, opposition to equal employment opportunity has intensified.

Nevertheless, it is difficult to see how the cumulative changes that have occurred in the role of women in modern societies can be reversed. While one or another factor that helped to transform the conventional role of women and to expand their options may temporarily be weakened, such a development will have, at most, a limited effect. Barring a drastic reorientation of social values, the changes that paved the way for women's increased work activity should quicken as younger generations of females, less bound by tradition, assert their claims. Even in the face of recent adverse economic trends and a retardation in public expenditures, adult women are continuing to reenter the work force, although at a rate that differs from one nation to the next.

These differing rates are the ultimate manifestations of national perceptions and actions toward the reentry process. While each of the five countries surveyed has initiated social policies with the explicit goal of fostering equality in the work place, with one exception, programmatic response and administrative enforcement has rarely been as vigorous as statutory pronouncements. Only in the case of Sweden has a national commitment to equality been effectively translated into reforms that govern the range of social relationships between men and women at home and in the labor market. Uniquely, the Swedish contribution to this report describes government policy as designed to "induce" women to enter the labor force.

Although Sweden has encountered obstacles in realizing this commitment, due to the persistence of traditional social attitudes and modes of behavior and to the high costs of providing auxiliary services to foster women's employment, the high rate of labor force participation of females of all ages is due in large measure to special incentives to women to retain or quickly resume their ties to the work force. It may take decades before the requisite infrastructure for true equality between the sexes is in place but, as of now, it appears that a nonreversible decision to move in this direction has been made.

In the other countries, the stance toward reentrants appears to range from neutrality to discouragement. Instead of governments' taking the lead, reentry has been a more or less spontaneous and autonomous decision, often without benefit of public support or patronage. Under such circumstances, to paraphrase Dr. Johnson, reentry may not be done well, but one is surprised to find it done at all!

A simple explanation for the differences between Sweden and the four other countries would direct attention above all to its relatively small and homogeneous population and a political consensus that for a long time has been generally supportive of social reform. Moreover, government, labor and employers often collaborate as partners, so that the initiation and execution of social policy is more coherent than in larger countries.

Despite significant differences in attitudes and behavior toward the return of mature women to work, France, Germany, and the United Kingdom demonstrate several elements in common. Each of these countries gives priority in practice to programs for unemployed and unskillled youth and adult males and to persons seeking upgrading in skills in high demand. Such programs usually offer benefits that include compensation for earnings loss, social insurance coverage, travel expenses, and household maintenance. Facilitating the reentry of adult women is not deemed worthy of special assistance. Despite increases in the work activity of adult women in these nations, they are still regarded as a peripheral labor supply that can be adjusted to fluctuations in demand. Together with policies aimed at opening and closing the spigot controlling the flow of guest workers, women remain the major balance wheel.

The pattern of female labor force participation in the United States resembles that of Sweden, insofar as there has been a sharp rise in women's work activity followed by a decline of exits from the work force during the childbearing years. The job market, which has been expanding rapidly since 1975, has seen a continuing disproportionate increase of women among the additions to the work force.

Since 1977 when President Carter entered the White House, the United States has expanded rapidly its expenditures for manpower training and public service employment. While women have participated broadly in both these programs, they have tended to be underrepresented in terms of their ratio among the unemployed and underemployed, and Congress has become increasingly restive about the assistance being offered those who need to become self-supporting.

Although the United States has established a series of measures to promote equal employment opportunity, they are not the equivalent of the national commitment to equality in all social relationships that underlies the Swedish model. Hence, while American women are not being actively discouraged from entering the labor force, they continue to be burdened with sex-linked inequities that prevent them from fully realizing their work aspirations.

NATIONAL INTERVENTIONS

Each of the reports provides the particulars of national labor market policies in response to the reentry or delayed entry process. While these responses reflect national choices which are themselves reflections of a country's values, political pressures, economic circumstances, resources, and demographic developments, certain common threads can be identified.

The reports indicate that facilitating reentry has three facets. The first involves the preconditions for employment, such as the establishment of more child care facilities and the removal of tax disincentives; the second relates to the provision of employment-related assistance such as guidance, training and placement; and the third pertains to measures affecting the level and allocation of labor market opportunities.

Preconditions for Reentry

Inadequate and costly day care arrangements, income tax penalties, and loss of entitlements are widespread inhibitors of women working. It would be incorrect, however, to assume that there would be a massive flow toward work in the absence of such deterrents, because many mothers would prefer to bring up their children themselves and, in the absence of financial need, delay reentry until their children no longer require continuing supervision.

Sweden's introduction of extended parental leave plus the option of working less than full time until a child's eighth birthday takes such preferences into consideration, although it also represents an accommodation to the inadequate number of child care places. It is instructive that France, with the most comprehensive publicly supported child care system, has a lower female labor force participation rate than the United States, where child care consists of fragmented ad hoc arrangements. One explanation for this difference lies in differential opportunity structures. No matter how favorable the preconditions for work may be, the lack of a strong demand for women workers in what they consider suitable jobs, both in terms of quality and scheduling, restricts reentry.

Ambivalence about exclusive attention to homemaking and child rearing creates enormous conflicts. Mothers are rewarded by family allowances or preferential tax treatment when they attend to wifely and maternal duties but are often penalized when they return to work. Moreover, the effective option of focusing on family-centered activities or on work is usually reserved to middle- and upper-class women who, freed of heavy pressures for income, can weigh what they prefer to do.

Increasing attention is being paid in Sweden, Germany and France to providing young working women with job protection during their child bearing period, but children are still quite young when the parent must return to work. While longer leaves may not be feasible in view of employers' staffing requirements, there is no evidence that a significant number of employers maintain contact with women who have left their employ to raise children in order to encourage their eventual return.

Reentry Assistance

The factors that lead to the decision to enter the market are of a different order than those that directly facilitate reentry. The major problems in the latter instance are twofold: limited access to opportunities for training or retraining, and insufficient attention to the orientation and support required to permit reentrants to evaluate their job readiness, learn about training and career opportunities, proceed confidently on job search, overcome anxieties, and deal with numerous job and family-related concerns. Despite lip service to equal employment opportunity, it is obvious that adult women continue to be regarded as an elastic labor supply that will automatically respond to the vagaries of demand. The lag between this perception and the development of new female attitudes and aspirations may turn out to be temporary, as more and more younger women seek to maintain close links to work. In the latter event, they will force a consideration of policies to help them realize their goal.

In the meantime, as long as the determination of recipients of government employment assistance remains family-based insofar as it favors household heads, wives are at a disadvantage in asserting a claim to reentry assistance. The Depression-inspired goal of spreading work has really never lost its hold on policy-making and, in most countries, women are not acknowledged as having the same claim to employment aid as their husbands, even when the latter are unemployed or underemployed and the woman's earnings could compensate in whole or in part for lost income.

Where public training programs are available to reentrants, they are rarely designed to serve this constituency alone. While some programs are focused on women, hardly any are limited to reentrants. Displaced homemakers in the United States are one exception, but women who have been deprived of income because of the loss of spousal support after many years of homemaking represent a singular group as a result of social security protection for wives.

Reentrants with access to training find that most programs, like the labor market itself, are largely segregated by sex, and this practice perpetuates occupational segregation. Recently, attention has focused on providing nontraditional training to women, but expansion has been slow because of the limited job openings; that which is available goes mostly to young women. Adult women generally have eschewed nontraditional training because they have been inculcated with conventional notions about the "proper" sex division of labor, both in and out of the work force.

Shortcomings in guidance were widely noted. These center around insufficient sensitivity to reentrants' special needs by employment service personnel, which has inhibited women from seeking assistance at the very place which should be their first point of renewed contact with the labor market. Where public policy is deficient, however, other mechanisms have often been developed in the private (voluntary and profit) sector that substitute for or complement public programs and, in certain instances, have become supported wholly or partially by public funds.

While employers have been willing to hire reentrants, relatively few have established special programs to assist this group, although reentrants are sometimes eligible to participate in programs available to all new female hires.

In most countries, trade unions are bastions of male supremacy, and only when government has taken the initiative with respect to equal opportunity have unions followed. Reentrants are in a particularly weak position because their relatively advanced years cause additional costs to employers to qualify them for deferred benefits.

Yet, despite the above-noted barriers and limitations, a range of innovative programs has surfaced that warrants consideration:

Preorientation programs that bring women up-to-date on labor market developments; provide them with occupational information on which to base their decisions about how to proceed; offer them opportunities to test their job readiness; and assist them in job search. In some countries, the absence of such government-sponsored programs has been ameliorated in part by services offered by voluntary providers, who often receive considerable public financial support, as in the case of associations in France where, in addition, "Retravailler" centers located throughout the country provide occupational information, guidance, and orientation exclusively for women returners. In the United States, similar organizations have emerged in the form of women's centers which primarily offer counseling and referral for training and placement.

Work experience and job orientation opportunities, usually subsidized, for women with practical skills who need to readjust to the workplace.

On-the-job training for women without skills or those whose skills are not in demand.

Expansion of apprenticeship opportunities for older women, particularly those with several decades of potential work life.

Counseling that not only pays attention to direct work-related problems but also deals with peripheral concerns that affect women's ability to deal with a renewed work role. These include financial problems, particularly with respect to tax obligations or benefits; alimony and child support; housing; social security, etc.

Attempts to motivate adult women to enter nontraditional occupations because of their superior earnings potential.

The provision of special programs for hard-to-employ reentrants to provide close supervision and support while the trainees work on projects specifically designed to develop saleable skills, positive work attitudes and eventual permanent placement.

In countries where nonworking women engage in volunteer work, attempts to capitalize on this experience by orienting volunteer-developed skills toward comparable market requirements.

Experimentation with job sharing and part-time career opportunities as transitional experiences during child rearing years, with the eventual option of continuing on a full-time basis.

An increasing commitment toward insuring the right to continuing training and education over a lifetime, especially in countries with relatively short periods of compulsory general education. Where the normal educational span is longer, as in the United States, there has been an expansion of opportunities for middle-aged homemakers to attend colleges and universities, including training in the liberal professions.

Attempts to translate homemaking skills into their labor market equivalents for use as job qualifications.

Manipulation of Demand

Job creation especially designed for the reentry population is a rarity. Sweden has taken some special initiatives to open opportunities for women, and these are often reentrants. American displaced homemaker programs have given attention to developing jobs that aim to utilize competencies developed in the home. These, like so many reentry jobs, have little present attraction and few future gains.

A policy of job creation for women through special subsidies and through plant location inducements is exclusively a Swedish phenomenon, except where on-the-job training subsidies are given for the hard-to-employ who may include some—but not many—reentrants. There is no question that in all countries, employers of large numbers of women may deliberately locate where a female labor force is available. Textile, apparel, and electronics manufacturing are examples. But such jobs frequently are low wage. In Sweden, locational subsidies are sometimes limited to employers' agreeing to open opportunities for women in nontraditional occupations.

Legislative commitments to equal opportunity have often been vitiated by the strength of the traditional ethos. Where progress has been made, young women and those already in the work force are the more likely beneficiaries, not middle aged homemakers. Adult women, because of early social conditioning, often defer to the prior claims of other groups, a sentiment that makes them ill-prepared to take action on their own behalf when they perceive the need for employment-related assistance.

RECOMMENDATIONS

Each chapter contains a series of proposals for improving the chances of reentrants and delayed entrants in specific nations. The following recommendations pertain to the major proposals and also include additional initiatives worthy of examination:

Since homemaking and child rearing confer social benefits and contribute to the gross national product, consideration should be given to certain forms of reward to mothers to facilitate reentry. One example is participation in the social security system (as is done in some countries) and/or in the unemployment insurance system during absences from work. In the latter case, benefits might be paid at the inception of job search. In addition, receipt of unemployment benefits would create eligibility for training programs that are now available only to the unemployed. A homemaker preference similar to veteran's preference might be worth studying and would counter women's criticisms of the latter as sex-biased.

Governments should consider foregoing inducements to increase fertility because they are unlikely to work unless women's access to education were restricted, a move that none is likely to propose. The more reasonable assumtion is that women will continue to have work aspirations, and accordingly the labor market should be restructured so that women are viewed as a normal component of labor supply.

Like any other large group, reentrants are diverse and require different types of assistance. Flexibility in programming is therefore essential.

Reentrants and delayed entrants who are most in need of assistance are the youthful hard-to-employ grown old. Women who have adequate educational qualifications and some work experience require training only if they seek to change occupations or to upgrade themselves. Updating may also be a factor but, at present, most reentrants have had work experience in female fields that have been shown to be easily resumed without further training.

Further training and continuing education is of value primarily to women with low qualifications (or none at all) or to professionals who wish to refurbish their skills. They appear to be of lesser value to other women who are job ready. Sweden's utilization of relief work as a countercyclical device can provide reentrants who are unable to find jobs with skill upgrading and work experience, which can improve their placement potential when the economy again moves ahead.

The principal form of assistance that argues for separate consideration of reentrants and delayed entrants to the work force is guidance and counseling, since relatively advanced age, remoteness from schooling and early work experience, and family responsibilities combine to present them with a series of problems unlike those confronting other job aspirants.

Child care systems are generally inadequate and, in any event, do not appeal to all mothers. It is possible that the establishment of high-quality centers with both a nurturing and educational component might encourage more mothers to use them. While such centers would be extremely expensive to operate, some of the costs might be balanced by the additional job opportunities generated—including jobs for reentrants.

Employers should explore the extent to which they could provide preferential employment opportunities for women who had previously been members of their work force but who had left to have and raise a child or for other family reasons. Such an approach might be mutually beneficial.

While women are exhibiting greater interest in paid work, men are tending to retire earlier. Of course, many women with interrupted work-lives cannot afford to retire early and may also be less jaded about work. But if the trend of males toward early retirement continues and low fertility persists, female reentrants may become a more attractive supply than at present, especially in occupations and industries where they have not heretofore been welcome.

Finally, it is important to recognize that improvements in reentry assistance do not of themselves enhance women's job opportunities. As the economies of industrial countries become increasingly open to both men and women workers, greater job competition between them is inevitable. Nontraditional training for women will be a frustrating exercise unless the job market is taut. Men will not surrender their hold on preferred occupations easily. If more men enter the service sectors dominated by women, the position of women workers could deteriorate by reducing their opportunities to obtain the preferred jobs. Reformulated, this means that broadened opportunities for women workers can never be dissassociated from improvements in the overall operations of the labor market. Only to the extent that the economy runs close to full employment and the proportion of good to poor jobs increases will opportunities for women workers, including reentrants, be improved.

2

Federal Republic of Germany

by JOCHEM LANGKAU and
MONIKA LANGKAU-HERRMANN

INTRODUCTION

Women reentering the job market are a problem group in the labor market
whose integration—according to the Labor Promotion Act of the Federal
Republic of Germany—is difficult under the usual labor market conditions
because they are either married or have, or have had, other reasons for
staying at home. Women who want to reenter the job market after an
employment interruption due to family obligations now have a particularly difficult time, given the current job shortage. In particular, prospects for
part-time jobs are practically nil. Consequently, women returnees currently are not finding a sympathetic hearing for their problems among
government officials, legislators, political parties, employers or workers.

The government's labor market policy in West Germany has set different
priorities. For the time being, the number one concern is unemployed
youth and unemployed males in the so-called active years, between the ages
of 25 and 45. For that reason, it is particularly important to point out the
long-term economic and social consequences which will be incurred if the
labor potential of reentrants, some of whom have above-average qualifications, is not utilized, and to devise strategies for a labor market policy which
would simultaneously create new job opportunities for them and provide
them with the means for a smooth reintegration into the labor market.

THE CURRENT AND FUTURE LABOR MARKET
SITUATION FOR WOMEN

Demographic Changes

The population of the Federal Republic of Germany has declined for some time. According to the currently available estimates, there will be approximately 4.7 million fewer inhabitants in 1990 than there were in 1976, among them approximately 2.7 million fewer women. This development is due to a decline in the birth rate which started in the middle of the sixties, falling from more than one million live births in 1965 to approximately 600,000 in 1975. The end of this decline, according to all currently available estimates, cannot yet be foreseen.

For the purposes of labor market policy, however, it is significant that the female population of employable age (20 to 60 years) will continue to rise until about 1990, because the large number of youths born in the postwar generation will still be entering the job market. This population group will increase by approximately 350,000, and their representation will rise from 63 percent to approximately 67 percent.

Labor Market Participation

In 1950, 8.5 million of the 27 million women in the Federal Republic were employed or were trying to find employment. This corresponds to a participation rate of 44 percent for 15 to 65-year-old women and a share of 36 percent of the total number of employed persons (Table 2.1). During Germany's reconstruction phase from 1950 to 1961, the women's participation rate rose to approximately 47 percent. There have been, however, only marginal changes in these rates since 1963, and the percentage representation of women in the labor force has remained almost unchanged since 1950.

Although the general participation level of women in the job market has hardly changed, over the last 10 or 15 years there have been changes in employment trends for certain groups of the female population which have led to considerable shifts in the composition of the female labor force. These shifts are mainly due to new trends among younger, older, and married women.

Young women between the ages of 15 and 20 are less frequently entering the job market and instead stay in school and obtain a qualifying education or vocational training. In 1950 and 1961 more than three-quarters of the girls of this age group were employed, compared to only 48 percent in 1976 and, according to predictions, as few as 38 percent in 1990. In other words, while the female population between the ages of 15 and 20 increased by about 27 percent during the last 15 years, the number employed or willing to work decreased by approximately 22 percent during that same period.

Table 2.1   Labor Force Participation Rates by Age, Sex, and Family Status, Selected Years, 1950–1990

Age	1950[a] Total	1961[a] Total	1961[a] Single	1961[a] Married	1961[a] Widowed/Divorced	1970[a] Total	1970[a] Single	1970[a] Married	1970[a] Widowed/Divorced	1976[b] Total	1976[b] Single	1976[b] Married	1976[b] Widowed/Divorced	1990[c] Total
Women (total)	44.2	47.2	81.7	34.9	39.7	46.2	69.9	39.1	43.3	48.3	62.7	43.9	45.5	48.5
15–20	76.7	78.2	79.5	55.0	58.3	64.4	64.9	58.2	–	47.9	47.2	59.9	–	38.0
20–25	69.9	71.9	90.4	49.0	77.1	67.1	84.4	54.2	79.2	68.8	74.9	62.6	80.6	64.0
25–30	50.1	50.7	91.4	39.0	73.5	51.5	88.9	44.0	79.9	57.8	83.0	52.1	79.2	56.0
30–35	40.2	44.6	89.9	36.2	71.7	44.9	89.2	39.1	76.5	51.8	87.4	47.3	77.1	51.0
35–40	36.7	46.3	88.8	37.9	67.5	46.1	88.2	40.8	70.3	51.0	87.4	46.9	74.2	52.0
40–45	35.9	45.4	86.3	37.8	56.1	48.1	87.8	42.0	71.8	51.3	88.1	46.8	72.8	55.0
45–50	36.4	42.3	82.3	35.6	46.7	48.4	86.4	41.4	64.9	50.9	88.6	45.3	69.0	53.0
50–55	34.5	38.1	77.3	31.7	38.5	43.0	81.6	36.5	52.8	48.1	85.8	40.9	60.0	50.0
55–60	29.8	32.8	68.8	26.6	82.3	34.7	74.7	28.7	39.1	38.3	77.5	31.4	42.7	40.0
60–65	20.8	20.9	40.4	18.4	17.8	17.8	37.6	15.1	22.3	14.7	31.7	12.7	14.0	15.0
Men (total)	92.4	91.7				89.3				85.0				84.1
15–20	84.5	81.3				66.9				52.8				40.0
20–25	93.2	91.1				86.8				79.9				70.0
25–30	94.4	96.2				94.0				90.6				88.0
30–35	96.4	98.3				98.1				96.9				97.0
35–40	97.3	97.8				98.4				98.4				98.0
40–45	97.2	97.1				97.8				97.9				97.5
45–50	96.7	96.1				96.2				96.8				96.0
50–55	93.5	93.8				93.6				93.3				93.0
55–60	87.5	88.7				87.3				85.4				85.0
60–65	73.2	72.3				69.4				52.3				57.0

Source: [a]Population census results 1960/1961 and 1970.
[b]Micro census results of May 1976.
[c]Prognos Company Basel: The Federal Republic of Germany in 1980, 1985, and 1990, Basel 1976.

These figures indicate not only an increasing willingness on the part of girls to obtain a qualifying education or vocational training, but also a more positive attitude on the part of parents towards better education and training for their daughters. The argument "a continuing expensive education for girls is not worth it since they will soon marry" seems to be on the wane.

While the number of female school graduates has increased by about 35 percent since 1960, the number of female graduates at the lowest possible level ("Hauptschule") has decreased; the number completing the middle level of education ("Realschule") has more than doubled; and the number of students graduating from the equivalent of college preparatory school (taking the "Arbitur" exam) has more than tripled. Almost half of the graduates from all of these three types of schools are now female.*

Only about five percent of all current female graduates registered with the labor administration for job counseling because they wanted to be employed right away, compared to 12 percent in 1969 and 22 percent in 1950. This development has been caused not only by the desire for better education and training but also, over the last four years, by the increasing necessity for advanced education and training. With a decreasing number of available apprenticeships for girls and of jobs for young women, further education often is the only alternative to unemployment.

Regardless of whether it is the desire for education or the labor market situation which is predominant in this decision, the current short-term relief for the labor market due to this development is obvious and could even be increased by introducing one additional mandatory year of schooling. In addition, better-qualified women will probably have improved chances in the future when competing with men in a job market that cannot be expanded much further, and they will more likely show a greater interest in utilizing their higher education and training levels, especially on a more continuous basis, i.e. with as short an interruption as possible. Yet, since better education and training, which women were forced into by current labor market conditions, came about at the expense of business-based training, this development cannot be seen in an entirely positive light.

For more than 15 years, women have constituted only one-third of the persons in business training in the Federal Republic. While developments with regard to female education and training in general and their chances in the labor market have been very positive, the situation has not been as favorable with respect to business-based training. A strong representation of girls in this area might be achieved with current new approaches—there are signs of success here and there—to attract girls to business-based training; simultaneously, employers are trying to offer more apprentice-

---

*The overrepresentation of female graduates which is currently still noticeable at middle-level schools and teachers' colleges is gradually disappearing.

ships. When choosing business-based training, however, girls continue to concentrate on relatively few job categories, mainly those generally described as typically female. This serves to insure the current work segregation of women for years to come. Almost half of all women in training decide on one of only seven vocations: every fifth female wants to become a saleslady or beautician; every tenth a doctor's or dentist's helper or office worker. Men tend to choose from a much wider variety of jobs.

Both the lack and the concentration of female business-based training will remain definite obstacles in the competition for attractive, stable, and well-paid jobs. Promotional programs and projects on the government level, such as "females in male jobs," can for the time being provide only a stimulus and must be conducted on a broader base to be effective. Otherwise, the fact that more than 40 percent of all female workers have completed no vocational training cannot be altered.

Marital Status

The work patterns of married women have undergone the most lasting changes in the past 15 years. Since 1961, the married female population of working age has increased by more than five percent, but the number of employed married women between the ages of 15 and 65 has increased by nearly 36 percent. Hence, the participation rate of married women in this age group rose by nine percent from 35 percent in 1961 to the current 44 percent. All age groups between 20 and 60 years were affected by this development: in the middle 1960s, the ages 40 through 60, in particular; thereafter, increasingly, married women in younger age groups (Table 2.1).

A number of causes are responsible for this trend, which is likely to continue in the future. One reason is the regressive birthrate which has already been mentioned. Other reasons are: improved child care opportunities for preschool children; improved education and vocational training of women; dissatisfaction with the role of housewife, alone; more flexible role sharing between marital partners; a better supply of jobs, especially part-time jobs for women; mobilization of the so-called manpower reserves through government labor market policies which were instituted as a result of a labor shortage until around 1972; and last but not least, the desire of married women to become financially independent or to contribute to family income.

The question of an interdependence between birth rates and employment of married women is of central importance in the current debate concerning the consequences of a population decrease. In this context, it must be pointed out that the number of mothers with children under 15 years of age who have nonagricultural jobs increased from about 1.3 million in 1962 to 2.3 million in 1977 (over 78 percent), and the number of mothers with children under six years of age, from 670,000 to 800,000. The participation rate of these groups during that period went up from 33 percent to 39 percent, and from 29 percent to 34 percent, respectively. Lower birth rates, therefore, seem to be only one of the reasons for married women's increased interest in holding a job.

In this regard, one group of women is of particular significance and has, thus far, been neglected in the government's labor market policies—barring times of extreme manpower shortage—even though it was mentioned explicitly as a target group for the Labor Promotion Act, namely, women reentering the job market. They constitute the main contingent of the so-called silent labor market reserve.

The labor force participation curve of women, as in the past, is still an interrupted line with a dip, which is typical of the age-related employment patterns of married women. Employment among married women in age group 20 through 25 reaches its peak when their education and training is completed and then drops drastically until age 35—approximately the period of time needed for childbearing and child raising. The curve then stabilizes until around age 50, when it drops again.

German labor force statistics give some indication of how many women stopped working, when, for what reason, how many times, and for how long. It is very difficult to draw conclusions from these data, however, as to how many of them will return to work one day, or how many would like to return to work but are unable to do so for lack of employment opportunities, for example. The labor potential of women consists of employed women, registered unemployed women, and women who have not registered with the Federal Institution for Labor but would like to return to work. The latter group would, by definition, be included in the unemployment statistics of the microcensus because it lists not only those registered but also those who are looking for employment on their own. It also includes those women who are planning to resume work but have not yet actually started to look. The comparison of the unemployment figures of the Federal Institution for Labor and those of the microcensus, however, reveal lower figures in the latter, even though they should be considerably higher given the wide spectrum of women included in the microcensus. Therefore, neither the unemployment rate for women calculated on the basis of data compiled by the Federal Institution for Labor nor the rate of women without income calculated by the annual microcensus give us sufficiently accurate information about the utilization of the female labor potential, or the size of the so-called silent reserve.

Estimates of the number of women who are currently or will be looking for employment without registering with the public employment agency are available. The German Institute for Economic Research, for example, in its most recent labor market projection, estimated the current latent labor potential to comprise 700,000 persons, of whom 70 percent are women, and 600,000 in 1985. In most cases, however, it was impossible to ascertain how this information was obtained. These figures are probably too low rather than too high, and a rise rather than a fall in the silent reserve figures should be anticipated because of demographic developments and changes in the employment patterns of married women. But even when using these figures, the rate of registered unemployed women plus the silent reserve would rise from 6.3 percent to 12 or 13 percent for 1977, a figure which probably gives a realistic indication of the utilization of the female labor potential.

Because of the lack of a precise definition of who belongs in the silent reserve, not much is known about its social structure—with the exception of some individual studies or bits of information—nor about the specific obstacles women run into when looking for a job; why they do not register with the public employment agency; what their earlier experiences with the employment agency were; what the attitude of their husbands is or was with regard to their job search; what their age, work and qualifications are; etc.—information which is important for the development of concepts regarding the reintegration of these women into the labor market. Thus far, new efforts in research or policy formulation have been made in this direction in the Federal Republic of Germany only when it was necessary to mobilize the silent reserve as quickly as possible in times of an overheated economy combined with a great shortage of labor. Given the current labor market conditions, the policy makers and the labor administration do not like to be reminded of this subject.

Sectorial Changes

The change in the sectorial employment structure which has been noticeable in developed economies for quite some time, i.e. a relative employment decrease in primary agricultural and secondary industrial sectors and a relative increase in the services sector, has occurred in the Federal Republic of Germany with respect to the employment of women. Between 1950 and 1976, the total number of employed women increased by nearly 1.1 million, or 12.9 percent, but the number decreased in agriculture by two million, 70.6 percent (Table 2.2). During the same period, an additional 500,000 women who were employed in private households stopped working. Yet, despite this enormous reduction of manpower there still was, on balance, an increase in the female labor force that must be attributed primarily to the uninterrupted capacity to absorb of the service sector, trade, local authorities, credit institutions and insurance companies.

The recessive economic development since the "energy crisis" necessitates a separate examination of recent sectorial developments in the job supply for women in order to determine trend changes in the long term. It is particularly striking that, in addition to agriculture, considerably fewer women are employed in the processing industry; the labor supply for women in trade is stagnating; and private households are now employing more females. Credit institutions, the insurance sector, and local authorities are still expanding at a higher than average rate.

Table 2.2 Employed Females by Economic Sector, 1960–1976 (numbers in thousands)

Economic Sector	Employed Females								Female Share of Total Employment		Changes 1950–1976		Changes 1970–1976	
	1950		1961		1970		1976		1950	1976				
	Number	Per cent	Number	Per cent	Number	Per cent	Number	Per cent	Per cent	Per cent	Number	Per cent	Number	Per cent
Agriculture & Forestry, animal care	2848.6	33.6	1961.5	19.7	978.2	10.3	837.0	8.7	54.8	51.9	−2012	− 70.6	−141	− 14.4
Energy & water supply, mining	26.2	0.3	36.5	0.4	39.0	0.4	46.0	0.5	3.2	8.6	+ 20	+ 75.6	+ 7	+ 17.9
Processing	2044.1	24.1	3114.4	31.4	3150.6	33.3	2638.0	27.5	28.1	28.6	+ 594	+ 29.0	−513	− 16.3
Construction	62.4	0.7	83.0	0.8	125.0	1.3	147.0	1.5	3.4	8.2	+ 85	+ 135.6	+ 22	+ 17.6
Trade	898.4	10.6	1653.7	16.6	1714.3	18.1	1713.0	17.9	43.7	55.3	+ 815	+ 90.7	− 1	− 0.1
Transportation & communication	144.1	1.7	221.4	2.2	164.5	2.8	286.0	3.0	11.1	18.7	+ 142	+ 98.5	+ 21	+ 8.1
Credit & insurance	78.2	0.9	205.3	2.1	313.0	3.3	378.0	3.9	32.9	48.3	+ 300	+ 383.4	+ 65	+ 20.8
Services	1004.7	11.8	1791.9	18.0	2107.2	22.3	2503.0	26.1	51.6	61.8	+1498	+ 149.1	+ 396	+ 18.8
Miscellaneous organizations & private households	791.8	9.3	428.3	4.3	242.4	2.6	259.0	2.7	88.0	64.4	− 533	− 67.3	+ 17	+ 18.8
Local government & Social Security	322.5	3.8	394.5	4.0	503.8	5.3	700.0	7.3	23.0	27.5	+ 378	+ 117.0	+ 196	+ 38.9
Unspecified	264.7	3.1	41.0	0.4	15.3	0.2	73.0	0.8	52.3	43.2	− 192	− 72.4	+ 58	+ 377.1
Total	8485.6	100	9931.5	100	9453.3	100	9580.0	100	36.1	37.2	+1094	+ 12.9	+ 127	+ 1.3

Source: Population census 1950, 1961, and 1970 and the micro census of 1976.

Upon examination of the individual areas within the industrial sector, it is evident that, since 1970, the consumer goods industry which heavily employs women now employs fewer females, especially in leather, textile and clothing, food, tobacco, wine etc., while the demand for female employees by and large has remained stable in the investment goods industries, where electrical and mechanical engineering firms are even offering additional jobs to women. The fact that employment in private households is expanding is probably largely due to the existing generally precarious job market situation for women as a whole.

Sectorial restructuring processes during economic change are primarily caused by demand and price shifts in national and international product and production-factor markets as well as by technological changes in the production process. The causes of the considerable reduction in female employment in consumer goods are probably to be found largely in the trend in this economic sector to move more and more toward highly capital-intensive production processes in order to remain competitive on the international market. Past strategies of employing cheaper female labor in peripheral regions wherever possible are no longer rational because of the growing international wage differential. Limited mechanization and rationalization possibilities in various sectors of the investment goods industry due to its high proportion of assembly work, and in the services, have in the past provided additional work opportunities for women.

There is no conclusive answer to the question of whether women's jobs are more easily affected by economic structural changes, on the one hand, and declines in the economic cycle, on the other, than those of men. A much more differentiated analysis on the business and industry levels would be necessary. The sectorial structural changes—reduction of jobs in agriculture, forestry, and production, and expansion in the service sector—have, in the past, had the same impact on employees regardless of sex, with perhaps some deviations in point of time. It must be noted, however, that the growth rate of the labor supply of women was 12.9 percent from 1950 to 1976 and 1.3 percent from 1970 to 1976, considerably higher than that of men (7.8 percent in the earlier period and a reduction of 4.1 percent in the latter), so that, on balance, the expanding economic sectors were able to counterbalance the reduction of female employment more easily than of men. There is, however, a question as to how female employees, more than 40 percent of whom currently have not completed vocational training, will be able to compete in the labor market in the future if the economy of the Federal Republic should move toward specialization in producing internationally competitive goods and services of high technical quality. This would require higher vocational qualifications on the part of women than they have been able to offer thus far.

The theory that women's jobs are more affected by cyclical changes than men's is in question since the most recent recession. During the recession of 1966-68, the number of female employees dropped at a greater rate than that of male employees, and during the period of cyclical overheating in 1972-73 the growth rate of female employees was markedly higher than that of males (Table 2.3). These findings led to the conclusion that women were used by businesses, enterprises, and branches of economic activity as a cyclical labor market reserve. The recession years of 1975-77, however, showed a different trend. Relatively more male than female employees lost their jobs and, in 1976-77, more women were hired than men. This trend reversal may be, among other factors, a result of the restructuring process in the job market for women in the direction of the service sector which, in the past four years, has not been affected as much by cyclical changes as the industrial sector.

Occupational Distribution

The changes in the sectorial structure of the German economy have had and still have a major influence on the occupational distribution of employees. The number of female family members helping out in a family business decreased by 52 percent between 1961 and 1976, and there was also

Table 2.3   Unemployment Rates and Employment Development by Sex, 1950—1976

Year	Unemployed (000)		Unemployment Rate		Annual Rate of Change in Employment	
	Men	Women	Men(%)	Women(%)	Men(%)	Women(%)
1950	1,756	613	10.8	11.5		
1960	178	92	1.3	1.3		
1961	118	63	0.8	0.8	+ 1.8	0.0
1962	107	52	0.7	0.7	−0.9	−1.1
1963	130	55	0.9	0.7	+ 1.3	0.0
1964	115	54	0.8	0.7	−0.5	−0.2
1965	106	42	0.7	0.5	+ 1.0	+ 0.7
1966	117	45	0.8	0.6	+ 0.3	−0.5
1967	335	124	2.4	1.7	−2.4	−3.2
1968	235	88	1.7	1.2	0.0	−0.4
1969	125	54	0.9	0.8	+ 1.2	+ 1.1
1970	93	56	0.7	0.8	+ 0.9	+ 0.6
1971	101	84	0.7	1.1	+ 0.8	+ 0.7
1972	141	106	1.0	1.4	0.0	+ 2.7
1973	150	124	1.0	1.5	+ 0.2	+ 1.7
1974	325	258	2.2	3.1	−0.5	−0.8
1975	623	452	4.3	5.4	−3.8	−2.6
1976	567	494	3.9	5.8	−0.9	−0.6

Source: Compiled from publications of the Federal Institution for Labor and micro census results

a decrease in the number of self-supporting females from about 760,000 in 1960 to 490,000 in 1976. Both developments influence the unemployment rate for women, which is currently above average, and also the percentage of dependent women which rose from 71 percent in 1960 to 84 percent in 1976.

In 1961, only every third gainfully employed woman was a salaried employee; today it is almost every second. The percentage of female wage earners, on the other hand, dropped from 39 percent to 32 percent. The trend toward salaried positions may have brought with it improved working conditions, an increase in average income, and more job stability; however, among both salary and wage earners in the private and public sectors, women still hold lower or, at best, mid-level, positions. In 1969 as well as in 1970, 94 percent of all female industrial workers were classified as unskilled or semiskilled, and only five to six percent as skilled workers. In contrast, half of the male workers are skilled and their share is constantly increasing, while the share of unskilled male workers is decreasing.

The situation is similar, although not quite as striking, in the case of salaried employees. In 1976, 58 percent of all female salaried workers in industry did not have their own area of responsibility or decision making on their job compared to only 16 percent of the men. The current trend indicates improvement, however, since in 1960, 77 percent of all female salaried employees were in the lower positions. There is an analogous disproportion in the public sector: nine out of ten female civil service employees and salaried employees in Federal agencies are subclerical or clerical employees.

The reasons for the above-mentioned qualitative job deficits with regard to women are obvious. On the one hand, there is a frequent lack of interest on the part of private and public employers to hire women or to promote them to positions for which they are qualified; there is a preference for male applicants of equal or less-qualified status for employment or promotion. There is also limited vocational and geographical mobility among women due to their double burden of family and job. The most important reason seems to be women's earlier mentioned lack of education and business-based training and its one-sidedness. The consequence of these educational and training deficits, which have been noticeable for quite some time, is a persistently lower vocational qualification level and a concentration of women in a few job categories, resulting in greater susceptibility to economically induced shifts in the job market structure. Since 1950, the number of female workers in agricultural jobs decreased by 72 percent, the number of female office workers rose by 170 percent, the number of women workers in scientific and technical jobs (with a preponderance in health and education-oriented jobs) rose by 176 percent, and, in commercial jobs with an emphasis on sales, rose by 123 percent. The number of female workers in production jobs, on the other hand, is hardly changing at all, partly because of opposite developments—increases, for example, in electrical engineering jobs and decreases in textiles.

The development of the structural share is analogous. In 1950, only every tenth female employee was an office worker; in 1976, every fourth. In 1950 only every 17th female employee had a scientific-technological job, now it is every seventh. In 1950 every 16th female employee worked in the commercial sector, now every eighth. However, only every twelfth woman now works in an agricultural job, while every third did in 1950. The structural share in the services and production by and large remained unchanged during that period.

There was a similar trend in the restructuring process for male employees. In comparison to women, it is striking that in 1976 every second male employee, yet only every fifth female employee, had a production job, which in turn indicates that the service sector is and probably will remain the main employment area for women (Table 2.4). A particular reason for concern is the fact that a more differentiated analysis has determined that, in 1976, 63 percent of all female employees worked in only eight job categories. By contrast, the vocational spectrum for men is much wider. The concentration of women in certain job categories has, over the last 20 years, increased rather than decreased.

The trend toward jobs in the service sector must be considered a basically positive one, because it is the growing market in the Federal Republic; the jobs are less subject to cyclical changes; and work conditions are generally better. Female employees, however, find themselves increasingly exposed to the danger of not profiting from these advantages, or profiting only to a

Table 2.4   Female Employees in Total Employment by Job Category, 1950–1976

Job Category	Female share of total number of employed persons (percent)			
	1950	1961	1970	1976
Scientific, technical and related skilled work	36.1	34.0	36.3	40.0
Public, business, and industrial management	15.5	15.3	15.5	16.1
Office and related	44.2	55.9	56.8	59.1
Trade vocations	41.0	51.3	55.5	60.0
Service	67.6	67.3	53.0	53.3
Horticulture, animal husbandry, forestry, fisheries, and hunting	54.6	−54.0	47.5	49.7
Production and related, including transportation and handymen jobs	17.9	17.2	17.3	17.8
Other	73.2	77.3	76.3	53.1
Total	36.1	37.4	35.9	37.2

Source: Compiled from publications of the Federal Office of Statistics.

small degree, compared to men, because they work more and more frequently in the less-qualified and less well paid jobs in the service sector. These jobs, moreover, are constantly in danger of decline subject to rationalization trends and measures relating to work organization (e.g. office work, trade, postal office, and telecommunication jobs). The job range for women must become wider and more balanced in this area as well as in production occupations, and high qualification levels must be achieved.

Part-Time Employment

In the past 10 to 15 years, part-time employment for women has gained considerably in importance in the Federal Republic. At this time there are no sufficiently accurate statistics available covering this type of employment to make them accessible for labor market analyses. The main problem is that there is no agreement yet as to what constitutes part-time employment, and there are statistical differences with regard to the extent of part-time work depending on the definition used. The number of female employees who were working less than 40 hours during the week of the micro-census report has risen by 1.2 million since 1960, and their representation among all employed women accordingly has risen from 21 to 34 percent. During that same period, the number of women who worked less than 24 hours per week rose by .9 million, and their share of the total went from 11 to 20 percent.

Part-time jobs are concentrated in trade, particularly retail sales, services, the public sector, and cleaning jobs, all of which together supply 40 percent of total female part-time employment. The Federal Postal Service has the highest percentage of women part-time workers. Agriculture still constitutes an important area for part-time work. In the production sector, it is the electrical engineering, precision tool, and the leather, clothing and textile industries which are the main employment areas, comprising approximately 11 percent of all female part-time employees.

It is a well-known fact that current part-time work opportunities leave much to be desired with respect to cyclical and structural stability, quality, and opportunities for advancement. It is a matter of some concern that heretofore hardly any initiatives have been made on the part of either public or private employers to provide more high quality part-time jobs by applying new measures related to work organization or personnel planning. It is suspected that industry and the public sector, in particular, have hardly exhausted their potential for part-time jobs. These areas, therefore, could make a significant contribution toward the solution of current employment problems for women, since almost one-third of the women currently registered with the Federal Institution for Labor are interested in working part time.

The discrepancy between the supply of part-time jobs and demand is becoming larger all the time. There are currently only eleven part-time jobs available for every 100 part-time job seekers. In addition to the positive effects that an expansion of part-time work for women and men, as well as a generally shortened work week, would have on employment policies, there are also the socio-political advantages which would arise from a better distribution of the burdens of household and child rearing between marital partners, especially with regard to women reentering the job market.

Regional Imbalances

Women who live in densely populated, growing regions of the Federal Republic like Munich, Berlin, Hamburg, or in the agricultural regions in southern Germany, have a better chance of finding a job than women in the so-called old industrial regions, namely the Ruhrgebiet and the Saarland, where heavy industry is still predominant. Generally, one can speak of a distinct south-north slope in job opportunities for women. Studies have shown that the share of employed women is always particularly high when regions have a high percentage of jobs in sectors considered predominantly female. This femininity mix of the regional employment supply consists, in the large industrial concentration areas, mainly of the service and trade sectors and, in agricultural regions, mostly of agriculture, leather, textile, clothing and food, tobacco, wine, etc. Regional specialization will most likely cause problems in the future, especially for women in agricultural areas, because the agricultural sector will continue to become smaller and the other sectors mentioned above will have to compete increasingly on the international market and will stagnate or even regress in terms of employment.

Incentives to draw service businesses, especially those of the public sector (agencies, research institutes, etc.) into peripheral areas, as well as selective incentives for fast-growing industrial production plants, could contribute toward a long-term stabilization of employment opportunities for women in rural regions.

Income

The obstacles, adverse developments, and discrimination against women in the area of job supply and demand described above influence the average level of women's salaries and wages in relation to those of men. In 1960, the share of gross wages and salaries of female employees was less than one-quarter of total gross wages and salaries, even though women's share of total employment was 37 percent and their share of work hours was 35 percent. The average gross annual wages and salaries of women were 38 percent below those of men. These percentages were only slightly different for 1976, when the income share of female employees was 26 percent and the employment share 37 percent. By that year, their work hour share had dropped to 33 percent and the discrepancy in average gross wages and salaries to 34 percent.

According to recent studies, equally important causes for this gross income discrepancy included women's lower average weekly work hours, lower quality jobs, and concentration in economic sectors with low wage scales. When these influences are excluded, the result is a net income discrepancy of about 17 percent. This figure approximates the real rate of income discrimination given a work and activity structure of equal value.

The situation changed in 1976. The influence of increasingly lower average work hours for females on their average annual wages and salaries was three times as strong as differences in job quality and occupational concentration. If these differences are excluded, the result is a net income discrepancy of approximately eight percent. Actual income discrimination, given equal jobs and structures of activity, is therefore becoming less significant. In terms of incomes, women suffer the greatest amount of discrimination, at the moment, in the food, tobacco, wine etc. industry, in crafts, and in small businesses; the least amount in the public service sector.

There seems to be a substitution relationship between income discrimination—lower income for work of equal value—and job discrimination—lower job quality despite equal or better qualifications: the more difficult it is to pay women a lower income than men for work of equal value because of standard job categorization criteria, the more often they are pushed into lower and mid-level jobs in spite of equal qualifications. It seems to be possible for women to obtain better-qualified positions only in middle- and small-sized businesses (where there is much room for arbitrary determination of wage and salary categories) at the expense of an income which is lower than men would receive for equal work.

Growth Rates, Labor Market Situation, and Unemployment

The leading economic research institutes in the Federal Republic of Germany claim that an annual growth rate of the actual gross domestic product of more than 4.5 percent must be achieved by 1990 if current unemployment of approximately one million per year, on the average, is to be reduced. This growth objective cannot be reached under current conditions, and it is more likely that average growth will range from 2.5 to 3 percent in the next few years. According to recent labor market predictions of the German Institute for Economic Research, this means that, in 1985, there probably will be around two million known and .6 million hidden unemployed.

In terms of job opportunities for women this means the following: until the second half of the eighties there will be an increase in the labor potential of women due to demographic causes, a rise in the number of married employed or would-be employed women, and a larger supply of women with better education and training. The increasing number of girls between 15 and 20 and of older employees leaving the job market are extremely unlikely to offset the numbers of employees entering the job market so that, on balance, an increase is expected in the labor force participation of women, including the silent reserve, and also in the demand for jobs on the part of women.

Assuming that the female employment share will remain at approximately 37 percent and the share of women among the registered unemployed will remain around 50 percent for quite some time, a total of about one million registered unemployed women, plus a silent reserve of 400,000 to 500,000 female job seekers, can be expected in 1985, according to estimates published by the German Institute for Economic Research. The official unemployment rate for women would thus rise from a current 6.3 percent to around 10 percent; if the silent reserve is included, the result will be an unemployment rate in the area of 13 percent. Moderating trends due to demographic changes are not expected until after 1990.

This quantitative dimension of impending unemployment among women is disquieting enough; yet the above-mentioned trends and analyses and current structural analyses by the Federal Institution for Labor with respect to female unemployment indicate additional, more qualitative aspects of underemployment among women. Accordingly, the danger of female unemployment will always be particularly high if:

they have not completed or have insufficient vocational training,
they are less than 25 years old or over 55 (Table 2.5),
they are looking for part-time employment,
they live in old, predominantly heavy-industry regions and have little mobility, and
they work in sectors which are affected by changes in the economic cycle or in sectors that are increasingly subject to pressures from international competition (mainly production).

Taking all these factors into consideration, the proportion of women among the unemployed is higher than their proportion of total employment.

REENTRANTS SINCE 1965

Age and Family Status

One of the first studies of women's return to employment in West Germany was done in 1965 by the Federal Institution for Employment.[1] It covered women who registered at labor exchanges as job seekers in April, July and October that year, after a break in employment of at least 12 months. Of the 19,200 women surveyed (7.6 percent of all newly registering jobseeking women in the period), 33 percent were under 30 years old; 25 percent, 30 to 40; 22 percent, 40 to 59; and 20 percent over age 50. Contrary to the

Table 2.5   Age Profile of Unemployed Persons by Sex, 1967—1976
(September of each year) (percentage distribution)

Sex and Age	1967	1970	1973	1976
Women				
Under 20	7.6	11.0	12.0	13.3
20–25	11.0	15.6	17.0	19.0
25–35	22.1	24.7	24.4	26.2
35–45	18.8	17.2	17.1	17.1
45–55	18.6	16.1	17.5	15.2
55–60	10.8	9.6	6.8	6.8
60–65	8.3	5.6	5.0	2.5
Over 65	2.8	0.2	0.2	—
Total number	109,925	43,663	112,762	461,752
Total percent	100.0	100.0	100.0	100.0
Men				
Under 20	4.7	4.4	7.0	9.4
20–25	5.3	6.3	10.2	15.3
25–35	13.8	14.3	20.7	24.8
35–45	13.5	13.9	16.3	20.3
45–55	12.0	13.9	15.5	15.6
55–60	12.6	16.4	8.8	6.5
60–65	20.9	30.0	20.4	7.9
Over 65	17.2	0.8	1.1	—
Total number	231,153	48,675	106,343	436,562
Total percent	100.0	100.0	100.0	100.0

Source: Compiled from publications of the Federal Institution for Labor.

assumption by Myrdahl and Klein that the reentry phase begins after child rearing at about 40 years of age, one in three of these returnees was under the age of 30 and one in two was under 40 years, ages at which child rearing is not necessarily completed.[2]

The findings of this study were confirmed by subsequent research between 1966 and 1970. Among approximately 100,000 women, the most frequent reentry age of those who had interrupted their employment for more than a year was 27.[3] A 1968 survey of about 2,200 women returning to employment after an interruption of at least a year demonstrated that one-third of the returnees were under age 30 and more than three-fifths under age 40.[4]

Data from a representative 1969/70 poll among 3,120 working and nonworking women aged 15 to 60 years regarding the factors determining their attitude to employment showed that nonemployed "women with children under the age of six not only more frequently expressed the wish to be able to resume employment, but also often have more concrete plans for reentry than women in the third phase of life, whose children have already grown up."[5]

A representative survey in the densely populated and industrialized Federal State of North-Rhine Westphalia found that almost one out of two women not in the labor force but seeking and capable of employment in 1968 was younger than 35 and one of five, as in 1965, was older than 50.[6]

A 1977 study shows that the age structure of women returning or wishing to return to employment did not change significantly with time.[7] It indicates that about 28 percent of nonemployed women who wanted or might want to resume employment are younger than 30, and 42 percent are between ages 30 and 40. The proportion of older women wanting to reenter employment has fallen markedly, however. In 1977, only seven percent of the over-50-year-olds wished to go back to work. Among other things, this was probably due to the fact that older women no longer felt capable of meeting the greater demands made on workers.

On balance, the surveys and analyses of the age structure of women deciding to return to outside employment have shown that in West Germany what Myrdahl and Klein call the third phase of women's gainful employment tends to lie before rather than after the age of 30.

The majority of women planning to resume employment are married. In the 1968 study, they represented 71 percent of the jobseekers, 61 percent of whom had husbands in full-time employment. The dominant ages at return ranged from 25 to 40.

Also overrepresented among reentrants, in comparison with the overall female population, were widows and divorcees (15 percent) who were primarily aged 50 or older. Only weakly represented were single women (13 percent), among whom under-25-year-olds predominated; most of this group had probably interrupted work for educational pursuits.

A 1974 survey found that married women comprised more than three-quarters of all returnees, aged 15 to 65 years.[8] Also, about 87 percent of all nonemployed women surveyed in 1977 who were definitely or possibly desirous of resuming work were married.[9] Only every sixth or seventh would-be returnee in West Germany is dependent on a job for support.

Prior Status of Returnees

The tendency of women workers to return to employment after a family-determined interruption has been found to be greater the later they had initially begun work. Relatively late entry is associated with longer and qualitatively superior vocational training, and this finding suggests that lengthier and better female vocational training in the future will shorten the break between the first and second phases of employment.

In various studies, hardly any discernible differences in school and vocational training records have been found between actual and potential returnees and employed women. As far as in-plant training is concerned, reentrants are more qualified since the proportion without vocational training is currently smaller than among female employees overall. Reentrants do not represent—as is often heard—an inferior component of women's labor potential; on the contrary, they are an example of the waste of well-trained resources. In addition, a qualified school and vocational education has been found to be the best guarantee that women who have interrupted employment for family reasons will be able to return to work.

Among women who have decided to return to work, salary earners are clearly overrepresented while wage earners, helpers in family businesses or the self-employed are underrepresented. "Salary earners—especially those in qualified positions—tend to want to return to work again sooner."[10]

The fact that white-collar employees are proportionally overrepresented among the returnees is probably due to the fact that, before ceasing work in the late 1960s, this group was more strongly concentrated in a small number of occupations than continuous female workers. Thus, according to the findings of the 1965 survey by the Federal Employment Institutions, two out of three returnees had previously been employed in service occupations, one-fourth of whom were in cleaning and housework, one-half in office or administration, and one-tenth in commercial occupations. Underrepresented among the returnees, on the other hand, were industrial and craft employees, in which only one-quarter had been employed. By 1968, every third returnee registering for job placement with the labor exchanges had formerly had an administrative or office occupation and every seventh a commercial one. At that time, salary earners, especially clerks and typists, had less trouble finding work again because of growing demand, whereas wage earners tended to have more trouble due to worsening economic conditions.

Among returnees in industrial and craft occupations, textile workers and processors dominated. Younger returnees came mainly from service occupations, while older ones more often had earlier been employed in the crafts. This probably was a result of general structural change from industrial to service occupations.

In 1968, almost 85 percent of the returnees previously had been in lower qualified salaried positions, lacking scope for decision-making and responsibility. In comparison, among all female salary earners, 70 percent were employed in these lower categories. This was analogous to the situation among wage earner returnees. Before their interruption, two out of three had been employed as unskilled workers—compared with only 46 percent of all women workers. Only one out of four had been a skilled or craft worker, compared with one out of two of all female wage earners.

Concentration of the prior employment of returnees among wage and salary earners in a small number of occupations and in lower ranks, although their schooling and vocational training probably was no worse than that of all women workers, must be traced to the fact that many did not choose employment and career advancement as their prime life objective. Employment was regarded as an interim activity on the way to the main one, marriage and child rearing. As a result, many accepted marginal employment and were stuck on the lower career rungs when they stopped working.

All women returning to work who have had inadequate work experience encounter difficulties in reintegration and in the further course of their employment. Data for 1966 show a highly significant connection between the time of exit from the labor force and the age of marriage. Returnees who originally began working when they were very young—mostly under 16 and without vocational training—had more work experience, while those who had had longer skilled vocational training stopped gainful work within a few years. From these findings it was deduced that a future drop in age at marriage and longer and more advanced vocational training for girls will result in a decrease in the average working experience of returnees. With time, however, the point of work interruption has shifted from marriage to the birth of the first child.

Reasons for Interrupting Employment

The main reasons for women giving up work clearly continue to pertain to family rearing, but there has been a shifting of weights over time. Thus in 1966, 44 percent of 45 to 65 year-old women who had stopped working at some time and then returned stated that this was because they married, while only nine percent gave the birth of the first child as the reason. The interruption was due to the war in 17 percent of the cases, and unemployment, health and further education accounted for about 12 percent.

In 1974, of 45- to 65-year-old women who had returned to work, marriage was the reason for the interruption of only 32 percent and the birth of the first child of 26 percent. Thus, it is apparent that marriage is ever less of a reason to exchange housework for employment, whereas the birth of the first child has become the determinant of the decision more and more.

In both 1966 and 1974, women who had given family reasons for interrupting work returned to work relatively less frequently than those who had given further training and unemployment as their reasons. In 1966, however, 42 percent of those women who had reentered the labor force gave marriage as the reason for stopping work, compared with only 37 percent of those questioned in 1974. In both years, 54 percent of the women who had interrupted work because of the birth of their first child later went back to work. It is possible that women who stop work to marry are under less financial pressure to resume work than those who have to contribute to the support of a larger family.

Duration of Absence from the Labor Force

The length of time women interrupt employment determines whether resumption occurs without problems and without a grave worsening of their working conditions. The longer the break, the larger is the gap in know-how and the psychological remoteness from working life. The greater the unfamiliarity with the vocational milieu, and the deficits due to atrophy of knowledge and skills or changed technologies, the more difficult is the entry process. The duration of the period of withdrawal depends on a number of factors:

the reasons for the interruption,
the age at the time of exit,
family status and the occupation of the husband, and
quality of the work previously done as well as the nature of initial vocational training.

The Federal Employment Institution showed that two out of three returnees in 1965 had interrupted work for only one to five years; 12 percent from six to ten years; and 20 percent for more than ten years. The tendency for the majority of returnees or would-be returnees to have had a break of one to five years or to be ready to undertake such a break appears unchanged over time. This finding is further evidence of the lack of realism attached to a third interruption phase of approximately 15 years described by Myrdahl and Klein, a duration during which, by present-day findings, all contact to one's vocation would be likely to be lost and a return hardly to be envisioned.

According to one study in 1966, the higher the educational and vocational attainment of the returnees, the shorter the interruption. A contradictory result was obtained in 1968 when it was found that the average duration of interruption for returnees with a qualified school graduation and above-average qualification levels in the work performed before the interruption was relatively the longest. The 1968 findings described women who registered as job seekers with the labor administration after an employment interruption of at least one year. In that year, this group probably was not representative of all returnees with similar attributes since most women with qualified training and above-average vocational activity were likely to have been able to find new jobs without resort to the labor exchange. Frequently the women who came to the labor exchanges were only those with a prolonged absence from work who had difficulty in meeting high job requirements. On the whole, it is more likely that the earlier findings are correct since they were based on a more representative survey. In any event, the group of qualified returnees, in particular, is extraordinarily heterogeneous, and generally applicable statements about them are very difficult to make.

The 1965 examination by the Federal Employment Institute found that returnees in service occupations frequently showed relatively longer durations of interruption (more than 10 years) than blue-collar workers. In the services, women in cleaning and household occupations returned sooner, which is not surprising since these activities are easiest to follow on a part-time basis and thus can be more readily combined with child rearing.

Women whose husbands were in full-time gainful employment returned to work relatively soon themselves. Widows and women with unemployed husbands, on the other hand, typically experienced longer interruptions. In their cases economic need is obviously the stimulus toward return to work.

Return to Employment

Of 15- to 65-year-old women employed in 1974 who had earlier resumed work, 65 percent stated they had sought reentry jobs out of financial considerations (emergencies caused by the death, unemployment or incapacity of their husbands, as well as the wish to raise the family's income and consumption level). Finances were more likely to be a reason for return for women with low standards of schooling than for women with qualified vocational training; for unskilled women workers than for skilled and salaried ones; for women with three or more children than for those with fewer or no children; and, finally, for older than for younger women.

One out of every ten returnees gave "enjoyment of working" as the reason for reentry: younger women more than the older, those with qualified training more than primary school graduates, and childless women more than those with children.

The possibility of obtaining part-time employment plays a decisive part in the decision to resume work. According to a 1968 study, half of the returnees sought a part-time job. These included more women whose husbands were in full-time gainful employment, older women, and those with long absences from work who have difficulty in adjusting to full-time work. The majority (42 percent) in the then favorable labor market situation did, indeed, find part-time employment.

Full-time employment tended to be sought, on the other hand, by single, widowed and divorced women; wives of unemployed, no-income and incapacitated husbands; younger women; and those with relatively short durations of interruption.

In 1968/69 in North-Rhine Westphalia, about 85 percent of non-employed women who were willing and able to work sought part-time jobs, a finding also confirmed in a 1969/70 study: "When return to employment is considered, it is almost exclusively in terms of part-time employment, and it appears to be presumed that there are enough part-time jobs available."[11]

1974 data show that 41 percent of employed 15- to 65-year-old women who had given up working at some time or other obtained part-time jobs at reentry, most particularly older women and women with children.

In line with these findings, expansion of part-time employment must be regarded as a central instrument of state labor market policy with the objective of preventing work interruptions, maintaining contact with one's vocation and easing the return to employment.

Particularly important in the discussion of women returning to employment is the question whether the employment interruption, its duration and the type of activity sought upon return involve vocational downgrading. In one study, half the women surveyed stated that their return to employment involved a change in occupations, but it was not possible to determine if this had resulted in qualitative demotion. In 1974, 53 percent of the women who resumed work after an interruption stated they had to accept a change of vocation. This affected the older more than the younger and wage earners more than salary earners.

In the latest study (1977), it was found that 39 to 44 percent of all gainfully employed females who had interrupted work for more than a year had changed vocations, compared to only 18 percent of those who had not left the work force. The conclusion to be drawn from this, therefore, is that interrupting employment demands a greater than usual measure of vocational mobility.

The current occupation of women in part-time employment, among whom there is a large proportion of returnees, is consonant with their vocational training in only 51 percent of cases, compared with 75 percent of those in full-time employment. Both indicators—above-average vocational mobility and inadequacy of occupation in relation to training—must be seen as proof of women's vocational down-grading upon their return to employment.

It has also been demonstrated that the likelihood of being in the same position when returning to employment as before leaving is relatively higher among wage earners than salary earners. Overall the frequency of gross occupational change among all female workers has diminished over time, although it is not possible to deduce shifts in occupational level upon return to employment.

From 1965 data it has been calculated that labor exchanges were involved with job placement for about one-quarter of the returnees. In other words, three out of four returnees found their way back to employment without the aid of the labor administration. It is very difficult to ascertain whether there has been any subsequent change in these findings. It is likely, however, that given present recessive labor market developments, return to employment without involvement of the labor exchange has become rarer. This is shown, inter alia, by the high proportion of women seeking part-time employment among the female unemployed. While the frequency of involvement of the labor exchanges is assumed to have risen, it is likely to fall again once the employment situation improves. Furthermore, the involvement of labor exchanges is likely to be greater among less-qualified returnees to work than among the qualified who even now very often still find jobs without labor exchange mediation.

REENTRANTS IN THE FRAMEWORK OF STATE LABOR POLICY

As a rule women returnees to employment are defined as a certain group of persons out of the labor market who wish to return to gainful employment after a more-or-less voluntary longer-term interruption in employment primarily in order to fulfill family care tasks but, in some cases, to pursue further education and qualification. Since those interrupting work for educational reasons are hardly likely to encounter difficulties in resuming employment, they will not be further considered.

The "voluntariness" referred to signifies that the interruption in employment was the result of a woman's own decision and not of the enforced loss of her job. Fulfillment of family care tasks means that the reasons for the employment interruption of these women were the birth and rearing of children as well as the care of older and ailing relatives. Apart from these, a great number of childless women give up employment because they want to or have to run their family households. Whether and how this latter group should be included in the labor market policy objectives is the subject of controversy. In any event, women no longer employed, with or without grown children, must be counted among returnees and thus in the labor market policy target group if changes in their personal status—divorce, widowhood, incapacitation or unemployment of the husband—force them to seek employment to support their families.

"Longer-term" in the context of the definition means that problems in returning to employment begin only when there has been a certain distance in time since previous employment.

Women returnees became a target group of state labor market policy in the 1969 Labor Promotion Act due to the fact "that their placement (in employment) is [made] difficult under the usual labor market conditions":

by factors which cause women to partially lose their qualifications and abilities during their absence from employment because they lack necessary vocational experience;

by factors rooted in economic and technological development which lead to changes in or lack of demand for the former vocations, qualifications and activities of these women so that they can no longer adequately meet the requirements of the market without qualifying retraining measures;

by factors which, with increasing duration of absence from employment, lead to strong psychological remoteness and alienation from the working world, which must be prevented or overcome by suitable measures; and

by factors and burdens lying in the personal and family spheres, be it children or relatives who have to be taken care of, or a husband who resists his wife's employment.

There is no system of employment statistics in the Federal Republic of Germany which periodically and with adequate accuracy registers the process of women's interrupting and returning to employment by socio-economic characteristics. The difficulties of such registration lie in the fact that returnees constitute a so-called potential labor market. In other words, apart from women who seek or find jobs on their own initiative or with the mediation of the labor exchange (i.e. those who have taken concrete steps towards returning to work), there are also women who (a) want to wait until later before seeking work, but are already thinking more or less intensively about it; and (b) have made one or several fruitless attempts to find work adequate to their qualifications or any type of work at all, but have for the time being given up the initiative although, on principle, they remain interested in resuming employment. In this context it is of minor importance whether the job shortage in the labor market is structural or cyclical. These two groups can be counted as part of the silent reserve.

Thus in any one period one finds entrants to work consisting of (a) those who have found employment, (b) the registered unemployed, and (c) the so-called silent reserve. It is impossible to determine how they are distributed among these labor market aggregates, however. It is only known that in 1974, for example, 92 percent of all 15- to 65-year-old women in the Federal Republic had at some time or other after leaving school been gainfully employed, but that, on average, only one in two women in any age group from 15 to 65 was employed when interviewed. That means that more women were giving up gainful employment than going back to it. Somewhere between these two pieces of data lies the proportion of women who have returned or are willing to return to employment; every percentage point of increase of female employment above 50 percent expands the female workforce by about 150,000 to 160,000.

There are no data about the number of women finding their way back to employment on their own initiative, nor recent statistics about the number of returnees who have registered as unemployed with the labor administration. There are indicators which show, however, that the number of returnees among the registered jobless recently has risen considerably. Tending to confirm this is that fact that, of some 500,000 jobless women in 1977, some 185,000 sought part-time employment, the greatly preferred form of employment among returnees.

Various research institutes currently appraise the silent reserve at 600,000 to 700,000 job-seeking women. The Institute for Labor Market and Vocational Research of the Federal Employment Institution defines silent reserve as that part of the potential workforce which is neither employed nor registered as unemployed with the labor exchanges and which, all experience has shown, would seek work if the labor market situation were more favorable. The institute takes the view that one can speak of a kind of involuntary, cyclically caused unemployment of a temporary nature.[12]

To define the silent reserve as being only cyclically determined is certainly a wrong approach. It can be proved that there is also a so-called silent reserve which is structurally determined, either because the labor market situation is unfavorable in the longer term (e.g. in remote regions or regions with a high proportion of shrinking industries), there are no child care facilities nearby, the distances to places of work are too long, or there is a lack of sufficient part-time jobs. A voluntary withdrawal of women from employment in these regions leads to long interruptions and almost insurmountable difficulties in finding work later.

The silent reserve both cyclically and structurally determined is currently probably far in excess of a million people in the Federal Republic of Germany. About 70 percent of these are women among whom there is, in turn, a large percentage who wish to return after interrupting employment but whose demands for jobs cannot be met. Cautiously estimated, the number of women who interrupted work because of family commitments and who would return to work if there were jobs for them must be put at about 500,000.

It would not be doing justice to the entire complex of problems if one spoke of the return to employment as being only a process of complete withdrawal and subsequent return, because this process is increasingly going on in other forms, e.g. the changeover from full-time to part-time employment after the birth of a child, later followed by full-time employment in the old or a different occupation. Part-time employment rather than complete withdrawal frequently involves a qualitative worsening of working conditions for the women concerned, as well as exclusion from the usual promotion opportunities. State labor market policy must also help these women so that they can "return" to the kinds of jobs which satisfied them initially.

There are often close interrelationships between a given labor market situation and a woman's decision to withdraw from or resume employment. Thus it is conceivable in an unfavorable labor market situation, for example, that:

women, even after they have borne a child, will delay withdrawing from employment or concentrate more on finding part-time work for fear of not getting another job later. In this situation, they are often willing to put up with a qualitative worsening of their working conditions;

women strive to get back into employment sooner than planned because their husbands' jobs and incomes have become threatened. In exchange for a rapid return, they frequently receive qualitatively worse working conditions than before their withdrawal;

women capitulate after several fruitless attempts to return to employment and withdraw from the labor market completely;

women frequently try to realize child bearing plans in periods when the labor market is tight; and

after fruitless job-seeking, women seek further training and qualification opportunities as a substitute.

When the labor market is favorable, on the other hand, the average periods of absence from employment are likely to be longer since the return to work tends to be seen as uncomplicated. The stable jobs and good incomes of husbands would perhaps be a disincentive for many women to return to work.

West German labor market policy has shown increasing interest since the 1966/67 recession period in determining the real factors in women's employment behavior since, in the ensuing years of enormous labor shortage from about 1972-73, nonemployed women with an unused potential of qualification and vocational experience, together with foreign workers, constituted the largest labor reserve. The purpose of most of these studies was, on the one hand, to estimate the potential that could be mobilized and, on the other hand, to discover the characteristics of this group of people so as to be able to chart suitable reintegration measures. It was clear that the primary objective was to develop economic and labor market policy designed for growth by identifying an available labor supply. Mobilization of women workers moved into the foreground particularly at times when general social and socio-political considerations and disproportionately rising social costs made it no longer desirable or tolerable to bring more than 3.9 million foreigners into the Federal Republic.

Women constituted a quantitatively important labor reservoir as well as one with certain qualifications which they had acquired through vocational training and earlier working experience and which was not being utilized or was underutilized at the time. Over and above this they fulfilled a flexibility function in the labor market. Quantitatively, they contributed to filling additional labor needs in boom times, withdrawing from the labor market during recessions, with no immediate resurgence into the market. Qualitatively, the labor market remained flexible because the female labor reservoir by and large covered the additional demand of the economy for relatively undefined run-of-the-mill qualifications. Foreign workers were brought into the country for similar purposes. The assured labor market flexibility contributed substantially to the remarkable adaptability of the German economy to world market structural and cyclical changes.

State labor market policy at that time defined women returnees as women who worked for a few years following relatively short educational and vocational training, then withdrew from employment at marriage or at the birth of the first child to devote themselves to family care. A low educational and vocational training level, little vocational experience, sights always set on the family as the main field of action, and employment more or less as a secondary, temporary phase of life were the characteristics attributed to them. Marginality was a constitutional element of this group, and that was the way the labor market policy of the time intended it to remain.

Emancipatory aims (such as enforcement of women's right to equal participation in the labor force, the raising of self-esteem by a satisfying occupation, the strengthening of financial independence) which can be achieved only by long-term planning of vocational and career patterns for women, leading to compatibility between work and family for both spouses, received minor attention and were considered at that time to be irreconcilable with the objective of economic expansion and a certain measure of labor market flexibility.

Unforeseen was the importance to the Germany economy of a long-term continuity of supply with sufficient qualified labor, a need which can now and in the future be provided only by women returnees. Sharpening of skills depreciated during an interruption as well as preparation for new occupations were as much in the foreground of this labor market policy program as was the increased establishment of kindergartens to lessen the double load caused by child rearing.

When recession set in again as a result of the so-called energy crisis, there was all the more public surprise when the number of unemployed women increased and the former mechanisms of women's quiet and frictionless withdrawal from the labor market into the silent reserve no longer worked as in the past and in the 1966/67 recession. From 1974, the number of registered unemployed women increased and, at the same time, the silent reserve also grew substantially. Overall, the number of women who would work if they could find jobs grew rapidly.

West German state labor market policy quickly set priorities at this time to the detriment of women returnees. Jobs have been and are currently being sought with priority given to juveniles and men in the so-called active ages.

Women are currently being conceded priority in labor market policy only if they depend on a job and an income (singles, divorcees, widows, women with jobless or incapacitated husbands). The cliche of the double-earning woman depriving the jobless breadwinning family man of work is popular again. Attempts are being made to dress up the unemployment statistics whereby women, especially those seeking part-time employment, are categorized as not really available to the labor market and thus as not really jobless. The labor market potential, defined in the boom times of the

1960s as those in employment plus the registered jobless plus all those wanting work although not registered as unemployed with the labor administration, was again changed to denote the number of employed plus the registered unemployed and, among the latter, only a core group of male and juvenile jobless needing priority solutions. The changed views proceeded to be rigorously applied as shown by the almost unfulfillable promotion conditions for female reentrants in the Labor Promotion Act in line with the Budget Structure Act of 1965, which will be referred to later.

Unfavorable to women in general and for returnees to employment in particular is the present tendency of state labor market policy to place in employment or to retrain those who receive unemployment benefits, so as to lessen the government's financial burden. Women are generally underrepresented in this group, and women returnees, as a rule, are not represented at all.

THE FEDERAL LABOR PROMOTION ACT (AFG)

The 1969 Labor Promotion Act (AFG) defines the objectives of state labor market policy. The measures provided for in the Act aim mainly at (a) sustaining a high level of employment, and avoiding a shortage of labor; (b) contributing to continual improvement of regional, sectorial, group and qualification employment structures; and (c) promoting and enhancing the employment opportunities of individual groups of workers whose placement is more difficult than usual under normal labor market conditions.

The Act explicitly covers women reentrants to employment as a target group to benefit from state labor market policy. It specifically demands action to integrate women in employment whose placement is difficult under usual labor market conditions because they are married or are or were housebound for other reasons.

The full employment objective of labor market policy is to be concretized in a way that, in boom and recession, achieves the highest possible utilization of labor potential. Labor potential in this sense covers not only those in employment and the registered unemployed but also all who do not register as jobless but are nonetheless willing and able to be employed. Thus, it is clear that the aim includes the quantitative full employment of women who wish to resume working after an interruption not resulting from job loss.

The Act does not in any way stipulate the policy that is currently being pursued, namely that labor policy is to alternate between a labor potential encompassing the silent reserve during boom times and excluding the silent reserve and registered part-time female job seekers, primarily returnees, during recessions.

In regard to women returnees, the qualitative targets of state labor policy are assumed to mean that under the Labor Promotion Act, the qualifications women have acquired must be preserved, enhanced and constantly adapted to changing demands, despite interruptions in employment for family care. These aims are served above all by advanced training and retraining provisions of the Act.

On the demand side, the Act requires suitable measures to ensure that women returnees be treated equally with other problem groups in placement in jobs that are stable and offer good income and advancement opportunities. These objectives are served mainly by the Act's provisions to promote work-introduction and integration as well as direct work creation measures.

In approach and intention, the Labor Promotion Act thus constitutes the central instrument for solving the problems of women returning to employment. Apart from the funds provided by the Act for promoting programs of employers, trade unions and other providers, there are practically no other activities aimed at helping women returnees.

The fact that the present extremely restrictive application of the Labor Promotion Act by state labor market policy is discriminatory, hectic, short-sighted and dictated by financial concerns may prove extremely harmful in the longer term. As overall labor market trends have already shown, after 1990 the Federal Republic must expect a worsening labor shortage. This scarcity should be countered now by dealing with the problems of women who want to return to work, thus ensuring an adequate and qualified potential work force ten years from now.

Trade unions and employer organizations—and, for that matter, the political parties—are presently only half-hearted, at the most, in demanding action to solve the special problems of women returning to employment, as an opinion survey has shown.*

The Federal Employment Institution

To achieve the Labor Promotion Act's objectives, the Federal Institution was given a number of different and selectively applicable instruments for active intervention in and shaping of labor market processes. Apart from career counseling and job placement, these primarily include measures to promote vocational training, wage cost subsidies to employers, and job creation measures.

Since 1971, the Federal Employment Institution's expenditure structure has clearly changed, in line with economic developments. After 1971, i.e. a year with a good labor market situation characterized by excess demand for labor, every third mark spent by the Institution went into improving the employment structure and measures serving the integration of problem

---

*An exception is the proposals of the conservative CDU opposition party for overcoming women's unemployment, presented September 18, 1978.

groups, and only every fifth was spent on jobless benefits. Wage cost subsidization and job creation measures, with just over one percent each of total expenditure, were extremely marginal. The bulk of the funds flowed into vocational training and retraining.

In 1977 the Federal Republic's economic situation was marked by about one million unemployed, some 70 percent of whom were benefit recipients. This development greatly restricted the Federal Employment Institution's scope to take active, differentiated and selective measures to steer and shape labor market policy. Only every sixth mark of its total expenditures was used for these purposes: 10 percent for vocational retraining, 2 percent for wage cost subsidies; and 4 percent for job creation measures. Fifty-six percent of total expenditure was for wage substitute benefits, representing more than a doubling of the proportion used for this purpose since 1971.

While there was a 206 percent rise in the Employment Institution's operations during this time span, wage substitution expenditures grew by 720 percent, whereas expenditures on vocational, advanced and retraining fell. Yet, despite substantial rates of increase, expenditures on wage cost subsidization and job creation were extremely small, only 6 percent of the total.

The structural shifts in the expenditures of the Federal Institution took place mainly at the cost of nonrecipients of benefits among the job-seekers, a high percentage of whom were women wishing to return to work who were most likely to have previously taken part in active, qualifying retraining and work introduction programs. This clearly points to a reversal in the priorities of state labor market policy, away from the forward-looking, vocation-qualifying, problem-group oriented and labor market relief measures toward a shorter-term policy of coping with the labor market crisis. Proof of this is the 1975 Budget Structure Act, which rigorously constricts the conditions for financing programs under the Labor Promotion Act and thus makes assistance to reentrants extraordinarily more difficult, if not altogether impossible.

Vocational Further-Training and Retraining Measures

According to the Labor Promotion Act, vocational additional-training measures serve "to ascertain, preserve, expand and adapt to technical developments, vocational know-how and skills, or to permit vocational advancement." Completed vocational training or adequate occupational experience is presupposed, and assistance is aimed especially at promoting " the entry or reentry of female employment-seekers into vocational life." Vocational retraining measures aim at "enabling the changeover into another suitable vocational activity, in particular to secure or improve vocational mobility."

Since the Act came into force, participation by women in the measures referred to has, generally speaking, been limited. With 62,500 new women participants (22 percent) in 1971, women were vastly underrepresented compared with the proportion of women employed. The number of new women participants subsequently grew to 70,000 by 1975. A recessive labor market began in that year, with a rapid leap upward in the unemployment rate. The same year, the Budget Structure Act was passed, which tightened the conditions of participation in the Federal Institution's promotion measures and greatly reduced the participants' sustenance benefits. This resulted in a halving of the entry of new women participants in 1977 compared to 1976: the ratio of female participants was 28 in 1977 compared with an employment ratio of 37 percent, a female unemployment ratio of 50 percent and a female rate in the silent reserve of 60 to 70 percent. Only 38,000 women entered further retraining courses sponsored by the Federal Institution in 1977. This indicated that the new priorities of the Federal Employment Institution's policy were being dictated mainly by budgetary and financial constraints.

No statistics have been published on the role of participation by women returnees in the advanced and retraining measures, although the Act specifically provides for them. According to the Federal Employment Institution, the number of women wanting to enter or reenter gainful employment among course participants has consistently fallen. In 1970, when the objective was to mobilize all possible labor reserves for a smooth growth process, every fifth woman participant belonged to this group. A publicity drive was mounted to try to get women to go back to work and to popularize vocational advanced training and retraining possibilities being offered by the Institute. There was no more talk of this in 1976, when only every 25th woman participant was a new entrant or reentrant to employment.

This development was due first and foremost to the changed labor market situation. Many women willing to return saw no point in taking on vocational advanced training or retraining—insofar as they were entitled to them—if there were hardly any prospects of their getting jobs. Other reasons were: restrictive participation entitlements; serious obstacles placed in the way of women whose husbands were employed in order to keep them out of the labor force; and a course offering which had little appeal to women with children, and did little justice to their specific needs and difficulties. Courses were frequently located far from their homes, had no childcare facilities, and gave practically no specific consideration to the entry situation.

Women participants in advanced training programs are known to concentrate more on courses dealing with adaptation of know-how and skills to changed vocational demands and less on vocational advancement. Returning women probably almost exclusively concentrate on the training goal of "adaptation of know-how and skills."

The fact that the number of women returnees participating in the

Federal Employment Institution's advanced-training programs falls far short of the very low participation of women in general, is due primarily to the extraordinary restrictive entitlement and financial conditions currently being applied for this group. Applicants with completed vocational training receive support only if they were employed for at least three years after their training; those with improperly completed vocational training receive support only if they were employed for at least six years afterwards. Although the occupation of housewife is recognized as a vocation under the terms of the Labor Promotion Act, it is likely to be difficult for women with qualified training but short employment experience, and those with short interruptions (e.g. of a year) to demonstrate three years of employment experience. Hence, they are forced to remain housewives for a further year. Returnees without completed vocational training are also likely to face problems because this group recently has been particularly affected by unemployment and therefore has a hard time accumulating six years of employment.

Overall, the regulations show a tendency toward lengthening the duration of absences from work if prior vocational experience was brief. This tendency is likely to increase the gap between women returnees and the working world, making the reentry process more difficult.

The condition that applicants receive sustenance benefit or costs repayment only if they have been gainfully employed in the three years preceding program enrollment is almost impossible to meet by women reentrants. This means that returning women who have ceased employment for more than a year, probably the majority, are thus excluded from the Federal Employment Institution's financial aid—a dog chasing its own tail.

The vocational experience regulation in which the occupation of housekeeping is recognized leads to the cited tendency to lengthen interruptions; with respect to financial benefits, on the other hand, the women returnees must be out of the labor force for less than a year if they want to take advantage of financial support for vocational advanced training or retraining. There is no semblance of rationality in this concept. Instead, it is a poorly thought-through action designed to apply the funds for vocation-qualifying programs in the foreseeable future exclusively to jobless benefit recipients, and to keep other groups, above all women would-be returnees, out of the labor market.

Women returnees who do not meet the above conditions are entitled to maintenance benefits if they are forced to work because of changes in their personal circumstances (divorce, death or incapacitation of the husband). Not only is this limitation irreconcilable with the aim of "best possible utilization of the labor potential," but the position of returnees who are forced to earn a living is further burdened by their having to commit themselves to working for a least three years after conclusion of the support. Failing this, they have to repay the stipends. This means that women returnees who refresh or adapt their vocational know-how and skills and who immediately marry thereafter and/or bear children must repay the benefits provided by the Federal Institution. This regulation is an intolerable constraint upon the scope of these women's decision-making. In general, the requirement that the recipient must work for three years after receipt of training is often irreconcilable with the interruption of women returnees, who often stop working several times.

Even if women returnees could satisfy all the conditions for receiving benefits, as a rule they are paid only 58 percent of their former net pay as sustenance for the duration of the support, because their integration into the labor market is regarded in most cases by the labor administration as desirable (zweckmaessig), rather than necessary (notwendig). If viewed as necessary, they would qualify for 80 percent of former income. Given women's generally low wages and salaries, the 58 percent rate often falls below the rate of social welfare benefits for the needy.

The same discriminatory conditions women returnees must satisfy to qualify for advanced training benefits apply in regard to vocational retraining (except work-introduction programs). There are no published statistics about participation by women returnees in vocational programs overall or in individual efforts. The fall in the overall number of female new entrants or reentrants participating in these programs, from 7,000 in 1970 to 1,600 new entrants in 1977, as well as the drop in the corresponding proportion of total women participants, from 11.6 to 4 percent, is not surprising, given the restrictive prerequisites, and throws a clear light on the borderline effectiveness of this program is assisting women's return to employment.

Currently, 69 percent of the women choose vocational advanced training measures and 19 percent vocational retraining. Every third new entry among the retrainees is a woman, as is every fourth among the advanced training participants. Participation in both programs has fallen by almost half since 1971. Currently, the crisis aspect in state labor market policy is being clearly overemphasized at the expense of future-oriented, vocation-qualifying activities.

Under the given institutional, financial and substantive conditions, the cited measures are hardly suited to eliminating the qualification and employment difficulties of women returnees. On the contrary, under the influence of the Budget Structure Act, they are more likely to contribute to enlarging their educational and vocational training deficits and to diminishing their employment opportunities. That jobless youngsters and recipients of benefits from the Federal Institution are presently receiving priority attention is indicated by the fact that in 1971, almost 43 percent of the new women participants in vocation-qualifying programs were more than 30 years old, which suggests considerable aid to women returnees, whereas now only 38 percent of the women participants are in this age group.

The educational and advanced training program of the Federal Institution also aims beyond the women reentry group, since a great proportion of participants are unskilled or semiskilled low-ranking wage and salary earners. Yet, in terms of quantity of courses, type of graduation, entitlement, and vocational replacement and utilization prospects, the courses are aimed predominantly at already qualified educational and vocational training graduates.

Working-In Subsidies, Integration Supports, and Wage Subsidies

Under the Labor Promotion Act the Federal Employment Institution can grant employers subsidies for employees able to achieve full performance on the job only after a period of work-introduction.

As a concept this instrument would be eminently suited to reintegrating those women in employment whose former occupations or vocations were no longer in demand. Under the present regulations, employers receive up to 60 percent of the net wage of such employees from Federal Institution funds for a maximum period of a year.

The second incentive for creation of jobs is "integration supports," which are paid to employers for "integration of job seekers whose placement is difficult under usual labor market condition." In the form of loans and subsidies, these also cover up to 60 percent of the net pay of such employees, in this case for a maximum of two years. Integration support is aimed explicitly at the absorption of problem groups, such as reentrants, into the labor market. It is more attractive to employers than work-introduction subsidies because the support period is twice as long.

Programs of indirect incentives to create jobs also include wage cost subsidies from various special Bonn government programs for invigorating the economic cycle, and are similarly structured.

By and large, the efficiency of these incentive programs in solving employment problems is thought to be low because:

funds are often claimed for hirings which would have been made anyway. Where production capacities are underutilized, wage cost subsidies are hardly likely to lead to lasting employment;

subsidized jobs are seldom of a lasting nature. There is, in fact, a kind of rotation whereby enterprises selectively employ women returnees whom they dismiss when their subsidies run out and replace with other women returnees in order to collect subsidies;

within the framework of valid allocation criteria, it is still possible for employers to choose younger and more qualified workers from the problem groups. This practice means that women returnees currently are likely to have fewer chances from the outset than members of other, mainly male, problem groups.

Hardly anything can be deduced from published statistics about the participation of women returnees in these programs. Insofar as women overall are concerned, there has been a clear rise in recent years in reintegration supports. While 1,400 women were supported by this measure in 1972, the number rose to 29,000 by 1977. In contrast, the use of work-introduction subsidies for the employment of women tends to be moderate, and is currently receding (presently covering about 4,900 women).

In 1972, 42 percent of all employees covered by work-introduction subsidies were women, which was an overrepresentation and most likely due to a shortage of labor at that time. In 1977, women's participation had dropped to 32 percent. There was an underrepresentation of women in both 1971 and 1977 among those covered by work-integration supports (about 28 percent).

The age structure of participants demonstrates that the instruments of wage subsidization currently give higher priority to younger jobless and benefit recipients than to women returnees. In 1971, 55 percent of all women newly provided with work-introduction subsidies were still over 30 years old, compared with only 40 percent in 1977. One in three of these women is currently between the ages of 20 and 25.

Direct Job Creation

Like wage subsidization, job creation plays a minor part in the Federal Institution's programs—even if funds from the federal government's special cyclical programs are included. It is fundamentally designed to assist women returnees find employment *if* they register as jobless with the labor exchanges. As part of this program, the federal government promotes the creation of jobs through subsidies to providers for types of work "which are in the public interest if these types of work were not to be carried out to the same extent or only at a later time." The Act provides for a subsidy of 60 percent of the wages or salaries to the providers.

There are no statistical data on the participation of women returnees in this program. Here, too, it is assumed that the labor exchange is negatively selective in regard to women, since it is likely to give priority work placement to recipients of Federal Institution jobless benefits whose placement in work eases the wage substitution burden. Hence women returnees, most of whom are not benefit recipients, have hardly any opportunities in this regard.

FACILITATING MEASURES

Childcare

Federal, Land (State) and local governments as well as the Federal Employment Institution have recently been engaged in providing adequate kindergarten place in the Federal Republic of Germany and have thus created crucial prerequisites for the greater work participation of women with children below school age and for a less problematical integration of women returnees in gainful employment.

In 1970, there were only 1.2 million places in these facilities, but there were about three million children aged three to six years. The potential supply ratio was thus only 40 percent. The situation improved substantially by 1976. There are now 1.56 million places and only 2.1 million three- to six-year-old children, due to the falling birthrate. Thus, the potential supply ratio has risen to 75 percent. If the birthrate continues its present decline, a supply ratio of almost 90 percent can be expected in 1990.

These supply ratios, however, give no indication of the actual usage of the facilities, especially the class-specific usage. It can be assumed that they are used predominantly by families in which women need not go out to work because of the husbands' good incomes. Moreover, there are still likely to be considerable imbalances in the availability of child-minding facilities in regions of the country away from the urban agglomerations. These facilities would be particularly effective in promoting the return of women to employment if more were operated in the form of all-day kindergartens. There are still great deficits in this respect. The number of places in day nurseries is also inadequate. The women returnees would certainly also be helped by more all-day schools or supervised home facilities.

Flexible Work Hours

Measures to make working hours more flexible can help women returnees to better harmonize family responsibilities with employment demands and thereby lessen their burden. Reference has already been made to the growing trend towards women's part-time employment, and that at present only ten percent of the demand for part-time jobs registered at the labor exchanges can be met. Also, the inadequate quality and stability and one-sided structure of part-time jobs were noted. It must further be pointed out that part-time employment is often resorted to by employers with the express intention of exploiting rationalization possibilities rather than, as would be desirable, expanding the availability of jobs overall.

It has also been pointed out how important the possibility of part-time work is to women's decision to return to employment after an interruption due to family responsibilities. Furthermore many women prefer part-time employment to an interruption. In addition, if men's part-time employment opportunities were expanded, a more equal sharing of family burdens by both spouses could develop.

The fact that a large part of the demand for part-time jobs in the Federal Republic of Germany could be met by converting full-time into part-time jobs is documented by fairly recent studies on the potential of additional jobs in industry.[13] Questioned firms indicate that by splitting full-time jobs they could create about 380,000 additional employment possibilities. If at least an equal part-time potential in the public and private services sector is included, the currently registered women for part-time jobs (about 185,000) and the majority of would-be women returnees in the silent reserve could be placed in employment. It would also be possible to offer such job opportunities to women presently working full time who prefer part-time employment.

Whereas the enterprises questioned appreciate the higher average hourly productivity, greater flexibility of deployment, lower illness and absenteeism rates, lesser incidence of work accidents and the better possibility of utilizing regional labor supplies provided by part-time employees, they see disadvantages, compared with full-time employment, in relatively higher fringe costs, expenses within the work-place and administrative costs.

This is where state market policy measures should play a role. It would be conceivable, for instance, for instruments of the Federal Employment Institution to be selectively applied as indirect incentives to create jobs, and for direct job placement in any conversion from full- to part-time positions. That is, if an enterprise changed over to part-time employment, it should receive subsidies for a certain period (perhaps one to two years) of a certain percentage of wages and salaries of the additionally hired part-time workers, i.e. a kind of part-time integration support aimed at offsetting the cost disadvantages of conversion to part-time employment. The direct job-creation measures of the Federal Employment Institution within the framework of projects and works in the public interest should also be aimed selectively and intensively at the creation of part-time jobs. This would also more effectively tackle the problem of vocational one-sidedness and under-qualification in part-time employment opportunities.

The present instrument of selective placement of part-time personnel, created by the Federal Employment Institution in 1970, does not alone suffice to achieve these aims. It is aimed primarily at women seeking part-time work for periods of weeks or part of a year in offices and administrations, in mercantile fields, and in health and education services. Placement in such occupations is made attractive to the female job-seekers because of the low taxation rate of 10 percent if no more than 20 hours are worked and no more than DM120 earned a week, and to the employers because they can save their share of contributions to social insurance if employment is for less than three months. Placement in such types of employment does, however, afford women who interrupted work the opportunity to stay in contact with their vocation and/or their old jobs. The number of such job placements has hardly changed since 1972, despite recessive developments in the labor market as a whole, and has even been rising of late (about 64,000 placements in 1977); as 74 percent of the placements, women are clearly overrepresented. This instrument for making working hours more flexible, which the majority of employers and employees welcome, has, in the past, helped women with children to coordinate family commitments and job demands and should be introduced, whenever possible, from the work organization point of view.

The same purpose is served by the currently existing opportunity for one parent to take up to five days off from work to attend to an ill child below the age of eight. The employer does not have to pay wages or salary for this time; a sickness benefit (*Krankengeld*) is paid instead.

Under longer-term aspects, a general shortening of the work week must be demanded, since this enables both spouses to participate equally in child rearing and employment. The latest collective agreements concluded in the Federal Republic (in the cigarette industry) and the current demands of the Metalworkers' Union for the North-Rhine Westphalian steel industry to begin reductions toward an ultimate 35-hour week point in the right direction. It hardly appears possible to stop this trend.

Finally, the imminent updating of the Mothers Protection Act (*Mutterschutzgeset*) will also contribute to making the worklives of married women with children more flexible, since this will introduce a paid maternity furlough of up to six months at a monthly taxfree salary of up to DM750, to be paid from public funds. Women covered will be protected from dismissal for the period. This measure will be of special help to women whose income contributes to the maintenance of a minimum family livelihood, and will give parents the breathing space needed to better organize the care of their children after birth, if both should want to continue working. Additionally, the demand for female part-time employees is likely to grow because of the falling overall female labor volume caused by this measure.

SUMMARY AND RECOMMENDATIONS

The following summary refers to the main areas in which the existing instruments of state labor market policy need to be more intensively or differently used to ease the return of women to employment. New measures are also suggested. All measures proposed derive from the problems dealt with in the preceding discussion.

1. The funds of the Federal Employment Institution for occupational upgrading and qualifying measures—advanced vocational training and retraining—must be substantially raised. With a view to an expected shortage of labor from 1990, especially qualified labor, much more needs to be done to improve the psychological outlook and technical skills of reentrants so as to enable them to fulfill new vocational tasks and demands.

2. There must be total cancellation of all the Labor Promotion Act's restrictive entitlement regulations that discriminate against women in regard to financial support of advanced vocational training and retraining

under the 1975 Budget Structure Act. This concerns above all the regulations about:

the required duration of employment experience;

the period of three years in gainful employment before participation;

the compulsion to repay stipends if women do not work for three years after participation;

the 58 percent rate of sustenance if the reintegration of women returnees is categorized as "desirable" rather than "necessary." The rate of unemployment benefit (*Arteitslosengeld*) should be the lower limit.

3. All conceivable efforts should be made to accelerate the division of full-time jobs to raise the number of part-time jobs available. These measures serve to prevent interruptions and shorten the duration of interruption. Already operating measures of the Federal Employment Institution, integration supports for problem groups and direct job-creation measures, must be intensified and oriented to this objective. With such action, additional costs to enterprises by the conversion of full-time jobs can be offset.

4. New ways and means have to be worked out to preserve women's contact with their occupations during interruptions. Both employing firms and the labor administration should contribute to this. A minimum demand in this respect would be for employing firms to keep their former women employees continuously up to date about the development of the enterprise, specifically at the vocational level, and for the labor administration to actively approach women exiters with informational materials about vocational developments, new vocational demands, possibilities of vocational further training and retraining, and about future prospects of returning to employment. Much will also depend on encouraging women willing to return to take concrete steps to find work or to undergo vocational qualification.

5. The content, standards and organization of the Federal Employment Institution's vocational qualification programs must be better tailored to the special situation and needs of women willing to return to work. In particular, care must be taken that courses are held at times when housewives with children can take part in them (mornings or evenings). Over and above this, more facilities must be provided for taking care of small children while their mothers are taking part in vocation-qualifying programs. Courses should be held as close as possible to the homes of the participants.

6. The career counseling and job placement services of the Federal Employment Institution should take more account of the particular informational, social and psychological problems of women returning to employment. If necessary, special counseling and placement services staffed by personnel especially schooled for this purpose must be set up. Even in times of recessive labor market developments, the labor administra-

tion should encourage women to take concrete steps to seek work and help them to establish vocational contacts. At the present time, the administration is doing its utmost to squeeze these persons out of the labor market.

7. The availability of child care facilities must be improved, especially at the day-nursery and all-day kindergarten levels. Publicly financed childminding by "day-mothers" must be expanded. More all-day schools must be established and qualified homework supervision promoted.

8. In the mid and long terms, measures must be developed aimed at preventing or shortening employment interruptions because of family care commitments in order to prevent women's losing contact with their vocations. In addition to the development of vocational and career patterns for families with children, which inter alia would have to provide for legally secured and agreement-regulated transition from full- to part-time employment of both parents, as well as measures generally reducing working time, it is necessary above all to bring women out of their present vocational marginality and awaken their interest in qualified vocational training and vocations offering good prospects. "Girls into male vocations" programs currently beginning to operate in the Federal Republic, which partially aim at eliminating cyclical and structural instabilities in women's vocational structure, preventing vocational one-sidedness, doing away with job and income discrimination and creating more advancement opportunities for women, are a step in the right direction. They need to be intensified so as to increase interest in them.

Efficiency Considerations

No cost benefit analyses of the macroeconomic efficiency of specific promotion of women's return to employment have been made in the Federal Republic of Germany.

There have, however, been studies comparing the costs of unemployment, on the one hand, and the cost of direct job creation measures by the Federal Employment Institution, on the other hand. This approach initially is only fiscal in the short term, since it can quantify the expenditures and revenue losses of the public budgets but not the value creation contributions or losses and other external benefits and costs, all of which are hard to quantify. According to these calculations, one jobless person currently costs DM20,000 a year, compared with DM18,500 for someone placed under direct job creation measures. Thus it is presently cheaper for the public budgets to place the jobless in direct job procurement programs than to leave them unemployed. A similarly positive appraisal would be likely with respect to the majority of recipients of transfer payments (e.g. social welfare recipients) if the positive social effects of gainful employment are considered. Since most women returnees do not qualify for transfer payments from public budgets, such a fiscal calculation is likely to be to the disadvantage of these women and can thus hardly be a suitable approach to assessing the efficiency of promotion of return employment. Here, indeed, a longer-term social cost/benefit analysis would be needed, which would compare, for a time span of 10 to 15 years, the economic *and* social costs and benefits of nonemployment of women wanting to return against those of programmatic assistance. In addition to the narrower economic and fiscal effects, more attention must be given to the effects of both alternatives on the family, to the work satisfaction of the women concerned, to problems of loss of qualification and rates of pay, to vocational socialization problems, to aspects of the longer-term security of the supply of qualified labor in the Federal Republic, and to other factors. Such calculations are not at hand nor have any yet been initiated. The interest of labor market research should, however, increasingly concentrate on these considerations.

NOTES

1. *Amtliche Nachrichten der Bundesanstalt fuer Arbeitsvermittlung und Arbeitslosenversicherung* 14, no. 3 (1966), p. 116 f.

2. A. Myrdahl and V. Klein, *Women's Two Roles* (London, 1968).

3. H. Kohler and L. Reyher, "Erwerbstaetigkeitsphasen von Frauen," *Mitteilungen aus der Arbeitsmarktund Berufsforschung* 3 (1970), p. 286–97.

4. H. Hofbauer, U. Bintig and W. Dadzio, "Die Rueckkehr von Frauen in das Erwerbsleben," *Mitteilungen aus der Arbeitsmarktund Berufsforschung* 9 (1969), pp. 713–33.

5. F. Weltz, "Bestimmungsgroessen der Frauenerwerbstaetigkeit," *Mitteilungen aus der Arbeitsmarkt- und Berufsforschung* 2 (1971), pp. 201–15.

6. Institut fuer angewandte Sozialwissenschaften (INFAS), "Frauenerwerbstaetigkeit in Nordrhein-Westfalen" (unpublished manuscript) (Bonn, 1969).

7. H. Hofbauer, "Die Untersuchung des IAB ueber Berufsverlaeufe bei Frauen," *Mitteilungen aus der Arbeitsmarkt- und Berufsforschung* 2 (1978), pp. 131–47.

8. E.g. "Aspekte der Erwerbstaetigkeit von Frauen," *Wirtschaft und Statistik* 2 (1977), pp. 87–92; "Unterbrechung und Wiederaufnahme der Erwerbstaetigkeit von Faruen," *Wirtschaft und Statistik* 4 (1976), pp. 3, 236–39.

9. H. Hofbauer, et al., op. cit.

10. F. Weltz, op. cit., p. 210.

11. Ibid.

12. Group of authors, "Der Arbeitsmarkt in der Bundesrepublik Deutschland 1978," *Mitteilungen aus der Arbeitsmarkt- und Berufsforschung* 1 (1978), p. 67.

13. W. Friedrich a.o., "Zu den Beschaftigungserwartungen, den Arbeitsplatzreserven und zum Potential an zusatzlichen Teilzeitarbeitsplaetzen in der Verarbeitenden Industrie and im Bauhauptgewerbe," *Mitteilungen aus der Arbeitsmarkt- und Berufsforschung* 2 (1978), pp. 235–51.

3

France

by GENEVIÈVE GONTIER and
ANNIE LABOURIE-RACAPE*

INTRODUCTION

A general rise in educational attainment and the growth of tertiary employment are the two principal explanations usually given for the steady increase in the labor force participation of married women in France since 1954.

French women have always worked but, in the past, their economic and productive activities were closely bound to domestic and household activities and were carried out within the confines of the family. The wives of farmers, tradesmen and craftsmen often still function in this manner, but a new phenomenon is women's work activity outside the home. When there are young children in the family, however, the difficulty of combining career and family often forces women to interrupt their work activity for some period of time.

The resumption of work activity, be it late or early, is a classic phenomenon which may be the result of a major constraint in the case of a single woman with dependents, or of a choice made by a married couple or a wife, usually in relation to economic, psychological or sociological factors. Reentry is often difficult, as stressed in 1976 by F. Giroud, then

*Françoise Laroche was responsible for the section dealing with legislation; Monique Appert, Cecil Baron, Marie-Claude Quiles and Sylvie Roger for the field surveys; Sandra Adams for the translation.

Secretary of State for the Feminine Condition, in her report "One hundred measures for women":

Today, it is usually between 35 and 54 years of age that women wish or are obliged to resume an activity that they had abandoned in order to raise their children. The older they are, the more difficult is reentry; but even before the age of 40: they may not be familiar with working conditions or have been absent from the working world for at least ten years; they have a poor perception of their opportunities; they are often in a psychological situation which aggravates their feeling of inferiority, particularly when the need to work is the result of rejection by the man from whom they are separated; and the knowledge they acquired as young girls is outdated . . .

In its choice of family and employment policies, the government must take into account changes in the behavior of women and couples, since assistance to women reentrants is related to both these policies.

In the framework of the Seventh Plan, measures were proposed to deal with the objective of facilitating the "conciliation between the employment of parents and the upbringing of children." Among other proposals were the development and improvement of services at the families' disposal and the protection of the employment of the mother or the future mother. Women also were the subjects of proposals made during the Year of the Woman in 1975: opening of the Civil Service examinations; priority in training programs; post-natal leave for women, etc.

Recent measures, however, show the actual preoccupations of Western European governments: first and foremost a concern with the declining birth rate and, second, anxiety over the increase in unemployment of persons under 25 years of age. The measures which can benefit reentrants are thus at cross-purposes to these concerns.

Three measures that have recently been adopted in France give an idea of current preoccupations: lengthening of maternity leave (from 14 to 16 weeks); parental leave which gives the father or the mother the option, under certain conditions, to interrupt work with the right of return; a 1978 extension of certain elements of the second National Pact for the Employment of Youth to single women with dependents. In the context of the economic recession can one hope for measures directed at facilitating—and thus encouraging—women to resume work? In spite of unemployment, reentrants have continued to join the labor market, but the latest statistics seem to show a slight slowdown in resumption. Discouraged, women are remaining outside of a market which, in any case, rejects them.

No study nor statistic provides precise information about female reentry, only some data on the basis of national inquiries, either from one year to the next or at five year intervals, indicates labor force entries and exits. These figures permit an evaluation of tendencies toward resumption of activity.

An exhaustive study for an analysis of the conditions and factors of resumption, as well as of the different measures susceptible of aiding reentrants, proved impossible. We, therefore, confined our inquiries to three areas. The first was an administrative subdivision in the Paris Region where the level of activity is high and the population very dense (20 percent of the French live in Paris and the seven administrative subdivisions which form the "Paris Region"). The second was the agglomeration of Lyon, which has nearly two million inhabitants and a very long-standing urban industrial and administrative tradition, being one of the large cities where a substantial part of the population depended on local industries before World War I, and did so to an even greater extent between the two world wars. This population, trained for generations in factory work and the organization of community life, had no trouble in entering the new industrial era after the First World War, nor in finding the essentially female personnel necessary for expansion of the service sector. Finally, we looked at the Calvados area which, in contrast to the first two, was essentially agricultural until the end of World War I, but has recently experienced rapid industrialization due to decentralization of the industries of the Paris Region. The large but poorly skilled labor force is made up, in the main, of untrained women. There is practically no service sector, except that which is specific to local public administration.

Although legislative proposals directed to helping women resume work exist, their impact is, unfortunately, very limited. Beside the traditional mentalities which tend to slow their realization, there is the additional barrier resulting from the particular structure of French residential patterns. More than three-fourths of the population live in cities of less than 200,000, which makes it extremely difficult to initiate efforts to help women who wish to reenter the labor force—efforts whose worth must be justified by the high rates of participation.

THE ACTIVE FEMALE POPULATION IN FRANCE

In March 1975, women represented eight million, or almost 37 percent, of an active population of 21.8 million.*

Between 1962 and 1968, the total active population increased by 1.2 million, and by 1.3 million between 1968 and 1975. This did not result from a postwar demographic increase alone, but was also due to a rise in female work participation and to immigration, which more than compensated for the decrease in the rate of activity of younger and older age groups.

Between 1954 and 1968 the proportion of women in the active population varied very little, but between 1968 and 1975 it rose from 34.2 percent to 36.7 percent. Due to the rise in the female work force, the total labor force grew more rapidly than the total population (139 inactives for 100 actives).

*Included in the active population are the unemployed seeking employment and the clergy; excluded are students, military contingents, the retired (both those who were salaried and those who were self-employed) and housewives.

This development of the labor force's resources, which has continued since 1975 in spite of an increase in unemployment, has transformed the character of the active population.

Between 1962 and 1968, the overall activity rate of women over age 15 remained unchanged. Actually this stability masked several movements which become apparent upon examination of age-specific activity (Table 3.1):

a reduction in the activity of the young as a result of the lengthening of education;

an increase in work activity at adult ages, probably due to both fewer exits and more entries; and

a reduction of the work activity of the elderly as a result of (a) the diminishing weight of self-employed and unpaid workers, particularly in agriculture (i.e. family aides aged 45 and over), and (b) the tendency toward a lower retirement age for employed workers.

Between 1968 and 1975, these movements continued, but the increase in the work activity of the adult women was such that the overall rate of activity went from 36.2 percent to 38.7 percent; and there no longer was the customary dip in activity between 30 and 45 years of age, demonstrating a profound change in women's pattern of activity. The rates of activity of widows, divorcees and single women, already at a high level, increased little; it was married women with children who mainly contributed to the growth of the labor force (Table 3.2).

Until 1977, the increase continued in spite of the economic crisis and female unemployment, but the overall rate of female activity had stabilized by 1978 relative to the preceding year, and the trend in the percentage of women seeking to return to work was diminishing. This may be a sign of a decrease in attempts to resume activity after a period of recession, unemployment, etc. by women who are discouraged and hesitant about their labor market opportunities.

A combination of factors have influenced the behavior of women with regard to occupational activity: dependents (number of children and age of youngest), level of training and qualification, and social class (defined by husband's profession). The period 1968 to 1975 was characterized by greater participation in economic activity of women with one or two children. Among women with two dependent children, the rate of activity was higher when the youngest child was seven years of age or over. Among all mothers, labor force participation was lowest when their youngest child was of preschool age. Obviously, the phenomenon of reentry tends to take place when women are released from certain family obligations.

The level of training, general or professional, acquired at school is one of the important factors influencing the participation of French women in the labor market. Women who left school before the age of 15 have a lower rate of activity than those who ended their studies after age 16. This was true

Table 3.1   Active Population by Age and Sex, 1962, 1968, 1975

	Women						Men					
	1962		1968		1975		1962		1968		1975	
	Total Active Population	Activity Rates	Total Active Population	Activity Rates	Total Active Population	Activity Rates	Total Active Population	Activity Rates	Total Active Population	Activity Rates	Total Active Population	Activity Rates
15–19 years	596,680	35.5	652,060	31.4	440,980	21.2	853,260	48.7	913,940	42.5	571,255	26.4
20–24	815,200	61.5	1,150,020	62.4	1,375,845	66.0	723,760	50.8	1,388,940	71.3	1,508,555	70.9
25–29	664,960	45.3	702,600	50.6	1,332,885	62.7	1,459,460	93.6	1,402,380	94.2	2,132,150	94.1
30–34	629,300	38.7	642,840	42.4	800,810	54.6	1,630,320	97.1	1,553,000	97.3	1,550,085	97.2
35–39	638,720	39.5	681,600	41.3	743,550	50.6	1,594,120	97.1	1,665,420	97.3	1,512,070	97.3
40–44	581,740	41.2	718,480	43.4	797,205	49.4	1,353,400	96.7	1,621,240	96.5	1,505,670	96.9
45–49	504,960	45.0	707,240	45.3	822,745	49.9	1,035,700	95.2	1,462,640	95.4	1,686,255	95.4
50–54	677,000	45.3	458,260	45.1	786,305	48.1	1,334,440	93.0	875,000	91.4	1,445,380	92.2
55–59	613,740	42.2	619,180	42.3	436,220	42.0	1,154,440	85.2	1,119,360	82.4	794,625	81.8
60–64	462,620	33.9	460,220	32.3	366,955	27.8	845,520	71.1	824,420	65.7	623,945	54.3
65–69	228,680	19.2	192,240	14.7	135,235	10.0	340,400	41.8	322,040	30.5	208,040	19.0
70–74	100,020	10.4	81,560	7.4	50,980	4.2	149,300	25.1	103,060	14.9	67,615	7.7
75 and over	71,640	4.8	57,220	3.3	42,470	2.1	105,080	13.5	64,200	7.9	37,030	3.8
Total all ages	6,585,260	36.1	7,123,420	36.1	8,132,185	38.7	12,579,200	75.3	13,315,640	73.0	13,642,675	69.5

Table 3.2   Rates of Activity of Women by Marital Status and Age, 1962, 1968, 1975

Age	Married			Single, Widowed, Divorced		
	1962 (percent)	1968 (percent)	1975 (percent)	1962 (percent)	1968 (percent)	1975 (percent)
15–19	41.9	43.4	49.5	35.3	30.9	34.6
20–24	45.2	51.2	62.2	74.3	71.0	69.1
25–29	36.2	43.1	56.5	79.0	80.7	84.3
30–34	32.0	37.0	49.6	76.9	78.1	83.9
35–39	33.4	35.6	46.1	75.5	78.3	81.5
40–44	35.0	37.4	44.4	74.4	76.6	79.6
45–49	38.2	39.1	44.2	72.6	73.3	77.2
50–54	38.4	38.4	41.5	68.2	67.5	72.6
55–59	34.6	34.9	34.8	60.3	60.8	61.5
60–64	26.7	25.3	21.5	45.1	44.3	39.6
65 and over	10.4	7.6	4.3	11.2	8.3	5.4
Total	32.4	34.2	40.3	41.6	38.8	40.1

in 1968 as well as 1975, whatever the current age. The differences are most perceptible between 25 and 35 years of age, however.

While a woman's age at the end of her schooling is a good indication of her level of training, the nature of the training (general or professional) and the specialty studied at school (sewing or industrial drawing, for example) are also factors that influence the interruption and resumption of work. Reentry can be facilitated when a woman has had good technical training followed by several years of work before exiting from the labor force, whereas a diploma in "general education" acquired at age 18 or 20 does not necessarily lead to meaningful work experience which can be of value later in life.

The rate of activity among married women varies by their husbands' occupational group. The highest work participation is among wives of junior executives and of other white-collar employees, closely followed by wives of senior executives. In this last group, the increase in the rate of activity of women under age 35 was the most perceptible between 1968 and 1975.

Considerable disparity exists in the rates of female work activity by region. The level of activity among women in the Paris Region and in certain recently industrialized regions is high compared to that of women in the north, east, and southeast. The size of the agglomeration has an influence, though relatively limited, on the rate of female activity, with a higher rate in urban communities than in rural.

It is probable that the future development of female work activity will be influenced by current transformations of the spatial distribution of the population: the decline in the rate of growth of the cities, which are losing their attractiveness; the growth of the agglomerations' neighboring rural communities; and finally, the depopulation of the completely rural zones.

In reality, none of the factors examined can be considered alone. The interruption and the resumption of activity tends to be "programmed" by the woman and by the couple, who take interrelated factors into account. In their economic calculation, they must consider their income, family allowances, taxes, and all additional expenses, for child care in particular.

The Structure of the Active Population

Since 1954, the active population, according to its distribution by sector of economic activity and occupational category, has been characterized by a decrease in the agricultural component, a rise in the proportion of wage and salary earners and the "tertiarization" of employment.* These last two changes have greatly favored the development of female participation despite limited part-time employment opportunities.

The growth of the proportion of wage and salary earners was already noticeable between 1962 and 1968 but, between 1968 and 1975, this increase accelerated. The 4.8 million nonwage or salaried workers in 1968— agricultural and nonagricultural—represented almost 25 percent of the employed; by 1975, their proportion had dropped to 18 percent.

In 1954, just over five million people, 28 percent of the active population, worked in the primary sector (agriculture) as landowners, family aides, or paid workers. By 1975, this percentage had dropped to 10 percent. The decrease was even greater in the active female population, particularly between 1968 and 1975.

Industrial composition. The tertiary sector included more than half the labor force in 1975: ten million people, 47 percent of whom were women. This is the sector in which employment has progressed the most, and which has provided numerous openings for women. In 1975, 66 out of 100 working women were employed in this sector, compared to 60 per 100 in 1968. The principal loci of women's employment are public administration, banks, insurance companies, etc., and the commercial sector. In 1975, the public service area employed ten percent of the active women, with which increasing feminization of this sector includes the national educational system, the postal and telecommunications systems and the public hospitals.

The highest proportion of female public employees is between the ages of 25 and 34. This fact reflects the guarantees and advantages offered to civil servants; women in this age group often have young children and are the principal beneficiaries of certain of these advantages (Table 3.3).

*The tertiary sector includes services, commerce, banking and insurance, and government.

Table 3.3   The Active Female Population by Age and Industry, 1968 and 1975
(percentage distribution)

Industrial Sector[a]		1968				
	Total	15—24 Years	25—34 Years	35—54 Years	55—64 Years	65 years and over
Agriculture	14.5	6.1	9.7	17.1	23.2	29.2
Secondary Sector	25.6	34.7	24.8	23.2	21.3	12.5
Food & kindred	2.8	3.6	2.6	2.8	2.3	1.4
Fabricated metal products	1.2	1.4	1.2	1.2	1.1	0.5
Machinery & mech- anical equipment	1.5	1.9	1.7	1.4	1.2	0.6
Electrical equipment	1.9	2.6	2.2	1.7	1.1	0.3
Chemical & allied products	1.6	1.6	2.0	1.7	1.3	0.7
Textiles	3.5	5.3	2.9	2.9	3.5	1.5
Apparel	4.1	7.0	3.0	3.0	3.7	3.1
Leather	1.1	2.0	0.9	0.9	0.9	0.4
Printing & publishing	1.3	1.3	1.4	1.3	1.1	0.8
Plastic products	1.1	1.9	1.3	1.3	1.2	0.9
Tertiary Sector	59.9	59.2	65.5	59.7	55.5	58.3
Other[b]	16.9	16.8	18.0	16.8	15.7	18.0
Commerce	13.8	15.2	12.4	13.7	13.2	14.7
Banking, insurance	2.4	3.3	2.9	2.1	1.3	0.6
Government	8.8	7.3	15.0	9.1	4.9	2.0
Domestic service	6.8	7.3	4.1	5.9	10.0	10.5
Total percent	100.0	100.0	100.0	100.0	100.0	100.0
Number	6,924,160	1,721,880	1,307,840	2,509,760	1,056,600	378,080

[a]Only industries with significant representations of women workers are included.
[b]Mainly business, industrial, health services, etc. Source: Census of Population.

The portion of actives employed in industry has changed little, but the proportion of women has risen slightly. The proportion of females diminished between the 1968 and 1975 censuses in two industries greatly affected by the recession—textile and apparel—which happen to employ the most women. On the other hand, the number of women in rapid growth industries, such as electrical and mechanical equipment manufacturing, increased. Consequently, although industrial employment has progressed little, the part played by women was important in the creation of employment between 1968 and 1975.

The proportion of women employed in industry is higher among the young than the old. Unlike the tertiary sector, industry employs young

Industrial Sector[a]		1975				
	Total	15–24 Years	25–34 Years	35–54 Years	55–64 Years	65 years and over
Agriculture	8.1	2.5	3.5	12.0	14.0	15.5
Secondary Sector	25.7	34.1	25.3	23.6	21.7	12.5
Food & kindred	2.7	3.5	2.3	2.7	2.6	1.7
Fabricated metal products	1.4	1.6	1.3	1.4	1.3	0.6
Machinery & mechanical equipment	1.8	2.1	2.1	2.0	1.3	0.7
Electrical equipment	2.7	4.0	3.0	2.3	1.6	0.5
Chemical & allied products	1.7	1.5	2.0	1.8	1.6	0.6
Textiles	2.6	3.8	2.3	2.3	2.6	1.2
Apparel	3.5	6.4	2.9	2.5	3.0	2.7
Leather	1.0	1.7	0.9	0.8	0.8	0.4
Printing & publishing	1.1	1.1	1.2	1.1	1.1	0.9
Plastic products	1.5	1.9	1.4	1.4	1.3	0.8
Tertiary Sector	66.2	63.4	71.2	64.4	64.3	72.0
Other[b]	20.3	21.2	21.7	18.9	19.0	23.2
Commerce	13.8	15.5	11.9	13.7	14.4	17.3
Banking, insurance	3.2	4.4	4.4	2.4	1.7	0.8
Government	11.6	8.3	16.6	11.7	7.9	2.9
Domestic service	3.9	3.3	2.1	4.2	7.6	7.7
Total percent	100.0	100.0	100.0	100.0	100.0	100.0
Number	7,675,755	1,619,570	2,021,820	3,040,035	169,425	224,835

women who interrupt their activity at marriage or the birth of a child, and who, if they resume work, do not necessarily go back to the same type of job.

As we have seen, the development of employment since 1954, and particularly since 1968, has greatly favored female activity. The tertiary sector absorbs a large number of young women who enter the labor market, and this sector seems to encourage the continuity of activity or an early resumption.

Occupational distribution. In 1975, out of 100 persons in the labor force (male and female), 38 were blue-collar workers, 26 were junior or senior executives, and 18 were office or commercial employees. The remainder

Table 3.4   The Active Population by Sex and Occupational Category, 1962, 1968, 1975

Occupational Category	Total			Female						Rate of Feminization		
	1962	1968	1975	1962	Percent	1968	Percent	1975	Percent	1962	1968	1975
Farm owners	3,011,600	2,459,840	1,650,865	1,166,880	17.7	932,060	13.1	566,405	7.0	38.7	37.9	34.3
Farm workers	829,600	588,200	375,480	97,260	1.5	61,000	0.9	43,710	0.5	11.7	10.4	11.6
Industrial and business owners and operators	1,996,560	1,961,980	1,708,925	723,160	11.0	685,040	9.6	570,875	7.0	36.3	34.9	33.4
Professionals and senior executives	761,040	992,800	1,459,285	126,420	1.9	186,200	2.6	338,615	4.2	16.6	18.8	23.2
Junior executives and technicians	1,490,500	2,014,100	2,764,950	585,040	8.9	816,740	11.5	1,249,440	15.4	39.3	40.1	45.2
Other white-collar	2,416,300	3,029,900	3,840,700	1,403,480	21.3	1,841,600	25.8	2,454,375	30.2	58.1	60.8	63.9
Blue-collar	7,024,040	7,698,600	8,207,165	1,519,580	23.0	1,569,760	22.0	1,839,845	22.6	21.6	20.4	22.4
Service	1,042,020	1,171,060	1,243,490	833,640	12.7	925,860	13.0	968,545	11.9	80.0	79.1	77.9
Other	592,780	522,640	524,000	129,220	2.0	105,260	1.5	100,335	1.2	21.8	20.1	19.1
Total	19,177,019	20,439,160	21,774,860	6,585,260	100.0	1,123,520	100.0	8,132,145	100.0	34.3	34.9	37.3

Source: Census of Population.

were primarily in agriculture, or industrial or commercial owners or operators. The distribution of active women among the various occupational categories is different—fewer blue-collar workers, more office and commercial employees, but the same proportion of executives—although women are more often in the lesser ranks than men (Table 3.4).*

Between 1962 and 1975, the greatest increases in the female work force were in the categories of office and commercial employees (from 21 to 30 percent) and, especially, of executives (from 9 to 15 percent for junior executives, and from two to four percent for senior executives). At the same time, women's representation has increased by more than six points in these areas. The number of women in agriculture has greatly diminished, while the proportion of blue-collar workers has increased slightly.

The increase in the employment of junior executives has been the greatest among women between 24 and 34 years of age, for two reasons: unlike blue-collar workers, women who have a career rarely abandon their job; and it is around the age of 30 that women who began at lower levels can hope to be promoted to the status of junior executive.

Working hours. In March 1976, 1,400,000 people (246,000 men and, 160,000 women), or 6.7 percent of the employed population, worked part time; that is, less than 30 hours a week. This type of work principally involves women, one-third of whom are farmers, family aides or self-employed. Among female part-time employees, one out of three is a domestic worker (mainly cleaning women); more than one out of four is an office or sales clerk.

The proportion of part-time workers increases with age but, between 1972 and 1976, growth was particularly evident among women 30 to 50 years of age and men over 60 (Table 3.5). Thus, the tremendous increase of female labor force participation between 1968 and 1975 in the 30- to 50-year age groups corresponded to an even more rapid increase in part-time employment.

Unemployment

The unemployment survey divides the unemployed into two categories: the PDRE, or those who answered "seeking employment or a position" when asked their occupation at the time surveyed; and the PMDRE, or those who answered "inactive" when asked their occupation, but who, in the course of the inquiry, said they were seeking employment (Table 3.6). This latter group (PMDRE) was distinguished from the former (PDRE) in several ways: one-quarter were seeking part-time work; two-fifths had not made

*Junior executives include instructors, health and social service workers, technicians and lower-level administrators. Senior executives include traditional professionals as well as high-ranking administrators.

Table 3.5   Part-Time Employment by Age and Sex, 1972 and 1976

Age Groups	Men		Women	
	Percent 1972	Percent 1976	Percent 1972	Percent 1976
15–19 years	2.4	4.5	4.0	7.1
20–24	1.3	1.1	5.0	5.8
25–29	1.1	1.3	8.9	9.3
30–34	0.7	0.9	12.8	13.6
35–39	0.2	0.6	15.0	17.6
40–44	0.8	0.8	14.7	17.9
45–49	0.8	1.3	14.9	17.4
50–54	1.2	2.1	16.5	19.3
55–59	2.6	2.6	18.3	20.4
60–64	4.7	6.2	22.0	23.4
65–69	9.7	14.3	31.8	31.5
70–74	15.4	22.8	39.1	33.8
75 years and over	25.6	32.2	43.7	35.2
Total	1.6	1.9	13.2	14.6

Source: Employment inquiry.

any effort to find employment in the month preceding the survey; barely 18 percent were enrolled in the public placement service (as opposed to 70 percent of PDRE).

Unemployment rates are usually calculated according to the relation of the PDRE to the whole of the labor force and do not take into account the PMDRE. Neither do unemployment studies based on statistics provided by the public placement service, since few women in the PMDRE category are enrolled in this service. Thus, the specifics of the labor market hardly cover latent unemployment of inactive women susceptible of resuming work but who have not yet taken the necessary steps to find a job.

Unemployment rates demonstrate the vulnerability of women, whatever their circumstances and training, and show a considerable increase in the unemployment of those under age 25. Women and the young, the very people who have been the most significant additions to the labor force, are those who have been the most severely affected by unemployment.

Between 1968 and 1974 the male unemployment rate remained stable, while the female rate increased. The increase in total unemployment between the two dates was thus due to a rise in the unemployment of women. After 1974, the beginning of the recession, female unemployment continued to increase, reaching 5.8 percent in 1976. Male unemployment also rose sharply during this period, reaching 3.2 percent in 1976. Between 1972 and 1976, the rate of unemployment among women under 35 years

Table 3.6   Percentage Distribution of the PDRE and PMDRE by Sex, 1972 and 1976

	P.D.R.E.[a]		P.M.D.R.E.[a]	
	March 1972	March 1976	March 1972	March 1976
Males	49.9	46.7	18.2	19.7
Females	50.1	53.3	81.8	80.3
Total percentage	100.0	100.0	100.0	100.0
Total number	450,600	910,800	342,700	439,100

[a]See Text
Source: Employment survey.

increased the most. In March 1976, one out of two unemployed women was under 25 (Table 3.7). Among the female PMDRE the proportion of women under 30 years increased, while the percentage of women over 40 dropped.

The total PDRE grew by 160,000 people between March 1976 and 1978, but the proportion of women in this group decreased. During the same period, the PMDRE, made up mainly of women, declined, from 439,000 to 370,000. These developments were primarily due to the decreasing number of reentrants among the unemployed population seeking employment: 18 percent in 1977 and 15 percent in 1978 (Table 3.8). It is possible that women wishing to resume activity expressed this intention less than before, having been discouraged by their first futile attempts to enter an already saturated labor market.

EXITS AND ENTRIES

Exits from the Labor Market

According to surveys in 1965 and 1970, 1,400,000 women between the ages of 15 and 64 who had been active five years earlier were no longer active; 17 percent were between 16 and 24 years of age; 28 percent between 25 and 34; and 55 percent between the ages of 35 and 64. Almost half of these withdrawals took place before the age of 35, but they continued past this age at a lower rate (FQP Survey).

Among the 7,900,000 women between the ages of 15 and 64 who were in the labor force in 1974, 570,000 exited in 1975, 200,000 (37 percent) of whom were under 30. These exits decreased in 1977; out of 8,200,000 working women in 1976, 500,000 had withdrawn from the work force in 1977, 170,000 of whom were under 30. The falling rate of exits between 1975 and 1977 occurred at all ages under 60, at which age the rates increased, showing a tendency toward a lower retirement age (Employment Survey).

Table 3.7   Unemployment Rates: Distribution of the PDRE and PMDRE
by Sex and Age, 1972 and 1976

	15—24 Years	25—39 Years	40—49 Years	50—59 Years	60 Years and Over	Total 15 Years and Over
Unemployment rate						
March 1972						
Males	3.6	1.1	1.1	1.7	2.7	1.7
Females	5.0	2.4	2.0	2.1	2.1	2.9
March 1976						
Males	7.7	2.4	2.2	2.4	3.1	3.2
Females	13.4	4.3	3.1	3.5	3.4	5.8
Percent distribution of PDRE[a]						
March 1972						
Males	33.4	22.4	14.9	15.0	14.3	100.0
Females	39.2	25.9	14.7	11.3	8.9	100.0
March 1976						
Males	35.4	39.9	16.2	12.8	5.7	100.0
Females	48.5	27.3	10.9	9.7	3.6	100.0
Percent distribution of PMDRE[a]						
March 1972						
Males	53.8	10.0	4.0	10.3	21.9	100.0
Females	30.5	34.6	20.6	10.1	4.2	100.0
March 1976						
Males	61.7	15.6	3.1	8.8	10.8	100.0
Females	39.0	36.6	14.6	7.8	2.0	100.0

[a]See text
Source: INSEE Employment survey.

According to a study made in Lyon and Caen, two out of three women
between the ages of 30 and 34 had interrupted their activity before the age of
25. Although this interruption was usually the only one, it was relatively
long. Two-thirds of the women between 30 and 34 who resumed work did
so after more than five years of inactivity.

Women generally stop working at the birth of a child. The interruption
may occur at the time of marriage, however; 15 to 20 percent of the women
who had their first child in 1973 did not work before the child's birth.
Afterwards, exits proceed gradually between the births of the first and
second child, and vary in degree according to the mother's occupation.
After the birth of the first child, the rates of exit of blue-collar workers were
twice as high as those of executives and slightly higher than those of white-
collar workers. After the birth of the second child, on the other hand, the

Table 3.8   Unemployed Population[a] Seeking Employment by Reasons for
Unemployment, 1974, 1977, 1978 (percentage distribution)

Reasons	April 1974	March 1977	March 1978
Dismissal	37.8	35.9	38.9
Resignation	17.8	15.3	14.4
Occasional employment	6.5	7.9	11.1
Retirement	0.9	0.9	0.6
Have never worked	15.9	19.3	17.4
Resuming acitivity	17.7	17.9	15.3
Other	3.4	2.8	2.3
Total	100.0	100.0	100.0

[a]PDRE and PMDRE do not include those who made no effort to find employment during the month preceding the survey, those unable to work immediately, and those seeking nonsalaried employment.

Source: Employment survey.

blue-collar rates are five times higher than that for executives, and double those for white-collar workers.

Entries into the Labor Force

The entries of women over age 30 into the labor market include both women seeking initial employment and those seeking to resume activity. The late entrants (first employment after age 30) are rare. Few women begin their work life after 35, and most young women work for at least a short time at the end of their studies. The number of women who have never worked declines with age. A 1964 study shows a rate of total inactivity of 23 percent for women born between 1918 and 1933, dropping to 10 percent for women born between 1934 and 1947. For the next generation the rates are even lower. Only six to seven percent of the inactive women surveyed in Caen and Lyon had never worked.

Women with no work experience come from families with a relatively high income and have, on the whole, a high level of education. It is most often marriage—less its date than its timing (at the end or middle of studies)—that is the cause of this absence of work. The training that these women received, which is often incomplete or unadapted to work activity, poorly prepares them for a late entrance into an occupation, which is, in any case, not an economic necessity. In answer to the question "Are you considering getting a job?," three women out of four in Caen, and two out of three in Lyon, said "yes"; but delays and the imprecision of their plans suggest that, for these women, work is very hypothetical.

In 1970, 521,000 working women 35 years of age and over had been out of the labor force in 1965; that means that one-fourth of all the women who began activity between these two dates were women over 34, representing seven percent of the female population employed in 1970 (Employment Survey).

The jobs that women hold when they first enter the labor force vary according to age. When the women begin working immediately after finishing their studies—usually between the ages of 15 and 24—the majority of them start as office employees or blue-collar workers. When they begin work later (35 years and over), the percentage of office employees is cut in half, while that of service workers almost triples (cleaning women and household domestics represent almost two-thirds of the last category). Because they are part-time and have flexible hours, these jobs are often sought by women without any training who resume work while they have small children.

Insofar as customary reentry to gainful employment is concerned, it is the degree of urgency which determines success. Two types of reentry can be distinguished: that which is the result of necessity (widowhood, divorce, etc. . .) and that which is the result of choice, a relative choice when economic necessity is very great, but which, nevertheless, permits a woman to organize and plan her return.

The Need to Return

The urgency of reentry. A sudden, brutal diminution of her family's financial resources forces a nonworking woman to find a job as quickly as possible in order to provide support. Twenty thousand female heads of family— widows, divorcees, and women separated from their husbands— began working between 1976 and 1977. The increase in the number of separations, divorces and legal separations (32, 862 in 1963 and 63,605 in 1975) brought about an increase in the resumption of work imposed by necessity. These resumptions, which oblige women to go from a situation of total economic dependency and security to an autonomous life, are often a source of great stress. When women have foreseen the change in their situation and have had several months to plan their reentry, it has a better chance of success.

In the future, these situations may be regarded differently, since marriage is seen less and less as an end in itself. Broken marriages tend to take place earlier, premarital pregnancies are more numerous and extramarital cohabitation more widespread. Moreover, young women tend to assume responsibility for themselves at younger ages and to assure their future either by not interrupting their employment at all, or by interrupting it only while their children are small, and by resuming it or another activity as soon as their children are of school age.

In the months following the death of their husbands, women with dependent children can receive life insurance benefits which permit them to meet their expenses for several weeks or months. For the most "favored"—most often the wives of executives—a company insurance policy assures a pension for the duration of the children's education. In lower-income classes where such insurance is exceptional, however, the mother has no resources after her husband's death except the state allocation to orphans and the Social Security (National Health Insurance) allocation to "single" parents.

Divorced or abandoned women must seek legal aid in order to receive child support, but the procedure is always slow and not always effective, since the payments are rarely sufficient when the husband's salary is low, and new procedures must be undertaken if the husband does not automatically assume his responsibility.

Thus, the situation in which these women find themselves obliges them to accept any employment readily available—most often as cleaning women—which will be compatible with their children's school hours.

Aside from husband's income, other advantages frequently disappear with his death: free lodging (in connection with the husband's occupation), insurance, etc. During the months following the departure or death of a husband, some companies "take charge" of the family by giving loans, prolonging certain of the children's benefits (camps, vacation activities), hiring the woman herself, or helping her to find a job. But these aids are not the general rule and exist only when the husband has not left the company. Furthermore, they are only temporary. The level of training of these women, their previous work experience, their contacts outside of the home during their break in work—all are determining factors in their reentry, which must sometimes be undertaken under conditions of extreme urgency.

Out of 21 women surveyed who belonged to this category, 13 had left school at or before the age of 14; two had outmoded training (such as corset making); and six had left school between the ages of 14 and 16. Two additional women with the highest level of training (end of secondary studies at age 18) had the greatest success in reentering the labor force, one as a sales manager and the other as a driving school instructor. Also successfully placed were those who had previously done office work. The women who had never worked encountered the greatest difficulty: they either found work as cleaning women or saleswomen, or they had not found jobs after searching three to six months. The aspirations of this last group often seemed utopian, especially those who had been in a higher income bracket and were without any work experience. Such women often seek jobs with human contact, such as serving as hostess or receptionist, working with children, or work in banks, insurance, etc. All these jobs are reminiscent and reflective of their homelife. It is difficult for them to imagine other activities, and it is in these cases that the intervention of a counselor or a training program can help them to make a more reasonable choice.

The presence of preschool children and the problem of child care that it entails creates supplementary difficulties in entry. The costs of day-care centers and "nourrices" are always high and available places scarce. If a grandmother is nearby and available, the best solution still seems to be to leave the children in her care, but this is becoming more and more rare. Among the women surveyed were some who were obliged to leave their children for the whole workweek with a babysitter far from the city where they lived; some who were seeking night jobs in order to be able to take care of their children during the day; and women who, instead of accepting a well-paid skilled job, were obliged to work as cleaning women because of the flexibility of the hours and proximity to their home—all "solutions" which render normal reentry difficult.

Paid training programs are not usually sought by women who wish to find immediate employment. On one hand, they fear that training stipends will be insufficient and that they will lose certain advantages accruing to paid workers; on the other hand, they fear being unable to find employment at the end of the program. Yet those who did follow a program preparing them for work, such as "Retravailler," or a refresher course for those who already had job qualifications, found jobs more easily. One example was an engineer's wife who had worked briefly in Poland as an architect and who, when widowed at the age of 32 with two children aged three and four plus three older children, became a driving school instructor after a paid training program.

All these women, whatever their social class, found themselves with a lower standard of living after the death or departure of their husbands.

Planned reentry. For certain women, reentry, though inevitable, may be less imperative, certainly less urgent, than in the preceding cases. It can be foreseen, and thus prepared for over a period of several months. This is the case for widows who receive a relatively high pension for several years, which diminishes as the children grow up. The desire to maintain their standard of living leads them to find a supplemental income; often they seek part-time employment.

Divorced or separated women who receive child support payments or complementary compensation often seek to resume activity several months or even several years after their divorce or separation, either because the amount of the payments is insufficient or will decrease as the children become older, because they are afraid the payments may stop, or because they simply wish to become independent. A woman also may fear that, upon an eventual remarriage of her ex-husband, he will be unable to support two households.

Perhaps the vast majority of women in this group are those who are separating from their husbands and who are seeking to resume activity because "the marriage is on the rocks" or because they are "having some difficulties at home." Such women are relatively numerous in all training programs, and even if they do not clearly express their reasons for resumption of work at the beginning of the program, they often separate from or divorce their husbands at the end of the program or shortly after resuming work. According to our survey, these women are slightly older than those in the preceding group and none of them have children under the age of seven or eight, which suggests that they waited until their youngest child reached this age before separating or divorcing. They often endure a difficult marital situation while the children are small, but as soon as their children are older and the women themselves are more mature and ready to face new circumstances, they envisage a return to work and make plans for reentry.

For these women, as for the preceding group, the quality of their reentry depends on the level of their training, their work and nonwork experience, and on the degree to which they have been able to acquire a certain amount of autonomy, or conversely, on the extent to which they have been in a state of dependency. In general, however, those with a low income found work much more quickly than those who were in a less pressing economic situation. This last group can be divided into those who had a high level of training and took the time necessary to find a job corresponding to what they wanted, and those who, unsure of themselves and lacking training and experience, decided not to enter the unknown working world.

It is for those women who have the time to plan their reentry that training programs, adapted to each case, have the most positive effect in facilitating the return to work.

The Reentry Decision

The elements of the economic calculation. With respect to the economic situation of the family or of the woman, several factors must be taken into consideration before the decision to resume work is made: husband's salary, the woman's expected salary, family allowances, taxes, and other outlays for such things as child care and work-related needs (restaurants, transportation, etc. . . .). To these must be added costs occasioned by the mother's absence from home (more frequent ready-prepared meals, or clothes, for example). These are not usually precisely calculated by the women, but they play a part in their decision.

According to one survey, 80 percent of the working women answered in the affirmative to the question "Do you consider, financially, it's worth working?" But to a second question, "Taking into account your supplementary expenses, have you calculated how much you actually earn?," 50 to 60 percent said they had made the calculation. Thus, one woman out of two claimed to have evaluated with precision the actual financial gain brought to the family by her work.

In low-income families, the family allowances make up the major portion of financial aid, while in the families of senior executives, financial aid is derived from tax deductions that rise in proportion to the number of children and income. Hence, for a family with four children—one under three, one between three and five, and two aged from six to nine—family benefits rise, when the woman does not work, to 17,500 francs for a professional or senior executive and to 18,970 for a blue-collar worker. Most aid to the latter is provided through the family allowances, while more than a half of the benefits for the senior executive comes from tax deductions. The family allowances and the method of calculating the income tax are intended to mitigate inequalities resulting from differential family size. This income redistribution is in fact more efficient when a woman does not work than when she is in the labor market.

In this two-sided game of family and fiscal legislation, the least-favored families are those in the middle-income bracket: on one hand, the tax reductions are of little significance due to an insufficiently high income and, on the other hand, certain family allowances are not received because the income is above that which qualifies them for allowances. Hence, it is not surprising to find the highest rate of female work participation among these families, often those in which the husband is a junior executive.

The addition of a second salary raises a family's income by 30 to 50 percent. In general, due to this second salary, almost all of the family allowance (determined by the family's resources) is lost, with the exception of the family allocation (discussed subsequently) and the child care allocation, from which only 50,000 families benefited in 1977. And the second salary considerably increases the tax burden because of its progressive nature. In a "model" family in which both spouses are blue-collar workers, the 1977 tax was approximately 2,460 francs per annum with one child and 1,850 francs with two children, 4.6 percent and 3.4 percent, respectively, of total earnings. In a "model" rich family in which husband and wife are senior executives, the tax reached 32,290 francs, 17 percent of earnings, when there was one child and 28,970 francs, or 10 percent, when there were two children. Thus for two-earner families, a redistribution of income occurs, but it is much less noticeable than in families where the woman is not in the labor force.

Reentry due to economic reasons. Two groups can be distinguished: one in which economic pressure is high and women declare that they would not work if it were not financially necessary; the second where the expressed reason is economic but is often modified by the women's claim that they would work even if they had no financial incentive.

In more modest income brackets, the resumption of work when there are at least two preschool children is relatively rare. The income of the husband is low and the expected salary of the wife is equally low. The combined incomes cannot cover the cost of child care. But in certain cases, either when the husband is partially or totally unemployed or when unemployment threatens, as is the case in certain areas of France gravely affected by the economic recession, young women resume factory work as soon as their second child enters nursery school. These are women who stopped work for a brief period, do not intend to have more children, and went back to the same job they held before the interruption. In fact, in calculating their wages, the companies take into account seniority accumulated before the interruption.

Reentry can be earlier, when a woman expects to receive a salary higher than that of her husband (for example, if she is a white-collar employee and her husband a blue-collar worker). If a family has more than three children, however, an early resumption of work is rare; the social assistance received by the family counterbalances the wife's low earnings and her work-related expenses. It is later, when the children are grown, that these women look for a fill-in job to supplement family income and "to help the children." In these families of modest income there are not such financial obligations as the purchase of a house or apartment, etc.

On the other hand, in cases where women at higher income levels gave economic reasons for reentry, 11 out of 13 said they would work even if it were not financially necessary. One example were women whose husbands have good jobs with high salaries but in a sector affected by the economic recession. It is fear of their husbands' unemployment or of lower income (notably in occupations where a part of income depends on the volume of sales) that encourages wives to resume work. Resumption takes place when the children are still young if the woman hopes to make a good salary; otherwise, the attempt to resume work is put off until the youngest child is eight or ten.

Another case is that of women of 35 or over who have three to five children, the youngest of whom is over eight years old. These women want to resume work because the family has made purchases—an apartment, furniture, trailer, etc. . . ; "Children cost more the bigger they get"; "The oldest no longer lives at home and the family allowances have diminished"; or simply "The cost of living keeps rising." In this category it is often when the youngest child "takes care of himself" that the couple makes large purchases and the woman seeks to resume work.

Reentry for other reasons. Among the 100 women surveyed, 21 did not give clear financial reasons to explain their reentry. Their reasons included the following: boredom; isolation; the need for outside contacts; "A woman must be responsible for herself"; "I can't stand being kept"; "You are not seen as being of any value when you are at home"; "You let yourself go when you stay at home"; "Now is the time to resume work—later it will be too late" (a woman of 37).

Three groups can be distinguished according to social class. The first is made up of wives of blue-collar workers in a low-income bracket: they are between 30 and 40 years old and have three rather than two children, the youngest of whom is between six and eight and can thus "take care of himself." Either these women have had vocational training, experience or interest—most often as office clerk, stenographer, typist—and they wish to find a similar job, or they have neither training nor much experience but have a great desire to work, and therefore participate in one or more training programs to acquire qualifications corresponding to their inclination. Often these women have done a lot of volunteer work while out of the work force, which facilitates their reentry. Some older women wait until their youngest child is 14 to 16 years old before resuming work, feeling that until then they are still needed at home.

In the more favored classes, we find two principal points of work resumption: when the youngest child is between six and eight, and when he is over 15. Reentry, however, sometimes takes place when the children are still of preschool age, especially among women with a high level of training who have had interesting prior work experience but were obliged to stop working because their husband's career required a move. As soon as they find satisfactory child care, these women tend to resume work. Others in a similar situation delay reentry because of their husbands' opposition or difficulties in organizing housework: "My husband never helps with the housework, nor do the children, who expect to be waited on." When they resume work, it is often, at least in the beginning, in a part-time job.

Reentry is often late—and sometimes never does occur—when family income is in a middle or high bracket, the husband is an executive, the woman has little or no work experience and a rather low level of general or vocational training. Whether the husband began his career as an executive because of his level of education, or he reached this position after a number of years through training programs and promotions, the distance between his preoccupations and those of his wife grows with time, if she concentrates on household and domestic tasks. Conscious of this problem, certain women between the ages of 30 and 35 seek to leave their "universe" by pursuing training programs that will enable them to resume a paid activity "of value." Some of them have a skill, but it does not correspond to the social standing of the family, such as a switchboard operator married to an executive in a large company, a skilled blue-collar wife of a bank employee, a saleswoman wife of a department store manager, a bookkeeper whose husband is an engineer. When these women seek employment, they usually do so in their husbands' field.

The Rejection of Reentry

The majority of the women who don't want to resume activity and refuse to envisage this possibility—even as an eventuality—are upper-class women. Very few have worked and they have a low level of general or professional training. The salaries they could expect, given their lack of qualifications, would be a negligible addition to family income.

The woman who said her resumption of activity was the result of "having a complex about being a 'kept woman'" found part-time secretarial work. Upon making calculations, she realized that, after subtracting all her supplementary expenses, she actually earned only 400 francs a month; consequently she decided to stop working and now strongly challenges the idea that woman should work outside the home for her own good.

For women who can be relieved of their domestic tasks by household help, the volunteer activities which they have outside the home are totally satisfying—officers of the P.T.A., nursery school aides, secretaries of young people's cultural centers. They have more responsibility than they would have in the jobs for which they would be qualified and often insist that they are not bored and that their cultural level permits them to participate in certain types of very gratifying activities.

Several young mothers of large families who seem satisfied and happy to stay at home with their children add: "After my children, I'll have my grandchildren." Some also prefer not to work and "restrain themselves." In other words, they do not incur additional expenses like buying a house or going on costly vacations.

Finally, there are women who were in well-paid jobs and who interrupted their work in order to raise their children. One of them, a graduate of a high-level graduate school (Hautes Etudes Commerciales) who worked for 12 years as a buyer for an importer, then in a legal office, said, "I prefer raising my children to studying files." She has four children between the ages of four and eleven and is involved in their upbringing. She may resume work, but for her this is a possibility for the distant future.

For women in lower-income families where they are more than three children, the "choice" does not exist: regular paid employment is not actually rejected, but cannot be envisaged simply because it would be of no financial benefit. These women seek jobs they can do at home such as babysitter or concierge—or jobs for a few hours a week, often undeclared, which bring in a small amount of money without entailing additional expenses nor loss of family allowances.

Timing

The time of reentry occurs at three different points, determined by the age of the youngest child: when he begins nursery school between ages four and five; when he reaches an age of autonomy at age seven to eight, and the mother knows she can return home an hour or two later than her child and that the short school vacations will pose fewer problems; or when the child is 14 years or older and is completely independent. Sometimes a mother waits until all the children have left home, but at that point the problem is more in terms of overwork (housework plus her job) than of child care.

If the salary expected by a woman is negligible in relation to the additional expenses her resumption would entail, or if it would represent only a small fraction of that of her husband, her reentry will be put off, at least until her youngest child no longer needs "babysitting." On the contrary, if her expected salary represents a relatively high percentage of her family's income, she will return to work quickly.

If, over the years, a husband has reached a position much higher than the one he began and higher than that his wife could expect to reach (she has not had this possibility since she has not exercised an activity), the woman will not seek employment since the jobs she would be qualified for do not correspond to the family's social standing.

The skill level of the employment the woman is likely to find is another determining factor of the success of reentry, but the nature and duration of her work experience before the interruption, independent of skill, are just as important. The working conditions, the atmosphere, the relationships with colleagues that she had before she exited from the work force are of great importance if the work is not too tiring, even if it entails no great responsibility.

Beside past work experience, a woman's nonwork activities are of great importance to her reentry. A woman who occupied her time during her absence from work with outside activities involving some responsibility is prepared for reentry. For example, the wife of the principal of a primary school who had practically never worked, and who had left school at 16, had helped her husband with the management of day camps. Extremely motivated, she entered a training program in accounting where she acquired indispensable technical competence and obtained, without too much difficulty, a job as manager of an activity center.

AID IN REENTRY

Legislation

The reality of the problem of women's reentry is well reflected in recent legislative developments relative to employment and training. Institutional and legislative measures for social protection, training and employment more and more frequently contain clauses designed to support women's access to training and employment—especially women for whom reentry is of an urgent nature.

Training. Traditionally, two Ministries are responsible for training: the Ministry of Education principally in establishments of primary, secondary and higher education; and the Ministry of Labor through the intermediary of the "Association Nationale pour la Formation Professionnelle des Adultes" (A.F.P.A.). Laws of 1971 and 1978 concerning continuing training complete this group of measures and partially use the network of educational establishments.

Adult education and training include the following:

L'Association Nationale pour la Formation Professionnelle des Adultes (A.F.P.A.) This is legally a private association but is entirely financed by the Ministry of Labor and is under its responsibility. Its purpose is to promote the entry or reentry of those seeking employment, young people seeking a first job and adults seeking a changed job orientation. In 1977, the A.F.P.A. enrolled 85,000 trainees in its 124 centers and various subsidiary branches throughout the country. The proportion of women has been growing slightly but remains small (13 percent in 1975, 15 percent in 1976, 16 percent in 1977). At the same time, the proportion of trainees over 30 years of age comprises less than 12 percent. The A.F.P.A. has places for 28,000 trainees at its disposal, but only about 1,800 of these places are reserved for women. The distribution of trainees by occupation shows a clear predominance of traditionally male skills: 33.7 percent in construction and public works, 28.3 percent in metallurgy. A policy of balancing the male/female ratio is gradually being adopted, however.

The Ministry of National Education. The G.R.E.T.A. (Groups of Establishments) permit the utilization of secondary institutions for continued training. The 400 groups provide training programs for adults on the local level, in accordance with the requests of the population and the needs of employers.

The National Center of Education by Correspondence (C.N.T.E.) has correspondence courses to prepare for secondary school, university, technical school and civil service examinations. The National Center of Pedagogical Documentation (C.N.D.P.) presents a monthly 12-hour televised information bulletin (Tele-formation) on training, and works in collaboration with the C.N.T.E. It is difficult to determine the public reached by this bulletin; about 12 percent were housewives. The training or pretraining courses of these two centers have an extremely variable public according to the subjects taught and the level. Different studies of their public made by the centers give general percentages varying between three and twelve percent who are housewives.

The universities are under the authority of the Ministry of Universities. Their aim is similar to that of the G.R.E.T.A., but naturally the level of studies is higher. They can organize training programs in all the disciplines leading directly to the exercise of a skill: computer science, secretarial work, languages. Some of them have particular programs for reentrants. Certain University Institutes of Technology also take part in the program of continuing training.

The Laws of 1971 and 1978. Any wage or salary worker or person seeking employment has the right to attend a remunerated training program. These are partially financed by the companies concerned, partially by the state, which assures the remuneration of the trainees. Four kinds of training programs are available; adaptation, conversion, refresher and pretraining. They are organized either by the A.F.P.A., the Ministry of Education, by organizations set up for this purpose by employers' associations, or by different semipublic or private organizations. These last two categories must be approved by the "Délégation à la Formation Continue" in order to receive a subsidy equal to the number of trainees (hours-trainees), which permits them to assure free training. On top of this, in order for trainees to be remunerated by the National Employment Budget, these organizations have to have an agreement with the prefecture of the region. The number of programs included in these two categories is too large and their variety too great to provide a detailed statistical breakdown.

The National Employment Agency (A.N.P.E.) Its main function is the orientation and placement of those seeking employment. It also sometimes organizes temporary and local refresher courses aimed at training workers to fill job offers that would otherwise be left vacant. In 1977, 3,300 trainees were prepared in this manner. Due to the traditionally female skills which these training programs often stress (tertiary and clothing sectors), women are in the majority (51 percent).

Employment. Since 1970, the counseling and placement services of the A.N.P.E. have been progressively reinforced by different institutions in matters of female employment.

The National Employment Agency (A.N.P.E.). This national public organization, created in 1967, is under the authority of the Ministry of Labor. Its purpose is to centralize job offers and requests and to give collective and individual occupational information to those seeking employment and eventually to orient them toward A.F.P.A. training programs or other courses, notably those created by the legislation for continuing training. This agency is also responsible for the creation of administrative files necessary for the paying of different allocations and allowances. The agency is found throughout the country. In 1977 it had 322 local agencies and 256 sub-agencies. Job seekers are welcomed by a member of the placement staff whose intervention is supplemented by an interview with a professional counselor, especially when there are problems of orientation toward a job or training.

Other institutions dealing with female employment. The Committee for Female Employment has been under the authority of the Ministry of Labor since 1965 and its finances noticeably increased in 1977. The organization includes representatives of employers' associations, unions, and family and women's associations, as well as other qualified people—in all, 32 people plus a permanent secretariat in the Ministry of Labor. It is a study group concerned mainly with legislative projects and also plays an important role in the distribution of information to different publics.

Between 1974 and 1978 the Secretary of State for the Feminine Condition and the Delegation for the Feminine Condition have also had an informational and public relations role in a wider field. Since 1978 there have been created: (1) the Secretary of State for Female Employment within the Ministry of Labor whose first actions and concerns are involved with informing women of the relationship between maternity and employment and also of the diverse job possibilities open to them; and (2) the Ministry for the Feminine Condition which is supposed to have the role of stimulating other agencies. In this capacity, the Minister for the Feminine Condition presides over an interministerial committee charged with "overseeing the government's policy concerning actions taken for women and with assuring the coordination of measures taken by the different ministries in this field."

Continuing training. In certain cases, inactive women can benefit from the 1971 Law for Continuing Training and, since 1978, measures taken to fight unemployment. Among the different kinds of training courses proposed for continuing training, the legislators have provided access to recycling programs to women not in the labor force: these have a maximum duration of 1,200 hours and a minimum of 120. They are organized by the A.F.P.A. or by a state-approved organization. All those 18 years of age and over enrolled at the A.N.P.E. have the right to enroll in such a program. The trainees benefit from Social Security and a stipend calculated according to their family situation. All those in a training program receive 90 percent of the minimum wage (in 1978, 1,888 francs per month based on a 40-hour workweek). For women, this remuneration may be higher in certain cases: mothers who have raised three children or who have a dependent child under three receive a stipend equal to 120 percent of the minimum wage; and mothers of one or two children and single women with one dependent receive a stipend equal to the minimum wage.

Current actions taken in the fight against unemployment. Initially concentrated on the employment of youth, these have been altered in such a way that certain categories of women can also benefit.

Employment-training contracts were created by the decree of the 4th of June 1975 in order to facilitate the employment of youth. Since April 1977 they have been accessible to widows and single women with a dependent child. The employer signs a contract with the state for a minimum of six months in which he agrees to assure a training program of 120 to 500 hours for the six-month program, and 500 to 1,200 hours for programs of one year. This program is either directly financed by the state, or the employer is reimbursed at the fixed rate of 24 francs per training hour. Also, the state will reimburse the employer 30 percent of the minimum wage during the six months following the contract, and 100 percent for the actual duration of the program. The employer agrees not to dismiss the beneficiary of the contract—except for cause—during the six months following the initiation of the contract.

The temporary measures of the Second National Pact for Employment (July 1, 1978 to December 30, 1979) contrast with the preceding program in that they concern not only unemployed youth but also women, regardless of age, who have been alone for less than two years (widows, divorcees, separated women, single women with at least one dependent child) and who are not employed. The measures provide:

A taking over of 50 percent of the employer's contribution to Social Security for a work contract of at least six months;

On-the-job training for four months, with at least 120 hours of training for manual work: the trainees receive 90 percent of the minimum wage (70 percent reimbursed by the state, the remaining 20 percent as well as training expenses may be partially deducted from the continuing training tax—equal to one percent of the total of the company's wage bill);

Occupational training programs (pretraining and entry to work); a maximum duration of six months with 80 hours of training, and remunerated at 90 percent of the minimum wage (for women these charges are covered by the state). The employers can either organize training programs which must be state approved, or participate in the financing of training by an organization, or in a training fund.

Employment training contracts which are open to women who have stopped working for more than two and less than five years after the birth of a child, and to all women between the ages of 17 and 26.

Access to training programs: priorities and costs. Training programs remunerated by the state (A.F.P.A. and state-approved programs) are free, and participants are covered by Social Security. The Law of the 3rd of January, 1975, gives absolute priority to widows and single women with one dependent child; the Law of the 9th of July 1976 enlarges this priority to women raising a child under three. Any expenses of training programs which may be incurred by the women are, like all training expenses, deductible from the taxable family income.

Women's employment and family income. Recent legislation has broadened the right to the following family allowances by eliminating reference to labor force status which formerly limited their application:

Le Complément Familial, established in 1977, replaces six preexisting allocations, certain of which were dependent upon the woman's being out of the labor force. A "complément familial" of 354 francs as of July 1978 is given to families having at least three children, or a child under three, and an annual income lower than a specified amount based on both family size and whether one or both parents are in the labor force.

"Les Allocations Familiales", which are given when there are at least two dependent children, have, since 1978, not been subject to conditions regarding employment. They are equal to 23 percent of the monthly basis of calculation where there are two children; 38 percent for a third and fourth child; and 35 percent for each additional child. The rates increase by nine percent of the monthly base when the children are between ages 10 and

15 years, and 16 percent when they are over 15 years. The monthly base was 850 francs as of July 1, 1978. For example, for a family with five children, two of whom are between 10 and 15 years and one over 15, the amount received was equal to 1,491.50 francs in July 1978.

The taxation of incomes is progressive, and the family income is calculated by adding the incomes of the different members of the family. Thus, the earnings of the woman increase the taxable revenue of the family and also increase the rate of taxation. On the other hand, the number of members of the household is taken into account in calculating the number of deductions. Hence whether the woman works or not, the couple has the right to two deductions, and each dependent child is allowed a supplementary half-deduction. The tax is related to the amount of income and the number of people, dependents or not, living in the household. A study of the effect of two earners on the family income, taking into account the income tax allowances, shows mainly that working wives' contribution results in a rise in the family income equal to 80 percent of the woman's salary.

Child care expenses are deductible from taxable income in certain relatively limited cases: they may be deducted by a single person in the work force with a dependent child under three when taxable income is under a given maximum (106,850 francs per year in 1976). The maximum deductible—1,800 F per year and per child in 1976—cannot be more than the taxable income.

Women's employment and child care. The continuation or cessation of work after the birth of a child usually depends on the possibility of day care. The government institutions available to women depend on the age of the child.

Children under three may be cared for by a collective day-care center, or by mother's aides in either family day-care centers or who are simply government-approved. These two sources provide about 35,000 places in the Ile de France (the total number of children in the area is 450,000). Working widows, divorcees, separated and single women have priority for their children. Whatever their marital status, women must give proof of employment in order to have the right to place their children in the centers.

Nursery schools take in children between the ages of two and five from 8:30 A.M. to 4:30 P.M. and usually have a canteen at noon and facilities to keep children until 6:00 P.M., as well as on Wednesday, the day off from school. This care is free. It should be noted that due to unequal geographic distribution and insufficiency of places, other forms of day care often are used (nonapproved aides, relatives, neighbors), as several surveys have shown (Table 3.9). One study in 1973 found that the average cost of keeping a child was 420 francs in that year. A family member paid to care for the child (50 percent of the cases) was paid about 350 francs, the same as a day-care center; an approved aide received 450 francs; a nonapproved aide, 350

Table 3.9   Type of Child Care Used by Working Women, 1973

Type of Child Care	Percent Employed Women		Percent Employed Women Not Caring for Child Themselves	
Mother	16		—	
Other family member	33		39	
Sitters	36		42	
Approved sitters		15		18
Day care center	7		9	
Household help	5		7	
Other means	2		2	
No answer	1		1	
Total percent	100		100	
Number of women	913		772	

Source: Institute National d'Etudes Démographiques.

francs; and household help who took care of the children as well as the housework were paid 840 francs.

French legislation allows for several kinds of work interruptions for employed women varying in length and type in accordance with the work contract.

Maternity leave allows a woman to suspend her work contract for six weeks before the expected date of the birth of her child and for ten weeks following birth. During this period the woman receives a compensation equal to 90 percent of her earnings (certain collective bargaining contracts permit continuation of total earnings). Following this period, the woman is reinstated in her previous position.

A woman also has the possibility, in some cases, of prolonging her absence by using postnatal leave, which is also open to fathers. Postnatal leave is provided 15 days before the end of maternity leave for the mother, or six weeks after the birth of the child for the father. A person can resign from his/her job without giving any other notice and, in the following year, he/she may ask to be rehired. He/she is given priority in rehiring and, if not rehired, receives priority of access to training programs.

Parental leaves were first provided in the Civil Service and now must be provided by companies with more than 200 employees. About one-third of employees in the private sector are covered, but companies with 100 salaried employees will be covered as of January 1, 1981. This type of leave simply suspends the work contract for one year. If a person is not reintegrated upon return, he or she is considered "fired" and thus has the right to severance pay, unemployment compensation, and participation in training programs.

Civil servants with at least five years seniority may ask for unpaid leave, normally to raise a child under eight or to care for an ill or handicapped child requiring continual care. The leave is granted for a maximum of two years and is renewable up to maximum total duration of 10 years. The individual must request his/her reintegration two months before the end of the leave and is normally placed in one of the first vacancies if the leave has not exceeded three years.

Job search. All job seekers have access to the placement services of the A.N.P.E. Women who have interrupted work activity for several years are allowed to benefit from public aid to unemployed workers (daily compensation 16 francs per day for the first three months and 15.20 francs afterwards) under the following conditions: at least three months enrollment at the A.N.P.E. and a diploma of technical or technological training or higher education obtained within the past year; or enrollment for six months at the A.N.P.E. and receipt of the baccalauréat (high school diploma), completion of a complete cycle of technological training, or completion of an occupational training (or pretraining) program within the past year.

Single women with dependents. In the event of widowhood or separation, assistance, usually of a temporary nature, is provided to aid entry or reentry either by guaranteeing a minimal income, maintaining certain allowances given to heads of family, or establishing priorities for employment or training.

Any person assuming the raising of a child alone has the right to the monthly allocation to orphans of 120 francs. Divorced women whose husbands have not paid child support ordered by the divorce court for one month may benefit from this allocation. In addition, all widowed, divorced, separated, abandoned or single people with at least one dependent child and all single pregnant women benefit for a year, or until the youngest child is three years old, from an allocation equal to the difference between the monthly family income, fixed at 1,152 francs plus 384 francs per dependent child, and the actual income of the single parent. Widows, divorcees, abandoned or separated women receive all the "family allowances" to which their husbands had the right if such women have the responsibility for at least two children.

Even if not personally insured, that is to say not employed nor in an approved training program nor enrolled at the A.N.P.E., a widowed, divorced, separated or abandoned woman continues to benefit for a year from her husband's social security. Under certain conditions, notably age, widows receive part of their deceased husbands' pension (in the normal social security contract, the woman must be at least 55 years old).

This review of legislation really takes note of theoretical possibilities, and does not show the *actual* situation of women seeking to resume work.

One must not lose sight of the limits of the legislation, the economic obstacles in its application, the individual difficulties encountered by women in claiming their rights. One must also take into account the actions of private associations who, in the area of information and training, complete governmental action and serve as intermediaries between women who are often isolated and disoriented and the official institutions whose functioning often appears complex.

Realizations

Within France there is a large number of organizations called "Associations under the Law of 1901" in reference to the year the law allowing nonprofit associations to be created freely was passed. They have legal recognition, are managed by an administrative council elected by their members, may receive contributions from their members, and they may receive public subsidies.

For about ten years, associations have been particularly active in assisting women. Totally dependent on donations in the beginning, they have often obtained subsidies permitting them to hire a certain number of people and to increase their potential for action. The sources of funds are varied; they may be of public, semipublic or private origin. Certain of these associations have a national membership (The French Women's Union, the Women's Civic and Social Union). Others are strictly local either because their objective is geographically limited or because they have just started. On the local level, public officials usually appreciate the steps taken by the active associations.

The easiest way to show what exists in France on behalf of reentrants is to follow a classic itinerary: information, training, orientation and placement (orientation comes before training or before placement). A certain number of women, however, do not follow this route: some resume work on their own; others, already informed, find their own training programs. It is impossible to make a complete list of everything that is done, but if we keep to the three areas chosen for this study, the agglomerations of Caen and Lyon and the department of the Val de Marne (in the Paris Region), we can get a fairly precise idea of the existing network.

Information

There is a certain number of public sources of information: town halls, social centers, the press (in all its forms), educational institutions, specialized agencies, orientation and leisure activities. Private associations which sometimes benefit from a government subsidy also furnish information. Certain profit-making organizations are also in a position to give different types of information. We will successively look at the principal organizations which reentrants use whether they are (1) organizations aimed specifically at women or (2) organizations open to the general public. It must be noted that according to social category, neighborhood, age, urgency of need, and information picked up through the grapevine, reentrants go to one or another source. It is generally impossible to know, even by talking to the people in charge, why and how a woman goes to one place rather than another.

Organizations aimed specifically at women are sometimes open exclusively to specific categories of women, while in other cases they are open to the whole of the female population. For widows, divorcees, abandoned women and women whose husbands are incapable of assuring sufficient family income, there are specific organizations. The National Association of Widows of Civilians was created in 1949 and receives public subsidies as well as contributions from members. It tries to bring about legislative measures to improve the situation of widows. The role of information is also very important; in 1975, there were 550,000 requests for information answered by 500 women, almost all of whom were volunteers.

The Syndical Federation of Women Heads of Family was created in 1967 and is also a federation of local associations. The objective of the federation consists of making the government recognize the position of a woman "head of family." At present its prime demand is that the public unemployment allocation be given to a woman "head of the family" whether she has worked in the past or not.

These associations are capable of aiding women who are in a state of urgency. They give them advice concerning formalities, direct them towards orientation and placement agencies, inform them of their rights, and especially give them moral support. Unfortunately, their budget is practically nonexistent and their vitality depends on donations.

The Women's Information Center (C.I.F.) was created in 1962, under the impetus of a woman's weekly magazine. It is subsidized by county councils, sometimes by city councils, and by different ministries. It has 23 principal offices and seven smaller offices in the provinces, about fifty paid staff members and 300 volunteer workers. Its objective is to give free information of interest to the female public in diverse areas: legal, social, cultural and practical. On the national level it answered 35,000 requests for information in 1977, about 1,500 of which concerned reentry.

The National Employment Agency (A.N.P.E.) receives only a few job or service offers relevant to reentrants. Placement personnel and professional counselors are absolutely snowed under with requests for employment from men, young people and people suddenly out of work, and are a bit negligent in helping reentrants who are reputedly difficult to place. The A.N.P.E. staff is not always capable of informing these women about the different training programs, aids, recycling or even of available jobs. Yet when a placement worker or a professional counselor is particularly sensitive to this problem (as is the case in one of the agencies in the Val de Marne), all the necessary information is assembled and given to the women concerned. This results in a huge demand for training programs, and reentry is facilitated. In many places, however, women who have not worked for a long time or who have never worked at all are unaware that the agency is there to inform them, and do not consult it.

Town halls have social workers who can inform women in an urgent situation or seeking employment information for the future. Job offers communicated by the A.N.P.E. are often posted. Women are accustomed to going to the Town Hall for various purposes; some towns and cities employ an aide especially for women reentrants (for example, the City Hall of Paris and those of several large Paris suburbs).

Every evening, national television broadcasts a program entitled "A Minute for Women" which treats different relevant subjects. In 1977, reentry was brought up at least three times. Every afternoon at the hour when women at home are watching television, "Aujourd'hui Madame" (Today) deals with a number of practical questions. Several times in 1977 the question discussed was resumption of work. Because the program lasts about an hour, a good deal of information can be given. Many women in the television audience telephone the organizers of these programs to obtain supplementary details. Direct studies show a large audience of women who have profited from the advice given. The national and local radio stations have also brought up these problems.

Information on the laws, decrees, training programs and possibilities of employment appear in the press, but all women do not read this type of news and some never open a newspaper. But the articles which appear in the "feminine" press—with a circulation of over ten million a month—do have an effect; women call, write and visit organizers of training programs and institutions capable of informing them in an efficient manner. Regional daily publications are widely read in the provinces, and when they give news concerning reentry—training programs for example—there are immediate results. Finally, advertising periodicals distributed free of charge often include announcements of various training programs. We have learned through our interviews that on reading these announcements, women realize that they can resume work.

Training

Training is often neglected by women. Some are in a situation of such urgency that they are obliged to find work immediately and do not even want to know about the possibilities of paid training programs; others find themselves too old and "rusty"; still others think, on the contrary, that they are sufficiently competent and do not have need for complementary training. The Women's Civic and Social Union and The Union of French Women are primarily engaged in making housewives aware of civic and employment problems or with allowing them to acquire a certain level of culture. They also organize reentry programs and promote diverse training, but the programs are relatively superficial, lasting between eight and 40 hours. They always take place in the afternoon and require a small fee.

Pretraining and worklife orientation programs are aimed at two types of women: those who have not decided to work (or return to work) but want to get out of the house or revive their intellect; and those for whom this elementary training is an indispensable base before real vocational training or a first step to work after an interruption of ten or 20 years.

In most Town Halls (at least in those of relatively large cities—in general more than 20,000 inhabitants) there are two kinds of courses: general education that goes up to the diploma given at the end of third grade (corresponding to the end of schooling at 16), which is indispensable when seeking office employment; and professional courses, access to which requires passing a test. The principal problem for reentrants is that most students in these courses are workers and the courses are given in the evening. Hence most homemakers are prevented from participating because of family responsibilities. Certain reentrants have, however, pursued these programs and have acquired the minimum preliminary knowledge necessary to profit from more specialized training.

A group of geographically close secondary schools (college preparatory, technical, general) under the direction of the headmaster of a high school provides continuing training programs (GRETA). There are about 400 GRETA in France. Regarding pretraining for reentrants, different institutions in the agglomeration of Lyon, for example, played a leading role in organizing refresher courses in French, typing, oral and written expression, introductory accounting and specialties in the sanitary and social sectors. These programs last a maximum of 120 hours and are not remunerated—but they are free. There are no programs of this kind in Caen nor in the Val de Marne.

The organizations which provide pretraining prior to reentry are the most varied: there are different associations in each administrative department, but their budgets and staffs are not the same. In the Calvados, for example, there is only one such organization aside from "Retravailler" (see below), and it is limited to about 15 women a year. On the other hand, in the Lyon region, several organizations have tackled this problem, each organizing several programs a year. Pretraining programs generally have three phases: intellectual reactivation by means of tests, orientation toward occupational training, and knowledge of the working world.

Retravailler is the best-known organization of this type. It has contributed by its dynamism and by its very existence to the awakening of the public conscience to the problem of reentry and has succeeded in stimulating the creation of numerous training programs. Founded in 1973 by Evelyne Sullerot, it is financed by a contract with the Regional Administrative Authority. But because of the insufficiency of the budget, a great many women must wait for several months to be admitted to training.

By 1979, Retravailler trained 7,000 people in France—6,000 in the Paris region, the first center established. There are 12 Retravailler centers in the provinces and two abroad. Some centers organize sessions outside of their home city (for example, in 1977 the Lyon center organized a session in Valence). The opening of a center in each of the 21 regions is planned.

The Retravailler training program is part time and lasts five weeks—about 120 hours. It provides tests of aptitude and skills (not knowledge); preparation for the working world, such as resumes, the work contract, collective agreements, the A.N.P.E., want ads; and finally, information about different jobs (for example, challenging preconceived notions) and group orientation with a professional counselor. In addition, there are individual contacts with staff members, who, with their knowledge of the local labor market and of the aptitude of each trainee, contribute to the development of satisfactory reentry. Most trainees are not remunerated but must pay a fee calculated according to the "quotient familial" which is obtained by dividing total family income by family size. This sum is never more than 1,050 francs and is very often much less.

Retravailler results vary slightly by region: in Paris, after a year, about half of the trainees had jobs; 10 percent were seeking jobs; 25 percent were in training programs; and the remainder were waiting for a training program. In the Lyon Region, one-third were working; one-third were in training; and one-third comprised women seeking employment, waiting for a training program, or who had, for the moment, given up the idea of reentry.

Retravailler is the most solid of all the structures to facilitate reentry. It has served as a model for all associations seeking to achieve the same goal.

The universities often have teaching programs for women who plan to resume work, either immediately or in the near or distant future. But they run into numerous difficulties, not all of which are budgetary. For example, program pesonnel have difficulty in convincing the university administrative council of the merits of such programs, whose level is relatively low and which seem out of place in an institution of higher learning. In addition, some women who enter these programs never really have the intention of resuming work, or consider it only a possibility in the distant future. They simply want to bring their knowledge up to date and get back into the habit of intellectual exercise. Such women are most often found in universities where the selection of trainees is less rigorous and the courses free or very inexpensive. The programs primarily cover information about the workplace and training. They generally serve a public of a high intellectual level and thus answer a very real demand.

The Women's Civic and Social Union launched elementary reentry programs in diverse departments, particularly in Lyon and in the suburbs. These programs are aimed at a public with relatively little training. Some cities' subsidies were renewed in 1978 and some not. The organizers are performing financial acrobatics in order to be able to continue.

No pretraining program provides stipends. They are all under the 120-

hour minimum set by legislation as the cut-off point for remuneration. If they do not go over this number of hours, it is because the Prefecture of the region which accords them an allowance (in 1977, 6 francs per hour per trainee) does so up to a maximum of 120 hours. The organizers have requested that the trainees be remunerated as for other programs (between 90 and 120 percent of the minimum wage according to the number of dependents), but even if this were done, they would run into another difficulty: it is now impossible for a person to be paid for two consecutive training programs, and about a third of the people trained in these organizations go on to an occupational training course which is indispensable in seeking a skilled job.

After having taken a pretraining or brush-up course, a woman desiring to resume work has several choices: she can enter the labor market; abandon this goal; or take a regular, more or less technical, training course. Those who enter the labor market directly after pretraining do so at a lower level than the others. Certain women, however, feel they need no pretraining and go directly into occupational training. These are often younger women who have been absent from the labor force for a short period of time, or women who have a good intellectual level and have had some nonpaid activity outside the home.

The brushing-up of school or work-related skills exists on several levels—from the executive to the typist. Cited below are a few examples of the numerous opportunities for reentrants:

The Center of Higher Industrial Studies (C.E.S.I.) is aimed at women engineers and at those with a Masters degree in science who wish to bring their knowledge up to date. The highly specialized program lasts one school year. At the end of the year the women, who also have a training course in a company, generally have very little difficulty in finding jobs. Most of the trainees are remunerated. Such programs exist in Lyon and in a number of large cities. About 20 women are trained in this manner each year.

The Parisian Center of Management trains executives and has a small program dedicated to the reentry of women university graduates. The Center is managed by the ex-director of a women's school of commerce and trains about 15 women a year.

A temporary employment agency, Manpower, provides full-time training programs of six weeks designed for women who have not worked for at least two years and who have secretarial skills (typist, shorthand typist, bilingual secretary, etc. . .). This private organization has no contract with public authorities and the trainees are not salaried, but the program is free and the women who pursue the courses are under no employment obligation.

One of the Employment Agencies in Lyon (A.N.P.E.) has taken the interesting initiative of putting a room at the disposal of women interested in brushing up their typing where they can use typewriters free of charge and at the same time meet other people who find themselves in the same situation.

Because they no longer wish to exercise the skills they have, because they never learned a skill, or because the knowledge they have is no longer useful, many women seek to learn something totally new. In the opinion of teachers, a woman over age 30 learns a new skill, intellectual or manual, much more quickly than a younger woman because she is more motivated and her nonwork experience is often useful. Some existing organizations encountered in the regions studied are the following:

The Chambers of Commerce play an important role in continuing training. In many departments, the instruction given is adapted more to members' requests than to the women's wishes. In Lyon, two programs, each lasting one school year, were created a few years ago. They train for two specific jobs: saleswomen-secretaries and secretaries-accounts, which are adapted to small and medium-sized enterprises and are uniquely for them. That is to say, they provide competence in all fiscal, commercial and legal affairs so that the trainee becomes capable of replacing a manager. One of the bases of this type of education is to give the trainees a feeling of complete devotion to the interests of the enterprise (for example, the ill effects of absenteeism are stressed).

Training programs uniquely directed to women in the process of reentry are organized in most universities, which can accept only a few trainees. For example, at Vincennes, near Paris, only 17 women were trained in 1977; at Lyon II the figure was a bit higher—about 60. Here the criticisms are the same as for the pretraining programs: the education provided is judged to be of too low a level for a university, since it primarily consists of courses in accountancy, secretarial skills and languages. The training programs last for 1,000 to 1,200 hours and can be taken in intensive (all-day) or extensive (several half-days per week) sessions. Figures on a national scale are unavailable, but the number of trainees in the programs is minute in relation to the number of women requesting places. In the agglomeration of Paris (a population of almost 10 million), there are about 15 universities, each of which, with the exception of special programs, enrolls about 15 reentrants, an extremely small proportion of total students.

G.R.E.T.A., already cited, also organize training programs which are more or less follow-ups of their pretraining. In an agglomeration like Lyon, where women's associations are very active, these programs are numerous; there were seven in 1977. They train frozen-products saleswomen as well as shorthand typists. In the Val de Marne the situation is quite different. The programs which existed in 1976 after the Year of the Woman were generally not renewed in spite of very vigorous efforts.

The I.F.O.C.O.P. represents multiple initiatives that exist on the departmental level: in the Val de Marne it provides training for mothers, aimed at women reentrants. Each year 120 women with the C.E.P. (Certificate of Primary Studies—end of schooling at 14) are trained as shorthand typists or assistant accountants. The programs are part-time and take place during school hours, with no classes on Wednesday or during school vacations. They last 460 hours.

There are many possibilities for training, about 2,000 on the national scale, which are not specifically directed to reentrants but which are open to them. Legally, all training programs are available to both sexes, but certain of them are, in fact, directed at males who are more interested in programs leading to industrial or very technical employment. The problem of lodging affects women more than men when the location of the program makes boarding obligatory. It is extremely difficult, given available statistics, to determine the percentage of women reentrants in these programs.

The Association for the Professional Training of Adults (A.F.P.A.), which is subsidized entirely by the government, trained almost six thousand women in 1977, more than a thousand of whom were over 30 years of age, but there is no way of knowing how many of these were reentrants. There are usually long waiting lists, often two years or more, for these programs. It is seldom that the trainees do not find work, since the A.F.P.A. programs have great prestige. In certain cities, however, some programs organized especially for women in traditional or tertiary professions have not been filled. The reason for this is probably lack of information, A.N.P.E. placement personnel being partly responsible. It is not necessary to be enrolled as a job seeker in order to take advantage of an A.F.P.A. training program, but many women are still not aware of this; and the A.F.P.A. centers are not equipped in terms of personnel or budget to meet the demands which might arise if they were better known.

Since January 1976, the National Employment Agency has organized training programs with the objective of giving job seekers complementary training to enable them to fill job vacancies which could not be filled in the usual manner of matching job seeker and job opening. A certain number of requests from enterprises suffice for the Agency to set up one of these programs. The firms then agree to "freeze" the positions for the duration of the training program—in other words, not to assign them to anyone they themselves might recruit. The A.N.P.E. does not provide this training itself, but calls in specialized organizations which are either approved or part of the A.F.P.A. The programs are relatively short (a minimum of 40 hours and a maximum of 500) since their purpose is simply to raise the level of a skill already known. The A.F.P.A. and the A.N.P.E. programs, like the reentry programs, operate on a national scale, but they offer an even greater number of training possibilities. The training programs having a contract with the Continuing Training Delegation (D.A.F.C.O.) are listed and brought up to date every year. Those interested can consult this listing in all local employment agencies. The offices of the Women's Information Center and the Committee for Female Employment possess, or should possess, this document.

Orientation and Placement

There is really no orientation or placement institution specifically for reentrants. Nevertheless, before beginning a program, be it training or pretraining, the interested person meets with a psychologist, an administrator, a therapist, or, very rarely, a professional counselor.

The only orientation which is designed for reentrants is that which they receive in a pretraining organization such as "Retravailler." Indeed, the administrators often encounter women who have been outside the working world for a long time and who need not only assistance but also better self-knowledge. During the program, the person in charge must be able to determine the skills and interests of the participants and the activities best adapted to their competencies. She may encourage one woman to train in the tertiary sector, and another to immediately seek employment in a different sector.

On the other hand, when women arrive at actual vocational training programs, they either have been advised by pretraining personnel, have learned about the program through advertising, were informed by the C.I.F., or they heard about it on the radio or read about it in the press. They sometimes choose a program simply because it is near home. The person who interviews them does not discourage them unless their level does not meet the requirements or their family or material situation does not permit their enrollment. At the end of the program, the women must find work. But at this time they are already oriented. Many programs end with a period of one or two weeks—sometimes a month—of practical experience in a firm. Either the woman or the organizers of the training program contact an employer, who accepts the individual under certain conditions: low or nonexistent pay, a particular work schedule, etc. . . . Very often this leads to a job offer. Indeed, and this is significant, this is a means by which employers learn to appreciate an older woman, who is perhaps less flexible and lively but often more conscientious and free of family obligations. A large number of work experience stints end in the hiring of the woman, and this, in a fashion, replaces the trial period. An organization of this type can aid reentrants but no more than other job seekers. In fact, a certain number of enterprises are familiar with these organizations and go to them when they are seeking reentrants, just as they go to vocational schools when they are seeking young personnel.

In all the centers of the National Employment Agency, there are one or more professional counselors (C.P.), but our survey found that practically none of the reentrants interviewed had had an interview with one of these specialists. At present, almost all reentrants have a training or recycling problem: those who go to the agency should systematically have an interview with a professional counselor who can inform them of training programs in the region. This would require an increase in the number of counselors, which is now largely insufficient. In the Val de Marne, in September 1978, there were 11 professional counselors for 9,417 job seekers.

As noted, reentrants present more placement problems than the ordinary public, and since the waiting list for interviews with professional counselors is very long, reentrants are rarely informed of the possibility of counseling. Our interviews with placement officials found that some of them are indeed concerned with this problem and know that certain employers, rather than negatively reacting to the age of the candidates, actually seek them out. Nevertheless, orientation for this group is practically nonexistent.

In contrast, social services aimed at those on the margin of society: women beaten by their husbands, prostitutes, ex-prisoners, the illiterate, the mentally handicapped, etc., always have a large counseling component. Thus, women who are outside the norm or whose general or professional training is almost nil achieve reentry. Although successes are rare, program staff manage to find employment in the industrial sector, even in critical cases, which allows these often traumatized women to get back on their feet.

Finally, it must be emphasized that a solidarity develops among the organizations whose aim is reentry of women. It is a solidarity of word of mouth, very characteristic of this type of organization, especially in the provinces. The vitality and success of an association or even of a specific training program often depends on one woman or a group of women who go out of their way in their work (be it training, counseling or welcoming), and who follow a certain number of women to the end of their preparation.

Yet the fact remains that in spite of legislative measures and the aids in training, information and orientation aimed at women who are obliged or desire to return to work, many of the women concerned cannot use these facilities due to two kinds of obstacles: difficulty encountered by women in gaining as much acceptance as men in programs open to both sexes; and traditional mentalities. In "One Hundred Measures for Women," Françoise Giroud describes the first kind well: "In theory they have the right to training but the application of the law is made more than difficult in practice." She cites in particular the length of the waiting time for a paid training program at the A.F.P.A. In the past two or three years, dismissals, restructurings, and the disappearances of companies have been so numerous that the A.N.P.E., snowed under by job requests, has had a tendency to concentrate on sending persons suddenly deprived of work to training programs although, since 1978, these programs are rightfully open to reentrants. In the Ile de France (Paris and the seven administrative subdivisions surrounding it) in November 1978, out of 3,320 trainees, only 60 were women reentrants.

In other respects, the measures of the National Pact for the Employment of youth and certain categories of women have not led to the hiring of many women. In the Ile de France during the same period, only five out of 650 employment training contracts were given women reentrants; in the Province-Cote d'Azur region, women were the beneficiaries of only 23 out of 1,800 contracts signed in the second part of 1978. In November 1978, in the Ile de France, out of 319 work experience opportunities, only one was reserved for reentrants; and out of 2,641 persons hired for positions permitting employers to refrain from paying social contributions, only 21 were women reentrants.

Another type of obstacle is due to a combination of types of behavior: women themselves, especially those who are not part of any association, and more specifically when their occupational category is low, traumatized by their situation and not knowing where to turn, often accept the first job offered and do not take advantage of available legislative measures since they are often ignorant of their existence. In addition, many people in positions of responsibility (men and women) still think that a woman's place is at home, and that, while it may be necessary to assist a woman in distress, a woman whose economic needs are not urgent should be discouraged from seeking a job, or taught to economize and to manage her husband's earnings, rather than encouraged to get out of her home and become independent. Some add that, if a woman wants to occupy herself, there are many volunteer activities which can give her a new outlook on life and make her feel useful.

Finally, it should be noted that all the difficulties stated above are even greater for women living outside Paris or other large cities because of the sparse distribution of firms and associations in the provinces and in rural areas. The chances of finding employment are greater in the big cities than in smaller agglomerations, and information, training and orientation structures are more developed. Also, women in urban areas are more used to employment. In middle-sized cities or rural areas, the traditional conceptions of a woman's role are still deep-rooted. Aid available to reentrants far from covers all of their needs and is rarely available to women living in rural areas. In this respect, the often used expression "the French desert" is apt in describing places outside the Paris region and the other large cities. cities.

All the measures in the realm of information and training should be reinforced. The C.I.F. should be given a budget increase to allow it to keep its present staff, mostly still volunteers, and to open agencies in all relatively large cities. The associations more specific to a certain category, such as the Federation of Women Heads of Family or the Association of Widows of Civilians, should be able to rely less on donations.

Women who wish to return to work should be able to obtain more complete information at the A.N.P.E. This would necessitate systematic meetings with a professional counselor capable of informing them of the training programs available to them, and requires a greater supply of counselors and placement staff than available at present. At this time, such personnel not only have too little time to interview and counsel women who have special difficulties, but they also cannot keep up-to-date regarding the various possibilities open to these women.

Parallel to this, it would be useful to develop programs of pretraining, updating of knowledge and skill reconversion. This would require reenforcement of existing measures with new actions suggested by the women interviewed and by the directors of some of the institutions contacted.

The type of aid proposed by them is at different levels. First and most urgent is the need to provide day care for the children of young mothers who must seek work. In the months following the death or other loss of a husband, a woman must have freedom to take all the steps her situation imposes: obtaining the diverse allocations for which she is eligible, enrolling as a job seeker or taking a reentry training program. Under present legislation and the practical situation in schools, particularly in small cities, a woman's access to certain facilities (the school canteen, afterschool care, day care centers, plus reimbursement of day care expenses) requires proof of employment outside the home or enrollment in an approved training program. She thus finds herself in a vicious circle: she cannot seek work or take a pretraining course unless she finds day care for her children, and she can find day care for her children only if she works.

After divorce, abandonment and especially widowhood, a woman, particularly of a lower class, sometimes finds herself with no resources, and with rent to pay and children to feed. If her family is not able to help her, she panics and takes the only job possible—cleaning woman. Since her income is low, she never manages to put aside enough money to stop work, even for a month for a pretraining program, which is not remunerated at the present time. All that is left for her to do is to find factory work. There is the possibility of a "pret d'honneur" (loan on trust), principally for professionals who wish to establish themselves. Assistance of this type, in the form of loans or aids, would probably permit more women to get past this difficult period and to reenter work at a higher level. Hence, it would be desirable to provide stipends for participants in training programs.

Widows often have the right to a relatively large sum of money but find themselves without resources during the months it takes to receive life insurance benefits or to sort out the payment of their inheritance. Even if there are no such difficulties, in many cases a special clause at the opening of a joint bank account prevents the survivor from withdrawing money. Also, a husband frequently has his personal bank account to which the wife has no right whatsoever. Most of the time speeding up the payment of the sums due would suffice to allow these women to start again without being obliged to take the first available job.

Certain associations favor the development of "social hotels," which would house widows or abandoned women and their children for a limited period of time in order to allow them to find work and housing within their new budget. These already exist but places are limited in number and reserved for special cases: women beaten by their husbands, handicapped persons, etc.

There are certain jobs suitable for the relatively aged (40 years of age and over) who have had absolutely no training and lack the energy necessary to acquire skills. They often take care of children or serve in a canteen. Just as there are jobs reserved for certain categories of mutilated or handicapped civilians or veterans, employment of this type could be reserved for these women.

Finally, in certain cases (women on the margin of society or near retirement age) where the probability is low of a training program's being worth the investment, systems of aid are recommended. These cannot replace training or employment possibilities unless the woman so desires, and should in no way be accompanied by an age limit for reentry.

A real priority in access to training must be established, at least for women who are obliged to resume work, and it would be desirable to impose on training centers a timed progression of the percentage of women. We can also visualize the distribution of "training checks" by the "Caisses d'Allocations familiales." These checks would be worth a certain number of free training hours and the women could cash them during the years they devote to child rearing. This would allow them to maintain or update their training and would thus facilitate eventual resumption of work.

Women in Rural Areas

Farm and rural residents are not the same. Certain farms may be situated near a large city or in a community with a population of more than 2,000. On the other hand, in rural areas the percentage of the population that is nonagricultural is high. In France in 1975, 27 percent of the population lived in rural zones, and 11.2 percent were farmers.

The problems of women with rural and agricultural status are very similar. They arise out of the often traditional viewpoints of these classes, the lack of information and training organizations in rural zones, and the inequality of economic development and centralization that places rural areas at a disadvantage. Finding work when one lives in a small community is extremely chancy. The participation rate of women living in rural zones is only 32.5 percent compared to 40.9 percent for the urban female population.

A difference does exist between these two groups, however, regarding the definition of "reentry." The wife of a farmer who is a family aide does not really cease work, although she is classified as being out of the labor force. She will usually resume employment by working outside the family business in order to increase the family income. Rarely will she take on the new responsibility of becoming her husband's business partner. On the other hand, women who live in rural zones but are not in agriculture and the wives of farm owners or of agricultural workers often find themselves in a situation similar to that of women living in urban areas with about the same difficulties in reentering the labor force.

There has been an exodus from rural and agricultural zones by women seeking employment in the cities. In addition, the activities of rural areas have been transformed. Nevertheless, a large potential female labor force remains. These developments are the result of a cumulative phenomenon: general economic transformation bringing about changes in the agricultural production sector and, at the same time, modifying the structure of female employment. These women no longer find employment in the traditional sectors (crafts, small business) and, once they are over 30, they are generally not prepared to perform nonagricultural work which is, in any case, not really available in rural areas.

Structures for information and orientation are almost always absent since they exist only in cities of a certain size. Rural women's access to these organizations depends on distance and the available means of transportation. On the other hand, training organizations have existed for a longer time and are closer to rural areas. At the present time, access to occupational training for women wishing to remain in their places of residence are developing for all rural residents on and off farms.

Women wanting to acquire or maintain agricultural skills are eligible for programs provided by syndical and professional organizations or by continuing training centers. Other programs facilitate the recycling of women towards para-agricultural activity or another sector of the national economy. Centers of the National Association for the Training and Occupational Improvement of Rural Adults—ANFOPAR—are unique in that the clientele is mainly female. The objective is to recycle rural adults and to place them in existing and new jobs in rural areas. Yet although the number of remunerated trainees has greatly increased in recent years, the number of women seems to have decreased.

The means of training available to nonagricultural rural women seeking reentry are practically the same as those of women leaving agriculture. They can also, like women from urban areas, go to G.R.E.T.A. or other approved establishments for pretraining, general, or vocational training prior to reentry.

Three major handicaps still exist in rural areas: an insufficiency of program information, unequal dispersion of training structures strongly penalizing underpopulated areas, and a persisting lack of openings for reentrants.

CONCLUSIONS

Female reentry to the work force is an indisputable fact. Data from a recent study indicate that the work life expectancy of a working woman aged 30 is

21 years, that of a nonworker, 16 years; at the age of 45, expectancy is 12 years for a working woman and six years for a nonworker. This means that even if the probability of reentry decreases with age, it is still appreciable.

Numerous factors, sometimes contradictory, explain this movement, and it is difficult to make predictions in this respect. Without a doubt, a slight slowdown in female work may occur due to the effect of the economic recession. Mothers who face difficulties in finding a job may put off their return to the labor force for several years. Nevertheless, it seems that the increase in female employment is the result of structural factors too strong to permit a reversal since it is so solidly linked to a transformation of family life. Such a transformation has brought about the separation of the family during the day and is, as Roussel remarks, "without a doubt, of all the structural transformations, that which best explains upheaval in families' way of life."

Whether they are obliged or have decided to resume work, women encounter numerous difficulties during reentry. Legislative measures, especially concerning the opening and remuneration of training programs or on-the-job training, particularly for women heads of the family, as well as the development of public or private associations capable of helping them, have, without a doubt, enabled numerous women to find successful places for themselves in the labor market. But these means are still seriously inadequate and have little effect on women living in agglomerations with a population of less than 100,000. Also, at present the government's priority efforts are directed at the population most affected by unemployment— youth under 25 years of age. In such a context, aid to women reentrants in matters of information, training and placement has scarcely been developing in recent years.

Indications are, however, that new measures or the reinforcement of certain existing measures would be of definite benefit to reentry. Women in a sudden situation of distress should be helped by giving them the breathing time necessary for successful reentry. This means speeding up the procedure of unfreezing and collecting child-support payments and widow's pensions; organizing a system of loans on trust in specific cases; and especially remunerating all trainees in programs capable of contributing to reentry. It would also be desirable to improve the handling of women by the services of the A.N.P.E., especially in the area of professional counseling.

Finally, one very important measure would consist of imposing on training organizations, if not quotas of female trainees, at least a minimum rate of progression in feminization. Also, credits for hours of training could be distributed to mothers so that they might maintain, refresh or acquire skills, thus minimizing handicaps resulting from prolonged concentration on domestic tasks.

BIBLIOGRAPHY

Brouard, Nicolas. "Espérance de vie active" à paraître. In *Population*, 1979.

Buttner, O. et Letablier, Marie-Therèse. "Le tertiaire, support de l'évolution de l'emploi de 1968 à 1975." In *Bulletin d'information* 29–30. C.E.E. (December 1977) Paris.

Charraud, A. "Activité feminine et famille: aspects socio-economiques." In *Données Sociales*, edition 1978, Paris.

Charraud, A. et Chastand, A. "L'aide a la famille en 1977: prestations familiales et réduction d'impôt." In *Economie et Statistique* 104 (October 1978) Paris.

Chauviere, M. "La galaxie des Associations Familiales." In *Information Sociales* C.N.A.F. July 6, 1978.

Cosse, L. "Du féminisme à la féminité." In *Le Monde*. October 4, 1978.

Cuvillier, R. "L'épouse au foyer: une charge injustifiée pour la collectivité." In *Droit Social* 12. December 1977.

"Données Sociales." INSEE edition 1978.

"Enquête sur l'Emploi de mars 1977." In *Collections de l'I.N.S.E.E.* D53, #250 (March 1978) Paris (résultats détaillés).

"Equipements et services collectifs nécessaires aux femmes qui travaillent." Rapport du Comité du Travail Féminin. In *Actualités du Travail Féminin.* March 1977, Paris.

Eymard-Duvernay, F. "Les liens entre les démandes d'emploi en fin de mois et la population disponible à la recherche d'un emploi." In *Economie et Statistique* #69 (July-August 1975) Paris.

"La formation des femmes en milieu rural." *Comité du Travail Féminin*. Paris: Ministère du Travail. November 1974.

"La France et sa population aujourd'hui." In *Les Cahiers Français* 184 (January–February 1978) Paris (Documentation Francaise).

"Groupe de travail sur les problemes spécifiques du chomage féminin." *Rapport de Synthese: Delegation à l'Emploi*. Ministère du Travail. May-June 1977.

Huet, Maryse. "Emploi et Activité entre 1968 et 1975." In *Economie et Statistique* 94 (November 1977) Paris.

Labourie-Racape, A. "Formations, emplois et carrières des femmes en France." In *Séminaire sur le rôle et l'influence de la formation et de l'éducation dans les possibilités d'emploi et de carrière des femmes en Europe*. Centre International de Pervectionnement Professionel et Technique. Turin. July 8-12 1974.

Labourie-Racape, A., Letablier, Marie-Therèse, et Vasseur, A.M. "L'Activité Féminine: Enquête sur la discontinuité de la vie professionnelle." *Cahier du C.E.E.* 11. P.U.F., 1977.

Laulhe, P. "Enquête—Emploi de mars 1978: Les repercussions d'un chomage important." In *Economie et Statistique* 105 (November 1978) Paris.

Luttringer, J.-M. "Les Institutions de la formation permanente et leur rôle." C.N.I.P.E. Armand Colin Formation. Paris 1974.

Marciano, J. P. "Une nouvelle étape de la libération de la femme." In *Le Monde*, October 17, 1978.

Michal, Marie-Geneviève. "L'Emploi Féminin en 1968. Rappel des resultats de 1962." In *Collections de l'INSEE* D25, #109 (November–December 1973).

Monnier, Alain. "La Naissance d'un enfant: Incidences sur les conditions de vie des familles." *Travaux et Documents,* Cahier 81. I.N.E.D, P.U.F., Paris, 1977.

Pohl, R., Thelot, C., et Jousset, M. F. "L'Enquête Formation—Qualification Professionnelle de 1970." *Collections de l'ENSEE D32,* #129. (May 1974).

"Population Active." Résultats du sondage au 1/20, pour la France entière pour 1962 et 1968. In *Recensement général de la population.* INSEE. Paris, 1964 and 1971.

"Population Active." Résultats du sondage au 1/5, pour la France entière pour 1975. In *Recensement géneral de la population,* INSEE. Paris, 1976.

"La reinsertion professionnelle des femmes en Rhône, Alpes." Délégation à la condition féminine. C.I.F. Régional Rhône—Alpes, Lyon. January 1977.

Revoil, J. P. "L'Emploi en 1975 l'impact de la recession." In *Economie et Statistique* 79 (June 1976) Paris.

Roussel, L. "Le mariage dans la société francaise. Faits de population—Données d-opinion." *Travaux et Documents,* Cahier 73. INED. P.U.F. Paris, 1975.

"Septieme Rapport sur la situation Démographique de la France" préparé par l'I.N.E.D.; Ministère du Travail. Paris, February 1978.

Seys, B. "Les horaires de travail en 1974." In *Economie et Statistique* 69 (July–August 1975) Paris.

Seys, B., et Laulhe, P. "Enquete sur l'Emploi de 1976. In *Collections de l'INSEE* D48, #210. (November 1976) (resultats provisoires).

Sullerot, E. "Les problèmes posés par le travail et l'emploi des femmes." In Avis et Rapport du Conseil Economique et Social. Paris.

Sullerot, E. "Retravailler après 35 ans." *Document de Travail de Formation de Formateurs.* Conseil Economique Européen—Fond Social Europeen. Bruxelles, 1975.

Sztokman, N. "Les Francaises et le Travail. Analyse des données du recensement de 1975." In *Annales de géographie* 484 (November–December 1976).

4

Sweden

by CHRISTINA JONUNG and BODIL THORDARSSON

INTRODUCTION

The steps and measures taken in a country to facilitate women's entry and retention in the labor force depend on how the authorities perceive the role of women in society. Should the prime responsibility for the upbringing of the children and the care of the home rest with women? Should market and nonmarket responsibilities be equally shared between men and women? Should each family be left to choose according to individual wishes?

In Sweden, as in other industrialized countries, the attitude to women's employment has undergone a rapid change during the last decades. The fifties placed an emphasis on the two roles of women—as a mother and as a wage-earner—and the conflict between the two.[1] Women were to be given the opportunity to choose one or both roles without severe economic consequences for the family. The typical life cycle of a woman could consist of three phases: a period of work before the birth of the first child; a period of intensive work in the home and with the children; and a return to the labor market when the last child started school. Social policy was expected to make the roles possible to combine by stimulating young girls toward an education and occupational choice directed to work in the market and

We wish to acknowledge the assistance of Ingrid Spetz and Ulla Wadell in conducting interviews with reentering women; Gudrun Ohlsson in typing; Anna-Lisa Thelander, Inga Persson and Eskil Wadensjo in providing advice; and numerous persons at different institutions who supplied information.

developing labor market policies supporting the return of women to the market by eliminating differential tax treatment of work in the home and in the market, increasing the possibilities for part-time work, introducing paid leaves in connection with childbirth, and by economic support for mothers with young children. This approach to women's problems was very influencial in the development of practical policies during the fifties and sixties.

At the beginning of the sixties, a reaction set in against this attitude of so-called "conditional liberation of women." It allowed women to work, the critics said, but only on the condition that it did not keep them from taking care of their children and attending to their duties in the home. The responsibility for the children rested with their mothers, who were expected to interrupt their careers when the children were small and to adjust their work load to family needs thereafter.

A research report, "The Life and Work of Women," published in 1962, was instrumental in establishing a new view which asserted that the man's role also must be considered in the analysis and the debate, since the problem of conflicting demands from family and work was not confined to women.[2] The problems were not women's problems, but sex role problems. The achievement of equality required changing the role of men as well as that of women. These ideas eventually were to strongly influence official Swedish policy.

Probably the most clearly formulated statement of the present Swedish policy goals with respect to sex equality is the one contained in the 1968 Swedish report to the United Nations regarding the status of women. Ten years later it still stands out as a fresh and radical view in this area. It states that "the aim of a *long term* program for women must be that every individual, irrespective of sex, shall have the same *practical* opportunities, not only for education and employment, but also, in principle, the same responsibilities for his and her own maintenance as well as a shared responsibility for the upbringing of children and the upkeep of the home."[3]

This report laid the foundations for the policies of the 1970s. The seventies can be described as the period of work towards the goal of equality for men and women. What elements must be contained in such a long-term program meant to give women and men the same opportunities to shape their lives?

There are two aspects of how equality is to be achieved that are brought out in the report and that form an important basis for the development of Swedish policies. One principle is that equality requires economic independence for men and women and possibilities for self-support for everyone. A woman should not be supported through marriage; a man should not have the obligation to support his wife; and both parents should share the responsibility for the support of the children.

Another principle underlying the Swedish formulation of equality policies is that equality requires changing the role of *both* the man and the woman. As long as the man does not assume his share of the duties at home, women will not be able to participate in the labor market, in unions, or in political activities to the same extent as men. Men should be educated and encouraged to take an active part in parenthood.

Present Swedish policy towards women is thus formulated on the basis that each individual should have the right to an education, to work and to self-support. The government should, through youth and adult education, labor market policies, family support, public day care, and other measures, actively promote a division of labor built upon equality between men and women.

This Swedish "sex equality ideology" has been reflected in the policies carried out. The main focus of such policies so far has been on removing barriers that hinder women from becoming full-fledged members of the labor force. Efforts have been made to remove marital, social welfare and tax regulations that treat women unequally and provide a disincentive to gainful employment. Equality in education and vocational training has been stressed. The authorities have embarked on an extensive program for building public day care centers. Sweden is, however, still far from the goal of providing men and women with the same practical opportunities for family life and work.[4]

The changing views on women's employment have been reflected in the altered and successively widened goals of Swedish employment policy. All through the postwar period, Swedish economic policy has had full employment as its main goal. The aim of employment policy has been stated to be full, productive and freely chosen employment for everyone. General stabilization measures proved insufficient to achieve this goal. Since the end of the 1950s, such policies have been supplemented to an increasing extent by selective labor market measures. Initially, the goal of labor market policy involved only overt unemployment. Policies were, however, to be sex-neutral, and women's equal right to work was recognized.

During the expansionary period in the sixties, there was a high demand for labor. Increased attention came to be paid to the so-called latent unemployed—persons who would have been looking for work if they thought that they could find a suitable job in their neighborhood. The vast majority of this group were women. Labor market policy was to include the additional aim of removing barriers to entry and of creating employment opportunities for those outside the labor force who wanted to work.

The policy goal formulations of the seventies have stressed the right to work for everyone. Employment policy has come to include the aim of increasing the general level of employment, not only of reducing the level of unemployment. In 1972, the Advisory Council on Equality between Men and Women was appointed by the Swedish government and placed directly under the Prime Minister. The instructions to the Council stated that its foremost goal was to secure the right to work for women. Policies directed toward the labor market were to receive highest priority. The focus was to be on unemployed and untrained women—often synonomous with re-entrants. With the establishment of the Council it was finally recognized that the achievement of full equality between the sexes requires measures specifically designed to support women in the labor market. A new task was thus added to the direction of employment policy—that of actively supporting equality between men and women.

WOMEN WORKERS

History has shown that the division of tasks between men and women and the attitudes towards sex roles are determined to a great extent by technological change and the demands of the labor market. This is also the case for Sweden. Employment policies for women and equality policies have been strongly related to labor market developments.[5]

The postwar period in Sweden was characterized by a continuous high demand for labor and relatively low unemployment, until the beginning of the seventies. At the same time, other changes in the economy meant that the demand for labor could not be met from the earlier sources of recruitment—men and unmarried women. The population stagnated due to low birthrates in the thirties. An increasing proportion of youth stayed in school; working hours decreased; and the married population increased. In the 1930s only about half of the women in the active ages were married; this was true for about 80 percent of the women over 20 in the 1960s. To find new labor, employers thus had to turn to married women to an increasing extent. Another possible solution was immigrant labor.

The increased emphasis on married women's "second" role and the creation of reentry possibilities during the fifties can thus be ascribed to the increased pull from the labor market. Mature women were reentering the market, but at this stage without much help from the authorities. Selective labor market policies were only employed on a very small scale, and the government had not yet started taking any responsibility in the area of day care for children.

Industrial employers, however, preferred immigrant labor, since many of the industrial jobs were considered male jobs and immigrants were viewed as more mobile than women. Immigration increased quickly. Net immigration was 10,000 in 1950-60, 19,000 in 1960-65, and 29,000 in 1965-70. The majority of immigrants recruited was employed in the manufacturing sector.

The largest expansion in employment in Sweden, however, has occurred in the state and local government sectors, which are responsible for education, health and hospital care, child care, old age care, and social work. The growth in these areas was especially rapid during the sixties, but has continued, although at a slower rate, during the seventies. This expansion of demand has been a special stimulus for women's work because it involves typical female tasks of education and care, and immigrant labor cannot usually compete. About half of all working women today are employed in the public sector.

Virtually all of the expansion in women's employment has been related to changes in the size of the sectors and industries that employ a large share of women.[6] From 1963 onward, over 100 percent of the increase of women in the labor force has been absorbed by increases in the number of municipally employed.

During the sixties the use of immigrant or female labor became an issue of debate. The labor unions were following a policy of wage solidarity—equal pay for equal work, regardless of the region or profitability of the industry or firm. One aim of this policy was to bring about rationalization and increased productivity that would ensure higher wages for all. As part of the policy there were labor market programs to relocate workers from contracting to expanding industries through the employment service, geographic mobility grants and training.

The fulfillment of a policy of wage solidarity required limiting the competition within low-wage groups. This was secured through a 1960 agreement among the labor market organizations for equal pay for equal work for men and women, an agreement in effect since 1965. It has meant that different wage scales for men and women have disappeared. Although immigrant labor could delay the desired structural changes by accepting low-wage work, once it became evident that the Swedish industrial sector had started to shrink after 1965, unions began to view women as an alternative to immigrants. They started an active policy pressing for investment in public day care and labor market measures to assist re-entering women. The debate also stressed that the use of immigrant labor required larger investments in housing, etc. In addition the large immigration during the sixties had made the Swedish society more aware of a multitude of related social problems. In 1967, the government took full responsibility for immigration and new stricter guidelines were issued.

The government report on long-term development till 1983 expects the new employment opportunities for this period to continue to be located primarily in the public sector. The net additions to the labor force will all be women. Demand is expected to take a direction whereby women will be absorbed without any changes in the male/female ratio in each sector.[7]

During the 1970s, Sweden experienced various changes in the functioning of the labor market and in the direction of labor market policies that affect new and reentering labor.[8] These include an increased stress on employment security within a firm. In 1974, a new law was instituted limiting a firm's ability to lay off workers. The emphasis of labor market policies has changed from employment service, labor market training and mobility grants to measures that subsidize firms to maintain their labor through government orders, stock build-up support, and training subsidies.

Consequently, layoffs and unemployment during the last recession were much lower than normal at that level of activity. Increased attention to internal labor markets and policies of employment security has, however, meant that less demand will be directed toward the external market and newcomers to the labor market. An increased share of the unemployment burden has been carried by those who are entering or reentering the labor market. Youth unemployment figures have soared, and they are especially high for girls. Employment security policies may thus serve to reduce the demand for reentering women in the future.

Labor Force Participation

According to the Swedish Labor Force Surveys for 1978, 1.9 million women aged 16 to 74 were in the labor force. This corresponds to 62 percent of the female population of these ages. There were 2.3 million working men, or 78 percent of the male population. Women thus accounted for 45 percent of the Swedish labor force.

Behind these figures lie sharp increases in women's labor force participation rates during this century (Table 4.1). Since the table includes only women working half time or more, the figures are lower than the labor force survey figures noted above, which include those in less than half-time schedules. Table 4.1 shows 1910 to 1930 as a period of fast growth in the female labor force. The period after 1960, however, stands out as exceptional in its very rapid growth in labor force participation rates for women.

Unmarried women, who were the first to leave household work and enter the labor market, were responsible for most of the supply of women to the

Table 4.1   Women in the Labor Force, Aged 16 and Over, 1900 to 1975

	Number in Labor Force[a] (thousands)	Percent of Labor Force	Labor Force Participation Rates[a]
1900	345	19	19.1
1910	416	21	21.2
1920	585	24	26.9
1930	732	27	30.7
1940	756	26	29.3
1950	805	26	29.5
1960	948	29	32.0
1970	1,207	35	38.0
1975	1,373	39	42.2

[a]Includes only those working half time or more.
Source: Population and Housing Census for respective years.

labor force in the period before World War II. Married women increased their labor force participation rate throughout the century, but the increase first became marked during the postwar period. After 1930, demographic developments consisting of an older population and increased marriage caused changes in the composition of the female population. Not only did more young women marry, but they married at younger ages and most of them had children, although fewer children per family. The change in age composition meant that the majority of the women in the active age-group were married women over the age of forty. The young unmarried women, who had earlier supplied female labor, quickly decreased in number.

The older women became the second group to enter the labor force. The census of 1945 still showed a low labor force participation of married women (11 percent). After that, the movement into the labor force started: the figures for 1960 were 26 percent; for 1970, 37 percent; and for 1975, 43 percent. These figures pertain to half- and full-time work and take no account of the large increase in part-time work that had occurred at the same time.

The changes in labor force participation rates for married women indicate that the life cycle pattern of work for married women has undergone significant changes during the postwar period. Trends in married women's labor force participation rates by age between 1900 and 1975 indicate that marriage and, in particular, the arrival of children used to result in a permanent absence from the labor force. The increase in married women's participation in the labor force started first among young women and, in 1940, the highest share of working women was in the 20-to-30 year group. During the postwar period older women began to stay in the labor force or to return after some years of absence. By 1970, peak participation after the downturn during the child-minding years was even higher for women aged 35 to 55 years than the peak at the earlier ages and, by 1975, the drop virtually disappeared, even when restricted to those working half time or more.

The most recent development in the labor market situation for women is that they tend to remain in the labor force or drop out only for a very short period, even when they get married and have children. The rapid flow of women into the labor force during the end of the sixties began to include younger women with children. The intensified inflow of this group has continued through the seventies. Since a great many of these women are part-time workers, their rapid inflow is best illustrated with figures from the labor force surveys. In 1977, 380,000 women with children under seven years of age were in the labor force, almost twice as many as in 1965. The labor force participation of this group increased from 36.8 percent in 1965 to 66.2 percent in 1977.

The major part of the expansion in employment during the sixties and seventies was in the form of part-time employment so that the growth in women's attachment to the labor force has been even larger than shown in the preceding table. Table 4.2 shows total labor force participation rates by age and marital status and the presence of preschool children for 1963 and 1977.[9]

The composition of the Swedish labor force has undergone some radical changes during the postwar years (Table 4.3). Not only has the share of women in the labor force increased, but the background of the women in the labor force has changed. In the 1950s, the majority of the women in the labor force were unmarried and unhampered by family bonds and children in fulfilling their career ambitions. The majority of the working women today are married and not infrequently mothers of young children; they must share their time and interest between family and work.

While the labor force status of Swedish women has continued to approach that of Swedish men in terms of participation rates, the expansion of the female labor supply is really not as large as it may appear from labor force participation rates. One reason is that a large majority of the recently entered female workers has chosen to work on a part-time basis. This was especially common during the sixties and seventies, the period of the great influx of married women. Comparable estimates of part-time employment for a longer time period are not available, but data from the Labor Force Survey indicate that, between 1965 and 1977, roughly 80 percent of the increase in female employment came about as a result of an increase in part-time employment. In the sixties, both short part-time work (less than 20 hours) and long part-time (20 to 34 hours) increased. During the seventies, short part-time employment has remained roughly constant

Table 4.2   Labor Force Participation Rates by Sex, Marital Status, and Presence of Children under Seven Years, 1963 and 1977

Age	Men		All Women		Married Women		Nonmarried Women with Children Under 7		Total Women with Children Under 7	
	1963	1977	1963	1977	1963	1977	1963	1977	1963	1977
16–19	62.5	56.7	59.6	56.1	40.5	67.8	56.5	52.5	42.1	53.4
20–24	81.2	83.4	64.9	77.1	45.0	71.2	68.2	68.9	33.6	66.0
25–34	95.4	95.2	55.2	75.0	48.7	70.6	69.4	74.5	39.6	67.4
35–44	96.9	96.7	56.5	79.9	52.0	78.4	48.6	75.3	36.6	62.8
45–54	96.5	94.7	57.4	78.4	52.3	78.2	72.3	67.6	45.5	63.0
55–64	89.6	79.7	39.9	51.7	31.6	51.0	–	–	30.1	55.6
65–74	43.3	13.0	10.9	4.8	8.8	4.6	–	–	–	–
16–74	85.2	78.6	49.4	61.1	44.0	61.9	63.3	71.9	38.0	66.2
16–64	89.9	88.0	54.5	70.6	47.0	69.8	–	–	–	–

Source: The Swedish Labor Force Survey, yearly averages 1963 and 1977.

Table 4.3   Distribution of the Labor Force Aged 15 to 64 by Sex and Marital Status, 1950 and 1975 (numbers in thousands)

	Married Women	Nonmarried Women	Total Women	Men	Total Labor Force
1950					
Number	235	576	811	2,286	3,097
Percent	7.6	18.6	26.2	73.8	100
1975					
Number	768	604	1,373	2,175	3,547
Percent	21.7	17.0	38.7	61.3	100

Source: Population and Housing Census 1950 and 1975.

while all of the increase has been in long part-time work. Since 1976, all of the increase in employment has been in the form of part-time work, and the number of women working full time has declined.

In 1977, 45 percent of women between the ages of 20 and 64 who were in the labor force were part-time workers. While part-time work also increased among men during this period, only four percent of the men in the same age group worked less than 35 hours weekly. Women comprised the absolute majority of the part-time workers (91 percent). The average time worked per week by women, 31 hours, was clearly shorter than the average time worked by men, 41 hours.

Who are the women who work part time? About three-quarters of them are married women who share their time between work in the home and work in the market, and almost three-quarters are between ages 25 and 54. Earlier, women above 35 years dominated the part-time employed, but the large increase in part-time employment during the seventies has mainly been in the age group 25 to 34. It is women with responsibilities for small children who entered the labor market during this period and found full-time work too burdensome to combine with bringing up children. About half of the part-time working women, and almost two-thirds with children under seven years, specify work in their own household as the prime reason for their work schedule. Another common reason is "don't want full time," which may also be related to sex role patterns and home responsibilities.

The attachment of women to the labor force differs from that of men in respects other than hours of work. Women interrupt their work more often than men, and they are more often absent from work. There are no data available showing how the frequency and length of women's labor force interruptions have changed over time, but labor force participation data indicate that women currently have fewer and shorter labor force interruptions than previously. Other information on the movement of women in and out of the labor force is provided by data on persons working all year and persons working part year. Because of the flow in and out of the labor force, the share of the population in the labor force at some time during the year is larger than the share in the labor force during an average week, and still larger than the share that stays in the labor force. This difference is greater for women than for men. A comparison of the figures for 1966 and 1977 shows that a larger proportion of women now remains in the labor force full year. The average number of weeks in the labor force has also increased over the period. The increased tendency of women to participate in the labor force in recent years has been accompanied by increased absenteeism. The increase in absenteeism is most pronounced for women with children under seven. Many women with children, who in earlier periods or in other countries would leave the labor force, now remain but take a leave of absence. The opportunity to take leaves has increased considerably; the paid parental leave has been extended somewhat; the right to unpaid leave has been enlarged, especially in the public sector; new opportunities for leave in connection with studies have been created. Many women have availed themselves of such opportunities. Thus, while many women now in the labor force are on leave to take care of their children, their situation is radically different from earlier years. They remain attached to the labor market and have a permanent job to return to when the period of homemaking is ended.

The Educational and Occupational Status of the Labor Force

A large expansion in the provision of education in Sweden has taken place in the last two decades. Today there are nine years of compulsory schooling. About 40 percent of youth are still in school at age 18, and about 20 percent of the 20- to 24-year-olds are engaged in some form of schooling. Women have participated in the general expansion of secondary and postsecondary education. A closer look, however, shows that women to a larger extent than men choose the shorter educational routes within each level. The direction of their studies is also different. While boys choose technical subjects, girls choose languages, social sciences and, within the occupational schools, training leading to health care and social work.

Education is one of the factors that affects women's labor force participation rates (Table 4.4). The level of education also affects the amount of time women work: women with a high level of education are more likely to work full time. The distribution of women and men in the labor force by education is thus more even than the distribution within the population. Although there are very small differences among the three broad levels— primary, secondary and postsecondary—women are overrepresented at the lower rungs within each level.

Over time, the level of education of the labor force has increased and differences between men and women have become smaller. Nevertheless in 1977, among persons aged 19 to 24 years, women were heavily overrepre-

Table 4.4   Labor Force Participation Rates of Men and Women Aged 16 to 64
by Educational Level, 1975 (percentage distribution)

	Primary Level (≤ 9 years)	Secondary Level (10 to 12 years)	Post-secondary Level (13 years and above)
Men	82	93	88
Women	58	74	76

Source: Living conditions No. 14, 1978.

sented in shorter occupational training. Since women with brief education
are those who have a greater tendency to drop out of the labor force, women
with insufficient educational experience dominate the reentry group.

Virtually all new female employment has been in the municipal sector.
As was true for the total labor force, the increase in employment in this
sector has been larger than the total increase of the female labor force. The
numbers of women have also increased somewhat in the state government
and the private sector. The distribution of middle-aged women workers
resembles the total female labor force. Today more than half of all
employed women work within the public sector, and a vast majority of
these within the municipalities. For men, however, private employment
still dominates.

The importance of the public sector for women's employment is also
apparent in the distribution of employed persons by sex and industrial
branch (Table 4.5). About half of all women are in community, social and
personal services, which primarily consist of public administration,
health, education and welfare. In terms of numbers employed, the only
major increase has occurred in this sector. Smaller increases can be observed
within the engineering industry and within banking and insurance.

The share of women within each industrial sector has remained re-
markably stable over the period on an aggregate level. The expansion of the
number of women within the labor force can be related almost completely
to the expansion of branches of the economy where women traditionally
have had a large share of the employment, such as social services. The only
major expansion of women's share of employment has been within the area
of health, education and welfare and, starting in the beginning of the
seventies, women have managed to increase their representation in the
engineering industry also.

Women in the Swedish labor market are concentrated in a small number
of heavily female-dominated occupations. These are in the areas of health
and education, clerical work and service work (Table 4.6). The greatest
change in the female labor market during the sixties and seventies has
resulted from the rapid expansion of "work in technology, natural and
social sciences etc.," which now dominates the female occupational

Table 4.5   Employed Persons by Sex and Industry, 1963 and 1977
(percentage distribution)

	1963			1977		
Industry	Men	Women	Percent Women	Men	Women	Percent Women
Agriculture, hunting forestry and fishing	15.3	8.7	24.9	7.8	3.7	26.3
Mining, manufacturing	38.2	22.4	25.4	35.6	15.8	25.5
Engineering industries	11.6	3.8	16.1	16.6	5.2	19.5
Construction	12.7	1.4	6.0	11.9	1.2	6.9
Trade, restaurants and hotels	11.8	22.9	52.9	12.2	17.4	52.4
Trade	10.9	18.5	49.5	11.2	14.9	50.5
Transport, communication	9.1	4.3	21.6	8.8	4.2	27.0
Financing, insurance, etc.	3.1	5.5	50.7	5.6	6.4	46.5
Community, social and personal services	9.7	34.6	67.5	17.7	51.4	69.1
Public administration, education, health and welfare	8.2	25.7	64.5	12.5	45.4	73.7

Source: The Swedish Labor Force Surveys, Yearly Average 1963 and 1977.

distribution. Within this area, health and sick-care and, to some extent, education are responsible for the large increases. Clerical work has also increased both in numbers and percent.

There are large differences between the occupational distribution of women of different ages. For women under 35, health care and education are the most important areas, employing about a third of the employed women in this age group. For women over age 45, the largest occupational area is service work, which includes cleaning and cooking. Clerical work also declines with age but to a lesser extent. Differences by age are partly due to changes in demand, but may also be due to the limited opportunities of women reentering the labor market late in life. Most of the occupations within the area of "technology, etc." require some occupational training.

The sex segregation of the labor market has only decreased slightly over the period, despite the large inflow of women to the labor market.[10] This is due to the fact that the growing occupations, to a large extent, have been those where women's share already was large.

Regional Differences

The demand for female labor has varied not only over time, but also among different regions of the country. It is easier for women to obtain jobs in the big cities where the labor market is varied and the demand in typical female occupations, such as services, clerical work and health care, is high. It is more difficult in the rural areas where farming, forestry and typical male industrial jobs are the principal opportunities. Labor force participation rates vary from 78 percent for women aged 20 to 64 in the county of Stockholm to 68 percent for the same age group in some counties in central and northern Sweden.

Yet, while the level of female labor force participation is higher in the big city areas, the trend toward women's increased work force participation has been prevalent in all areas of Sweden. For women in the age group 25 to 54, the upward trend in labor force participation has been quite similar in all regions. If anything, the increase in the rural counties has been stronger, and thus the differences in labor force participation rates between different regions in the country have diminished over time.

Unemployment

Women have a higher rate of unemployment than men. This is true for all age groups, but the unemployment situation is especially problematic for teen-age girls. The smallest differences between men and women occur in the years when the return to the labor market takes place. Women in their middle years do not appear to have much difficulty in finding jobs.

Existing differences in unemployment can be explained by women's greater inflow into unemployment. In the sixties, the duration of a spell of

Table 4.6   Employed Persons by Sex and Occupation, 1963 and 1977

| | 1963 | | | 1977 | | |
Occupation	Men (percentage distribution)	Women (percentage distribution)	Percent Women	Men (percentage distribution)	Women (percentage distribution)	Percent Women
Work in technology, natural sciences, social sciences art and letters and fine arts, etc.	13.5	15.9	40.7	21.3	27.5	48.0
Administrative work	2.3	0.4	8.3	3.1	0.6	11.0
Accounting and clerical work	4.9	18.3	68.4	4.5	22.1	78.3
Commercial work	8.1	13.3	48.9	7.8	9.3	47.7
Agriculture, forestry and fishing	15.3	8.3	23.9	7.9	3.5	24.3
Transport and communications	8.4	3.5	19.5	8.2	3.2	22.8
Manufacturing, machine maintenance, mining, etc.	43.3	14.7	16.5	41.9	10.0	16.4
Service work	4.2	25.3	77.8	5.1	23.9	77.9

Source: The Swedish Labor Force Surveys, yearly averages 1963 and 1977.

unemployment used to be shorter for women than for men. Today women and men who become unemployed on average are unemployed a similar number of weeks. The greater frequency of women's unemployment is due to women's mobility in and out of the labor force and to their larger share of the new and reentering group (Table 4.7).

Reentrants are officially defined as those out of the labor force for more than one month, which means that women who drop out only for a short time as well as some part-year workers are included. On average during the seventies, 30 percent of unemployed women have been "reentrants" compared to about 20 percent of men. Also, new entrance is a slightly more common cause of unemployment for women than for men. For the age group 25 to 44, as much as 42 percent of the unemployment can be related to reentry.

Although the frequency of unemployment for women is higher than for men, the difference has diminished over time. This is due to fewer spells of unemployment per individual rather than fewer persons experiencing unemployment during a year. It can probably be explained by a more permanent attachment of women to the labor force and lowered incidence of part-year work.

Women's unemployment rate is less sensitive to changes in the level of activity than that of men. Thus, the difference between the male and female unemployment rates is smaller during recessions than booms. One reason for this is that women tend to work in sectors that are less affected by business cycle fluctuations. Another reason is that women—at least this was the case in the beginning of the seventies—have a greater tendency to drop out of the labor force during a period of unemployment.

An increased emphasis on employment security and extended attention to the internal labor market during the seventies has meant that a small share of labor demand has been directed toward the external markets. This can be expected to affect negatively the unemployment rates for the entering and reentering groups. Layoffs and unemployment during the last recession were much lower than normally would have occurred. Surprisingly, this has also been true for entrants and reentrants. However, they have had to bear a much larger share of the unemployment burden than earlier. Within these groups, it is youth whose share of unemployment has increased, while women aged 25 to 54 have not experienced any increase in their share of unemployment.[11] Thus, despite the rapid rate of entry of women to the labor market, it has been possible to absorb them through the development of demand and with the help of labor market policies.

INFLUENCES UPON REENTRY

The Potential Labor Force

Apart from students, there is a pool of women consisting of those who are principally occupied by household work who could be drawn into the

Table 4.7   Unemployment Rates and Reasons for Unemployment by Sex and Age, 1977 (in hundreds)

Sex and Age	Unemploy- ment Rate	New Entrants		Reentrants		Work Finished		Start or Production Reduction		Temporary		Other	
		Num- ber	Per- cent	Num- ber	Per- cent	Num- ber	Per- cent	Num- ber	Per- cent	Num- ber	Per- cent	Num- ber	Per- cent
Men													
16–24	3.2	25	18	25	18	38	28	15	11	2	1	23	17
25–44	1.2	4	3	27	20	33	25	28	21	5	4	22	17
45–54	0.9	1	3	6	16	12	32	11	29	2	5	3	8
55–64	1.1	0	0	5	11	14	32	12	27	2	1	4	9
16–74	1.5	30	8	64	18	97	27	67	19	12	3	53	15
Women													
16–24	5.1	31	18	35	21	54	32	13	8	0	0	22	13
25–44	1.7	5	4	59	42	27	19	15	10	2	1	14	10
45–54	1.2	3	7	12	26	12	26	10	21	1	2	3	7
55–64	1.6	1	2	9	21	7	16	12	28	1	2	5	12
16–74	2.2	39	10	115	29	99	25	50	13	5	1	44	11

Source: The Swedish Labor Force Surveys, yearly averages 1977.

labor force. The proportions of women of all ages who were occupied in their own household dropped continuously between 1963 and 1977. The largest unemployed groups, both in terms of number and percent, have been women of childbearing age and women over the age of 55. Not all of the women engaged in household work will have a long period out of the labor force. A low labor force participation rate can be the result of many women leaving the labor force for a short period of time or a smaller number of women dropping out for a longer period. The size of the part-year labor force indicates that there is considerable movement in and out of the labor force and that middle-aged women without any labor force experience during a year amounted only to about 15 percent in 1977.

Many part-year workers hold only short temporary jobs. Women with very intermittent labor force experience (i.e. with jobs of short duration, such as vacation substitutes, etc.) are in many ways similar to women who have dropped out completely for a longer period. They have no experience that can be evaluated to fall back upon nor any firm attachment to a working place. Information on women's last steady job may therefore be more relevant to the problem of reentry.

A 1975 study of the population not employed at that time, including the unemployed, estimated that 31 percent of all women aged 16 to 69 could be considered a potential work force (students and persons incapable of working were excluded).[12] Many of these women had had labor force experience years earlier: about 30 percent had been out of the labor force for more than ten years, and an additional 30 percent had their last labor force experience between three and ten years earlier. About one-fifth had never worked, but this group probably contained many young persons on their way into the labor market. Almost two out of five of the women had worked for more than ten years when they were in the market, and one-third had experience totaling between three and ten years. No less than about one-fifth of all Swedish women between the ages of 16 and 69 in 1975 would thus seem to have fulfilled the definition of possible "reentrants"—i.e. had not had any steady job for three years or more.

Of course, not all of these women are willing or ready to start working (Table 4.8). As many as one-fourth of the women wished to start work within six months. Not surprisingly, the younger the cohort, the smaller the share that wanted to remain housewives. Women aged 25 to 34 constituted 37 percent of all women who wished to return to the labor market, but relatively few women in this age group were ready to start work in the near future because of the presence of young children.

Only about 20 percent of the women who wished to start to work within six months were actively engaged in job search. The fact that many women who desire to work do not actively search for a job or register as unemployed is a problem that has long existed in Sweden and is termed "latent" or "disguised" unemployment. The Labor Force Survey has tried to capture this type of unemployment by asking persons out of the labor

Table 4.8   The Desire to Start Working among the Potential Female Work Force
Aged 25 to 55, 1975

Age	Want to Start Work Within 6 Months	Want to Start Work Later On	Don't Want to Start Work
25–34	20	59	20
35–44	27	45	28
45–54	28	18	54

Source: The economically inactive population survey in spring 1975.
Statistiska Meddelanden AM 1977:11.

force if they would have looked for a job if they thought a suitable job were available in the local community. (Since 1976 this question has been changed to whether the person would have wanted to and have been able to work during the week.) One of the aims of employment policy has been to reduce this form of unemployment in addition to overt unemployment. This policy appears to have been successful judging from Figure 4.1, which shows latent unemployment among women aged 25 to 54.

The reason why women do not actively search for a job is that they evaluate the probability of finding one to be very low—either due to lack of vacancies or to their own limited qualifications. Of those women in 1977 who said that they would have wanted to work and also would have been able to work, 63 percent indicated the absence of suitable job openings in the local labor market as the reason for not searching; 27 percent did not search because they felt they were unlikely to qualify for a job.

The survey of the economically inactive population also provides some background on the potential labor force, of whom 80 percent are women. About 40 percent of these women had children under seventeen years and about 27 percent were mothers of preschool children. Among those who indicated that they wished to return to the labor market, no less than half had preschool children and almost three-quarters had children under seventeen years of age.

The educational background of the potential labor force—unfortunately not divided by sex—was low. About 76 percent had only a primary education; 19 percent, a secondary education; and five percent, a post-secondary education. Hence, there is quite a difference between the educational status of those in the labor force and those outside. However, the educational level among those in the potential labor force who want to work in the market is higher than among those who wish to remain outside, but this may largely reflect an age effect.

Figure 4.1   The Share of Latent Job-Seekers among Women Aged 25 to 54, 1964—1977

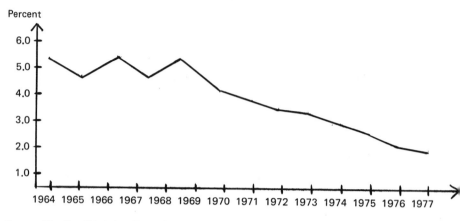

Source: The Swedish Labor Force Surveys.

Family Circumstances

The choice between home work and market work for a woman is related to her family situation. A single woman cannot choose to devote all her time to household chores. In most cases, she has to work in order to earn money with which she can buy the market products she needs. For couples living together, there is the opportunity for specialization with one person primarily responsible for maintaining the home and the other for obtaining market earnings. Women living alone thus have a stronger incentive to enter the labor force, which is reflected in their higher labor force participation rate and their lower share of the potential labor force.

The value for a family of having one member working at home will depend upon the extent of homemaking duties. The main determinant is the presence of children, their number and ages. Women's most common explanation for not working is the care of children, which is related to the woman's age and to the age and number of her children.

Consequently, the ability of young women with children to return to the labor market depends on the availability of arrangements for the care of their children. In the 1977 Swedish labor force survey, almost half of women 25 to 34 years old who indicated that they would have liked to work during the survey week referred to problems in arranging child care as the basic reason for not working (Table 4.9). This has been confirmed in other studies. The provision of child care facilities must therefore be a priority if women are to be able to stay in or return to the labor market.

Table 4.9 Women out of the Labor Force Who Wanted to Work during the Survey Week, by Age and Reason for Not Working, 1977 (percentage distribution)

| Age | Women Who Wanted to Work But Who Could Have Worked | | | Women Who Wanted to Work During the Survey Week Who Were Unable to Work Because | | | | |
	No Suitable Vacancies in the Local Area	Limited Opportunities to Get a Job	Other	Child Care not Available	Household Duties	Studies	Health	Other
20–24	33	7	9	33	4	4	7	2
25–34	34	9	4	43	2	2	5	1
35–44	51	16	6	14	1	2	8	1
45–54	50	22	7	1	4	1	13	2
55–64	48	25	6	0	4	0	15	4

Source: The Swedish Labor Force Survey, yearly averages 1977.

The effect of the family situation on the work decision was also revealed in interviews. Two life situations characterized the decision to return to the labor market: a divorce or when "the children are old enough to handle themselves." Possibly women who drop out of the labor force are women who strongly prefer to care for their children full time themselves. One of the women expressed this attitude: "I don't want anyone else to look after my children."

Economic Situation

The higher the income of the husband, the greater the opportunity for his wife to devote herself to homemaking. No relationship has been found, however, between husband's income and his wife's participation in the labor force, except that husbands of part-time workers have a higher average income than husbands of full-time workers. While a number of reasons besides securing a certain income level enter into the decision to start working, economic necessity may be important in deciding the amount of time one wants to devote to paid work.

Among the women interviewed, divorcees and a woman with an unemployed disabled husband said that they primarily worked for family income reasons. While most of the married women stated that economic aspects in the sense of securing a certain standard of living were an important factor, other reasons relating to their own personal development were the main driving force. Of course, the addition to family income was appreciated, and occasionally this had changed the opinion of an initially negative husband. All women interviewed said they would work regardless of the income of their husband.

Married women emphasized such economic motives as being able to support oneself, and having money of one's own so as not to have to ask for money, as important positive factors in the work decision. This was also a finding of Rita Liljestrom and her colleagues in their study of reentering women. Women stressed the personal value of their earnings, while their husbands pointed to the financial benefits for the family.

While women do not work primarily out of economic necessity, this does not mean that they are not influenced by economic considerations. Where there is a choice, the profitability of working will exert an important influence. The higher the net income to be earned by devoting a given number of hours to market work, the larger will be the net additions to family income and the larger the funds that the woman, herself, can control. The tax and transfer systems can be manipulated to induce or discourage women from working. High tax rates and transfers related to family income in connection with high costs of day care may serve to limit the economic benefit from work. About five percent of the inactive women who did not wish to work gave "It does not pay" as an explanation. This answer has been found to be most frequent among women with small children who would have to bear child care costs as a condition for work. It is not only the availability of child care but also its price that is a decisive factor in the reentry of this group of women.

Education and Occupational Training

Women out of the labor force have a lower level of general education on the average than those in the labor force and, to an even larger extent, have less vocational training, since vocational education has a stronger positive influence on women's labor force participation than does general education. Older women out of the labor force, in particular, either lack occupational training or their training is often obsolete.

Many women emphasize insufficient occupational training when asked to identify their problems in reentering the labor market. This answer does not always imply that they lack such training. Some reentrants interviewed had vocational training but they were so lacking in self-confidence that they were afraid to use it after many years out of the labor force. They preferred to obtain additional schooling and enter different areas of work. A substantial proportion indicated that they would be willing to train for a male occupation (although an overwhelming majority preferred female jobs). Adult education, possibilities for recurrent education, occupational training especially directed at women, and a stronger emphasis on occupational training for girls must be important ingredients in policies to enable women to reenter and remain in the labor market.

The Local Labor Market

The importance of education as a barrier to entry for women is related to the level of demand in the local labor market. Studies of local labor markets with a strong demand for labor and very high female labor force participation rates show that the relation between education, occupational training and labor force participation rates is very weak. If the demand for labor is high relative to the supply, women can find jobs even without a substantial amount of education.

The data from the labor force surveys suggest that women's low evaluation of the possibilities of securing a job in the local labor market deters many of them from looking for a job. This is the main reentry barrier for older women for whom child care is no longer a major problem. Women often have a geographically limited labor market since they are tied to their place of residence due to their husbands' jobs. Only 13 percent of the women in the potential labor force who wanted to start working could conceive of moving as a means to find a job.

Another problem for women is local transportation. Often they have no access to a car and consequently have to rely on communal transportation or take a job within biking distance. This is more often a problem for older women.

The level of economic activity, general employment policies and regional policies have special implications for reentrants. In addition, a wider range of occupational choices would counter limitations due to women's low geographic mobility.

Work Aspirations

One reason why it is difficult for women to enter the labor market may be that they have specific requirements for the jobs they are willing to accept, requirements that are not filled by the available openings. We have already noted one of these requirements: the job has to be fairly close to home. The majority of the women interviewed accepted a commuting time of no more than 20 to 40 minutes.

Another limiting factor may be job content. Different studies of women outside the labor force show that they are less willing than men to accept shift work and tempo work and that, not unexpectedly, they are looking for jobs in the typical female areas of health, social work, services and clerical work. Although quite a few women have manufacturing experience, one reason why many women do not look for such jobs may be unfamiliarity. In a study of women in male industrial jobs, it was shown that women who have entered such jobs are much more satisfied with their working conditions than men, both in terms of wages and work environment.[13] The authors' interpretation of this finding (and similar ones from other studies) is that women's aspirations are at lower levels than men's. Women compare their situation to that of other women and to their own experiences in the home, while men's expectations are derived from their own experiences and those of other men. As a consequence, women generally demand less of a job than men do, both in terms of wages and work environment.

This squares with the information from our own interviews. Even considering that many women had limited resources, it was striking how low their demands were both with respect to what they asked for at the employment service and what they asked of a job (and of their husbands!). Often they expressed readiness to take *any* job. The women who had reentered, all of whom had low-level jobs, often expressed gratitude for their great luck in acquiring a job. Even if they had other preferences, they were satisfied; they felt they could not demand more, although one woman advised other women job seekers, "Don't be afraid to make demands and show what you want."

There was, however, one demand that was almost universal: the job had to be part-time. "I will take anything as long as it is part-time." In the labor force surveys, the persons out of the labor force who wanted and could have worked during the survey week were asked what working hours they desired. In 1977, only about one-fifth wanted a full-time job. A somewhat smaller share (16 percent) of women with children desired to work full time, but there was no difference between women with preschool children and women with older children.

The choice of part-time work is usually related to household demands and a desire to adjust working hours to children's school hours. The sexual division of household tasks was considerable in the households of women interviewed. There was a virtual consensus among the women that the wife should be the one to adjust her working hours to family demands. Quite often, however, this belief was based on economic rather than biological grounds. Several women spontaneously remarked that "The woman should adjust her hours because she is the one who earns less." Often the demands from home seem to be demands that women have placed on themselves: "I can only accept a part-time job because I can't think of reducing any of the housework I am now doing." In households where wives had reentered, husbands quite often helped out but the women still had the main responsibility.

Policies to adjust women's expectations to available labor market opportunities have to work on two fronts. Women need better information about available job and training opportunities, qualifications demanded, and possible negative aspects of part-time jobs. But employers, too, need to be made aware of the existence of a potential labor force and informed about the qualifications and demands of available labor so that they do not search for labor that is simply not available.

Other Factors

A recurrent theme in studies of women who enter the labor market is the strong appreciation women show of the social values of work—self-development and job satisfaction, contacts with fellow workers, and improved self-esteem. Although many women liked being with their children, they often felt isolated and locked up at home. "Home is an isolated world." On the job, women meet the outside world and it is easier to make contacts. "At home you only speak about cleaning, diapers and children. At the job we speak about everything." "At work you have spontaneous contacts with fellow workers. At home you have to use your own initiative to make contacts, which is much more difficult." A job and money of one's own provide women with self-confidence and make them feel more independent. "I think a woman feels she is valued more when she goes to work. You need to get out to gain self-confidence."

Going to work can provide women with positive values that may be hard to obtain at home. With the part-time jobs that most women demand, the positive values of the world of work can be acquired without giving up too many home activities. In the majority of cases, the husband and the children have positive attitudes about the woman's work. This is not surprising since, in most cases, the wife has adjusted her hours to family demands and has retained most of the home responsibilities.

POLICIES AFFECTING REENTRY

Problems related to reentry can be approached from two different policy directions. One is to let women drop out of the labor force to care for their children while they are small and then provide education, occupational training and labor market information to assist them when they wish to reenter. The other is to enable women to combine market work and a family life while remaining in the labor market. Thus, general employment, tax and family policies are of utmost importance as far as reentry is concerned.

Employment Policy

We have earlier pointed to the importance of a large demand for labor for women's opportunities to enter the market, since women still usually are secondary family earners. An important prerequisite for maintaining women in the labor market is adherence to a full employment policy. Full employment has been the stated goal of Swedish economic policy throughout the postwar period. As described earlier, this policy first applied to both women and men workers; it later added the removal of barriers to entry for those outside the labor force; and finally included measures specifically directed toward women.

Due to the limited geographical mobility of women, the regional distribution of demand is very important. Since the end of the 1960s, regional support in the form of grants for investments in machinery and for the training of new personnel in development areas has been an ingredient in Swedish employment policy. In the seventies this has been complemented by hiring sex quotas. As another element in the policy for regional balance, the counties and local communities have been asked to take a greater responsibility in employment planning. Employers are expected to be encouraged to use the local potential labor supply before attempting recruitment from other communities or abroad. This policy is of direct relevance for women's reentry opportunities, since women comprise the majority of the potential labor supply. The local authorities, the employment board and employers have cooperated on local labor force investigations to identify labor demand, potential labor supply and barriers to entry. In the same general direction, another policy that has been in existence in some counties is the requirement for compulsory reporting of vacancies to the employment service.

Another factor reflecting demand and affecting the reentry of women is the wage women receive. Wage policy in Sweden is traditionally a matter between the unions and the employer organization. The main principle of the Swedish Confederation of Trade Unions (LO), which represents blue-collar workers, has been a policy of wage solidarity. It involves, first, equal pay for equal work regardless of region or the profitability of the industry or the firm. Second, it aims to raise very low wages through relatively higher percentage increases. This policy has probably contributed to raising women's wages relative to men's in the manufacturing sector where the ratio of female to male earnings has risen from 68.8 percent in 1960 to 87.1 percent in 1977.

Another reason for the improvement of women's relative pay in manufacturing during the 1960s is probably the 1960 agreement on equal pay for equal work for men and women reached between the labor market organizations, which has been in effect since 1965. The agreement has resulted in the elimination of different wage scales for men and women.

Most women, however, have not entered employment in manufacturing but in the municipal sector where there are many low-paid jobs. Women's market wages have grown over time along with the growth in the economy, but the evolution of the overall difference between men's and women's wages is difficult to trace due to lack of data. In 1976, the overall difference between the earnings of full-time, full-year working men and women was 26 percent. But one must bear in mind that almost half of all women work part time.

Tax and Transfer Policy

The Swedish tax and transfer system has developed in ways that have served both to encourage and discourage women's work in the market. Since work at home is not taxed, increases in the level of taxes serve to increase the value of nontaxed nonmarket work. In Sweden, the tax pressure on households has increased very rapidly during the last decades, which should have served to make households devote more of their time to home activities. A household, however, can affect its income and tax-burden not only by the amount of time devoted to market work, but also by the way family members divide the labor supply.

Until 1971, Sweden had a system of joint taxation whereby a wife's income was added to her husband's. With the wife as the family's secondary earner and progressive taxation, the wife's contribution was decreased by the increasing marginal taxes. In 1971, a system of individual taxation was adopted under which each individual is taxed separately on his or her own income. The immediate marginal effects on the wife's income were thereby reduced. A small deduction for two-earner families should serve to reduce the marginal effects further. The aim of this change in taxation was to remove the financial barriers to entry inherent in the tax system and to encourage women to enter paid work. It probably contributed to the large increase in labor force participation that occurred between 1971 and 1973, despite an ongoing recession. The combination of very high marginal tax rates and a system of separate individual taxation makes having two earners very profitable for most families. It will almost always be more profitable for the family to have the wife enter the market than for the husband to increase his earnings.

The profitability of working is affected not only by taxes but by income-related transfers that the family may lose if the wife enters the market. A further influence is the cost of child care that the family may have to bear. The Swedish housing benefit is an allowance toward rent that is dependent upon family income, the amount of rent and the number of children. If the wife in a low-income family enters the market, the housing benefit is reduced and, in most cases, disappears. If there also are children in need of day care, the benefit from the wife's market work will be reduced substantially. If subsidized day care is available, the wife's "marginal" tax rate will probably be lower than that of her husband, but if she has to pay for private care the benefit from working is bound to be quite low.

Thus reentry is most profitable for women without small children. The housing benefit has the further effect of making the incentive to enter the market stronger for a woman with a high-income husband, since she has no transfer income to lose. The fees at public day care centers are not sufficiently progressive to outweigh this effect.

The financial incentive to work is lowest among single mothers. Low-income families with children can receive welfare benefits when the mother is not working. Usually this affects only single mothers, since the family income for couples living together costomarily will be too high for welfare benefits if the mother does not work. In 1977, a single mother with two preschool children received on the average about $5,000 in social welfare payments and housing benefits (depending on her income), and would have to pay fees, although low, for day care. Single parents get priority in public day care. A low income or part-time job means little added income, since 85 to 90 percent of wages would disappear in the form of lost transfers and increased costs.

This illustrates a dilemma for policy-makers. On the one hand, they wish to enable the wives of low-income husbands and single mothers to remain at home with their children by providing them with financial support. On the other hand, this will severely limit these women's opportunities to improve their financial situation by going to work and will impose regressive marginal effects.

Child Care Policies

Since 1939, employers have been prohibited from firing women because of marriage or pregnancy. A paid leave of absence for six months for childbirth was instituted in 1955. The government has successively taken over some of the economic burden connected with having children. Cash benefits are available in the form of a basic child allowance available for every child regardless of the parents' income—today amounting to about 2200 kronor per child per year plus the aforementioned housing allowance. Free tuition through the university level, free school lunches and free maternity and child health services are also provided.

Swedish children do not start school until the year they become seven and, during the first couple of years, the school day is quite short. Since the early seventies, a three-hour preschool is available for all six-year-olds whose parents wish them to attend. There is thus a considerable time period for which child care has to be arranged. It was not until the mid 1960s, however, that public day care for children of working parents came to be recognized as a public responsibility in Sweden.

The first element of the present child care system is the parental leave which replaced the maternity leave in 1974. The parental leave makes it possible for either parent—the mother or the father—to stay home when a child is born or for parents to divide the available times as they see fit. In 1978, the available leave amounted to eight months, during which the parent who stayed home received an amount corresponding to 90 percent of his or her regular income, the highest income groups excepted. (This is the same amount received under health insurance.) An additional month is available at the minimum level of compensation (32 kronor/day) if so desired. The first six months have to be used as full-time leave sometime during the child's first year. The last three months, however, can be used at any time until the child is eight years old, e.g. when the child starts school. It can also be used to pay for a shortened workday, corresponding to a six-hour workday during one year.

In 1978, a new law went into effect which gives parents the right to additional but uncompensated leaves of absence. As long as the child is under one-and-one-half years old, one parent can remain at home full time. Up until the child is eight years old, a parent has the right to ask the employer for a three-quarter workday. A further provision gives parents of children under 12 the right to 12 to 18 days of paid leave to care for sick children.

An extended leave for child care enables a woman to have children and still stay in the labor force and keep her job. The opportunity to shorten the workday has been instituted to enable children and parents to spend more time together. At the same time, it will facilitate women's ability to combine work and family life. Extending the opportunity for child care leaves to fathers is a recognition of how vital shared home responsibilities are to equality in the labor market. The number of fathers availing themselves of the opportunity to take a leave of absence is still small, but has grown steadily. In 1977 about ten percent of fathers used the parental leave for an average period of approximately 40 days. Leave for the care of sick children has tended to be shared more equally between parents.

It was not until 1965 that Sweden started to expand public day care facilities. Since then there has been a fast and continual increase in the number of places, which nevertheless, still falls far short of demand. Swedish women have entered the labor market despite the lack of public day care for children rather than due to any efficient day care system.

By far the most common way preschool children are cared for in Sweden is by their own parents. Somewhat over one-half of all children from birth to six years of age are cared for by their mother. Not quite one-fourth are in some form of public care. The remainder are privately cared for by relatives, a private day mother, or a hired maid. The number of places in public child care corresponds to roughly 40 percent of children of mothers who usually work half time or more. After-school facilities are even less available. About eight percent of all children seven to twelve years of age are in public after-school care, representing 15 percent of those estimated to need such care.

The provision of day care facilities is the responsibility of the municipalities who receive state subsidies for this purpose. Public day care is provided both in day care centers and in the homes of child-minders hired by the community. Fees are heavily subsidized and much lower than what one has to pay in the private market, even by parents in high-income groups, although the fees depend on income and are progressive. Demand is high and the queues are long in most areas. Single mothers and families with very low income get priority in the distribution of places. The availability of subsidized public day care is a stimulus toward reentry. For many low-income women with small children, a place in public day care is a precondition for going to work.

It should be emphasized that in Sweden public child care is viewed as a service for working mothers *and* a measure to stimulate a child's personal development and to provide important social contacts. Thus the goal has not been confined to expansion of the quantity of places, but also has been to insure that a high quality of care is provided.

Educational Policy

A common route to the labor market for women is via reentry to the educational system. During the sixties and seventies a variety of reforms were instituted that have expanded the opportunities for adult education on all levels. Women have been a target group for these reforms since their education has tended to be shorter than men's, they lack vocational training, and there are greater generational differences in female schooling than male.

Adult education is now available in a variety of forms. Local communities run adult education free of charge both on a full-time and part-time basis for the different diplomas provided in primary and secondary school. Interest organizations and unions run study circle programs and evening courses. There are correspondence institutes, and radio and TV have also experimented with adult education courses. The so called "people's high schools" are boarding schools that traditionally have been geared toward adult education. Another special form of education is labor market training, which represents labor market, rather than educational, policy. Since all these different programs are government supported, tuition is nonexistent or very low.

Women have been in the majority in municipal schools for adult education ever since their inception in 1968. In the spring of 1978, about two-thirds of the students were women. The educational background of the women in adult education is lower than that of men, and women's representation is largest at the primary level and in shorter educational training at the secondary level.

When educational opportunities expanded, it was difficult to reach persons who had very brief primary education. Experimental programs were organized to determine how to remove obstacles to study for such persons. The programs involved recruitment of students to study circles and courses through outreach at work places and in residential areas.[14]

Housewives were one of the target groups for these programs. About 37 percent of those contacted wished to start studies in one of the subjects offered (Swedish, English, mathematics and social studies). They were less interested in studies than women who were already working, however. Interest in studies decreased with age, inferior levels of education, increasing family size, and lack of work experience. The program provided collective child care, and financial support for child care was also available, but child care still proved to be a problem for many women.

The rules regulating financial aid for studies and for entry into higher education consider the care of children to be equivalent to work in the market. In 1976, new rules for the support of adult education were put into effect. If someone wants to begin studies for the primary or secondary school level and has either worked or taken care of children for four years, he/she can apply for financial support during the period of education. For a former housewife, the support amounts to 2100 kronor a month of taxable income. (In addition, 750 kronor is available as a loan.) Studies can be full time or half time (support is adjusted accordingly).

Due to limited resources, somewhat more than half of those applying for such support received it in 1977/78. This amounted to about 15,000 persons.[15] Among the factors positively affecting the opportunity to receive aid are limited prior education, the amount of work (or child care) experience, handicaps, difficulty in studying during leisure time, burden of support, and difficult working conditions. Wives with high-income husbands are not excluded from receiving such aid, but their husbands' income is of importance in determining their amount of support. For those studying at the secondary level or in higher education, an advantageous system of government loans is also available. Here, however, there is a direct means test.

Three-quarters of those receiving support for adult education are women and the majority are between 30 and 40 years old. In the county of Malmohus, close to 20 percent of the women receiving adult education support for the first time were former housewives.

Since 1969, persons over the age of 25 with five years of work experience have been eligible to enter certain areas at the university level, even if they do not have a diploma from secondary school. Today, only four years of work experience are required. In certain areas, persons with work experience are given priority or special preference. At the university level, too, care of children is regarded as equivalent to work experience. In 1977, 45 percent of all women were admitted on the basis of the work experience rule, more than one-fifth of whom had entered on the basis of work at home.[16]

The educational problem of women who have dropped out of the labor force is not so much that their knowledge has become obsolete, but that they tend to be those with an initially low level of education. They therefore face serious difficulties when they attempt to return to the labor force. Opportunities for women who have worked at home to return to school and receive financial aid while studying have been progressively improved during the seventies, and should have opened up an important route to return to the labor market for many middle-aged women.

Future Trends in Reentry

In each successive generation, the share of women remaining in the labor force has increased. This means that the problem of reentry of women to the labor market will automatically diminish over time, since fewer women will be potential reentrants. Today, the participation rate for women in the reentry age groups (25 to 54) is 75 to 80 percent. Yet there will still be a substantial number of women in need of reentry programs in the near future, since most of the women out of the labor force, especially in the younger age groups, wish to return to the labor market and many women hold only temporary jobs.

Future entry of women into the labor market will depend upon how the factors influencing reentry develop and on what policy changes occur. For the time being, there are no signs of any reversal of past trends. The Swedish long-term planning report for the period 1978–1983 expects continued increases in the labor force participation rates of women. Since the labor force participation rate in the Stockholm area already has reached a very high level, it is calculated that there will be a slight slowdown in overall expansion relative to past trends. In the age groups 25 to 54, the predicted female labor force participation rates for 1983 lie between 85 and 90 percent.[17]

Women will constitute all of the net addition to the Swedish labor force for the next five years. If the predictions of labor force participation are to be fulfilled, the demand for women's services must continue to increase. The long-term planning report expects the new openings created during the next five years to be in areas with a high proportion of females, mainly the public sector. The new and reentering women can thus be absorbed without any significant changes in the proportion of women in the various sectors. Regional imbalance is not expected to be great enough to serve as a limiting factor for the entry of women.

Difficulties in reentering the market are strongly related to the length of the drop-out period. Many of the women who drop out of the market today will probably stay out for a much shorter period than earlier generations. Data on the extent of leaves in connection with childbirth indicate that the majority of women return to work rather quickly.[18] In 1976, almost two out of three of all women who gave birth started to work within a year. Of the women who could be considered to be in the labor market before childbirth (i.e. had an income above the minimum insurance level), four out of five had returned to work within a year. The tendency to return to the labor market was greater the higher the income of the mother, which again indicates that women who drop out are those with low incomes and, most likely, low education and job qualifications as well.

The number of children in a family is a factor that affects the length and number of dropout periods. The fertility rate in Sweden has fallen successively since the middle of the sixties to an all-time low of an average of 1.65 children per woman in 1977. Women today who are between 20 and 30 years of age have a fertility rate that is substantially lower than earlier generations, and this development should serve to reduce the likelihood of exit. A 1978 population projection predicts that the fall in fertility will not continue, but will increase slightly to 1.8 in 1985.[19] This is not likely to produce any significant changes in drop-out periods or reentry. More probable is that an increase in fertility will occur as women find it possible to combine family and market work and reforms in this direction continue. In fact, a substantial number of younger women may have postponed having children because the present system of paid leaves makes it advantageous to wait to have children until one is firmly established in the labor market. The long-term report estimated that even with the predicted increase in fertility rates, available and planned expansion of child care services will be sufficient to permit the expected rise in women's labor force participation.

A likely pattern for coming generations of Swedish women is that they will not drop out of the labor force when they have children, at least not in the traditional sense. Swedish family policy has aimed at creating opportunities for women and men to combine market work and family life. Women can now stay out of the labor market for a substantial period without having to risk the loss of their jobs. After that period they can adjust their working hours to family needs. Thus we can anticipate that women will continue to enter and stay in the labor force, but on a part-time basis. The rate of absence will increase due to the new possibilities for child care leaves. More men probably will work part time also, especially those in high income groups, but the increase in male part-time work will be slow. For some number of years, we will have women reentering after a longer absence from the labor market, but this will be a diminishing problem. Instead, women's new pattern of employment will accentuate other problems, since their reliance on part-time work most probably will intensify occupational segregation and limit women's advancement opportunities.

LABOR MARKET PROGRAMS FOR WOMEN

One of the most important means used to fulfill the Swedish goal of full employment has been that of selective labor market policies. Ever since the end of the 1950s, such policies have supplemented the use of general policies and have been increasingly utilized.[20] In 1977, the budget of the National Labor Market Board, which is the government agency responsible for the execution of labor market policy, corresponded to roughly three percent of the GNP and to nine percent of the government budget. Currently, labor market programs are primarily devoted to information, vocational and geographic mobility, job creation, regional development assistance, rehabilitation, and other measures on behalf of the hard-to-employ. The direction of policies and the emphasis on different programs have changed over the last two decades as full employment policy has changed.

The focus of labor market policies is upon the employment situation of the individual. The official policy statements point out that full, productive and freely chosen employment is in the interest of both the individual and society. The achievement of this goal requires differentiated and selective policies. When labor market policy was expanded during the 1960s, its role in stabilization and in achieving structural changes was especially stressed. In addition, the goals of economic growth and a more equal income distribution were seen as being fostered by a more active labor market policy. It was also pointed out that a massive economic effort to reach full employment was justified by the intrinsic value of work. The stress on the value of work itself has meant that, in Swedish policy, measures directed at job placement for the unemployed have priority over cash benefits.

In the early sixties, a program of vocational and geographic mobility was strongly emphasized. The most important part of this program was labor market training. Labor market policies were also to have a role in facilitating the move from work in the home to work in the market. The major structural changes and substantial mobility during this period gave rise to negative public reactions which resulted in an expansion of regional policies during the latter sixties.

While the role of labor market policy in facilitating structural changes through occupational and geographic mobility was retained into the seventies, other elements have been added. Now, labor market authorities are expected to selectively create employment opportunities in connection with layoffs and shutdowns. It has increasingly been recognized that groups with special difficulties in finding jobs, such as the elderly, handicapped, women and youth, may need additional support. In a country with a decreasing share of the population in the productive ages and a more restricted view on immigration than in the past, the potential labor force, i.e. those not looking for work who could be activated under special circumstances, is gaining growing attention. The goal of full employment has come to be transformed into the goal of "jobs for all." As a result, the employment service grew rapidly during the early seventies in order to better match the desires of workers and employers and to activate persons out of the labor force.

The labor market developments during the seventies have emphasized job security. New laws have increased the cost of laying off labor and, as a consequence, new measures during the last recession enabled firms to retain their employees, and an increasing share of the current budget of the NLMB has been in the form of training subsidies for employers.

Women in the Programs[21]

Women reentering the labor market have not been identified as a special target group for labor market programs. The different sub-groups toward whom policies have been specifically aimed are women, youth, the elderly and the handicapped. Reentrants will be found in two of these groups, women and the elderly job seekers. Lately, new entrants have also been treated as a special group. However, since no measures have been designed to serve exclusively reentering women but usually apply to other unemployed groups as well, the discussion will focus on those programs of major interest to reentrants. This means primarily programs of labor market information and vocational and geographic mobility as well as certain relevant employment creation measures and regional development programs.

Although measures are not restricted to reentering women, activities have been developed and changes of routine have occurred in light of their special needs. In the 1960s, measures regarding women were concentrated on increasing female employment and facilitating the reentry of women to the labor force. In the 1970s, these policies have been coupled with an increased interest in supporting the women in the labor market.

Until recently, a main guideline for labor market policies was that men and women should be treated equally and that measures should commonly apply to both men and women. Neutral treatment, however, usually means that the stronger group will be favored: women will get fewer places in training since there are fewer women in the market; relief work traditionally has been developed within typical male occupations, etc. With the establishment of the Equality Council in Sweden, it was acknowledged that full equality between men and women may require labor market policies specifically aimed at women. A number of special programs for women have since been developed, and the focus of the policy has slowly changed from the problem of enlarging women's employment to the problem of achieving equality in the labor market.

In 1977, the NLMB adopted a special program which clearly states that work for equality in the labor market is an important task for labor market administration.[22] This program stipulates that the employment service shall consider the wishes and qualifications of the applicants without reference to obstacles in the form of traditional sex barriers in the labor market. The employment service shall also stimulate applicants to choose occupational training irrespective of sex.

The Organization of the Labor Market Board[23]

The responsibility for planning and carrying out Swedish labor market policy decided upon by the government rests upon the National Labor Market Board. This is a separate government agency with central, regional and local offices, whose governing body is appointed by the government. Representatives from the labor market organizations form the majority of the Board, which includes a member representing female labor.

At the local level, the Employment Service is the basic unit for labor market policy. The Employment Service provides several types of assistance, including information, placement and job planning. Job planning includes job preparation information and decisions on labor market training.

The program for equality in the labor market decides how the goal of equality is to be carried out within each organization. Equality is the responsibility of all officers in every aspect of their work. In external contacts with other authorities and organizations, with business firms, or with individuals seeking work, traditional attitudes with respect to sex have to be discarded. The program is focused on the achievement of equality rather than the problems of reentry per se. The switch of focus can be seen in the fact that some equality officers previously were "activating" officers, responsible for programs to support women's reentry. Nevertheless, since the main target group for labor market policy is the unemployed and the untrained, it is obvious that the problems of reentering women or of women with very intermittent work patterns still loom large in equality work.

Placement Services

Let us follow a women contacting the Employment Service to help her search for a job after several years out of the labor market. First, she is provided with printed information in the form of vacancy lists, course catalogues, publications and a number of folders containing brief information about the different offerings of the Employment Service. Earlier, a special folder directed to women called "Take the chance now. Get yourself vocational training" informed them about rules for labor market training, sex equality grants and regional quotas for the employment of women. This folder has been discarded in favor of material not directed exclusively to women.

Experimental appointments of special employment officers for women have also been made. Since women have more limited market opportunities and experiences than men, they usually need more assistance and more intensive search. Thus, for a period of three years at the beginning of the seventies, one hundred placement officers were added to the staff and assigned to assist women seeking employment. The experience of this pilot program was not altogether positive. Instead of increasing the resources available to women, there was a tendency to reorganize internal patterns of work, placing the responsibility for attending to women's issues upon these officials and ignoring women in other areas. During periods of high unemployment, the placement officer was drawn into the regular activities of the office, with not much time left to initiate special actions for women. This program was discarded, and currently questions of equality are expected to be the concern of all placement officers in connection with their daily tasks.

A study of the effects of the intensified placement service for women was undertaken at a district office in the south of Sweden which received extra personnel during 1976-77. Although the preliminary results of the study indicate that the risk of remaining unemployed diminished and the length of the unemployment period was shortened, this was the case for both men and women. This finding supports the reorganization of work, since it means an increased number of personnel will result in an increase in the time spent on men as well as women.

Let us now return to the woman in the employment office. All the printed information may seem a bit overwhelming and difficult to understand, especially for the reentry woman with a limited knowledge of the labor market. Many of the women interviewed indicated that they found the first visits at the employment service unsatisfactory, and that it took too long before they got a chance to have a personal talk with a placement officer. Until then they were usually unaware of the different possibilities open to them.

The placement officer can help women to study the vacancy lists and give suggestions for employment. Since many job seekers have a very unclear idea of their own capacities and qualifications, it is difficult for them to judge different job offers without help and support. Sometimes it is enough to visit a work place. The officer can also contact an employer. If the job opening is in another city, the job seeker can get travel assistance for herself and accompanying children. If the woman accepts the job, she receives support for transportation and moving costs for the entire family. Among movers receiving such support, the proportion of females increased from about 20 percent in 1963 to 46 percent in 1977.

Occupational Guidance and Worklife Orientation

Still other efforts may be needed before the woman finds a job that suits her. Our interviews show the great need for disseminating educational and labor market information among reentering women. The lack of knowledge pertains to labor market requirements and their own qualifications; self-evaluation is often very low. Job preparation information may be provided in a variety of forms: the woman may have a discussion with a placement officer, a career adviser and/or a psychologist and sometimes a test of skill will be given. The purpose of such interviews is to give the Employment Service information about the woman's preferences, earlier job experience, education and special demands (e.g. hours of work). The task of the career adviser is to inform the woman about working life and different education and vocational training programs.

Since many of the job seekers have similar problems and need similar information and support, the Employment Service has organized experimental guidance groups on the premise that it may be helpful and stimulating for those in the same situation to meet and talk about their problems under some leadership. At the same time, employment officials have an opportunity to provide more information than would be possible in individual talks. A guidance group consists of eight to ten job seekers, a placement officer and a psychologist. The meetings generally last about two days. The discussions concentrate on what to consider and what actions to take when choosing an occupation. So far this program has been tried only on a small scale—about 300 groups have been in operation during a year. The experience has been positive, and the activity will be expanded.

Some women may be in need of even more thorough occupational guidance and information about the labor market. A special course on "working life and training," aimed towards uncertain and inexperienced job seekers, has been developed within labor market training to serve this need. This type of course can also be arranged for other groups such as youths, immigrants, the handicapped or men leaving their normal occupation. The course is regarded as a more intensive form of occupational guidance and placement. It involves a group of about 12 persons, lasts for four to six weeks, and includes both a theoretical and a practical segment. About one week is devoted to studies of the labor market, social rights, unions, health problems, occupational information, training and employment opportunities. There is also plenty of room for individual guidance and psychological tests. The great advantage of this course is the opportunities it offers for practical experience. The participants use the next couple of weeks for practical work in at least two different fields like industry, commerce or health care. The length of the practical experience can be extended for a few more weeks if desired.

The organization of the course provides another advantage. It can be used to break traditional occupational barriers for men and women by planning women's practical experience in male-dominated industry. A course for men can be arranged with practical experience concentrated in nursing and care. In this way, occupational choice can be widened for both men and women. Further, the participants get a chance to try a nontraditional occupation before making any definite decision. Groups of women or men enter a workplace dominated by the other sex with respectability conferred by virtue of being part of a public program.

Around 11,000 persons started a working life orientation course during the year 1977-78, compared to about 155,000 who started any form of labor market training during the same period.[24] Of those participating in working life orientation, women constituted about 65 percent. On average, two-thirds of the women were older than 24 years. Several women interviewed had participated in such a course. Some received job offers at the place of their practical training. The basic aim of this course, however, is not to provide immediate employment, but to help insecure persons find out what sort of job they want. Often the women go on to a regular labor market training course or go back into the regular school system. Follow-up studies have found that, in general, participants in the working life and training course are more satisfied with the information they receive about education and work than participants in other forms of labor market training. A majority of the participants had followed the advice received in the information course, and it was they who were especially content with the education or work they entered after the course.

The Kristianstad project. The working life and training course is a major ingredient in an experimental program geared towards unemployed and reentering women originally introduced in the county of Kristianstad in southern Sweden. In 1973, the Equality Council proposed the introduction of selective compensatory measures in labor market policy for women to be tested during a transitional period. One of these programs aimed to prepare and guide women through their entry to working life. It also had the additional aim of stimulating and facilitating the entry of women to male-dominated jobs. The project used already available labor market measures but combined them in a new and more systematic fashion. These were information, introductory courses, practical experience and training in various forms.

When the project was initiated, a business upturn had started and there was a high demand for labor from the manufacturing sector. In the Kristianstad region, a great number of women were unemployed or were potential reentrants outside the labor market. At the same time there was a large number of vacancies in male jobs within the metal and wood-working industries. The Equality Council, the County Labor Board, the local Employment Office, the authorities of the municipality, the companies and the trade unions all cooperated with the program in order to entice women into male jobs.

The following actions were the essential elements of the program. Firms that were willing to take on women in formerly all-male occupations were recruited, and jobs suitable for the experiment were selected. Information about the project was spread by advertisements in the press, and special information folders were distributed, addressed specifically to former housewives and others with little experience of working life. During a one-day information meeting, women in the community were then further informed about the experiment and the training and employment opportunities it could offer. Interested women were prepared for work by attending a working life and training course with practical experience provided in the participating firms. After the course, those women who so wished were employed at the firm of their choice. A special advantage of the program was that women got the chance to enter the firm as a group, rather than having to take the step individually, and that the trade unions cooperated with them from the start.

About 40 percent of the women attending the information days got a job. Most of them were in the age group 30 to 39. Several of them had no vocational training and only elementary schooling; as young girls they had worked in various low-level jobs and, after some years, they married, had children, and became housewives. The principal factor in their decision to reenter the labor market was isolation and lack of outside contacts at home. Other reasons were a desire to have money of their own rather than being economically dependent on their husbands and, in some cases, the wish to secure a better standard of living. The positive aspects described by the women themselves, after their reentry, were greater self-reliance and social relationships on the job.[25]

The reaction to the program from all parties involved has been positive. It has now been extended to all counties and is carried out on a more regular basis. The project has involved a large number of firms, local communities and representatives of labor organizations. At the end of 1976, 2,000 women were known to have received placement through the program. Many more had been reached by the day-long information and introductory courses. Due to the recession and a low demand for industrial workers, however, its use has been limited during the last few years.

Labor Market Training

One labor market policy measure which has grown in importance over time is occupational training for adults. At the outset, this training was only available to the unemployed, but in 1963 criteria for acceptance to training were changed so that persons in danger of becoming unemployed or with placement difficulties were also eligible. They must be above the age of 20 and registered as job applicants at the Employment Service. For women who wanted to return to the labor market this was an important change.

In the first years after the new policy was established, training was utilized by a large number of reentering women, but the proportion of reentrants in training became successively lower thereafter. In 1969, as many as 40 percent of the women in labor market training were former homemakers. In 1975, women with this background comprised only seven percent of the total. This reflects the increase in the labor force participation rate of all women that had occurred over the period, which meant that trainees were more likely to be unemployed women than homemakers.

The objective of labor market training is to assist the unemployed and to generate a supply of trained labor. The training programs are directed toward improving the situation of groups in the weakest position in the labor market. The aim of "a job for everyone" demands that training efforts be especially designed for groups outside the labor force or in an unstable labor market situation. Newcomers to the labor market, e.g. women who have been working at home and youth with little work experience, need labor market training to strengthen their labor market position. Recommendations of an official investigation of labor market training programs carried out in 1974 especially emphasized that resources be sufficient to cover the need for training women entering or reentering the labor market after a long period at home or with incomplete occupational training.[26] This investigation also noted the importance of widening the range of occupations available to women, and recommended that labor market training be used for this purpose. Since the traditional female occupations usually require a shorter training period, they are readily chosen without consideration of alternatives.

It is important for the Employment Service to actively inform women about alternative training possibilities, especially in nontraditional occupations. Practical experience in the worklife orientation courses can be used to cover areas not dominated by one sex. The County Labor Boards are also empowered, in consultation with labor market parties, to give priority in training to applicants from the sex that is underrepresented in the particular occupation. The effect of this new policy has been minimal, but an increase in the proportion of women training in the agricultural, forestry and fishing sector is noticeable, as well as a slight decrease in the proportion of women training for medical and health services. Follow-up studies have shown that if a single woman follows a male-dominated course she is more prone to drop the course than a woman following a traditional course. It is therefore recommended that several women together take a male-dominated course.

Courses are run by other authorities, firms or organizations also. Follow-up studies have shown that if a single woman follows a male-dominated course, she is more prone to drop the course than a woman following a traditional course. It is therefore recommended that several women together take a male-dominated course.

National Board of Education. The courses arranged by the National Board of Education (NBoE) are especially arranged for labor market training and are held at 50 special training centers throughout the country. Decentralization makes it easier for women to enter training close to home. The courses are generally directed towards specific occupations, except for certain preparatory courses, and the majority involve retraining. Preparatory courses, continuation courses and adaptation courses combined constitute only a small part of the total.

The NBoE runs about 300 different kinds of courses, mainly directed toward the manufacturing sector, although recent labor market developments have led to the creation of more courses directed toward the service sector; and such courses currently constitute one-third of the total. At the end of the sixties, a special course for persons insufficiently trained in general subjects was also introduced.

The courses are of different duration, ranging from two weeks up to a year, and schedules can be changed according to individual need. Flexibility in scheduling may be necessary for persons with home responsibilities.

In certain occupations, reactivating courses for persons who have had training but have been out of the labor force for some time are arranged by the employer in cooperation with the NLMB. Most of these have been in the medical and health services area, e.g. nurses or physiotherapists, where there has been a shortage of trained personnel. Each year the county councils (the health authorities) look through the register of specific types of personnel and try to get in touch with those who are not active in their occupations. Through these contacts, which are made through the Employment Service, the women get an offer to participate in a reactivating course, usually about eight weeks long, before reentering work. During the training period, "stimulation pay" is given, jointly financed by the county council and the NLMB. The pay is somewhat higher than the regular support for labor market training but is substantially lower than the regular salary for the job.

A study of 20,000 persons who completed labor market training courses during the last half of 1972 found that the women's ages ranged from 18 to 54 years, with a mean of 33 years. Homemakers comprised about 20 percent of the trainees compared to seven percent in 1975. The majority of the women had been in the labor market prior to training, in office work, retail sales or in hospital employment. Most of the women studied had only seven years of basic schooling, and very few had any vocational schooling. While half of all the women trainees chose vocational training, this was true for two-thirds of the housewives. Almost half of the latter selected training in service occupations in order to become home service workers, and one-third chose office work. In comparison with all women in the program, reentrants selected shorter courses.

About two-thirds of the reentrant group had a job after three months, a more positive result than for others. Also, they had a shorter period of unemployment and a low drop-out rate. Only ten percent left the course for other activities, usually to care for their children.[27] A possible explanation of the favorable employment situation of the reentrants lies in their selection of an occupation, since home service workers have been in great demand. Other follow-up studies that have concentrated on the employment situation three or six months after finishing the course have found that women trainees generally fare somewhat better than men since a higher percentage were employed.[28] This is related, however, to women's large representation in occupational training for health care and other occupations that have relatively low unemployment rates.

Problems encountered in connection with training included unaccustomedness to studies and lack of previous knowledge, especially among the elderly and women with little education. Combining homemaking, including child care, and studies was a problem for all of the women. Nevertheless, considerable interest was expressed in continuing training after the end of the course.

On-the-job training. Training on the job is arranged and contracted with enterprises and generally financed by contributions to the employer in the form of a wage subsidy for the training period. This type of training grew rapidly during the seventies and has a variety of goals. On several occasions, training subsidies have been introduced to stimulate new employment of groups with structural problems. In 1972-1974, training subsidies were offered to firms which hired and trained women and youth above their normal level of recruitment. All together 13,000 persons were covered by this form of training subsidy, roughly 2,000 of whom were women over the age of 25.

School courses. Courses within the ordinary educational system include local adult education, people's high school and ordinary high school. Students in this type of training are predominately women. Stipends are available to persons entering such education as necessary preparation for later vocational training arranged by the labor market administration. Persons with only elementary schooling can attend the same programs free of charge, but without receiving stipends.

In 1976, the Labor Market Board, together with the government's commission on employment and the National Board of Education, started a pilot project in one county in order to raise older person's share of labor market training. The experiment took place between October 1976 and May 1977. All job-seekers above the age of 45 who could not be placed by the Employment Service were informed about the opportunity for labor market training. At the same time, they were invited to a meeting to learn about the labor market training being offered where they were provided with information about the training, the learning capacities of the elderly, and successful results of training older people. A further purpose was to give these job seekers an opportunity to discuss and exchange views with others in the same situation. A special information folder was published

entitled "Take the chance now. Get yourself vocational training. Information from the Employment Service for you who are over 45." Visits to a
training center were arranged. The employers in the district were informed
about the project and asked to cooperate in the efforts to find jobs for these
individuals.

Although the pilot project was not restricted to women, they were in the
majority among the job seekers concerned (78 percent); 55 percent of the
women were in the age group 45 to 59. At the end of the experimental
period, a little less than half of the women were either employed or in
training, all of whom were aged 45 to 59 years. The main reason given for
not applying for training was age, i.e. the feeling of being too old for
studies. Another reason was that there was no suitable training. The number
of participants in labor market training in the area increased during the
period, and women almost doubled their share.

Persons participating in labor market courses receive stipends subject to
taxation during their period of training. The grant amounts to 150 to 200 kr
per day and is about equal to the wage of a low-level industrial job. Earlier,
support was means-tested against the income of the spouse, but since 1976,
eligibility is unrelated to husband's income. There are also special
allowances for travel expenses, course fees and expenditures for instruc-
tional materials and working clothes. Single parents reentering the labor
market after an interruption can get special housing support. A recent
innovation provides parents without training opportunities in their home
area with support for their children's maintenance and education and for
the rental of an apartment at the center. At present, this program covers
about 200 individuals at 23 places.

The Equality Grant

The equality grant is available to an employer who hires and provides on-
the-job training for women in typical male occupations, or hires and trains
men for typical female occupations. The employer can then get a wage
subsidy for each hour of training, which now is equal to eight kronor (in
some counties 14 kronor). The subsidy is available only for a limited
number of occupations: three for men and nine for women (in some
counties the range of occupations is larger).

An employer who hires someone of the "right" sex for one of these
occupations and works out a plan for training is eligible for the subsidy.
The union representatives must give their consent and participate in the
planning and implementation of the training. The person employed has to
be hired through the public employment agency and the subsidy is not
intended for internal recruitment of women who wish to change jobs. The
subsidy is available only where there is a shortage of workers in the
particular occupation in the local labor market. Thus, if men are available
for the occupation, there can be no subsidy for women willing to enter.

Although not directly aimed at reentrants, equality grants can serve to widen the potential labor market for women and increase the number of possible openings for reentrants.

The use of the equality subsidy has been quite rare—for only about 250 persons a year, and only once for a man. In 1975, only about one percent of all women in training were involved in equality grants. The overwhelming proportion of these women were trained in metal and precision-tool manufacturing or welding. There are several reasons why employers have not been interested in the subsidy. First, the amount of the subsidy has been considered too low to compensate for training and administrative costs. Secondly, in many areas unemployed persons were available and, due to the restrictions mentioned above, the subsidy could not be used.

The National Labor Market Board has not been satisfied with the effectiveness of this measure. Proposals have been made to increase its use by raising the amount of the subsidy, expanding the number of applicable occupations and eliminating its restriction to situations where no other job seekers are available. So far these proposals have not been accepted by the government.

Relief Work

If a job cannot be found for a woman on the open market and she is not interested in labor market training or there is a waiting period for the course she wants, she may be placed in relief work as a temporary solution. Relief work is arranged for applicants at the Employment Service and has the aim of leveling the demand for labor.

Traditionally, relief work has been arranged in the typical male areas of employment but, during recent years, special relief work has been arranged for youth and women who lack work experience, since they have represented an increasing share of the unemployed. County Labor Boards have been instructed to plan relief work for women and men in correspondence to their share of the unemployed. At the same time, relief work is supposed to be used to encourage men and women to try nontraditional occupations.

As a result of this new policy, women's share of relief work has grown rapidly during the seventies, although the major part of the increase has been among women under the age of 25 (Table 4.10). Nevertheless, in 1976, unemployed women had a lower probability than men of being placed in relief work.[29] With regard to other labor market policy measures, no such difference could be observed.

A special program combines the development of relief work with opportunities for labor market training for employed persons. This has been operating within the nursing sector since 1972 and, in 1975, it was extended to the entire municipal and county-council sector. This program has a twofold purpose. First, it gives employees, chiefly women, an opportunity to obtain basic or further training in their particular occupa-

Table 4.10 Women's Share of Relief Work, 1970—1977

Year	Total Number (in thousands)	Percent Women	Percent Women Over 25 Years
1970	9.6	4	98
1971	14.0	5	86
1972	23.1	9	70
1973	25.2	16	57
1974	17.8	19	58
1975	12.9	18	61
1976	21.5	31	27
1977	24.9	35	20

Source: The Labor Market Board.

tion. Second, unemployed youth or other new entrants can gain worklife experience as they replace employees on leave for labor market training.

The trainees get their salary from their employer during the period of training. The Employment Service selects unemployed persons to replace those in training, and the employer has the responsibility for providing the substitute with adequate work. If a short introduction course is needed, it might be included in the relief work. The substitute's salary is in accordance with the existing standard agreement. In order that the municipality shall not bear all the costs, the state subsidizes 75 percent of the outlays for the relief workers. From January 1973 to June 1978, about 20,000 persons were trained under this program and about 15,000 persons replaced them.

Regional Policy

Since women often are tied to the local labor market due to their husbands' work, regional policy especially directed towards their needs can be an important tool for reentry to the market. Regional development grants are available for new enterprises or for the expansion of already existing ones in regions where the level of employment is low. They can be used for investment in buildings and machinery or for the education and training of new personnel. Increasing the demand for labor is important for new entrants to the labor market, although this is not always particularly helpful for women since most of the jobs opened in this way are in traditionally male fields.

In an effort to direct more of the demand created by the regional grants towards women, firms receiving regional development support have been required since 1974 to hire a minimum of 40 percent of each sex.

Companies are required to file recruitment plans for new hires when they apply for a grant. The recruitment plan is formulated by the firm in cooperation with the County Labor Board and labor market organizations.

The results of this measure have been quite favorable. Although it is possible for firms to apply for an exemption from the rules, most of them have made recruitment plans in accordance with the regulations. Local authorities report that firms are now more actively considering opportunities to employ both men and women and, when reconstructing or expanding their plants, they generally include personal facilities for both men and women. During the first two years of the program, women's share of employment in the participating firms increased from 19 percent to 21 percent, which is somewhat greater than the increase in corresponding company branches in the country as a whole. The proportion of women in the national labor force during this period also increased and rose at a faster rate within the development regions.

Changes in attitudes towards employing women as industrial workers have taken place all over the country. It is therefore hard to judge to what extent the recruitment pattern is a result of the quota requirement or whether it would have occurred without it. It is clear, however, that the quotas have forced firms to plan their recruitment policies more deliberately with regard to sex. They can no longer, by habit and tradition, continue to hire men only. Also, when women feel more hopeful that there is going to be a demand for them in male occupations, they tend to be willing to enter them. In the development regions, the share of women in education and training for male-dominated occupations is higher than in other areas of the country.

Summary

There are no measures designed exclusively for reentering women. Reentrants, however, have been counted among the unemployed for a long time and have been eligible for services and training provided by the Labor Market Board. Activities have also been developed in light of the special needs of this group. In practice, it is difficult to distinguish the problems of reentering women and women who have been in the labor market intermittently, employed in various jobs. This type of experience is of little value in looking for steady employment.

Many women find a job directly without contacting the Employment Service (Table 4.11). Through friends, advertisements or sometimes through their children, they find out about available openings and then contact the employer directly. Often some short training is provided by the employer, e.g. for home service workers, day care mothers, nurse's aides. Moreover, the Labor Market Board has limited resources, which means that not every interested woman gains access to a guidance group, a worklife orientation course or occupational training. The aids are available, but it is

Table 4.11 Unemployed Women by Means of Job Search, 1977

	Women	Percent
Employment service	80	53.3
Employer	21	14.0
Advertisement	13	8.7
Other	4	2.7
Employment service and employer	12	8.0
Employment service and advertisement	14	9.3
Employer and advertisement	1	0
Employment service and advertisement and employer	6	4.0
Total	150	100.00

Source: Information from the Labor Market Board Nr 1978:17.

up to the individual employment officer to decide who can benefit most from the different programs.

For many women, the visit to the employment office is one of the first steps taken on the way back to the labor market. Therefore, the manner in which women are received there is very important. Many women feel that they are not given enough support and help from the Employment Service and that it takes too long before they get a chance for a private talk with an employment officer. Many women may expect to be completely taken care of once they have applied to the Employment Service, and their lack of self-confidence prevents them from asking questions or making demands.

When I looked for a job, I knew there were different courses one could start, but the employment office didn't suggest any and I didn't ask.

The employment officer must take time to fully explore job-seeking women's desires and possibilities and must be aware of the lack of confidence that is characteristic of the reentering women. Information about the different labor market programs ought to be given, even if a woman does not explicitly ask for it. Once women get such individual counseling they are very satisfied.

Although I think it took loo long before I got the help I wanted, eventually I found out about the different possibilities and I feel I have received a great deal of help. I am very satisfied now.

The main problem of reentering women is their lack of labor market experience, but generally they also have a low level of education. The women are handicapped by their inadequate knowledge of labor market requirements and prospects. To this is added their uncertainty about their own preferences and qualifications, which is accentuated by their low self-confidence. The working life and training course is one attempt to fill this need of basic knowledge about the labor market. This type of course, as well as the guidance group, also aims to overcome psychological barriers and build up self-confidence. Those women interviewed who had participated in such a course much appreciated this type of help.

I was very satisfied with the course. It gave good information about the labor market and then I got to know other women in the same situation which I felt as a support.

As reentering women often have only six to eight years of elementary schooling and shorter periods of experience in low-level jobs, the program of labor market training provides an important means of helping them to obtain better jobs. Both the possibility of further studies within the ordinary school system and vocational training at one of the training centers of the NLMB are used by women to a high degree.

Women in regional development areas often face considerable problems due to a low demand for female labor. In such circumstances, the attitude that the jobs are to be reserved for men easily gains ground. Hidden unemployment is large, as was demonstrated when Algots Nord, a textile firm, opened a branch in an area in northern Sweden with low female labor force participation. Within a few days after the announcement of the location, the number of applicants at the Employment Service increased sharply, and middle-aged and elderly women were preeminent among those who registered as job-seekers.

The concern of many reentrants is often just to find a job—any job. In the sixties, labor market policy focused mainly on bringing women into the labor market. As the share of reentrants has fallen and more and more women are in the labor market, the focus of interest in the seventies has shifted somewhat towards the situation of the women within the labor market. While new programs still center on the unemployed and untrained, efforts to find jobs for women have been coupled with a larger interest in the types of jobs they get.

POLICY RECOMMENDATIONS

1. *The profitability of work.* The tax and transfer system must be such that the family's living standard can be significantly improved by the woman's work since, if the financial benefit from her work is low, the woman will be less interested in employment. Still more important, the more she can earn through her market work, the easier it will be for her to convince her husband that her job is important and rewarding.

2. *Child care.* The reason why women drop out of the market is to care for their children. If women with children are to be able to stay in the labor force or reenter the labor force, high-quality child care must be provided. As

increasing numbers of women enter the labor market, the opportunities for informal private care are reduced and collective care becomes all the more important. Public subsidized child care is one way to make high-quality day care economically accessible to single earners and low-income families.

3. *Labor market information.* Labor market programs which provide women with vocational guidance and information about labor market requirements should receive high priority. Because of their limited labor market knowledge, reentering women should have access to immediate individual counseling at the Employment Service. It is important that the counselor provide women with information about both labor market openings and educational and training opportunities. Information to employers about the qualifications and demands of women who have worked at home should also form a part of a program of labor market information with regard to reentering women.

4. *Education and training.* Work at home should be counted as work experience in determining eligibility for training courses. Reentering women should be one of the groups given priority in schemes for the upgrading of educational and vocational skills. Those pursuing schooling should be eligible for public child care services, even if they have no income during the period of study.

5. *Working hours.* Swedish women have entered the labor market as part-time workers. For most of the reentering women, part-time work has probably been a precondition for employment. Women want to be able to adjust their working hours to family needs. If women are to be able to enter the labor market on a large scale, there must be ample opportunities for part-time employment and flexible work hours.

Cost of Assistance versus Alternative Policies

In Sweden most of the cost-benefit analyses carried out with respect to reentry measures have concerned the provision of public child care. With the market wage estimated as the wage for a female industrial worker, analysis shows positive returns if the woman has only one child, no matter whether she works full time or half time. If she has two children requiring day care, positive returns require full-time work. If there are three preschool children, the costs of day care give a negative result at this market wage.

Interruptions in labor force participation and absence from the labor market make women unable to invest in on-the-job training and advance and obtain high earnings in the future. It also makes women less prone to enter high-paying male occupations that may require an uninterrupted career. Gustavsson has shown that labor force interruptions do cause reductions in future earnings, both for men and women. The provision of day care that enables women to stay in the labor market thus has long-run benefits in the form of raised productivity and earnings in the future.[30]

Although the state and local governments subsidize the cost of day care, in return they receive increased tax revenue, and outlays for welfare benefits are reduced. The net financial effect for the government and community depends upon whether the woman is married, the number of her children, her income and her husband's income. The provision of day care for single mothers provides the best financial result for the local community because it results in the largest reduction in social welfare and housing benefits.

All of these calculations assume that there is a net demand for labor and that, without the effort to activate women, production would not take place. An alternative to the use of the local female labor supply when there is a shortage of labor is to induce persons to move to the area of shortage. Usually, however, the investment required to activate the local potential labor supply by building day care centers is far lower than the investment in housing and community services required to bring in male workers and their families from other communities.

The number of children is a crucial factor in determining the profitability of public day care. Considering, however, that the majority of families with preschool children have only one child in that age group and that only a small percentage have more than two, and further taking into account the long-run benefits of child care, the use of public child care to assist reentering women is most likely a very profitable investment. This is reenforced by the fact that full-time workers often are given priority in the queues for child care centers. This result, however, assumes a demand for labor and full employment and does not take into account any costs incurred to maintain demand.

The profitability of such measures as information, guidance groups, training, etc., crucially depends upon what is assumed as the alternative employment situation if the activity is not undertaken. Assuming that a woman would never enter the labor market at all without this assistance, the payoff period is very low, from a couple of months to a couple of years, depending upon the period of training. If the women would have entered the labor market anyway, or perhaps a little later on, the payoff period will be longer. It is up to the employment officer to select those women for guidance and training who cannot be placed without such activities.

For older women without small children, measures to facilitate reentry will most likely be profitable. For women with children, the cost is higher. For women who have several preschool children and who need labor market assistance in addition to child care there might be an economic loss. For the group of potential reentrants as a whole, considering both short-run and long-run benefits, the provision of child care and other reentry services is very likely to be a rewarding investment for society.

Measures to assist women's reentry to the labor market are thus not a roundabout way to redistribute income to low-income families. Rather they are a way to secure a more efficient use of available resources and will result in a net gain to society. This does not mean that they will be distributionally neutral. Who will lose and who will gain in the process will depend upon the design of the tax and transfer system; the users of the different services; etc. Without further knowledge we cannot say whether the net distributional effects of reentry measures in Sweden will be from high-income to low-income families or the other way around. The only fact we know for certain is that bringing women into the labor market will result in a more equal distribution of income between men and women.

Current Concerns

Policies in the near future are likely to continue to stress equal opportunity and increased efforts to make it possible to combine work in the market with family concerns. There are, however, a few current policy issues that will have implications for women's possibility of reentering the market and which may serve to reduce their opportunities.

One issue is the organization and financing of public day care in the future. As concern about a growing public sector and tax pressures has increased, voices have been raised in favor of increased use of fees for such public services as child care, which is now heavily subsidized. If fees are raised significantly and this policy is not combined with other measures that can counteract this action, the result will probably be that many women will find the net financial gain of their own work too low and will drop out of the market or postpone their entry until child care is no longer necessary.

Another proposal is a cash transfer to all families with children under three years of age. This would enable many women to stay home who now work out of financial necessity and who are induced to do so because of subsidized day care. It is argued that many of these women would prefer to work at home and receive their subsidy in cash. Furthermore, this proposal would extend child care allowances to all and not only to those who can find a job and can get a place in public day care.

A child allowance in cash may cause some women to drop out of the labor market, but may also induce others who had felt they could not afford to hire child care to enter. A crucial factor in such a reform is whether child care fees would be raised, and whether there would be a reduction in the expansion of public child care. In such a circumstance, the possibility of women staying in and reentering the labor market would be reduced.

Another policy issue concerns structural changes in an economy that has recently experienced severe structural problems. Several traditional areas of production—ship-building, steel manufacturing, the wood and pulp in-dustry—are problem areas that will have to reduce their employment in the future. Most likely, personnel will move from contracting to expanding industries, and discussions of future labor market policy have already begun to place an increased emphasis on improving mobility within the labor market. Such a policy focus may have both positive and negative influences on opportunities for reentering women. The policy emphasis on employment security and the use of local labor supply, which has been advantageous to reentering women, may be lost if geographical mobility is to be stimulated again. However, a more mobile labor market and more external recruitment should help all groups that are trying to enter the labor market.

CONCLUSIONS

While Swedish policies have been successful in bringing women into the labor force, there are still large differences in men's and women's labor market situation in terms of earnings, jobs, work time, etc. While opportunities to stay in the labor market have increased and periods of withdrawal have been shortened, making reentry less of a policy problem, new problems have developed and other problems have become accentuated.

Women have, in fact, not left the home. They still bear the main home responsibilities and carry that burden with them out into the market. The result is that they work part time in jobs that allow enough flexibility to make home and market work possible to combine. A new pattern of employment has developed whereby the arrival of children no longer means that women drop out of the market completely, but instead drop out partially. The problem of reentry has been transformed into a new problem, that of a part-time attachment to the labor force.

Part-time work is a good solution for many women who otherwise would not be able to work at all. But part-time work creates its own problems. It is often provided in traditional female occupations; and the jobs are often unskilled, do not offer opportunities for promotion, and keep women at the lower levels of the decision hierarchy. Moreover, social benefits are usually less comprehensive.

Women's part-time work creates a new entry problem. What can be done so that women with part-time jobs have opportunities to enter male areas of work, reach top decision levels, return to full-time jobs, and receive high earnings? What can be done so that partial attachment to the labor market for a period does not have to mean dropping out completely from interesting well-paid jobs? This requires among other things the establishment of part-time job opportunities and flexible work hours in many more occupations and at all levels.

As long as women, alone, continue to carry home responsibilities, they will remain at a disadvantage in labor market competition. Equality in the labor market can only be achieved when men and women equally share the time costs of having children. It must become just as common for men as for women to drop out for shorter periods, stay home when the children are sick, and reduce their work effort to part time when family needs call for it. At that time we will also find more women in positions of influence in society.

NOTES

1. See Myrdal-Klein (1956).
2. A shortened version appeared in English in 1967, "The Changing Roles of Men and Women," edited by E. Dahlstrom.
3. "The Status of Women in Sweden," Report to the U.N. (1968), p. 5.
4. For further information on such policies see Sandberg (1975), Baude (1977) and Liljestrom (1978).
5. See e.g. Qvist (1974), A summary in English (1975/76), and Kyle (1979).
6. See e.g. Silenstam (1970).
7. SOU 1978:78.
8. For a discussion of this development, see a recent government study of labor market policies, SOU 1978:60. A summary is available in English—"Labor Market Policy in Transition" (1978).
9. Marital status no longer gives accurate information on the living situation of women, since many couples live together without being married, according to the information from the Population and Housing Census, 1975. Among unmarried women with children, about half are actually cohabiting. Among women with children under 7, about 90 percent are married or living with someone, and 10 percent are single.
10. This is discussed in Jonung (1978).
11. See footnote 8 above.
12. "The economically inactive population in the spring 1975" (1977).
13. Liljestrom et al. (1978).
14. The experiments are described in SOU 1974:54.
15. The data in this section were provided by the central student grants committee (Centrala Studiemedelsnamnden).
16. We are thankful to Peter Stenkula, Nationalekonomiska Institutionen, Lund, for providing us with this information.
17. SOU 1978:78.
18. SOU 1978:39.
19. SOU 1978:78.
20. For a discussion of Swedish labor market policies since 1960, see SOU 1978:60 or "Labor Market Policy in Transition" (1978).
21. This and following sections build upon Jonung (1979).
22. "Equality in the Labor Market" (NLMB 1978). See also Rollen (1978).
23. The Board and its activities are described in the annual report, which is available in English,—"Swedish Employment Policy 1977/78".
24. Information received from the Labor Market Board.
25. Liljestrom et al. (1978).
26. SOU 1974:79.
27. Dahlberg (1975).
28. Meddelande fran utredningsenheten, AMS, 1978:9.
29. Wadensjo (1978).
30. The different cost-benefit studies of day care have recently been summarized by Gustavsson (1978) in a study for OECD.

REFERENCES

Baude, A. "Public Policy and Changing Family Patterns in Sweden 1930-77." In *Social Policy and Sex Roles*. Edited by J. Lipman, Blumen and J. Bernhard. London: Sage Publications, 1978.

Dahlberg, G. *En registerstudie om kvinnor i arbetsmarknadsutbildning*. Pedagogiskt centrum i Stockholm Y:64, 1975.

Dahlstrom, E., ed. *The Changing Roles of Men and Women*. London: Duckworth & Co., 1967. (Boston: Beacon Press, 1971.)

Gustavson, S. *Cost-Benefit Analysis of Early Childhood Care and Education.* Mimeograph. OECD, 1978.

Jonung, C. "Sexual Equality in the Swedish Labor Market." *The Monthly Labor Review* (October 1978).

———. *Policies of "Positive Discrimination" in Scandinavia in Respect of Women's Employment.* Research Series of the International Institute for Labour Studies. 1979.

Kyle, G., *Gastarbeterska i manssamhallet.* Stockholm, 1979.

Labour Market Policy in Transition. Summary of a report from the Expert Group for Labour Market Research at the Swedish Ministry of Labour. Stockholm, 1978.

Liljestrom, R., *The Integration of Family Policy and Labor Market Policy in Sweden.* Paper presented at the Wellesley Conference on Equal Pay and Equal Opportunity, May 1978.

Liljestrom, R., Furst-Mellstrom, G., and Liljestrom-Svensson, G. *Roles in Transition.* Stockholm, 1978.

Myrdal, Alva, and Klein, Viola. *Women's Two Roles: Home and Work.* London: Routledge and Kegan Ltd., 1956.

Qvist, G. *Statistik och politik.* Landsorganisationen och kvinnorna pa arbetsmarknaden. Stockholm, 1974.

———. "The Landsorganisationen (LO) in Sweden and Women on the labor market (1898–1973). In *International Journal of Sociology* (Winter 1975/76).

Rollen, B. *Equality in the Labor Market—a Task for the National Labour Market Board.* Paper presented at the Wellesley Conference on Equal Pay and Equal Opportunity, May 1978.

Sandberg, E. *Equality is the goal.* The Swedish Institute, Stockholm: 1975.

SOU 1974:54. *Vidgad vuxenutbildning.* Stockholm, 1974.

SOU 1974:79. *Utbildning for arbete.* Stockholm, 1974.

SOU 1978:39. *Foraldraforsakring.* Stockholm, 1978.

SOU 1978:60. *Arbetsmarknadspolitik i forandring.* Stockholm, 1978.

SOU 1978:78. *Langtidsutredningen 1978.* Stockholm, 1978.

The National Labour Market Board. *Equality in the Labor Market.* Solna, 1977.

———. *Swedish Employment Policy 1977/78.* Solna, 1977.

The Status of Women in Sweden. Report to the United Nations, 1968. Stockholm: The Swedish Institute, 1968.

Wadensjo, E. *Selection of Applicants for Labor Market Programs.* Meddelande 1978:49. Nationalekonomiska institutionen, Lund.

STATISTICAL SOURCES

Arbetskraftsundersokningarna (The Labor Force Surveys), 1963–1978. Stockholm: SCB.

The economically inactive population in the spring 1975. Statistiska Meddelanden AM 1977:2.

Folk- och bostadsrakningarna (The Population and Housing Census) 1900–1975. Stockholm: SCB.

Levnadsforhallanden (Living Conditions). Stockholm: SCB, 1974.

Meddelande fran utredningsenheten, AMS (Information from the Labor Market Board). Stockholm, 1977–78.

5

United Kingdom

by SHEILA ROTHWELL

INTRODUCTION

The most significant change in the composition of the labor force in Britain over the last 25 years has been the increase in participation by women, and particularly by older and married women. Women's employment is, however, officially seen in the same way as the employment of any other section of the population. Government policy aims at full employment—at providing opportunity for everyone seeking to work and at meeting employers' demands for labor. There is no official policy of encouraging the employment of men rather than women, or of husbands rather than wives. This is seen as a family decision: it is not the business of government to put any obstacles in the way of those who wish to enter employment, nor, by the same token, should government necessarily be expected to provide any special facilities to enable certain groups to do so. Those wishing to reenter employment will receive help in the same way as those entering for the first time. "Everyone is in the queue" and enactment of the Equal Pay and Sex Discrimination Acts (together with the establishment of the Equal Opportunity Commission) should have ensured that women's employment opportunities are equal with those of men.

Nevertheless, "employment" is still largely seen in terms of the male breadwinner and male norm, full time and continuous throughout a working life of 16 to 65, with other patterns (of intermittent, part-time, or seasonal work) still regarded as peripheral and secondary. The development of the resources and policies of the Manpower Services Commission has recently facilitated a more segmented and interventionist approach to the labor market with the identification of certain priority groups (such as unemployed 16 to 19 year olds and long-term registered unemployed) and the development of special programs designed to meet their needs. Racial minority groups (about three percent of the population) are another official target group attracting considerable government resources. By default, if not by deliberate action, the employment problems of mature women reentrants tend to be relegated to the back of the queue.

The reasons for this are rarely made explicit, but women are obviously seen as having alternative occupations open to them, and they represent no threat to law and order if unemployed. The only sign of expressed policy preferences have been government speeches about the need for more attention to the needs of the family, and the woman as the center of this. Cynics observe that family policies tend to be stressed whenever there is a particularly loose labor market (as at the end of World War II) with the aim of keeping women at home; on the other hand many feminists (and others) would agree with the need for family policies to be developed in a wider context.

The declining economic condition in Britain in the mid 70s has had a dual impact on women's employment. The effect of inflation on family budgets has meant that two wage packets are often necessary to maintain an adequate standard of living, so that labor supply has increased as more women have to enter the labor market or to stay in it. On the other hand, demand has been reduced through government policies aimed at controlling inflation by drastic reduction of public expenditures. Opportunities for public sector employment, especially in central government and in local authority health and education services—all traditional areas of female employment—have recently contracted or ceased to expand. Decline of certain manufacturing industries, especially clothing and textiles, as well as certain branches of electrical engineering, has also hit women's work. At the same time, reduction of public welfare expenditures has meant that some women have been prevented from working through the need to care for young children or to look after sick or elderly relatives at home. Cuts in education budgets have made it doubly difficult for women to obtain grants for further education to equip themselves for reentry at a higher level. Nevertheless, some of those concerned over the training of engineers and technicians—or the supply of students for higher education—may be beginning to consider women.

Certainly in spite of adverse economic conditions—partly cyclical, partly structural—women's employment overall has continued to increase. This has also been largely in spite of, rather than because of, the attitudes and policies of the trade union movement, which is still male dominated and oriented, even though "women's issues" have received more attention and support at a national level over the past few years. Nor is it the result of a strong feminist movement which in Britain has been slow (compared to the

United States) to develop or make any major impact on national life, at least in political pressure group terms. It has, however, been able to exert significant pressure at key points—during the passage of the sex discrimination legislation through parliament, for example.

Women's employment, whether stimulated by the women's movement or the pressures of the consumer society, brings a measure of economic independence which in itself contributes to the raising of feminist consciousness. These factors, together with rising educational standards and a falling birth rate, are probably the most significant aspects of the underlying dynamic of the reentry of mature women. The extent of successful reentry may be largely attributed to the availability of part-time work.

THE LABOR MARKET BACKGROUND

Population

Women make up 51.3 percent of Britain's population. More boys are born than girls, but women outnumber men in middle and old age. The age structure of the population shows that during the next few years more young people will be entering the working age group and fewer old people leaving it. The fall in births since 1964 has already had an impact on the numbers in primary schools and on teachers, and its effects are spreading to secondary education; in the early 1980s it will begin to affect higher education.

Annual births have fallen by some 30 percent during the last 10 years. It is thought that many women have been deferring childbearing, especially the more educated and the wives of nonmanual workers. Yet comparing 1971-1975 rates with those of the previous decade, the fertility rates of women over 34 years fell by about 50 percent, and those of the age groups 30-34 by 39 percent. On the other hand, most recent figures indicate that the birth rate has begun to rise again: 55,000 more births are now expected up to 1981 than were forecast a year ago. The increase is chiefly, but not entirely, the result of the increasing number of women in the childbearing age group.

Marriage had been increasingly popular over the period of 1950-1971, but the number of marriages has fallen recently and the average ages at which men and women first marry (25.1 years and 22.9 years respectively in 1976) are no longer decreasing. Ninety percent of the population marry at least once during their lifetime; 31 percent of women marry before the age of 20.

Getting married and starting a family are no longer so closely connected as they were a few years ago: more births are likely to occur in marriages of between three and seven years' duration. The increasing tendency for women to remain in gainful employment after their marriage and before beginning childbearing, and to return to work when they are no longer actively engaged in rearing young children, can be interpreted as either cause or effect of this.

Average family size has fallen over recent years: the biggest drops have been in births to manual workers of third and later children, but the patterns are similar for all classes. Estimates of completed size vary from 2.3 to 1.8 children. The majority of women have completed childbearing by the time they are 30.

The number of divorces has increased, especially since the Divorce Reform Act 1969 (England and Wales). In 1976 there were 10.18 divorces per 1,000 married females (all ages), compared with 3.2 in 1966. Remarriage rates also are high.

The increase in the number of single parents with dependent children is one of the most striking facts to emerge from the demographic picture of Britain in recent years. Between 1971–1976, the number of one-parent families increased by about a third (averaging 6 percent per annum). The main part of the change is attributed to broken marriages, but there has also been an increase in the number of unmarried mothers. It is estimated that by 1976 one-parent families constituted 11 percent of all families with dependent children, compared with 8 percent in 1971; 88 percent of these families were headed by a woman. Nearly a third of female lone parents are under 30 years and another half are between 30 and 45 years. Almost two-thirds of divorced mothers are in the 30- to 45-year age group.

Economic Activity

Between 1950–1973, women accounted for most of the net increase in the British working population, which now totals about 26 million with a female representation of nearly 40 percent. In Britain more women go back to work after having children than in any other E.E.C. country; about two-thirds of British women in their forties and early fifties are economically active. Female labor force participation rates for the population aged 15 and over rose from 35 percent to 46 percent between 1951 and 1975 while the male rate dropped from 88 percent to 81 percent (Table 5.1).

1976 statistics show that the overall female activity rate increased to 60 percent by age 24, then declined to 51 percent among women aged 25 to 34 years, followed by a gradual increase to a peak of 66 percent at ages 45 to 54, as women gradually reentered the labor force. The rate then declined slowly, but even at ages 55 to 59, over half the women were economically active. There was a sharp decline after age 60 as women retired.

The proportion of the economically active married women in 1975 was 55 percent at ages 20 to 24; 48 percent at 25 to 34 years; and 66 percent at ages 35 to 55, declining thereafter. The striking increase in the activity rates of married females has been more marked in some age groups than others, i.e. 35 to 54 years. The activity rate for those aged 25 to 34 is the lowest for all adult groups below the normal retiring age (34 percent in 1966; 48 percent in 1975) (Table 5.2).

Divorced women have a markedly higher activity rate than married

Table 5.1   Great Britain: Economic Activity Rates[a], Population Aged 15 and Over, 1951 — 1991 (actual and projected)

	All Males	Females		
		All	Married	Nonmarried
1951	87.6	34.7	21.7	55.0
1961	86.0	37.4	29.7	50.6
1966	84.0	42.2	38.1	49.2
1971	81.4	42.7	42.2	43.7
1975	80.6	46.3	49.0	41.6
1981	79.3	48.0	51.9	41.6
1991	79.9	50.6	56.2	40.6

[a]Economic Activity Rate: Proportion of working or unemployed members of population in relation to total population.
Source: Department of Employment.

women of all ages, and very slightly higher than widows up to age 60. It is, however, noticeably lower than that of other single women. Activity rates of divorced women have also shown a considerable increase since 1951, but a leveling off after 1966 (possibly due to increased financial provisions), so that divorcees' economic behavior has come to be closer to that of married women with similar domestic responsibilities than to that of single women. In general, the numbers of economically active nonmarried women declined overall between 1971-1976, especially in the 35- to 44-year age group.

Types of Economic Activity

Of the nine million economically active women in 1971, over 400,000 were unemployed (25 percent for sickness). Of the 12.5 million inactive women, over nine million were housewives; three million were retired; and 300,000 were students.

The labor force (defined as all those working and seeking work) is estimated to have increased by 600,000 between 1974 and 1977. A third of the total new increase was made up by young people, and a further third by married women.

Statistics of the working population (which excludes the unregistered unemployed) show that just over half (72,000) of the women's increase (130,000) was absorbed into employment in 1977.

The Warwick group concludes that in the case of males and married females, activity effects contribute much more to the change in the labor force than do population effects. For nonmarried females, however, there is

Table 5.2 Great Britain: Historical and Projected Changes in Married Female Activity Rates by Age, 1951–1991

Age	1951	1961	1966	1971	1975	1981	1991
20–24	36.5	41.3	43.5	46.7	54.6	55.7	55.7
25–34	24.4	29.7	34.3	38.4	47.8	49.6	52.7
35–44	25.7	37.1	48.6	54.5	66.4	70.3	75.1
45–54	23.7	36.1	49.8	57.0	66.3	70.9	77.9
55–59	15.6	26.4	38.4	45.5	49.8	54.8	60.2
60–64	7.2	12.8	21.3	25.2	26.6	29.1	31.5
65 +	2.7	3.3	5.5	6.5	5.4	6.1	7.1

Source: Censuses of Population 1951, 1961, 1966 and 1971.
DE Gazette, April 1978—based on EEC Labor Force and other survey data.

a strong population effect. At the sex-marital group level, only the activity effect for married females makes a positive contribution towards the change in the total size of the labor force. About half of this contribution is then offset by the activity effects of males and nonmarried females. The only significant, positive population effects are for the 25- to 34-year age group, due to the immediate postwar increase in the birth rate.

Women Reentrants

The figures of "ever worked" show that in 1976 only four percent of the 25- to 44-year age group and seven percent of the 45- to 54-year age group had never worked, so it is likely that most of the mature women entering the labor market in the 1970s were in fact reentrants. The 1971 census found that 87 percent of all women of working age had worked at some time in their lives. A proportion of women have always worked more or less continuously throughout their childbearing period—this proportion was higher in 1971 than a decade earlier, though it was still low in absolute terms.

Analysis of differences in activity rates by age group, using Census of Population data, points to considerable movement by married females in and out of the labor market. For example, a comparison of married females, aged 25 to 29, classified as economically active in 1966, with those aged 30 to 34 in 1971 shows a net movement of 139,000 married females into the labor market from that one age group in a short period, an increase of 25 percent (Figure 5.1).

More light is thrown on the extent of reentrant activity by detailed cohort analysis of activity rates using unpublished data from National Insurance

Figure 5.1   The Employment of Women under 20 and Aged 30 to 34, in 1960
over a Ten-Year Period

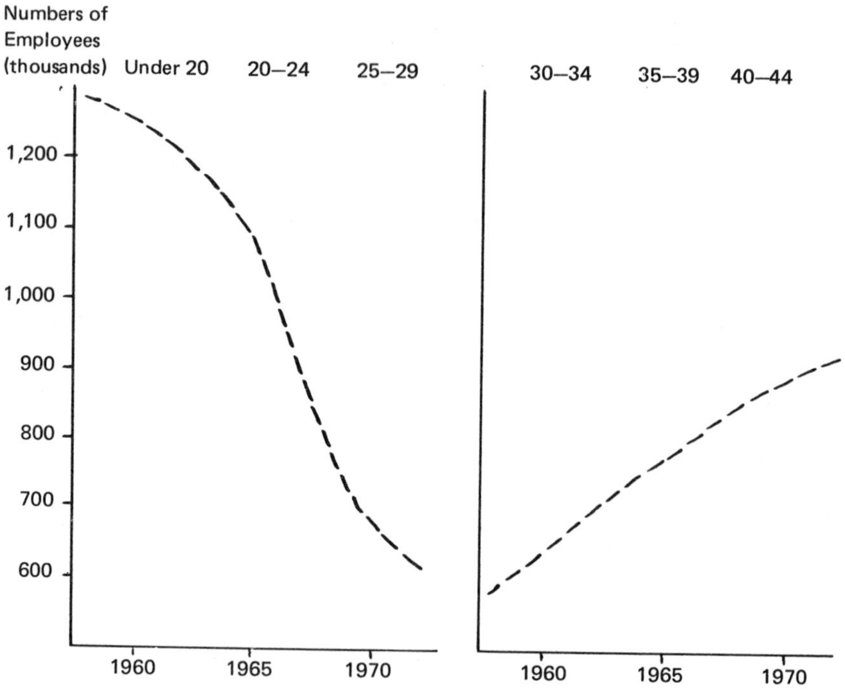

Numbers of
Employees
(thousands)

Source: DE Gazette, June 1961, September 1966 and September 1971;
in T.S.A. Training Opportunities for Women, MSC, 1976.

cards, 1970-1974. This establishes that there is a large amount of coming
and going in and out of the insured labor force by married women at all
ages, but especially in the childbearing years among those under 35 years of
age, and especially among those who had opted out from paying contributions. In general, up to 1977, young married women would pay contributions and claim maternity allowance but leave the labor market after the
birth of their first child; they were then likely to opt-out of paying the full
rate when they returned, particularly if they worked part time. In 1971, 3.7
million, or 75 percent, of all married women employees opted not to pay
full rate contributions, particularly those with low earnings and in low-
income families.

The pattern over the 1970-1974 period shows a rising trend in entries of
opted-out married women for all age groups under 60 years. They had a
much larger absolute turnover than the opted-in: 1.1 million (out of 3.6
million working at the end of the year) compared with .4 million (out of 1.3
million) in 1973/74.

Table 5.3 Estimated Working Rates for the Female Population of Great Britain, Selected Dates (percentages)

Age	1961	1966	1971	1976
Under 20	72.1	64.7	52.4	56.4
20—24	63.8	58.0	57.5	62.2
Under 25	68.1	61.5	55.1	59.5
25—34	39.6	38.9	41.3	50.9
35—44	44.9	51.6	54.7	65.8
45—54	45.6	53.6	57.8	66.0
55—59	37.5	44.8	48.4	52.2
60 +	10.0	12.1	11.5	10.5
55 +	16.8	19.8	19.6	18.8
Average	38.6	40.7	40.5	44.8

Note: The working rate is the proportion of an age category of the population who are members of the working population (either employed or registered as unemployed).

Source: Census of Population Statistics, in "Increased Labour Force Participation and the Growing Employment Opportunities for Women" by Colin Leicester. Paper presented to Workshop of 6 Countries Programme, Paris, November 1978. (mimeo GN No.115, Institute of Manpower Studies, Sussex).

The data also show that nearly half of all "opted-outs" employed in May 1974 had worked continuously during the previous four years (mainly older women); a quarter had interruptions of at least eight weeks but no whole year out of the labor force. Three out of four opt-outs, aged 25 to 34 years, were working after a recent interruption. The percentages with an interruption of at least one year were highest among the 25-to-39 age groups, reflecting women returning after childbearing; a higher proportion had been out for three years than one year. The age group 35 to 39 years shows a peak of activity, particularly of those with short durations of employment.

Estimated working rates for the female population by age, at selected dates since 1961, have been used by Leicester to analyze net changes on both a "time-specific" and "cohort-specific" basis (Table 5.3). The analysis shows changing patterns of reentry, a more extensive attachment to the labor market by girls, and an increasing rate of withdrawal for older women. Such changes may be accelerated or slowed down by the employment opportunities experience.

Economic Activity and Dependent Children

The extent to which dependent children are associated with low female activity rates is clearly seen in all measures used, especially among women

Table 5.4   Percentage of Women Working by Age, Number of Dependent Children, and Whether Working Full-Time or Part-Time[a], Great Britain, 1976

Age	Number of Dependent Children[b]							
	None	1	2	3+	3	4	5+	Total Percent
16–24								
Working full-time	65	15	3	[NIL]				53
Working part-time	4	15	12	[2]				6
All working[c]	69	30	15	[2]				59
Number (=100%)	1399	261	123	20				1803
25–34								
Working full-time	74	17	9	8				25
Working part-time	11	24	30	28				24
All working[c]	85	41	40	37				49
Number (=100%)	523	479	873	490				2365
35–44								
Working full-time	57	31	21	14				29
Working part-time	20	37	43	39				36
All working[c]	78	69	65	54				66
Number (=100%)	378	450	635	448				1911
45–59								
Working full-time	33	21	18	[13]				29
Working part-time	27	41	35	[29]				30
All working[c]	61	63	54	[42]				60
Number (=100%)	2176	536	198	88				2998
Total								
Working full-time	50	22	14	11	10	15	7	33
Working part-time	17	31	34	33	35	32	22	25
All working[c]	68	53	48	44	45	48	28	58
Number (=100%)	4476	1726	1829	1046	718	226	102	9077

[a] Full-time students who worked in the reference week are not included as working.
[b] Because of the comparatively small base numbers, the percentages for women with 3, 4 or 5+ children are not given by age group.
[c] Including a few women whose hours of work were not known.
Source: General Household Survey, 1977, Table 6.2.

aged 25 to 34 years. Married women under the age of 40 with no dependent children have similar rates to unmarried women of the same ages. Where children are very young, or there are several in the family, the rates are lowest—three-fourths of the children under five years have mothers who do no paid work. The most extreme differences are for women in their twenties, where a wife with no dependent children is more than four times as likely to be economically active as a mother with one or more dependent children (Table 5.4).

The number of working mothers with young children increased by 63 percent between 1961 and 1971. The largest recent increase among reentry women is among those with young children and those with three or more dependent children. Labor force statistics of 1971 show that 49 percent of women with a youngest child aged 5 to 10 years were economically active, compared with almost 20 percent of those with children under five (12 percent in 1961). By 1976, these rates had increased to 60 percent and 26 percent respectively. Two-thirds of married women with a youngest child aged 10 to 15 years were working in 1976.

Statistics of employment of lone mothers in 1971 showed that 45 percent of those with at least one child under 16 years (212,000) were employed. The large increase in the 70s in the numbers of divorcees probably has resulted in some rise in this group, although only ten percent of nonmarried women with *young* children are divorcees.

Distribution of Women within the Labor Force

All the available information about women's position in the labor force points to their being concentrated in industries and occupations which are largely female, and that this pattern has changed little throughout the century.

In 1974, almost 60 percent of women working full time were employed in three nonmanual occupational groups: clerical, professional and related, and selling. Many were also employed in such manual occupations as catering, cleaning and other personal service. Women are underrepresented in managerial, technical and skilled manual occupations. Less than one working women in 12 is a skilled manual worker; for men the proportion is five out of 12. One in five men works in the professional and managerial groups—but only one woman in 20 (Table 5.5). Mothers are even more likely than married women without children to be in low-skill jobs.

The Warwick Study predicts the only significant manual employment growth will be in transferable semiskilled occupations that require a fair degree of training*, such as catering and machine-tool operating. Overall, greater growth in nonmanual occupations is expected—especially in managerial and technical groups—with only a small net growth in clerical occupations.

Sixty percent of all working women are employed in the tertiary sector, and over half of these are in only four industry groups where they constitute the majority of employees: professional and scientific services; distributive trades; miscellaneous services; and insurance, banking and business services. (Table 5.6).

There is a similar picture of concentration in a few industries in the manufacturing sector (in food, drink, tobacco, electrical engineering,

---

*In 1971 the largest gross inflow into this group came from females of all ages who stated that they had no occupation a year ago.

Table 5.5 Great Britain: Employees by Occupation, 1977

Occupation	Number in NES Sample		
	Men	Women	Percent Women
Managerial (general management)	1,895	185	8.9
Professional and related supporting management and administration	5,758	837	12.7
Professional and related in education, welfare and health	5,346	9,843	64.8
Literary, artistic and sports	757	252	25.0
Professional and related in science, engineering, technology and similar fields	6,775	517	7.1
Managerial (excluding general management)	6,116	897	12.8
(Part) Clerical and related	7,998	22,112	73.4
(Part) Selling	3,619	5,131	58.6
Security and protective service	1,890	145	7.1
Total Nonmanual	40,154	39,919	49.9
Total Manual and Nonmanual	106,621	65,668	38.1
Total Manual	66,467	25,749	27.9
Miscellaneous	2,218	121	5.2
Transport, operating, materials moving and storing, and related	12,188	645	5.0
Construction, mining, and related not identified elsewhere	5,620	13	0.2
Painting, repetitive assembling, product inspecting, packaging and related	5,311	4,811	47.5
Processing, making and repairing and related (metal and electrical)	22,041	1,109	4.8
Making and repairing (excluding metal and electrical)	5,683	336	36.9
Materials processing (excluding metals)	4,010	1,420	26.2
Farming, fishing and related	2,275	220	8.8
Catering, cleaning, hairdressing and other personal services	4,423	13,692	75.6
(Part) Security and protective service	618	100	13.9
(Part) Selling	530	103	16.3
(Part) Clerical and related	550	199	26.6

Source: New Earnings Survey 1977, Part E Table 135 (1% sample).

clothing and footwear). In the primary sector, women constitute less than one-fifth of all employees. The pattern of employment of reentrant women is the same, with the exception of insurance and banking, where the majority of female employees are under 30 years of age.

Further decline in manufacturing industries is expected, along with expansion in the service industries, particularly those now employing a majority of women. The exception is distribution, where a marked decline is predicted.

Table 5.6   Great Britain: Employees by Industrial Sector, 1977

Industrial Sector	Number in NES Sample Men	Women	Percent Women
Agriculture, forestry, fishing	1,795	331	15.6
Mining and quarrying	2,975	138	4.4
Food, drink and tobacco	3,762	2,451	39.5
Coal and petroleum products	344	65	15.9
Chemicals and allied industries	2,732	954	25.9
Metal manufacture	3,681	442	10.7
Mechanical engineering	6,565	1,153	14.9
Instrument engineering	838	404	32.5
Electrical engineering	3,966	2,209	35.8
Shipbuilding and marine engineering	1,391	101	6.8
Vehicles	6,002	757	11.2
Metal goods not elsewhere specified	2,954	1,081	26.8
Textiles	2,302	1,761	43.3
Leather, leather goods and fur	163	113	40.9
Clothing and footwear	694	1,979	74.1
Bricks, pottery, glass, cement, etc.	1,640	539	24.7
Timber, furniture, etc.	1,553	385	19.9
Paper, printing and publishing	3,141	1,324	29.7
Other manufacturing industries	1,695	878	34.1
Construction	9,635	681	6.6
Gas, electricity and water	2,442	597	19.6
Transport and communication	10,443	2,232	17.6
Distributive trades	8.483	9,504	52.8
Insurance, banking, finance and business services	4,217	4,158	49.7
Professional and scientific services	9,028	19,233	68.1
Miscellaneous services	5,982	7,117	54.3
Public administration	8,198	5,081	38.3

Source: New Earnings Survey 1977, E Table 135 (1% sample).

Public sector employment increased by almost one-quarter between 1961 and 76; a large part of this rise is accounted for by the employment of more women, many services being in the public sector.

Hours of Work and Part-Time Employment

The most significant aspect of women's employment in the United Kingdom—and certainly of reentrant women's employment—is the increase in the number of part-time workers from about one-third of all working women in 1971 to more than two-fifths in 1976. This accounts for a large proportion of the total increase in women's employment. The U.K.

has the highest proportion in the EEC. Little more than five percent of men work part time.*

In 1976, 83 percent of all part-time female workers were married, compared with 64 percent overall, and 51 percent of all married working women were part-timers. This is closely related to the numbers and ages of children. Lone mothers, however, and women from ethnic minority groups are not only more likely to work, but are more likely to work full time. The upward trend in the proportion of part-time workers is now moderating, and a slower rate of increase is projected; it may nevertheless still account for 45 percent of the female labor force over the next few years.

Regional Differences

Female activity rates in Britain are highest in the West Midlands, South East and North West, and lowest in more rural areas—Wales, South West and East Anglia. Part of the variation is the result of regional differences in age, marital and employment status but is more closely connected with differences in industrial structure and employment opportunities, as a regional study of South Yorkshire showed. Participation is higher generally in conurbations, and there is some evidence of a higher propensity to return among women in depressed areas.

Unemployment

Unemployment in Britain has increased throughout the 70s to a level not known since the Second World War, from under 300,000 in 1966 to over 1,270,000 in 1976—a rate of 5.4 percent (excluding school leavers), or 6.4 percent on a U.S.-adjusted equivalence basis (1.38 million in 1978). Long-term unemployment is greatest in the largest metropolitan counties.

The most recent increases in unemployment have been greatest among young people and women. Between January 1976 and January 1978, the number of men registered as unemployed increased nine percent, from 981,000 to 1,070,200, while the number of women increased 53 percent, from 270,500 to 414,500. In January 1978, women made up 28 percent of Britain's registered unemployed. Since a large proportion of women seeking work do not register, the number of women actually unemployed is far higher than the official figures suggest, the difference between the two rates being estimated by the Warwick Group as being two and one-half to three percentage points. There are now signs of an increasing propensity to register, and this is likely to rise further as eligibility for benefits rises.

Relatively, unemployment has risen most rapidly among women aged 25 to 50, although two-thirds of all female unemployed are under 30 years of age and 44 percent are under age 20 (Table 5.7). One analysis of the effects of

---

*The normal working week in Britain is regarded as 40 hours, but part-time work is usually defined as under 30 hours a week.

Table 5.7   Estimated Unemployment Rates of Women by Age, January 1976—
January 1978

Age	Percent January 1976	Percent January 1978
16–17	12.0	15.6
18–19	8.0	10.6
20–24	5.3	8.3
25–29	3.0	4.9
30–39	1.5	2.6
40–49	1.2	1.9
50–59	1.7	2.4
60 +	0.2	0.2
All ages	2.9	4.5

Source: DE Gazette, May 1978, p. 585

cyclical unemployment concludes that some groups of married women—
chiefly those of an age to have dependent children—suffer more from
recessions than men, and particularly at the state of rejoining the labor
force after child-rearing. Growing numbers of company early-retirement
and redundancy schemes mean that more women over age 50 are likely to
become unemployed in future.

Forecasts

Most official and other forecasts predict an increasing and continuing high
rate of unemployment, in the 1980s of from eight to ten percent. They also
expect the supply of female labor to continue to increase and to constitute
42 percent of the labor force. The Department of Employment expects this
increase to continue to be mainly among older married women, but the
Warwick Group also emphasizes the increasing numbers of single women
in their twenties who will be economically active. The more able of these
women are expected to be particularly likely to be hit by declining
opportunities for higher-level employment in education and health services. The Institute of Manpower Studies (Sussex) is optimistic about
women's employment prospects generally, predicting that they will continue to enter new industries in the service sector, putting to advantage
their work experience and ready transferability of skills.

Pay

Average weekly earnings of women remained a fairly stable proportion of
men's earnings in manual and nonmanual occupations in the 1950s and

1960s. Between 1970 and 1976, however, largely as a result of the Equal Pay Act, earnings of women have increased on average much faster than those of men. The most recent figures, however, show a slowing-down and partial reversal of the trend towards narrowing the differential, particularly among nonmanual employees, which moved from 63 percent of men's earnings in 1970 to 75 percent in 1977 and 72 percent in 1978. In money terms, the gap has steadily widened.

The lack of continued improvement in women's average earnings with increasing age is in marked contrast with men and may partly be attributed to their discontinuous employment. The gap between male and female earnings is at its peak for workers in their forties.

The distribution of earnings of men and women is also very different. For example, in April 1977, 44 percent of full-time women workers earned less than £45 a week, compared to only six percent of men; and only 25 percent of women earned more than £60 a week, compared with 73 percent of men. Moreover, mothers (who are most likely to work part time) have particularly low earnings: an analysis of 1974 data found that only eight percent of employed wives with a child below the age of five, and 13 percent of those with a child aged five to ten years, earned more than £30 a week, compared with 53 percent of childless married women aged 16 to 44 years, and to 93 percent of husbands of employed wives with young children.

Education and Qualifications

The majority of children start school by their fifth birthday and remain there until they are 16, thus completing 11 years of compulsory education. There are only marginal differences in the levels of educational attainment of girl and boy school-leavers. Slightly fewer girls stay on at school after the age of 16, but they are more likely than boys to obtain some sort of training—chiefly secretarial—before entering employment.

The numbers of women obtaining higher-level qualifications is now increasing, and a marked rise is forecast for the near future. Only a small proportion of women study mathematics, science and technical subjects— the majority still take languages, literature and history. While graduates will be unlikely to obtain posts at as high a level as in the past, they are expected to continue to be more likely to obtain employment than the unqualified.

Significant Trends

To summarize the salient trends of the population and labor force statistics and their implications for reentry, it is only necessary to quote the "Demographic Review" (1977) which was commissioned to examine British population changes over the past 30 years and their implications.

Earlier marriages and the shorter period spent in reproduction mean that most women will have finished childbearing when they are in their early 30s, and their youngest child may well be of school age by the time women reach age 35. At that age, the most recent female life table gives a further expectation of life of 43 years, of which 25 will be spent whilst the woman is of working age. Many of these women will be seeking work, some part-time and others full-time. There may well be a need for re-training women returning to gainful employment after a period of absence from the labor force when they are engaged in rearing young children. . . . In the immediate future, Great Britain is faced with two contrasting trends: a working population which is becoming younger and will be increasing, and a population of pensionable age which is also increasing but becoming older and more liable to the illnesses and disabilities which normally accompany old age. If present trends in the employment of married women continue, the demand for new jobs will be proportionately greater than the increase in the population of working age. And if women continue to be employed in the occupations which provide personal service, and if family size remains low, there will be a need for them to turn increasingly from the provision of services for the younger dependent population to providing more services for the elderly dependent population.

INFLUENCES UPON REENTRY DECISIONS

Psychological Factors

The complexity of the motivation of housewives to undertake paid employment is still underresearched in Britain. Controversy remains about whether women should be asked "Why do you" or "Why don't you" work outside the home.

The majority of women with children (including many of those who go out to work) still define themselves as housewives. Recent research among both "depressed" and "normal" groups of women in London has demonstrated that internal and external pressures to conform to a housewife image, on those with young children especially, are still strong and often highly conflictual. They are found among women of all ages, in a variety of class situations and marital circumstances, although those without a husband may experience countervailing "breadwinner" pressures.

It was a difficult decision to make. A man has to work; a woman has to choose between a job and the family.

If I went out full-time I wouldn't be able to keep house and garden tidy. I still feel it's my job to keep the house proper.

Conflict arises for many women from the realization that home and children are not sufficient. The isolation, dependence, and endlessness of domestic drudgery, which is often felt, is made more difficult to bear by feelings of guilt arising from the belief that they *ought not* to have other needs, that family *should* be sufficient.

Two or three times I have nearly gone back to work because of my sanity. I have little contact with other people—we're very cut off here. It's no challenge looking after kids and doing housework.

Some research evidence indicates that the self-concept of girls and women is situational and that, once marital goals have been satisfied, a secondary need for achievements and self-fulfillment, often outside the home, emerges as a next stage.

I wanted to learn and didn't want to go back to factory work. I wanted to get satisfaction within myself, to know myself and my capabilities. I felt I was a half-made person. So I went to college and found myself doing things I didn't know I was capable of.

Replies to interview questions about work motivation generally stress that the chief reason for working is financial, but most women also link this with other factors (such as the desire for social contact or the desire to use qualifications) and are ambivalent about whether they would continue to work without financial need. "Boredom in the home" and "satisfaction of doing a job" have been found to outnumber financial reasons for nonmanual and highly educated women, and many undertake voluntary work for this reason.

Just couldn't survive on social security, there was no choice in it.

The main reason for going back was mental stimulus—definitely not money. I've got plenty of company at home—I'm always busy but I needed mental stimulus. I always wanted to go back to work, in fact I never wanted to stop.

It is of course necessary to be very cautious in interpreting financial motivation. It may relate to a woman's desire for some money of her "own," and thus less dependence on her husband; or it may relate to an overall feeling of the family being under financial "pressure," and is of course highly subjective and relative, depending on the previous or expected standard of living.

I love the money but I'd always want to work. I like working in a shop—you meet everybody. I hated being stuck on my own with the children—my husband kept me very short of cash and I never felt safe till I went back to work.

There is little evidence of great career motivation among reentry women, apart from a few who are qualified or qualifying, either because they do not want a career or because they do not expect one, perhaps perceiving themselves as having forfeited such aspirations by their decision to have a family. Low work expectations by many women seem to support, and carry over into the workplace, the feelings of guilt and ambivalence experienced by their failure to conform with the housewife role. These expectations may also account for the relative lack of demand by women for assistance in facilitating their return.

Husband's attitudes are obviously a major factor:

Eddie is opposed to me working. He has this old fashioned idea that I should be at home with the children.

My husband's been super—really good—he had more confidence in me than I had.

Decision to return? Inflation! It got hard to manage. I asked my husband would he mind.

Many women are well aware that their working may make their husbands feel insecure:

It was all right when he was working; he could see my job as a sort of hobby. But when he went to college and wasn't earning, he wasn't happy about it.

And this may be a further reason (apart from the social security system) why wives of unemployed husbands are *less* likely to be working.

Loss of husband or anticipated marriage break-up is clearly a strong motivation to work (though less among widows than other single mothers).

It's been in my mind for ages but the precipitating factor was P. leaving. I went out straight away and had a job within two weeks.

This does not necessarily mean that the decision is approved by family and friends, who tend to criticize working mothers for neglecting the family, unless there is urgent financial need. But they appear to have less influence on the final decision.

Some friends, no, call them acquaintances, they wouldn't be friends now anyway, thought that I was a bitch for going out to work and abandoning my kids so soon after P. left.

My mother couldn't understand why—why wasn't I satisfied with a family and a husband.

Some, however, resent Women's Lib social pressures:

Women like me are made to feel "cabbagey" if we don't go out to work—I'm not working because I'm responding to that pressure—I'm working because I need the money.

The mixed motivation of many women was summarized by one widow:

I need to get out for money, company and *prestige*. You're useless and a parasite at home, and you're devalued as a housewife. You need your *own* standing in the community. But there are so few things open to women. There's nothing I can do to earn a high standard of living for the family, compared with a man.

Domestic Responsibilities

The major reasons for women stopping work, not working, delaying reentry or "stopping and starting" all relate to pregnancy, child care and domestic responsibilities. Most mothers with young children prefer not to work but intend to do so soon, while those currently looking for work now tend to be those with school-age or recently grown-up children.

Less than a third of children under five years receive any form of organized care. The gap in provision is greatest for two- to three-year olds. About a third of women with dependent children say they would go back to work earlier if satisfactory arrangements could be made, but it is likely that standards of "satisfactory" would be high (Table 5.8).

I would work if there was no financial need. But only short hours while I felt socially responsible for the children. If the youngest had been put in school early, just for me to return to employment, I probably would have felt guilty. I don't believe in depriving children of a mother's company (well not for money anyway, if you don't need it). I probably have a different attitude from most women anyway.

There were no nurseries or playschools convenient. A few hours a day would have done the youngest good, as the older two had each other. He had no other children when they were in school and missed them.

Since 1960 there has been an overall threefold increase in child care provisions for children under five, from an estimated 300,000 places in 1961 to 900,000 in 1973 and nearly 1.25 million in 1977, which must have facilitated reentry. Official statistics distinguish between part-time and full-time places, but even full-time (where provision is declining) does not normally cover the adult working day or school holidays.

National policy is that day care provision should be available for certain priority groups, including children of working lone parents, but in 1976, priority waiting lists alone amounted to over 12,000 places. Top priority recently has tended to go to children "at risk" from "battering," but usually only after some evidence of it. One young divorcee admitted:

I would like to think that my mothering is primary and work-life is secondary but, if truth is known, work is an escape . . . I think more of us ought to stand up and say we're bored with mothering and we all occasionally feel like cracking our children . . . I think I understand baby-battering . . . most mothers feel like it and if only more people admitted it . . . It gets on my wick . . . I never actually have smashed him but my friends were very understanding and said to ring them if ever I felt like it because they knew how I felt.

Financial problems mean that community nurseries run by charitable foundations and local groups, as well as employers' work-site nurseries, often have difficulty in surviving. There are a few creches at some colleges of further and higher education (during term-time), but only at the discretion of the authorities who finance them; the University Grants Commission does not allow money to be used for this purpose.

I had already started the course, but had to give it up at the birth of my child as there were no nursery facilities at the University College and I could not afford to pay for an outside nursery on the grant. (Unmarried mother)

It is estimated that over a million mothers require some form of after-school care, and even more require holiday care for their children. Provision for after-school care is very scattered and variable. Many working women express their worries about their children during nonschool periods. They often limit their working hours to fit with "taking and

Table 5.8 Influence of Satisfactory Child-Care Arrangements on Reentry

| | If Arrangements Available | | |
	Would Work Earlier than Intended (percent)	Would Not Work Earlier than Intended (percent)	Number (=100 percent)
All children at school	34	66	301
Some of the children at school	37	63	564
None of the children at school	31	69	393
Total	34	66	1258

Source: General Household Survey 1976, Table 6.26.

collecting" and stop work in the holidays, although single mothers cannot often risk this.

An extra hour would bring in a few extra pounds which we could use, but now I take the kids to school and collect them. That's important. The children have to come first. Besides I couldn't afford to send them by bus—that'd be £7 a week! There's nowhere they could wait from 4 till 5—if only there was a library or a Wimpy bar even . . . (Divorcee)

I was out from 8 am to 6 pm with the job. It would have been very difficult if the boys hadn't gone to my Mum's for five weeks as I wouldn't have been able to work and would have had a very low income. Without my parents I don't know what I'd do in the summer holidays. (Widow—student)

The school holidays are awful . . . When there is a local holiday play scheme. . . the kids are put on their honor to go down there. Other times I pay girls to come and just be here. There are people around if there are problems, next door for instance.

The majority of working mothers appear to manage with a variety of ad hoc arrangements, chiefly because they prefer their children (of all ages) to be looked after by husbands, family and neighbors.

I wouldn't leave him with a child-minder. I'd have to give up work, sell the house and take it from there . . . that's talking about the desperate. I think in fact that my mother will see Tom through his childhood. (Young separated mother, with 8-month-old baby)

Some arrangements are of extraordinary complexity:

My Mum does two nights, on night duty, and my Dad works from 8 am till 1 pm, and starts again at 5 pm. Mum went to bed at lunchtime before her nights, then Dad looked after Ian till 5 pm when I came home and took over. During the school holidays he had to be left for an hour in the mornings twice a week until Mum came home. Then she'd go to sleep and he'd play. It was a worry as I didn't know how good he'd be, but he seemed to be able to cope. I phoned him from the office and he'd answer. He's beginning to accept things now. (Young divorcee)

Family and friends are also relied on to help with sick children—a universal worry of working mothers.

His shift work comes in handy. My husband can help if the children are ill, and he can take them to hospital appointments if we arrange the times right.

Another problem that I've had is with the children. They've been ill a couple of times, mumps and chills, so I've had to stop working then.

There's a very good neighbor living across the road who would be only too glad to watch them for me.

That so many working women still choose to describe themselves as housewives is also an indication of the objective realities of their lives: that housework is *work*, that it takes up a lot of time, and it is *their* responsibility. "Domestic responsibilities" are cited nearly as often as child care, as reasons for not working.

Many working women report that they are continually struggling to "catch up":

The house definitely takes second place. It never looks as tidy and polished as before. I do get tired. We hardly ever go out in the evenings.

One recent study found the time spent on housework varied from 48 hours (the only woman in the sample working full time) to 105 hours a week, with an average of 77 hours. Domestic help is difficult to obtain, even for the minority who can afford to pay for it.

Apart from occasional child minding and washing-up, most women report little help from their husbands in cooking and preparing meals, washing and ironing, mending or shopping. Some studies (mainly of middle-class couples) have found the extent of the husbands' help increasing with the proportion of outside working time by the wives. Husbands' reports of the amount of help they give often focus on gardening, home repairs and decorating. Single mothers often face problems—or expense—here.

I am expected to do *all* the housework—washing, ironing, cooking, shopping, cleaning, feeding the dogs etc., etc. even though I leave at eight in the morning (he's still in bed) and get home at six. It's not so bad coping with the boys, but they bring their friends in too. But I've *got* to finish the course.

I feel I haven't used my husband enough. He really does want to help more. He has offered to take the washing to the launderette—I think I'll take him up on that.

I'm not so sure about my husband if he had to cook his own meals too often. I've got a friend whose husband works shifts and she is out at work, and she pays out extra so he can have meals in the canteen before or after his work so as not to have the disasters in the kitchen you get when a man copes!

Of course, the desire to "buy things for the house," or homeownership itself, is the principal financial motivator to work for some women.

The care of older relatives can also be a barrier to returning and often arises just as child care responsibilities are diminishing. Single women, too, often give up work for this purpose, or, in spite of financial need, may never enter the labor market until their elderly relative dies. Cuts in public spending on community care may mean this will become, in the future, a more significant factor in women's ability to return.

Mobility and Housing

The journey-to-work time—and cost—is a major constraint on various aspects of women's reentry decisions. "Within easy travel distance" is generally rated high in any list of factors that make a job attractive. Drastic public transport cuts in recent years, particularly in rural areas, have severely limited some women's opportunities. Travel time of 20 minutes each way is often seen as a maximum because "I have to get back for the children." Women's problems are exacerbated because they are less likely than men to have the use of a car for the journey to work, and over twice as likely as men to go by bus or to walk.

I must keep an eye on the family . . . I wouldn't have taken this job when they were smaller. (She is working five minutes by bike or 15 minutes' walk from home.)

I wouldn't go into Reading—couldn't get home quickly enough. (Reading is 20 minutes by regular bus service from her house.)

Married women who move because of their husbands' careers may have more frequent reentry problems, loss of seniority and a "nonlogical" career pattern. Conversely, managers' assumptions of lack of geographical mobility for women, who are regarded (rightly or not) as tied to the location of their husband's jobs or child's school, is a major handicap to women obtaining promotion or in access to many higher level jobs.

The ability to find a house near the job may be as important as that of finding a job near the home, particularly for those returners without a husband and under financial pressure. Reports on single mothers reveal desperate problems of homelessness and its relevance to other reentry problems, reinforcing the vicious circle of deprivation. Residential employment rarely provides a long-term satisfactory solution for those with children. The "Over-forties Association" is as much concerned with accommodation as with employment problems.

Employment Factors

Women would not have been able to return to work in such large numbers had there not been a demand for their labor, whatever the range of factors facilitating supply.

All the evidence shows that women do better in a tight labor market, since employers then set out to attract them; otherwise women are generally regarded as a "marginal" or "reserve" pool of labor. Nevertheless, for many unskilled and semiskilled jobs, employers still prefer women. Traditional beliefs in their "greater dexterity" and affinity for domestic type work, clerical and personal services, mean that for some jobs, employers prefer them to men (of any age) and welcome the stability and maturity of older women, compared with school-leavers. (One employer taken to an industrial tribunal by a man claiming discrimination said the job was so simple even a monkey could do it, so it was appropriate for an older woman). Women's lack of unionization and industrial militancy is often cited as another factor.

It is difficult to find much evidence of employers' schemes to encourage their female employees to return to them after a break for child rearing, other than telling them that they will be welcome to apply again, or giving them a leaflet when they leave. Most say other procedures would be bureaucratic and time-consuming to administer, but there is some evidence of "keep-in-touch" pools operating through the personnel department of large local employers of female labor, with a continual flow of school-leavers/ pregnant employees/returners.

I had worked there previously, so I just applied for a job and they sent for me within a fortnight.

The existence of a "reinstatement" policy, such as that introduced in the Civil Service in 1976 which guarantees favorable consideration of would-be reentrants (though not necessarily a job) in relation to their skills and existing vacancies, could be helpful in other organizations. Those leaving are given an application form and told retraining will be given.

Recent legislation providing for compulsory maternity leave has certainly facilitated reentry at this stage, but not for those women who want a longer break. Some collective agreements are starting to improve on this, especially in local government. The "right to return," however, means to the same or equivalent post; most returners do not want full-time work.

Examples of a few schemes (mostly in the 1960s) where employers deliberately and successfully set out to attract older women have included giving attention to the wording of advertisements—not asking for "older people" but describing the job; designing simpler application forms than those used for school-leavers; and changing interviewing and induction systems to provide "sponsored" reentry. A shoe manufacturer in a rural county found that recruiting systems based on neighborhood social groups and personal contacts were more effective than "faceless" newpaper advertisements and he hired rooms in village halls and pubs to explain available job opportunities.

The extent to which women are able to vary their hours from the basic norm of the nine-to-five day, Monday to Friday, will probably affect their return to work more positively than any other single factor. The majority of returners have school-age children and therefore have a strong preference for hours that fit in with them, or that are less than full time in some way. The big clearing banks have a variety of schemes: some women have fixed-term contracts on two or three peak days of the week, and some work alternate weeks only. In the National Health Service, some areas have established "nurses banks" in which people can "deposit" a statement of their skills and the hours they would be available for work.

The decision to go back to work was not difficult. It was finding the right hours to fit in with the kids that was difficult. Then I got this part-time clerical work and I work at lunch time in order to make up the hours so that I'll be home in time for the children.

Flexible working hours have been slow to develop in the U.K. as formal systems (estimates are four percent over all), *except* in office employment— primarily in the commercial, financial, and public administration sectors and particularly in London and the South. Where they have been insti- tuted, they are usually popular with married women (who sometimes work only "core" time), but transport problems often do not make it feasible in smaller towns. Informal flexibility is widespread, often at the initiative of women themselves—especially "early leaving" arrangements.

Women's shift working in factories is at present still restricted by the Factories Act (1961), but exemption orders are readily available. The most popular shift with young mothers is the evening "twilight" or "house- wives" shift (about six to ten pm), as husbands are then at home and even single mothers find it easier to make sleeping than day-care arrangements for young children. Night work also is popular with those under financial pressure because they can earn as much in a few nights as a week on day shifts, eg. nursing auxiliaries.

I did the 5pm to 10pm evening shift when the children were small, and my husband looked after the kids, but only for a year . . . It meant that my husband had to put the kids to bed five nights a week—he didn't like to change nappies!

Despite legal entitlement to certain employment rights of those working 16 hours or over, part-timers generally have very much lower security and fringe benefits, particularly where these are linked to longer or continuous service. Full-time reentrant women, for this reason, do no always get the same fringe benefits as men. On the other hand, employers who do have proper sick pay and holiday schemes for part-timers find greater stability. Synchronization of factory holiday closures with school holidays or with other local firms to allow husbands, wives and children to be on holiday together is now more common. In addition, transport may be provided by employers for the "school shift mums" or the "twilight" shift in areas where there is a shortage of labor and/or transport. A few also provide it to the shops at lunch time—or else encourage shopkeepers to trade on-site on an isolated industrial estate.

The majority of managers are ignorant of the extent of family responsibilities of their women employees, and only a small minority make special arrangements to take account of the different patterns of women's working lives. Comments of the women are often along the lines of "beggars can't be choosers"; and while they are well aware of and bitter about the exploitative rates of pay, they feel (unless they are in real financial hardship) that what the jobs lack in financial reward they make up for in convenient hours, nearness to home, and contacts with people and outside events. There is therefore little expressed demand for improved conditions—other than more scope for work within school hours.

I feel that I ought to get paid better because I'm doing four jobs in one, and it's a lot of responsibility, there's one table waiting for coffee, another waiting to pay their bills, another waiting to order. I feel that £13 a week for doing all this, as well as helping with the washing up, is ridiculous. The cafeteria seats about 30 people and I work for 20½ hours but I can't afford to chuck it up.

The only change that I can suggest that would have made things easier for me is if a firm could offer me a job on a flexible 40 weeks a year, so that I would be able to fit in my labor time to suit the children. This would be of great advantage to many women in my position.

Financial Factors

Clearly the need for more money, as well as the recognition that accompanies the status of wage-earner, is the major incentive to women to return to work in a period of rapid inflation. Retail prices were rising at an annual rate of over 25 percent in 1975, and the rate was still only just below 10 percent in 1978. While rates of increase in average earnings have generally kept ahead of price increases, families with children (and particularly low-income families) have become relatively worse off in recent years with respect to both the cost of living and their tax liability.

Labor market statistics have already illustrated women's low pay and its relationship with the presence of young children and part-time work. A recent report comments that "Women who can earn high hourly wages are more likely to work. So low pay has a double effect on women's earnings; if they do work, they don't earn much, but they are also not so likely to work."*

The British system of taxation (P.A.Y.E.) is based on the assumption that, for the purposes of tax, the wife's income (earned and unearned) is deemed to be the husband's. Since both can get tax allowances, the system is, in fact, relatively generous to families in which the wife takes paid employment and is particularly so where the wife is the sole breadwinner, because of the anomalies created by the transfer of the married man's tax allowance. Despite a recent modification (favoring working couples), it

---

*R. Layard, D. Piachaud, M. Stewart et al., "The Causes of Poverty." Royal Commission on the Distribution of Income and Wealth, Background Paper No. 5.

remains a steeply progressive system of taxation; and the marginal tax rate created by the interaction of tax, national insurance contributions and means-tested benefits is still the most awesome obstacle for the low paid to overcome. Unless they can make a giant leap out of poverty, low paid workers often have very little incentive to work or to earn a few pounds extra. Part of the problem lies in the very low level of the tax threshold.

A new system of tax-free cash benefits (payable to the mother) is shortly to be fully phased in, including a special weekly allowance payable for the first and only child in one-parent families. "Means-testing" rules, however, will prevent single mothers on supplementary benefit from taking full advantage of this program. No tax relief is available for child care costs.

National insurance contributions in fiscal 1978 amounted to 6.5 percent of any earnings between £17.50 and £120 per week for an employee, and 10 percent (+2 percent) for an employer. They act as an incentive to some part-timers to keep their earnings below this level (this often involves working less than 16 hours a week and thus losing certain legal job security rights). Before April 1977, married women (and widows) could elect not to pay full contributions; but this is now being phased out, except that those who had previously opted-out and continue to work pay only 2 percent on earnings. While married women are thus being required to contribute equally to the scheme as workers, they still cannot claim for dependents in the same way as men. (They will, however, be credited with "home responsibility" credits towards pensions if they are employed for 20 years and take up to 20 years to look after children.) Part-timers are unlikely to be eligible for unemployment benefit, even if paying full contributions, unless they register for full-time work.

Welfare Benefits

Britain's social security system is still based on the assumption of the single-role family with the breadwinner husband and the homemaker wife—that is, on the assumption of the wife's dependency. Most benefits are means-tested; thus an important consideration for a woman returning to work is the negative effect this will have on the family's entitlements. These are principally supplementary benefit (S.B.), family income supplement (F.I.S.), rent rebate, rate rebate, free school meals and free welfare milk. Some allow a certain amount of a wife's or of a lone parent's earnings to be ignored or "disregarded"—but £4 to £6 only.

Family Income Supplement is payable to a low-paid head of household in full-time work whose family includes a dependent child. Only the husband in a married couple can claim. Forty-three percent of people claiming F.I.S. are lone parents—nearly all of them women. The definition of "full-time" work has just been reduced from 30 to 24 hours a week, and it is estimated that this will bring another 10,000 one-parent families within the scope of F.I.S. and off S.B.—probably at very little net increase in cost.

Under British law, husband and wife have a legal responsibility to support each other and the children. When a marriage ends, the husband is usually ordered to pay about one-third of his income to support the wife and sometimes to pay extra for the children. Women claiming Supplementary Benefit may sign over authority for the court to remit to the DHSS and sometimes to pay extra for the children. Women claiming supplementary benefit may sign over authority for the court to remit to the DHSS ment. This is not always agreed if the maintenance is higher than the benefits; in any case the amount received is fully deducted. Nonclaimants may well find it difficult or impossible to enforce rights to maintenance. Alternatively, they may get only an occasional lump sum rather than a regular payment.

He is supposed to pay £15 per week but we saw none of that last winter, and he's ill and out of work again so I don't suppose there'll be any this winter either. Because I'm earning they don't seem to care whether I get it or not.

It has been estimated that about half of separated/divorced mothers get regular allowances from the father of the children. In 1975 the average receipt was about £9 a week: "This makes less difference between poverty and sufficiency than working or not working."

Child care costs must affect the economic viability of mothers returning to work, although there is no generally agreed average figure for these. One survey found working mothers spending 20 to 30 percent of their earnings on child care, while one expert (Piachaud) argues that care costs for a child under five may amount to 50 percent of the mother's earnings; this calculation should probably be limited to a maximum of £25 per week at present. Care of sick children may mean loss of earnings.

If they became very ill and needed me at home I'd report myself sick to the exchange and then would get paid from them just the same. If I reported the children ill, I would get time off but I wouldn't get paid.

Even care by family and friends may involve disguised expenditure in the form of extra presents, meals or reduced rent to a lodger. Many working mothers spend more on labor-saving devices, convenience foods and repairs, so that possibly 10 to 20 percent of earnings goes for extra housekeeping costs. Extra clothes are another item, apart from travel expenses.

I pay my mother £4 a week but fares are going up all the time and as I'm doing two jobs, by the end of the week I do feel shattered. (Divorcee, part-time waitress, and barmaid two nights, earning £20 a week)

I wondered about getting a suit for teaching practice, but it didn't seem very practical, so I've bought a new vacuum instead. I may lash out on a typewriter next year. I could type my own thesis, and it would be useful for other things later.

A woman's earnings will often determine whether or not the family's income is above the poverty line. A couple is far more likely to be poor if the wife is not working. Overall, it is estimated that the number of two-parent families with incomes below £40 a week would have doubled and the numbers living below the supplementary benefit level would have trebled if it had not been for a wife's earnings. Only five percent of working wives actually earn more than their husbands, but about a third contribute 20 to 50 percent of the total family income. Moreover, among mothers who did not work, 94 percent of single-parent families had incomes below the poverty line, compared with only 20 percent where the mother earned over £30 a week.

Increasing numbers of single parents (especially those with young children) are now in receipt of supplementary benefit although, relatively, rewards for working have risen faster than benefits available in recent years. When they do work, single parents work considerably longer hours than working mothers in two-parent families, which suggests that the social security system deters part-time work by single mothers, particularly when child care costs are taken into account. While some women may overcome those costs, others may easily face a situation where it is not economically viable to work for earnings which vary widely (from £20-£80), although they may choose to do so to avoid the stigma of claiming.

I didn't realize that one human being could do that to another. They humiliated you and made you feel *so* high. That made my mind up not to live off Social Security and that I would need to go back to work.

Widows are in a more fortunate position if they are out of the work force, because those in receipt of widows' benefits can keep their income above the S.B. level. Once a widow starts to work, her widowed mothers' allowance is not reduced, but it becomes taxable along with any earned income. And, because of the "poverty trap," her increased gross income results in lower rebates and welfare benefits. Consequently if child care costs are included, a widow is in much the same position as any other single mother and, unless she can avoid these costs, she needs high earnings to cover them. She is also likely to be in a less-favorable position regarding government retraining grants. One interviewer observed:

Coupled with this genuine love of homemaking is the wry observation that it doesn't pay her, as a widowed mother, to go out to work. She reports with accuracy and exasperation the penalizing of her pension income, free school meals, rate rebates, etc. if earnings creep to a reasonable level.

Wives of unemployed husbands are 33 percentage points more likely to be out of the labor force than the wives of employed husbands. "About half of the families of unemployed men receive supplementary benefit which, after disregards, is reduced pound-for-pound for any earnings of the wife. This creates an incentive for wives to stop work when their husbands become unemployed," says one report. Detailed calculations of an average couple's net financial position show that this would be rational if the wife earned more than about £9 a week (depending on various circumstances).

Wives with low-earning husbands are under pressure to go out to work. Yet financial incentives, especially if child care costs are included, are relatively low. For instance, if the husband earned only £40 gross, the family would stand to lose £10.33 in welfare benefits if the wife earned £27 or more gross. This, of course, assumes that the family is claiming all the benefits to which it is entitled, which is not necessarily a realistic assumption. If both husband and wife earn two-thirds of average incomes for men and women, the family's gross earnings increase by £39 but their net income by £26.18. This is more than if the husband increased his earnings, even allowing for additional child care costs, because of the wife's extra tax relief and earnings disregards allowed on benefits. For comparison, when a wife and husband earn average incomes, the marginal tax rate on the increase in gross income is much lower.

Once a married woman's children have grown up, some of the factors that create the financial disincentives to taking paid work are removed. The most obvious is child care costs, though these will normally cease at an earlier age. Also the family will stand to lose less by way of welfare benefits because their entitlement to such benefits will, in any case, be reduced.

Despite the importance of a woman's earnings in reducing family poverty, the interaction of tax and national insurance contributions can eat away at the extra income gained. If there is no great increase in family income, then a woman is under correspondingly high pressure to stay at home.

Educational Factors

Every study shows that the more education a woman has had, at every level, the more likely she is to be in employment, and the higher her earnings are likely to be. Women who are reentering the labor market now at around age 30 to 50 are those who were born between 1930 and 1950 and left school between 1945 and 1965. This generation, growing up during and after World War II, has been described as the "lost generation" in terms of educational opportunities. Most of them would have left school by the time they were 15 and gone straight into employment. Some are now rather bitter about this.

When we left school we were just trained skivvies—we'd only done cookery and housecraft and things so I wasn't trained for anything. (34-year-old)

Greenhalgh's analysis of a sample of 8,000 households taken from the 1971 General Household Survey found that 69 percent of married women had no formal qualifications (77 percent of the widowed, divorced and separated group, and 45 percent of single women); 25 percent had school or other qualifications; and six percent had higher qualifications (degree or diploma).

How far, then, are women who are planning to reenter the labor market now able to improve on their low educational base, to add to their minimal vocational qualifications or to change direction? Conditions for this are only slowly beginning to improve, since the British formal higher educational system remains highly selective on the basis of qualifications gained in the last years of secondary school, and largely geared to the education of 18- to 24-year olds. There is still very little flexibility to meet the needs of mature students. Part-time courses are few for university degrees and only slowly increasing for other qualifications, except as part of full-time employer-sponsored day-release or college-based sandwich schemes. Unit-based or module courses are only beginning to be developed in some subjects, and transferability between courses and institutions is still difficult. (A study of credit-transfer feasibility is beginning at Exeter University). Teaching methods are aimed mainly at the young.

Formal classifications of high, further and adult education are beginning to break down in practice in a few areas, but the distinctions remain to hamper change and confuse students. There is now great public focus on expanding facilities for postschool school education for adults of all ages: but talk is tending to exceed development so far.

Remedial education. Some women really need basic education in functional literacy and numeracy before they can make progress in any area. A recent government-funded National Adult Literacy campaign has helped, and the Training Services Division of M.S.C. also finances "work preparation" and "Communication Skills" courses of this sort, in cases where they are diagnosed as vocational need.

Community education groups have been pioneering outreach programs both for urban communities and for rural areas. Education for parenthood is often a way-in for women—the Liverpool "Home Link" scheme has developed in this way, out of child development classes started at a local clinic on an isolated housing estate.

"Nonvocational" education. Statistics show that the proportion of women enrolled in courses has increased steadily over the years. But adult education, traditionally defined as "nonvocational," remains the only area of postschool education in which women outnumber men. They form the majority of students in evening-only and part-time day courses. A significant proportion of these women is over age 30, and many are over 50.

Recent increases in fees have led to a marked slowing in the rate of increase of enrollments; those most likely to be hit are the older women who are below average in income, education and confidence. A wide range of courses in arts and crafts, linguistic, domestic, cultural and recreational activities are covered by this classification. Women attend them out of interest and self-development in the first place, but in practice the classes often act as a stepping stone to attendance at a more demanding course leading to a qualification.

The only thing I looked forward to each week was the evening class. I went to classes on anything just to keep sane—otherwise I would be terribly depressed. (Now completing teacher-training)

Courses for returners. The problem of transition from a period of home-making to the world of work is, for many women, a combination of lack of confidence, mental "rustiness," and sheer ignorance of the educational, training, or employment opportunities available and how to find out about them. A variety of courses are springing up to meet this need, but it is not known how many there are. Ruth Miller has listed about 70 in twenty-four educational areas of the country, but is certain that this is an underestimate. Pioneering courses were those developed at the City Literary Institute, London, at Hatfield Polytechnic, and at Manchester (with some E.E.C. funding).

These courses probably represent the most significant single development in the education available to women reentrants. They demand no entry qualifications and, in general, give women an opportunity to regain their self-confidence, learn how to study, find out what courses or jobs might be available, and to acquire interpersonal skills and insights. The names—"New Opportunities," "New Horizons," "Return to Work," "Foundation"—give some indication of their focus. Students stress the value of the courses in developing confidence and enabling them to plan their time and their future in a new way.

Most of the courses are short, part-time, and informal, allowing scope for group learning and for tutor counseling, and many try to provide creche facilities. They may be held on one or more days (or evenings) a week, and length varies from six or eight weeks to one academic year. Daytime classes are usually between ten and three to fit in with children's school hours.

There is no national pattern or central information point, although the Equal Opportunities Commission is starting to coordinate these programs, since a clear demand for information has emerged. Whether there is a course depends entirely on whether there is someone in the education system with enthusiasm for helping potential returners. Many classes start in response to demand from potential students—but some have found it difficult to get off the ground owing to lack of finance for initial publicity. Once this is overcome, word-of-mouth is usually sufficient to ensure a steady supply of students. Many courses say they could easily double their enrollees, given the resources.

The Burnham system of financing further education courses on a points basis, according to the level of the course, means such low-level courses are not attractive to administrators and do not have many resources available to them, unless a special arrangement is made, as by the Inner London Education Authority. As "bridging" courses they tend to fall between vocational and nonvocational sources of finance. Recent cuts in educational spending have tended to exacerbate the difficulties.

In some areas these courses have developed as part of a university continuing education program; in others they have been part of a range of activities of a polytechnic or a further education college. They may also develop within courses of a community education service or of an established adult education center such as the City Literary Institute in London (one of the pioneers of such courses, with about 100 students currently in various full-time and part-time classes). Classes run by the Workers' Educational Association may also develop along these lines.

Students more often tend to go on to further education than directly into employment, although obviously this varies with the focus of the course and the motivation of the students.

It was a great help talking about my situation and hearing others' problems. I got a great boost from one woman who had gone back to office work and survived the experience! (Student at Bracknell suddenly forced to go back to work because husband's income became insecure)

"Return to Science" at Southwark College, London, helps women start in science from scratch, while some courses, such as "Polymaths" and "Polyphysics," are direct feeders for prospective higher education students. A few polytechnics run a "Polyprep" course of their own to help students by introducing them to learning to overcome anxieties before starting a higher education course. Older women in particular find these valuable.

The scope to progress gradually is important: "At each stage I thought I'd never make the rest," said one woman who was about to graduate.

Another significant recent development is the government request to certain local education authorities to develop special courses to prepare mature students who lack the normal (2 "A" levels) qualifications for entry to higher education. These will be aimed chiefly at ethnic minority groups, to prepare them for teacher training entry, but they could be of great value to women returners as well, if developed on a larger scale.

General Certificate of Education. The statistics of mature students in further education show that many of those taking Ordinary and Advanced level subjects in evening and daytime courses are women over 30 years of age. Most of these take the normal examinations and learn in mixed age groups, but some prefer the "adult equivalent" syllabi and validation, as developed at Sheffield and elsewhere.

Some subjects can be taken through correspondence courses: the National Extension College (Cambridge), the Barnet "Flexistudy" scheme and the "Open College Programme" are variants of these. They all attempt to minimize students' isolation to take advantage of modern aids to learning, and to suit the needs of mature students in different, and developing, ways. The "Open College" program is really moving to a more adult qualifying approach.

I did an O level statistics course at the local tech. and I was the only 'oldie' in the class. I hated it, used to dread going to classes. I felt really out of it. If I tried to talk to them they all giggled. I really *hated* it.

Adult residential colleges. There are seven long-term adult residential colleges in the U.K., where people over 21 who left school early "can catch up on missed education opportunities in the leisurely and civilized atmosphere of a mini university campus." There are no entry qualifications, and selection is by interview. Full-time one- and two-year (mostly) courses are taken that lead to diplomas or certificates validated by a university, and many students go on to gain further forms of higher education. Some day students are now accepted.

Hillcroft College in Surrey has a unique history of successful provision for reentrant women, but in most of the colleges less than a third of the students are women. The newly founded Northern College in South Yorkshire aims deliberately at achieving a balance through both its mix of courses and provision of facilities (including child care).

When my divorce was completed and I decided that I wanted to develop myself and my knowledge, I went to see an old friend of my family who works for the Extramural Dept. He advised me to enter a residential course in a mature students college. He gave me tremendous support. He got in touch with the Warden of the College, acquired the necessary forms, and also supplied me with one of the three references that was needed. (Student at Coleg Harlech)

Vocational and technical courses. It is possible for women to obtain places, if they wish and know how to do so, in a variety of technical and business studies courses. An important reorganization of almost all these courses (apart from those leading to City and Guilds certificates) is taking place under the auspices of the newly established Technician Education and Business Education Councils. This has resulted in a more clearly defined hierarchy of progression from one level to another, and within each level there is a modular system; linked around compulsory core subjects is a range of options to complete the package. Once these courses become more widely implemented and publicized, there should be more scope for women to obtain vocational qualifications in stages to fit in with their family cycle; but it will be important for the BEC and TEC diplomas to become fully integrated into higher qualifications systems and to meet the needs of professional bodies or they could become additional "dead-end" routes for women.

Degree courses. Universities are now much more welcoming to mature students than previously, especially the newer universities. (Only about 12 percent of students are currently over age 26.) "Mature" students are defined as people over 21/23/25 who have been out of education for at least three or five years. The normal entry requirements may be waived for them, to allow admission by interview only, by special exams, or by submission of an essay. In 1978, two official statements of encouragement were published outlining the "alternative" provisions, or rather describing all the hurdles of the "mature entry" schemes. Lucy Cavendish College at Cambridge accepts only mature women students (with formal qualifications).

The Open University (O.U.) is specially designed for mature students (over 21). On average, 12 to 20 hours a week for about 34 weeks a year are needed. No formal qualifications are required, but the course is very rigorous and demanding and prospective students are often encouraged to undertake preparatory courses. Students choose from about 120 courses at four levels in six faculties, and study at home through correspondence courses involving a variety of modern multimedia techniques. There are about 265 study centers around the country where students can meet their tutor counselors and course tutors, and some subjects include a week's obligatory residential summer school.

Large numbers of housewives have successfully taken the courses, and numbers are now increasing. One or two pilot schemes of group study for OU have been found to be highly successful in reducing the dropout rates, especially of older women of limited educational and social background— for example those at Rowlinson Adult Education Centre in Sheffield, who found the support of the group vital in overcoming lapses of confidence, domestic crises, and isolation of study.

Transfer arrangements to OU from polytechnic degree and diploma courses and from some universities now exist; the reverse is also occasionally possible.

I'm going to university in the only way I can. If I went back to Glasgow I would only get a grant for two years because of dropping out before. (O.U. student; also works evening shift in a factory)

The OU has kept me sane, honestly. But the degree is not an aim. I don't feel I have the mental capacity to get the degree. The idea is to grow with the course but I've got reservations about whether I could grow that far! (Ex-computer operator)

Polytechnic degree courses are particularly attractive to returners, as they are often more vocational in approach and aim to meet labor needs of the area in which they are situated. There is a CNAA (national degree-validating body) rule that no course may have more than 10 percent mature students, but the rule is not generally enforced. Proportions increase every year and may be around 30 percent. Enrollment of women over 30 in these courses is not as high as men but is increasing, and many polytechnics now run part-time degrees. N.E. London Polytechnic has developed a course attracting mature students based entirely on the students' own need: the

Degree or Diploma by Independent Study. A few universities and polytechnics have an "associate" student scheme by which a student is admitted to one or more course units in the college's existing program.

Degree courses can also be taken at the new Institutes of Higher Education which are attracting larger proportions of mature students, partly because entry requirements are easier, and partly because many of the courses are modular and recently developed to meet student demand. There is, however, criticism of the quality of some of these courses, and the labor market value of the new Diploma in Higher Education is still uncertain.

I had a proper interview, with all the youngsters. That was all right, I was more confident then, I even felt a bit motherly towards them—some of them turned up with their mums!

Recent reorganization of the teacher-training program into a graduate entry profession has been facilitated by the dramatic decline in demand for teachers resulting from demographic changes. Teacher training has become increasingly popular with women returners over the past 20 years—partly because it fits in with their domestic circumstances and child-rearing skills, but also because of its earnings potential and its job satisfaction. During the shortages of teachers in the 60s, colleges were encouraged to provide courses for returners, and grants were made readily available (even for part-time courses).

Most remaining colleges still welcome mature students and some have special courses for them but, overall, the raising of entry qualifications and the cuts in funding are hitting women especially hard. Colleges specially for mature students have closed; others are now sited too far away from women who are running a home as well.

Grants for education. The financing of higher education students in the U.K. is based on a system of grants that appears much more generous than that of many other countries, but it tends to work against mature students, particularly married women. Grants are awarded by local education authorities and are divided into "discretionary" and "mandatory" (courses thus designated by the D.E.S., for which a grant is automatically payable). Mature students accepted into a full-time university or CNAA course will obtain a mandatory award which covers the payment of tuition fees and a sum toward living expenses, based on certain conditions. Dependents' allowances may be payable if the students are both "independent" and married before the start of the course. If living with their husbands, or if they have not been working during the past few years, they will not get the full mature students allowance. This can hit the family budget hard, or deter women who want to qualify precisely because they have been out of the labor market. Single parents are in a better position for claiming the full amount, and there is a special DHSS hardship fund. On the other hand, unmarried students will not get child dependents allowances, and students compelled to leave the course because of pregnancy or childbirth will lose entitlement to a mandatory award on return.

I had to convince the Education Authority that I was a special case so that they would produce my grant for one year. (It was no more nor less than a begging letter.)

Grants for most other "nonadvanced" courses are subject to the discretion of the local education authorities, who are exercising this much less generously than previously in the present situation of financial stringency. This may mean that amounts awarded are much lower or that other conditions are imposed—often indirectly discriminatory—such as setting lower maximum age limits for eligibility. Some authorities limit awards to courses unlikely to attract women thus no grants may be available for secretarial, nursery nursing, or even social work courses in some areas. No grants are usually available for 'O' and 'A' level or other low-level courses, even if these are necessary to qualify for entry to others for which a grant would be available. Women on supplementary benefit, or indeed any on very low incomes, are hard hit by this, unless fees can be waived or reduced. Mandatory grants are not available for part-time courses, and discretionary grants, if paid, are often very inadequate. In general, policy towards nonadvanced courses seems to be based on the (questionable) assumption that students will be in the 16 to 20 age group, living at home and dependent on their parents.

The major Research Councils, which finance most postgraduate courses, impose an age limit of 27 years, which can only be waived "in exceptional circumstances." This can be a particular handicap for reentrant professional women who find they have need of a second qualification to compete in the labor market to compensate for the lack of "years of experience" qualification, and to up-date their specialized knowledge.

The first year was murder. I hated every minute of it and didn't know if I was coming or going. For the first time in my life I felt I couldn't cope. Myrna (a friend) and I moaned together and said we only stayed because we'd spent the grant. Then I passed my exams and I thought, Well, fancy that! Now I'm taking Honors. I feel as if I could take on anything now!

REENTRY POLICIES AND PROGRAMS

Legislation

The Equal Pay Act, 1970, and the Sex Discrimination Act, 1975, represent the major expression of Britain's policy toward the position of women in the labor market. Discrimination on grounds of sex is unlawful in the fields of employment, education and training, and in access to a range of other goods, facilities and services. Discrimination on grounds of marriage is unlawful in employment.

Special exceptions enable training to be afforded by employers (or training bodies) to one sex only, for the performance of particular work where none or very few of that sex have done that work in the past year. Training bodies may also provide special training for those in need "by reason of the period for which they have been discharging domestic or family responsibilities to the exclusion of regular full time employment." The Equal Opportunities Commission was set up to "enforce the law in the public interest." The education, training and employment problems of women returners have been listed as a priority, from the beginning and in all its discussions with official organizations; and in its publications on good practice, the EOC has called attention to the needs of returners and the scope for special provision for them under the Act.

The Employment Protection Act, 1975, also makes important improvements for women returners in its protection of pregnant employees against dismissal, its provisions for a six-week paid maternity leave, and its entitlement to return within a period of 29 weeks after birth, with unbroken pension and seniority rights. Conditions of eligibility for maternity rights include, at present, two years of continuous service.

Government Training Policies

Government responsibility for, and expenditure on, training has been increasing steadily in Britain over the past 25 years, with growing recognition of the part training has to play in aiding national economic recovery. Powers are largely vested in the Manpower Services Commission, which aims to identify and meet the training needs of the nation as a whole, of firms, and of individuals. It also runs the public employment services and has three operating divisions: Employment Service, Training Service and Special Programs.

The 1973 Employment and Training Act enabled the MSC "to include arrangements for encouraging increases in the opportunities available to women and girls for employment and training." Its 1976 publication, "Training Opportunities for Women," revealed many limitations in skilled, technical, and managerial training, and the "training of girls and women" was listed as one of MSC's priority areas. Initiatives, however, have been concentrated on school-leavers rather than returners.

In general, MSC has, until recently, tended to resist provision for special sections of the population or to concede that women's training needs differ from men's. A more "segmented" approach to the labor market is now being developed, and there is greater emphasis on meeting employers' needs, so careful matching programs will be needed, although there is potential for women to get more training if existing schemes are made more readily accessible to reentrants.

Industrial training boards. The major industries have their own Industry Training Boards (including representatives of both unions and employers), which are financed from a levy of firms in the industry and from MSC. The jobs which women "happen to" occupy, however, happen to be those requiring little training. Industries where women predominate (such as textiles, clothing, distribution) are mostly low-skill, low-pay industries, and training is mostly on-the-job and lasts only a few weeks.

I rove and draw the flax, and the girls next door to me in my room trained me—there wasn't anybody else to train me; you just learned from your mistakes and got quicker and better.

Nevertheless, some Boards are starting to develop special programs for women only, under encouragement from MSC, but the few schemes so far have concentrated on school-leavers and offer nothing substantially new to assist reentrants as such, although some could be utilized by them. The only exception is the recent grant-aid proposal of the Food, Drink and Tobacco ITB. Under this, up to 20 grants of £500 would be available to companies employing or training women as managers or supervisors, following unemployment for domestic reasons for at least five years. The women will normally have been back in employment for no more than a year and be over age 30. Before grants can be paid, further criteria, relating to the level and quality of training and subsequent appointment, would have to be met. Practical guidance will be given by the Board on ways in which companies can facilitate the recruitment of older women to posts of responsibility.

In skill training, traditional age-limits mean that females tend to miss out twice—as girls "because they will soon leave and have a baby," and as reentrants because they are beyond the age for trainees and have not had the experience to justify further training. The normal entry to skilled craft or technician work in industry is by apprenticeship at 16, for three to five years. Recent discussions over revision of skill-training requirements have progressed little beyond "recognizing the need" for flexibility with regard to mature entrants.

Training opportunities schemes. The MSC-financed TOPS scheme is the program most suited to meet the training needs of women reentrants and most widely used by them. Between 1973 and 1977, numbers trebled, and women now constitute 43 percent of all completing trainees. In 1977, 40,881 women completed TOPS courses, a large proportion of whom were older married women.

This program was specifically developed to meet the needs of those wishing to acquire a new skill, update a rusty one, or train for a new occupation. It is open to men and women:

who are at least 19 years old and have been away from full-time education for a total period of more than three years;

who intend to take up employment using the skill for which training is given;

who are unemployed at the moment or who are willing to give up their job to take a full-time training course;

who have not had a government training course during the past five years; and

who are suited to the course they choose. (Previous experience, ability and potential are assessed.)

The course must last at least one month and not more than one year. Courses are available in over 800 subjects, but the scheme does not so far cover degree courses, normal training for the professions, or training for a specific employer.

TOPS courses range from bricklaying to electronics and from typing to management. They are held in Skill Centers at over 700 colleges and at employers' establishments; most people are able to train locally. Some courses are exclusively TOPS-provided and run; others are "infill" in that TOPS grants are available for students in existing vocational college courses.

The vast majority of women trainees (over 80 percent) have taken clerical, commercial and secretarial courses in colleges of further education. Many women also take hotel and catering courses or nursery nursing. More should be encouraged to do computer training, some of which may be based on the premises of employers in the future.

At a postqualification level, occupational health nursing and vocational guidance counseling courses are attended by ex-nurses and teachers. Personnel management courses are also popular with ex-teachers. The numbers of applicants for professional training have steadily increased, and more women have started to take TOPS management courses. Some reorientation courses for managers and redundant executives would also seem to be appropriate for women reentrants.

Only an occasional woman trainee is found on the craft or lower-skill levels. Only 817 women attended skill-center courses in 1977 (mostly younger unmarried women in hairdressing courses).

How can women get these jobs if they want experienced people? If you had a place for women to go to learn computers and machinery and so on, perhaps at night . . . so women could walk out and get a job. There's nothing like that here. Everything is becoming computerized now so they should let women do it. You see a job and say, "I'd love to do that," but you can't as there's no one to learn you. Just like an apprenticeship . . . there should be something for people to learn at whatever age.

She then asked whether I knew about any courses women could go on to learn about men's jobs. I told her about TOPS courses theoretically being open to women now. She was amazed: "Oh I never knew that! Do you mean to say I could be earning about £25 a week and *learning* something instead of just plugging along in that school?! I'm going to find out about that this afternoon!" (School cleaner, Scotland, with invalid husband)

Research into the experience of clerical and secretarial trainees in different parts of the U.K. has remarked the predominance of mature women, and has distinguished three main groups: (a) the highly motivated (for financial and/or career reasons), (b) those with equal interests in their families (no career ambitions, real preference for part-time jobs), and (c) those with no real intention of working (doing the course for the money, something to do, with a vague idea of preparing for the future).

A high proportion of the divorced, widowed and single parents are said to be in the first group, although it is thought that some were training prematurely before they could really cope with all their other pressures, and this inhibited their progress. The third group is often referred to as rather disparagingly as having the "married women syndrome," but many women do now have the idea of preparing to reenter even if unaware of the difficulty of maintaining skills over an intervening period without practice.

Surveys have found that quite often women really didn't want secretarial training but that nothing else seemed available, and it was usually difficult to transfer once in a course. They were often aware, however, that it provides a highly marketable qualification in an urban area and represents the first opportunity some women have had to obtain a white-collar skill.

I felt really great. I felt I was achieving something. It was as if someone had put two roads to me—if I chose this road I could be a full person . . . if I chose the other road I would be a half-made person . . . And here I was on the road to being a typist. (Young, separated mother)

Both refresher courses and beginners courses are available in most areas, but staff have often found that women who really needed only refresher courses have been so lacking in confidence that they have not disclosed previous experience and have taken the longer courses. Criticism that courses are too intensive have been expressed by women and by employers.

Those with home responsibility and those without previous office experience have found it most difficult to get work ultimately. Provision of "confidence training" in "self-presentation" techniques might help.

A recent MSC review of the scope and effectiveness of TOPS has recommended: better publicity of the range of courses available; more part-time provision; more short-term preparation-for-work courses to improve employability; and more attention to assistance in finding a job and bridging the training/job gap. On-the-job training may also be available, with a newly hired trainee continuing to receive the TOPS allowance or part of her wage for a short period. These improvements, if implemented, should meet many current criticisms.

Wider Opportunities for Women courses. A major recent TOPS development is the pilot 'WOW' schemes financed by the E.E.C. Social Fund. These are designed for women likely to enter manual or semiskilled occupations. They must be women who meet normal TOPS requirements, who have not worked outside the home for a number of years, and who do not know what they want to do.

Courses last 4 to 12 weeks, and so far have been run in Birmingham and Cardiff—some have been part-time. Students, mostly aged 25 to 35, try a variety of both job and training samples in the college and with local employers as a means of assessing their own strengths, weaknesses, likes and dislikes. There are talks by outside speakers, group discussions and individual counseling.

Preliminary evaluation found that the courses had been highly successful, in terms of their objectives of building self-confidence and giving information about opportunities for jobs, training and education. At the end, more of the students than expected were planning further training rather than taking a job directly.

The courses were extremely difficult and time consuming to set up initially (as well as expensive to run, in view of the high overhead) because of the variety of different job samples and visits to organizations, but they were relatively easy to repeat and continue after that. It has not yet been decided, however, whether they will be provided on a national basis.

Other work preparation courses. Wider Opportunities Courses (WOCs) of up to 12 weeks had previously been run mainly as "work preparation" for young people (and some adults) in skill centers. It is proposed that more, shorter (about three weeks) work assessment courses of this nature should be developed in the future, especially in urban areas of high unemployment. Short "transfer of employment" courses (mainly for redundant executives) may also be expanded. All these developments could assist women returners.

Other Reentry Training

Professions. Refresher courses for careers in the professions are more widely available than retraining at other levels—mostly at the initiative and expense of public sector employers, especially in the health and education services, and at the initiative of professional organizations and local colleges, usually in response to demand by women. Single mothers who have professional qualifications, or the ability to obtain them, are unlikely to be as well able to afford them as women married to high-income husbands. Many, however, obtain TOPS grants for preentry courses.

Employers. Employers in private industry have developed very few programs of their own for reentrants—only a minority express any willingness to consider this on a formal basis. Even less is done in service industries than in manufacturing. Most of the latter allow no more than a short period of "sitting next to Nellie" for women to regain their old skills, to operate a slightly different machine, or assemble a new product.

I have received no formal training for the job, but I was taught as I was going along. They said that they wouldn't drop me in at the deep end, and then handed me the work force wages!!!

I took a job as a hospital relief night cook [She relates how she went to the interview deeply conscious that she offered no qualifications] but the lady interviewer said— well you cook for your family without poisoning them don't you?

For higher-level work, most companies say they will provide training as necessary for individuals, and some managers interviewed by the EOC (in a survey of the 500 largest employers) cite the occasional example. They feel that existing provision is sufficiently flexible to cover individual needs, but are not necessarily aware that the weekend or even week-long residential course can preclude participation by women coping with family responsibilities, and particularly single parents.

Public sector employers may offer slightly more scope. The Civil Service reinstatement scheme says "retraining will be provided." British Airways encourages their ex-stewardesses to return and runs refresher courses for them.

Camden Council's radical 1978 equal opportunity policy hinges on a positive approach to staff development and training. It identifies three groups of women employees: continuous and career minded, career minded returners, and noncareer returners. It proposes alternative training schemes, which should facilitate career reentrants' chances, either within or by direct entry from outside. Some resources have been made available "to enable any woman employee to attend a relevant training program of her choice. It is essential that women be positively encouraged to enroll for such courses and such encouragement should be part of the function of the supervisor/manager in career development interviews." Every employee will have the right to an annual interview in this regard.

Voluntary organizations: trade unions. Most of the educational and training activities of unions are of course related to those who have already reentered the workforce and to training in union activities. Nevertheless, their basic education courses, correspondence, and weekend day and residential courses may provide the only educational and training opportunities some women ever have, and may create the stimulus necessary to demand and obtain more in other spheres. The increasing attention now being paid to the position of women in unions could facilitate this, although part-timers' participation is inevitably likely to be low. Public sector unions are giving more attention to training needs of part-timers, eg. school meals, child-minders, and home-helps.

Professional organizations. The Medical Women's Federation has long been active in pushing DHSS to meet retraining needs of women doctors, and it has recently organized a very successful one-week refresher course at Nottingham Medical School (with some financial support from Regional

Health Authorities). Most of these organizations act as support groups or providers of information rather than as devisers of programs specifically to assist reentrants. The support and information functions may be those most needed by returners.

Voluntary Societies. A few organizations exist to help middle class and professional women reenter employment by providing information and guidance. Most were founded in the late 50s or early 60s when there was a great demand for women workers.

One example is the National Advisory Center on Careers for Women. Traditional national womens' organizations such as the Women's Institute, Townswomen's Guild, Federation of Business and Professional Women and Soropotimists are now taking slightly more interest in educational and vocational training activities than they did in the past.

As some voluntary organizations develop they attract government or charitable funds and are able to take on paid staff and to train others—often mature women—both paid and unpaid. The Pre-School Play Groups association and the Citizens Advice Bureaus are two examples of this. The former ran over 1000 courses in 1975-1976 for nearly 20,000 students who attended one-and-a-half to two hours once a week for five to ten weeks.

I haven't got any qualifications at all but that's never stopped me—lots of the other playgroup leaders are trained teachers—I should be trained really, but I've done lots of courses though, and I've got lots of experience.

So far, there are not many examples of radical organizations as such setting out to help women obtain vocational training or to run courses for them, although they do provide "Know your Rights" types of courses. Moreover, they have developed pressure groups for child care and have drawn attention to the financial, legal and housing needs of single parents, to low pay, to child poverty, etc. Their achievements, even if limited, have done much to facilitate reentry for women, especially those in financial need and unable to express their demands.

Guidance

The single most crucial need of mature returners is advice and counseling on what to do and where to go. Most of them will have received very little help previously, and after a few years at home they feel out of touch and unsure of their abilities to cope—often to a totally unjustifiable extent.

I think it's a big step going back to work, though, and it's got a lot to do with confidence. I never really had time to think about it, but I can see that with other women.

Almost all those who seek to build the confidence of reentrants and help them make positive career plans have to take account of the women's marital, personal and financial problems as well, whether or not they have been trained to do counseling.

Educational guidance. Those women who are aware of their need of a course in preparation for reentry may well be bewildered by the range of help available and may need assistance in deciding where to start. Various educational guidance services for adults are now developing to meet this need. Some of them are still in the planning stage, under the auspices of newly created Local Development Councils for Adult Education. They aim to coordinate guidance for adults on everything available in all the universities, colleges and centers in the region. Some are attached to university continuing education departments, as at Sheffield where a network of local volunteers (each able to provide guidance in specialized areas) has been developed.

Another educational guidance service for adults has been set up at Hatfield Polytechnic to supplement the Careers Service on the campus, and this links with local colleges. Almost 500 adults from the entire county and beyond contacted it in its first year and welcomed it, since they had had nowhere else to go for independent advice. The importance of the counselor not "selling" any particular course, or college, but genuinely helping the client to meet her own needs is also stressed by the successful Educational Resource and Information Centre at Cardiff in Wales, set up on the initiative of an O.U. tutor and MSC-financed.

Services have developed in other areas out of the enthusiasm of an individual college advisor or adult education tutor. Many of these advertise in unorthodox places such as launderettes, child welfare clinics, super-markets and bingo halls, as well as the more conventional places such as libraries and job centers. Some operate from a shop, or a caravan, or even through local radio.

Occupational guidance. The most likely starting place for women seeking immediate reentry is the nearest Employment Office or Job Center, especially for manual work or lower-level white-collar jobs. In addition to placement facilities, these offices have employment advisers who are trained to advise applicants with special needs on the range of job and training opportunities available, and to refer them when appropriate to other agencies. In the past, the caliber of advice received here has not been highly rated, nor has that of the Professional and Executive Recruitment branch of the service, to which qualified women are likely to be referred, and which runs a range of support and information services. Nevertheless, some women have been helped by staff who have understood the needs underlying the casual inquiry and have provided support.

I inquired about TOPS courses and so on, but she sensed I was keen on teaching and encouraged me. She persuaded me to go back to the FE place and see about Highers and to come back to her if I didn't get anywhere. She was helpful and said I shouldn't rush into a job I wasn't happy in . . . So she had quite a lot of influence on me, and if she'd said "Well we've got this and this. . ." I'd have probably gone. But I went back to the night school and I never went back to the Job Center. (Marriage breaking up; Glasgow)

Women who are not sure what to do may be referred by either of these agencies or go on their own initiative to an Occupational Guidance Unit (also run by the public Employment Service). These are potentially of great help to women returners, one of the special client groups for which the service was designed. It is free and confidential service for people who wish advice before choosing their occupation. Although apparently admirably suited to the needs of reentrants, the O.G.U. is not widely used by them. While the numbers of women users have steadily increased from 20 percent in 1966 to 33 percent in 1975 and 40 percent in 1977, only about 10 percent of them are in the age group 25 to 39, and only four percent over 40 years, nationally—but there are wide regional variations. Officials feel that the chief value of the interview to reentrants is as a confidence-building exercise.

They did say I was aiming too low. (A divorcee who used O.G.U. when seeking to change jobs)

One reason for lack of use of O.G.U. by reentrants is their ignorance of its existence and its limited accessibility. It is obviously an expensive service in terms of staff resources and time, and there is some reluctance to increase publicity unless further resources can be found for its expansion, since overall demand is already high.

One step forward could be to develop the use of computer-aided guidance (CASCAID, developed in Leicestershire for middle-ability school-leavers) at least as a first stage, and this is being explored, along with other forms of partial self-help guidance and information. The Careers Occupation and Information Service is beginning to open up job libraries to the public, giving them full access to all the literature available in the offices.

Careers Offices are spread widely throughout the U.K. and are run by local education authorities to give help and advice to those in (full-time) school, further or higher education. Although the service is now available to anyone, including adults, not all offices have developed this side of their work or have done so as effectively as Harrow and Sheffield. Yet their potential is admirable, particularly if liaison with the employment and training services, in relation to job opportunities and TOPs courses, could be improved.

For someone like me who has chosen to have babies first and then a career there's no advice. Everything is for young people and there's nothing for us.

Placement

The majority of women taking courses do so with the intention of finding employment afterwards, but in the process usually realize that this will not be easy. They are not always aware of college careers services, or else find that vacancies are suited only to the young. Those still at home rely on the "grapevine" or newspapers and usually try the various public and private agencies.

Employment Service Division. The government employment service holds just over one-third of all unfilled vacancies in the economy; this includes nearly one-half of all manual vacancies and one-fifth of non-manual. The service is entirely free and has recently become much more widely used, chiefly by women returning to the labor market. This has resulted partly from modernization of the service ("goodness me it has changed—fitted carpets") but chiefly from the development of self-selection methods in the new Job Centers where a comparison between 1973 and 1977 showed that placing of clerical and related occupations was up by 70 percent, compared with other offices, and 38 percent overall.

Since 1975, vacancy cards no longer have stated the sex of the employee, but there is some sign of an increasing tendency to stipulate upper age limits. One study found 28 percent of vacancies had upper limits, of which 45 percent stipulated "under age 30" and 77 percent "under 45 years," so that women reentrants could easily be deterred. This was especially the case for jobs in distribution.

If I apply for a job the first question is "What experience have you got?" and the next is "How old are you?"—I'm 42—and then I've had it. If you've been with kids for years how can you possibly have had the experience they're looking for?

The second tier of the placing service—the employment interview—gives more scope for personal advice, although information on reentrants as such is not recorded. Development of various computerized vacancies and some matching systems (such as CAPITAL) may, in time, further help some returners by bringing forward a wider range of vacancies than officials offer.

The Job Center gave me a week at the Merry Chef in the office. That was nice but it didn't go on. They are the best, at least they will go through their files. The others say "No, nothing", and don't even look.

Very few temporary or part-time vacancies are normally listed at the public employment service, and this immediately restricts its usefulness to many reentrants, unless they make their own adaptations.

Professional and executive recruitment. Only about 20 percent of the 21,000 qualified women registered here are over 30 and little attention seems to be given to their special needs, apart from advise on TOPs courses. Yet PER apparently provides a range of services to help job search, including half-day seminars and two-day self-presentation courses. These could be more useful if oriented to women's needs, especially for shorter hours. It charges fees to employers, but those interested in interviewing senior women seem unlikely to use the service.

Special Temporary Employment Programs

Many women have opted out of paying full insurance contributions and do not register as unemployed. They may not therefore be eligible for the range of MSC special programs aimed at helping long-term unemployed and administered through Area Boards. The new STEP is aimed at providing 25,000 jobs in a year for those aged 19 or over, registered unemployed for six months or more (40 percent women), and those aged 26 or over unemployed for a year or more (17 percent women). They are paid wages at the local rate (subject to an MSC maximum of about £65 a week). Jobs are provided by encouraging sponsors to come forward with projects providing worthwhile work, which would not otherwise be carried out. In this way, unemployed teachers may obtain employment in connection with the special programs for young people.

Indications so far are that other older women—especially the unskilled— are getting little help from this scheme and are unlikely to do so unless it is expanded to provide the training, counseling and remedial education they need.

The Private Secretarial Agencies

These agencies place a significant proportion of reentrants to clerical work, especially in London and other large cities where demand is high. Some specialize in part-time or temporary posts. Many have deliberately set out to attract returners: "Manpower" for example, has recently introduced a flexible work scheme that will enable women reentrants to take unpaid extended leave, if they want it, but be guaranteed a similar job on their return. Some private agencies have an advantage to employers over government services in that they employ the staff themselves and thus remove the problems of overhead expenses and of meeting requirements of the employment protection legislation.

At the local level, many small private agencies have grown up over the last few years, often run by women returners who have experienced the problems of reentrants, know the local labor market, and match demands for domestic, nursing, secretarial and other services with women's needs to earn something near home a few hours a week.

Other Methods

Most surveys find that women make a lot of use of newspaper advertisements (much more than men) and of direct application to an employer, especially if they have heard of a possible vacancy from a friend. These are usually reported as the most successful methods.

No, I got the job with no trouble at all—they always like housewives at the mill, and I knew a lot of people there.

It took me about four months to find the job, but I wasn't really trying to be quite honest. Then someone else showed me the ad in the paper, and I thought I'd go along to see about it. He told me that I had the job. I could have fallen through the floor, I was very surprised.

I happened to see a card in a shop window. I went in and was given the job straight away—I wondered what was wrong with it!

It just happened, I was taken on as a Temp secretary while somebody went on holiday and it sort of evolved from there. They were busy and I agreed to become permanent when they asked me. It just happened; I wasn't looking for work.

Looking back on reentry, women often recall their poor interview technique and lack of confidence, but some find the best training is to take the first job that comes and move later if necessary, having gained both confidence and experience.

You feel that the length of time you've been out of work you have to prove yourself all over again. I felt I was being written off. It was no good sticking to the unvarnished truth—you were giving all the "wrong" answers to the employer. You had to gloss over things a bit.

I shall feel so much more confident this time. Before, I didn't even want to go to an employment agency. I was in awe of them. They seem so sophisticated, and they give you tests—at least the Job Center doesn't do that. I knew I could do a job, and do it well, but I'd lost the confidence to go out and sell myself. In the very first week at the shop a lot came back.

RECOMMENDATIONS AND CONCLUSIONS

Proposals for improving facilities for mature women reentering the labor market can be broadly divided into two categories: (a) those aimed at helping the women themselves, and (b) those aimed at modifying the external factors which affect their decisions. The first group relates mainly to the personal level, the second to household and national levels. Some of these facilities will be more appropriate to the period of preparation for reentry, others at the point of reentry, and some in the year or two after getting a job.

Proposals to Help Women Themselves

Confidence. The primary need is that of confidence building, especially for single mothers and those who have been at home for a long period. Given this, women might be readier to demand—and obtain—a range of other services, rather than accepting societal norms of a woman's place and feeling guilty about needing "special" facilities.

Personal counseling or group discussions with others in the same position can provide this. Short "bridging" courses are admirably suitable and need greater development in all parts of the country at lower as well as higher levels. "Assertion training" needs to be a specific element in most vocational training (refresher, induction or in-service) for mature entrants.

Information. The demand for better information about the jobs, education, and training available in a particular locality is evident in the increasing number of local advisory services and networks growing up in the interstices of the official systems. These are extremely valuable, not least by virtue of their independent status, but with better and more stable funding and more coordination could be even more useful.

The Employment Service is often women's starting point, but it needs further structured coordination to overcome the present duality of separate employment-related and education-related advice systems that face re-entrants. This could possibly be achieved through the Careers Service which, with better resources, should be able to help adult women find their way through the jungle of jobs, courses, and advice centers, or direct them to another local service which can do so.

The establishment of a Center of Problems of Career Change (possibly through development of the recently established National Institute for Careers Education and Counseling, sponsored by CRAC and Hatfield Polytechnic) would help to provide a national research forum and a source of information on good practice. It could, for example, draw on the experience of the admirable resettlement services provided by H. M. Forces, even though it would be difficult to develop on a scale sufficient to meet the needs of the several hundred thousand women reentrants.

Educational qualifications. Many women are aware of the need to qualify for reentry. They could be helped considerably if institutions and qualifying bodies relaxed traditional regulations to allow greater flexibility regarding:

(a) age limits and formal entry qualifications;
(b) timing—hours of the day, days of the week, numbers of years, requirements for continuous years of attendance (three days over four years may be easier than four days over three years);
(c) course units and examinations or credit allocations; and

(d) transferability of qualifications and credits within and between institutions.

Course content and teaching methods could be better related to adult needs, and there should be more short reentry, preparatory and refresher courses. Clearer ladders of progression are needed from lower- to higher-level qualifications, particularly those which are of direct vocational relevance.

Many of these proposals to make higher education opportunities accessible to women with family responsibilities have already been detailed by EOC in its response to the D.E.S. consultative document *Higher Education in the 1990's*. This puts forward various models of future development based on alternative predictions of student demand—given an increase of 18-year-olds in the early 1980s, followed by a sharp diminution thereafter. The proposals range from a contraction of the institutions on the one hand, to a widening of their scope to attract mature students on the other. Mature women as such are almost totally neglected in the D.E.S. document, but very many responses by official bodies have stressed the needs of this group.

Much of the scope for these developments is already in the hands of the institutions themselves (and teaching unions see the relevance of them to their interests in protecting members' jobs), but the central organizations must give a more positive lead. The establishment of the National Advisory Council for Adult and Continuing Education in England and Wales (and a similar council in Scotland) could also provide a welcome impetus, if women's needs were specifically diagnosed within each of the Council's priority topics. At present, it has too few resources or powers to be able to achieve any major change—at least in the near future. The rate of progress of Local Development Councils also appears inevitably slow, although they offer the best potential for establishing an educational advisory and guidance service in every region.

Changes needed in regulations for student grants that indirectly restrict the opportunities for mature reentrants, are:
(a) designation of a wider range of courses for mandatory awards;
(b) modification of the regulation refusing grants for courses for which a student would previously have been eligible; and
(c) removal of the upper age limit for research grants and of age and certain other restrictions on the granting of local authority discretionary awards.

A system of entitlement of every person to "x" months of postschool paid education or training over a lifetime could enable women to benefit when they are most likely to need it—often after, rather than before, rearing a family.

Training. Women, especially those with children, need to acquire training as well as other qualifications: basic communication skills may be a prior need. Thus the same proposals can be made, especially the stress on greater flexibility over timing and content: more part-time courses, and allowance for a period to bring a skill up to a previous level, as well as to improve and develop it further. There is also scope for much more use of sections 47 and 48 of the Sex Discrimination Act by MSC and designated training bodies to provide training specifically for reentrants, and resources should be allocated for that purpose. Since training is increasingly seen by employers as a government-financed activity, there is no reason why conditions of eligibility for grants, subsidies, etc. should not include a minimum proportion of reentrant training at every level, other than traditional reluctance to be directive, to condone quotas or to encourage an increased supply of women.

There is an additional need for the rethinking of traditional sex-stereotyped attitudes toward certain masculine skills to give women the necessary preliminary training to enter male occupations. The EOC is particularly concerned that MSC should encourage women to train in new technologies, especially in microprocessing, but currently reported budget plans show little likelihood of this.

In-service refresher or reinduction courses are particularly needed by mature reentrants. For qualified women, graduate trainee schemes could be modified relatively easily. For those who show particular ability but have mixed job histories, accelerated promotion schemes could be devised (similar to those for high-flier young men) to involve a rotation of temporary assignments at various levels. Some scope might be readily available in the jobs of women out on maternity leave. The need for accelerated experience is often greater than the need for more formal qualifications for many returners, and this could be provided in a training "package." On the other hand, some unqualified reentrants soon demonstrate their abilities and within a year or so are performing quasi-management functions. With appropriate training and recognition they could progress further.

Responsibility rests mainly with employers, and large employers in the private sector (as well as the public sector) should all have specific schemes involving keep-in-touch registers and reentry training. Problems of incompatibility between existing staff and reentrants or late entrants to a highly structured internal labor market could be partly overcome by allowing some credit for years spent in domestic responsibilities. In many cases, only adjustments of age assumptions are needed. In others, pre-promotion training courses can be the answer rather than postpromotion, which tends to be the usual practice; ability testing might help indicate potential here. Attention may also be needed to assist reentrants and existing employees to develop successful work-group relationships, since there is evidence of the importance of this in job stability.

Much in-service training is held off the job, so even were a new woman entrant deemed eligible, she would be unable to attend if it were on the weekend, outside working hours, too far away, or involved overnight absence from home. This problem may be overcome by enabling women to plan ahead sufficiently or by finding an alternative course (or site).

Training allowances are usually good, but "vocational" needs redefinition to remove present anomalies and to include study for a lower-level qualification essential for entry to a directly vocational course.

Placement services. In a period of labor surplus there are obviously problems for anyone seeking employment. Nevertheless, recent improvements in placing school-leavers indicate that, where a special group is identified, it is possible to improve its chances in the labor market. The same could be done for women reentrants if more account were taken of their needs and motivations and if more part-time vacancies were available.

The success of the Job Centers through the self-selection system may indicate that further development of self-help and computerized systems would be even more valuable—particularly for those who "just want a job" and not necessarily of the same sort they had before they married. It means that women do not have to nerve themselves to queue up, ask advice, or expose their inadequacies before an unknown official over the counter.

They might, however, be more willing to do so if the employment advisers in the local offices and in PER had more training in assisting women reentrants and would:

(a) take initiatives with employers and training bodies on their behalf;
(b) liaise with local educational advisory bodies;
(c) identify and register the needs of a particular group of women and develop some local scheme to meet them (not necessarily in traditional female occupations);
(d) recognize those with pressing financial needs and guide them toward high-paying opportunities and away from their own low evaluation of themselves;
(e) advise about interview techniques and self-presentation; and
(f) advise about transport facilities and travel-to-work times, about childcare facilities, and even about home-helps when needed. They should also assist applicants in arranging flexible hours and/or parental leave with the prospective employer. Advice on tax or social security may also be needed.

Reentrants and employers should be encouraged to regard attention to these facilities as normal and mutually beneficial rather than special favors or handicaps. Employment service staff are in a position to convey this attitude and could do so more easily if it were recognized public policy (as with school-leavers).

Proposals to Improve Other Factors Affecting Reentry

Public policy is still that of discouraging mothers from working unless absolutely necessary, although it has modified slightly from the 1945

Ministry of Health circular to that of 1968, which states that "day care must be looked at in relation to the view of medical and other authority that early and prolonged separation from the mother is detrimental to the child; wherever possible the younger pre-school child should be at home with his mother." Thus, although children of working mothers are a priority group for nursery care, no pressure is put on such mothers to work (and this policy was endorsed by the Finer Report); in the eligibility conditions for supplementary benefit, they are not obliged to register for work as unemployed men are. Yet single mothers may be caught in a threefold poverty trap of no child care facilities, means-tested benefits, and unsuitable hours, with very little scope for any choice between preferences.

Child care. More research is needed into women's preferences between more child care facilities or more part-time work, but for many there is no choice—or no provision for either.

Clearly more facilities are required both for preschool and for school age children—and they need to be provided by employers and educational establishments, as well as by local authorities, voluntary bodies and private agencies. Local authority responsibility is needed to ensure that provision is adequate to meet local needs for children of all ages, and to facilitate coordination and extension in quantity and quality of what is currently available: "quantity"—in terms of numbers of centers and hours of opening, including school holidays, and "quality" in training of staff and in combining care and education into one preschool service, as a few "nursery centers" are now doing.

Financial facilitation: Earnings. Incentives to return would be greater if pay scales gave more recognition to reentrants' years of experience, either by giving some credit for the period spent out of the labor market (as in teaching), or by counting years prior to marriage and treating the interim as a temporary cessation of work. Obviously this would be easier where women returned to the same employer.

Other suggestions (to recognize the value of women's work through fair job evaluation schemes and to improve the position of the low-paid through the establishment of a national minimum wage) go beyond the focus of this study and could reduce chances of reentry. Nevertheless, payment for part-time work at a pro-rata proportion of the full-time rate for the job would certainly improve incentives for many reentrants.

Tax. There is a danger that there will be some pressure to abolish the wife's earned income relief in order to encourage married women to stay at home. While it is unfair that a family should receive extra tax allowances for a dependent wife and an earning wife at the same time, the anomaly would be best resolved by phasing out the married man's extra tax allowance and replacing it by some system of individual personal allowances for both husband and wife (possibly combined with a "home responsibilities" cash payment where appropriate).

Reentrants' financial problems arising from the low level of the tax threshold and lack of progressiveness at lower levels could be overcome by the introduction of further lower tax bands on a wider range of income.

Other minor reforms currently promised will give greater recognition to the earning wife. The treatment of child care costs as allowable work expenses would directly benefit some, especially those with higher earnings. Action should be taken by the Inland Revenue to reduce the present lengthy delays in putting people into their proper tax coding, which can act as a very real disincentive to taking a job.

Welfare and Social Security benefits. So long as the assumption of dependency remains, the notion that unpaid domestic work is the role of women will remain. Nevertheless, some reforms could be made, and the case is recognized for making the supplementary benefit disregards on wives' and lone parents' earnings more generous. This could be done either by means of a higher flat rate disregard than now or by introducing a tapered disregard.

In the case of lone parents, a nonmeans-tested benefit similar to the widow's benefit (but noncontributory) would create more of a financial incentive for lone parents to take paid employment. Proposals for higher child benefits seem the only effective way to deal with many of the problems created by other means-tested benefits. More limited reforms would be a review of level of disregards allowed for wives' earnings, or a further reduction of the "hours" eligibility for F.I.S.

Working hours. There is no doubt that greater flexibility in working hours is the single greatest demand from women reentrants in Britain. This can mean part-time, flexitime, late shifts, job-sharing schemes, extra paid or unpaid leave, or simply other than full-time or "different from standard" working hours. Employers benefit from having a wider pool of labor available and are enabled to meet their own peaks in demand during the day, week, month or year. But it should apply at *every level*—even management jobs can be limited to smaller areas and telephone contact with home maintained; increased shift working in services as well as manufacturing implies varied management hours, too. If careful preliminary thought is given to administration and planning, under-used plant or higher costs should not result. Indeed, now that one major overhead—national insurance contributions—is proportionate to earnings, it need not be more expensive to employ two part-timers and, given their higher productivity in some occupations, it is likely to be cheaper.

More positive trade union attitudes to negotiating agreements over a greater variety of working hours could be helpful to members of both sexes. This could overcome some union ambivalence over part-time work, which is opposed because it undercuts negotiated terms and conditions (even if more attention is given to insuring pro-rata terms by some unions) but accepted because it provides a useful marginal element of workers who can be the first to be let go in times of labor surplus.

Government Statistical Sources

More basic statistical information is needed by most government departments on the patterns of women's lives: how soon and how often women start and stop paid employment; how long and why they remain housewives; what hours they work on return; and how these features relate to other aspects of the labor market, to family or national circumstances. This may necessitate some revision of standard surveys and careful planning to ensure that questions in new inquiries for specific purposes are formulated in a way that is relevant to women's lives. Without this information, future planning of the economy is inevitably handicapped.

CONCLUSIONS

Women's reentry to the labor market in Britain is often spread over several years, with an "in-and-out" period while the children are young, followed by a "part-time" phase, which may become full time as the children become older or leave home. This pattern depends on the woman's job ambitions, on the family's finances, and on the local labor market. Women without husbands seem more likely to work full time or to seek to qualify themselves for better-paid or more satisfying jobs; but policy initiatives based on financial need may be dangerously selective in categorizing some women or families as "more deserving," except in so far as they attempt to bring them up to the same level, so that real choices may be exercised.

The government has not started to consider the impact of its policies on the family; and there is a danger that when it does, there will be greater social and financial pressure on women to stay at home. Yet there is little evidence that women have any desire to do so full time; even some of those with young children would prefer part-time work, if satisfactory arrangements could be made for child care. There is every indication that women in their thirties will continue to return to work (a million between 1976 and 1986) on a shorter working week, and that many will successfully find jobs in the developing service industries. The chief question that remains is: Will they continue to be a secondary work force, with little training, no promotion, low pay and benefits, and limited to a few occupations? If they do not, will they be in more direct competition with men than they have in the past, and what will be the effect of this?

National concentration on male unemployment can be only a short-term expedient—the numbers of women seeking work can hardly be ignored much longer—and government attention needs to be given to developing industrial, employment and social policies that are appropriate to the needs of different types of families, on the assumption that both men and women are likely to have parental responsibilities at some stage and that both are likely to seek paid employment for the greater part of their adult lives.

BIBLIOGRAPHY

Central Policy Review Staff. *Services for Young Children with Working Mothers.* HMSO, 1978.

Central Statistical Office. *Social Trends No. 8, 1977.* HMSO, 1977.

Civil Service Department. *Employment of Women in the Civil Service.* 1972.

Department of Education and Science. *Adult Education.* (Report of Russell Committee). HMSO, 1973.

——. *Statistics of Education* 1976 Vol. 3. HMSO, 1977.

—— and Scottish Education Department. *Higher Education into the 1990s.* 1978.

Department of Employment. *Employment Gazette.* HMSO, June 1977, April 1978.

——. *Women and Work: A Statistical Survey.* Manpower Paper No. 9. HMSO, 1974.

Department of Health and Social Security. *Report of Committee on One-Parent Families.* (Finer Report). Cmnd 5629. HMSO, 1974.

——. *Social Assistance.* July 1978.

Equal Opportunities Commission. *Annual Report.* HMSO, 1976, 1977.

——. *Fresh Start.* 1978.

——. *"I want to work . . . but what about the kids?"* 1978.

——. Research Bulletin (forthcoming).

——Catalogue of free publications.

Equal Pay and Opportunity Campaign. "Work and the Family." 1978.

Fonda, N., and Moss, P., eds. *Mothers in Employment.* Brunel University, 1976.

Home Office. "Equality for Women." White Paper, Cmnd 5724. HMSO, 1974.

Hunt, A. *Management Attitudes and Practices towards Women at Work.* O.P.C.S. Social Survey Division. HMSO, 1975.

——. *A Survey of Women's Employment.* Government Social Survey. HMSO, 1968.

Leicester, C. "Increased Labour Force Participation and the Growing Employment Opportunities for Women." GN No. 115. Institute of Manpower Studies, University of Sussex, 1978.

Lindley, R., ed. *Britain's Medium Term Employment Prospects.* University of Warwick Manpower Research Group, 1978.

Greenhalgh, C. "A Labour Supply Function for Married Women in Great Britain." *Economica.* August 1977.

Manpower Services Commission. *Training Opportunities for Women.* 1975.

——. *Annual Report.* 1977–78.

——. *Review and Plan.* 1978.

——. *TOPS Review.* 1978.

Michaels, R. *New Opportunities for Women.* Hatfield Polytechnic, 1973.

Miller, R. *Equal Opportunities: A Careers Guide for Men and Women.* Penguin, 1978.

————. "Second Chance Education." Good Housekeeping Editorial Bulletin. 1978.

Moss, P. "Forward from Finer: Jobs for Lone Parents." 1977.

National Advisory Centre on Careers for Women. *Returners.* 1975.

National Council for One Parent Families. *Annual Report.* 1977–78.

Nissel, M. "Taxes and Benefits: Does Redistribution Help the Family?" Policy Studies Institute. 1978.

Oakley, A. *Sociology of Housework.* Martin Robertson, 1974.

Office of Population Censuses and Surveys. *General Household Survey,* 1976. HMSO, 1978.

————. *Demographic Review 1977.* HMSO, 1978.

Ollerrenshaw, K. and Flude, C. "Returning to Teaching." University of Lancaster, 1974.

Page, N. "The Mature Woman and Opportunities for Employment—The Manchester Experiments." 1977.

Peltman, B. "Woman Power: an Underutilised Resource—Bibliography and Review." MCB Monograph, 1977.

Royal Commission on Distribution of Income and Wealth. *Report No. 6: Lower Incomes,* Cmnd 7175, and *Background Paper No. 5, The Causes of Poverty,* by Layard, Piachaud, Stewart et. al. HMSO, 1978.

Services Resettlement Bulletin. *Resettlement Handbook.* Institute of Army Education, 1978.

Supplementary Benefits Commission. *Annual Report.* Cmnd 6910, 1976. HMSO, 1977.

Trades Union Congress: *1978 Report.*

————. "Report of 44 TUC Women's Conference." 1978.

————. "Statement of Priorities in Continuing Education."

————. "Charter for Women at Work."

6

United States

by ALICE M. YOHALEM

INTRODUCTION

Although a commitment to "maximum employment" was legislated by the United States Congress as long ago as 1946 and iterated in the Full Employment and Balanced Growth Act of 1978, fears of inflation have severely limited actions to stimulate demand. Instead, attention has focused upon structural defects that have impeded the employment of specific population groups. From the 1960s, employment policy has placed emphasis upon remedial services to assist these "target" groups to negotiate the labor market. This was a shift from primary reliance on macroeconomic policy for stimulating employment to a therapeutic strategy to treat segments of the population who, even in the best of times, have been demonstrably unable to secure places for themselves with the job market.

An array of employment and training programs was developed, and targets fluctuated with changing diagnoses of labor supply pathologies and with periodic pressures for aid by diverse constituencies. Over time, recipients have ranged from adult males, displaced by technological innovations, to youth, the poverty-stricken and minorities—often overlapping categories—who are currently the principal beneficiaries of employment-related assistance.

Programmatic response to the employment problems of women *in the aggregate* has been minimal. Instead, women have been dealt with in terms

217

of other attributes, such as youth, minority status and low income, that are deemed to transcend gender as determinants of need. The fact that being female is itself a barrier to progress within the labor market has been recognized, not through service interventions, but through a national commitment to equal employment opportunity as expressed in various governmental measures. Yet even if the goals of these initiatives were strictly enforced, which they are not, serious problems would remain because early social conditioning and differential treatment in the educational system have produced sex-linked aspirations that have effectively limited the number of women with employment qualifications on a par with men. Nevertheless, American women's preparation and expectations are beginning to show a closer resemblance to those of men, and anti-discrimination measures are giant steps toward protecting women from prejudicial practices that have prevented them from competing with men on equal terms. At the very least, these edicts are symbols of changing societal attitudes toward women's right to engage in gainful unexploitative employment.

A concentration upon the employment problems of men, particularly young men, is commonly justified as holding promise of a greater payoff than attention to the problems of women essentially because of different assumptions about work attachment. Young men inferentially will be continuous long-term workers, so that expenditures on their training and upgrading are warranted as a fair price to pay to produce the prime labor supply for the future. Investments in services for women are deemed less rational because women have tended to maintain weaker lifetime linkages to the labor force than men. Because of presumptions about female labor force interruptions and withdrawal, in conjunction with inferences about working women's supplementary role as wage earners, policy makers have judged that the employment problems of most adult women who reenter the labor force do not create sufficient inconvenience to individuals or families nor disequilibrium in the market to require the kind of comprehensive services that were established for the manifestly hard-to-employ.

The fact that the jobs available to reentrants are principally of low quality in terms of wages, fringe benefits, regularity of employment, working conditions, job security, and advancement did not give rise to concern because most of these women have been wives of employed husbands, and policy makers saw no urgency to allocate funds to help individuals unlikely to become charges upon the public treasury or clamorous claimants for attention.

Reentrants who are in financial jeopardy because their husbands are chronically unemployed or underemployed or who are themselves low-income household heads have been eligible for government-funded training and other assistance if unable to obtain employment on their own, although eligibility has not necessarily assured the provision of aid. Nonwhite and Hispanic women are overrepresented among both of these groups.

In recent years, increasing numbers of all reentrants or delayed entrants to the labor force have been women without husbands or wives whose husbands have been unable to provide adequate family support. Not only have many of the jobs that previously lured mature women back to the labor force been insufficient for those who have to provide sole or substantial family support, but reentrants are competing with an expanding pool of younger women who are demonstrating a strengthened attachment to work. All married women can no longer be viewed complacently as a labor reserve that will readily expand or contract according to the demands of the market. More and more of them appear to be committed to continuous work activity, and sizable numbers of reentrants and delayed entrants to the labor force expect their renewed or belated participation to last until retirement.

While the number of jobs held by women has substantially increased since 1960, the number of women job seekers has increased even more rapidly. The fact that additions of women workers to the job rolls imply sustained demand for female employees, and that some amount of adult female unemployment reflects initial job search after reentry, does not mean that the job aspirations of most mature women are being fulfilled. Apart from underemployed women and those among the unemployed who cannot find jobs, there are many potential workers among homemakers who are discouraged from entering the labor force by the conviction that their job search will be futile. The substantial reservoir of women who would like to work is not reflected in unemployment statistics that ignore persons who have either abandoned job search or who do not undertake search because they fear rejection in the market. The true measure of unemployment is not job search but job aspiration. Women's desire to work cannot be accurately measured because it is suppressed in the face of bleak prospects.

The extent to which reentrants' work aspirations can be fulfilled depends ultimately upon the degree to which the American economy provides sufficient employment opportunities for all potential workers. At the present time, slackening economc growth and rising inflation are provoking grave concern about the nation's ability to create and maintain enough jobs to meet the needs of the population of working age. The fulfillment of the work goals of women who wish to resume or belatedly enter market work is closely dependent upon the stance of the government toward solving the nation's economic problems. If inflation is fought by forswearing policies designed to generate and maintain full employment, potential reentrants are likely to be among the prime victims because many women will refrain from trying to realize their work aims.

It is not beyond the realm of possibility that insufficient job opportunities and fears of the labor market consequences of increased reentry could engender policies to actively discourage married women from engaging in market work. The rise in adult female labor force participation is being cited as a cause of persisting high rates of teenage unemployment, particularly among nonwhites, although there is no conclusive evidence that these groups are job competitors. Whether the unavailability of adult women would stimulate the employment of male teenagers in occupations which women have traditionally filled is moot, although young females may be acceptable substitutes. Aside from the injustice of making women the scapegoats for a situation that is fundamentally due to neglect and indifference on the part of the society as a whole, any serious attempt to impede the employment of adult women undoubtedly would meet strong resistance, in light of the transformation of American women's attitudes and behavior.

In the long run, demographic and behavioral changes linked to women's relation to work may obviate the need for programs to assist reentry or delayed entry to the labor force as continuous female work attachment approaches the norm. In the meantime, a considerable segment of young women will probably withdraw from the labor force and, when they are ready to return, they will be at a disadvantage relative to women and men who have remained at work. Policies to meet their employment needs go hand in hand with attempts to fashion a full employment economy.

WOMEN'S WORK: TRENDS AND INFLUENCES

Labor Force Participation

Reentry of American women to the labor force assumed major proportions during World War II when large numbers of married women took paid jobs in response to strenuous recruitment efforts to expand the civilian work force.* Although many women withdrew from the labor market after the war, either because their jobs were eliminated or they wished to commence or resume family-centered activities, the female sector of the work force never regressed to its prewar level. Once the downward trend of the immediate postwar period was reversed, the influx of women to the labor force proceeded at a rapid rate. The size of the total labor force grew from about 64 million to 103 million between 1950 and September 1978, and over 60 percent of the growth was generated by females. Accordingly, the ratio of women per 100 men in the labor force rose from 41 to about 71, and women's representation in the work force increased from 29 percent to 41 percent.

The role of increased population in the expansion of the female labor force has been less significant than women's growing propensity to work. The adult female population, 20 to 64 years of age, increased by 17 million,

*In the United States, the "civilian labor force" broadly defined, consists of persons, other than military personnel, who have been employed during the survey week and unemployed persons who were available for work and had looked for jobs within the preceding four weeks. Employed persons include those who worked for pay and unpaid workers in family-operated enterprises who worked for 15 weekly hours or more.

or 39 percent, between 1950 and 1977, but the number of women of these ages in the labor force rose by 18.5 million, or 115 percent. In contrast, the growth of the adult male labor force of these ages—up to 11.8 million or 30 percent over the same period—did not keep pace with a 37 percent increase in the number of males, aged 20 to 64 years.

Population projections indicate that women will outnumber men throughout the remainder of the century as they have done since 1950, and that the numerical gap between the sexes will widen further. The declining youth population in combination with a surplus of adult females has important implications for reentry into the labor force. Some number of mothers will undoubtedly continue to exit from work, and a shortage of young workers and possible insufficiency of adult male workers could enhance their reentry job opportunities. At the same time, these circumstances might strengthen female work commitment if they lead to more attractive employment for young women.

The expansion of the female work force was not uniform among all age groups. Most of the growth in the 1950s was attributable to women aged 45 to 64 years, many of whom resumed working or initially entered the work force during the war and remained at work thereafter, or had entered employment after the war in response to job opportunities in expanding sectors of the economy which traditionally employed large numbers of women. By 1960, 45-to 50-year-old women had the highest labor force participation rate among women aged 20 years and over, in a marked shift from a decade earlier when 20- to 24-year-old women were in the lead (Table 6.1).

There has since been a subsequent rearrangement of the age pattern of female labor force participation as the largest increases shifted to ages below 45. The 20- to 24-year-old age group regained its traditional front position by 1970, and the participation rate of women aged 25 to 34 years advanced sharply and has continued to escalate mainly due to increased work continuity and shorter absences from the labor force. Acceleration of labor force participation among women aged 20 to 44 years has been accompanied by a decreased rate of growth in the work rate of 45- to 54-year-old women and a drop in the 55 to 64 year rate, possibly due in some measure to growing competition between older reentrants and young continuous workers.

The labor force participation rates for nonwhite women customarily have been considerably higher than those for white women. In 1954, the nonwhite rate was 46 percent compared to a 33 percent white female rate. In recent years, however, there has been a narrowing of the racial differential as the result of a sharp rise in white women's work rates. The change has been greatest among women between the ages of 25 and 64, particularly in the 35 to 44 year range where the nonwhite rate rose from 58 percent in 1954 to 67 percent in 1978, at the same time that the white rate grew from 39 percent to 63 percent.

Table 6.1   Civilian Labor Force Participation Rates by Sex and Age,
           Selected Years, 1950−1978

| | Female Participation Rates | | | | Male Participation Rates | | | |
Age	1950	1960	1970	1978[a]	1950	1960	1970	1978[a]
Total, 16 years & over	33.9	37.7	43.3	51.0	86.4	83.3	79.7	77.6
16 and 17 years	30.1	29.1	34.9	44.9	53.1	46.0	47.0	47.6
18 and 19 years	51.3	50.9	53.6	61.3	75.9	69.3	66.7	70.4
20−24 years	46.0	46.1	57.7	68.5	87.9	88.1	83.3	85.5
25−34 years	34.0	36.0	45.0	64.2	96.0	97.5	96.4	95.5
35−44 years	39.1	43.4	51.1	63.1	97.6	97.7	96.9	96.0
45−54 years	37.9	49.8	54.4	58.9	95.8	95.7	94.2	91.3
55−64 years	27.0	37.2	43.0	42.5	86.9	86.8	83.0	74.1
65 years and over	9.7	10.8	9.7	8.2	45.8	33.1	26.8	20.6

[a]November 1978.

Source: *Employment and Training Report of the President*, 1978; and U.S. Department of
        Labor, Bureau of Labor Statistics, *Employment and Earnings* 15, no. 12 (Decem-
        ber 1978).

Work Experience. Since women have been especially prone to intermittency of work and to labor force withdrawal and reentry, their numbers in the
work force over the span of a year tend to be much larger than their
participation in one particular period. In 1976, 44.7 million women, 16
years old and over, worked at some time during the year, 6.3 million more
than the average size of the female labor force at any one time, and double
the excess of males with work experience over male labor force participants.

     The work experience rate of women of all ages to 65 years increased
betwen 1950 and 1976, in contrast to that of men which fell in every age
group, except 16 to 19 years. Although the largest proportion of females
who work during the year has tended to be in the 20 to 24 year age group, the
greatest percent increase between 1950 and 1976 was shown by women aged
25 to 34 years, up 51 percent.

     In recent years, a proportionate increase in female part-time and part-
year employment has occurred simultaneously with an increase in the
percentage of female year-round, full-time workers. More than half of the
45 million women with work experience in 1976 were employed year-
round, and over two-fifths of the total worked full time (35 hours or more
per week) year-round (50 to 52 weeks). The incidence of full-time, full-year
employment increased with age, reaching a peak of 55 percent at ages 55 to
59. Thus, while the largest proportion of women with some amount of
work experience in that year was in the 20 to 24 year range, women of late
middle age showed the greatest tendency to work year-round at full-time
jobs.

Fifteen million women, or one-third of all those with work experience in 1976, worked at part-time jobs, mostly for fewer than 50 weeks. Largely due to family demands, women aged 25 to 44 years were more likely to work part-year than younger or older women. Part-time jobs, on the other hand, were most common in the youngest age group where work tends to be combined with school attendance, and in the oldest, where it is combined with retirement. However, in every age group, at least one-quarter of all women with work experience were employed part time.

The great majority of women working part time report that they do so voluntarily. This was the case for four-fifths of the 11 million women who were working part time in November 1978. The remainder would have preferred full-time employment if it had been available.

Many women move from part- to full-time jobs as they become older and their household responsibilities decrease. The National Longitudinal Survey of women who were 30 to 44 years old in 1967 found a rise in the proportion of full-time employees between 1967 and 1972 among women who were working both years. Full-time employment among white women in the survey rose from 64 to 78 percent of the total during the five-year period, and among black women, from 65 to 70 percent.[1]

Unemployment

Unemployment among women tends to be higher than among men, and has been on the rise since 1970. Although the number of employed women rose by 112 percent between 1950 and 1977, the number of unemployed women rose by 211 percent. Women represented 32 percent of the unemployed in the earlier year, but 48 percent in the latter. The highest percentage of unemployed adult females has consistently been in the 35 to 44 year age group where the disparity between male and female unemployment rates is widest (Table 6.2). However, the incidence of unemployment among women progressively decreases with age. Lower rates of unemployment for older women partially reflect the tendency of reentrants to exit from the labor force when job search is unproductive, as well as a low rate of voluntary job change at advanced ages.

The November 1978 unemployment rates for wives with unemployed husbands, 16.6 percent, and for female family heads, 7.8 percent, were much higher than the rate for wives with employed husbands, 5.1 percent. Not only are both of the former groups of women under greater pressure to obtain jobs, but they include a disproportion of nonwhite women whose unemployment rates, in general, are considerably greater than those of white women.

Men under the age of 65 in 1977 had a longer median duration of unemployment (eight weeks) than their female contemporaries (six weeks). While the period of unemployment lengthens with age among both women and men, all adult women tend to spend less time on job search

Table 6.2 Unemployment Rates of Women and Men by Age, Selected Years, 1950—1977

Year and Age	Percent of Labor Force Unemployed			Ratio of Women's Unemployment Rates to Men's
	Both Sexes	Women	Men	
1950				
16 and 17 years	13.6	14.2	13.3	1.1
18 and 19 years	11.2	9.8	12.3	.8
20 to 24 years	7.7	6.9	8.1	.9
25 to 34 years	4.8	5.7	4.4	1.3
35 to 44 years	3.8	4.4	3.6	1.2
45 to 54 years	4.2	4.5	4.0	1.1
55 to 64 years	4.8	4.5	4.9	.9
65 years and over	4.5	3.4	4.8	.7
Total, 16 years and over	5.3	5.7	5.1	1.1
1960				
16 and 17 years	15.5	15.4	15.5	1.0
18 and 19 years	14.1	13.0	15.0	.9
20 to 24 years	8.7	8.3	8.9	.9
25 to 34 years	5.2	6.3	4.8	1.3
35 to 44 years	4.1	4.8	3.8	1.3
45 to 54 years	4.1	4.2	4.1	1.0
55 to 64 years	4.2	3.4	4.6	.7
65 years and over	3.8	2.8	4.2	.7
Total, 16 years and over	5.5	5.9	5.4	1.1
1970				
16 and 17 years	17.1	17.4	16.9	1.0
18 and 19 years	13.8	14.4	13.4	1.1
20 to 24 years	8.2	7.9	8.4	.9
25 to 34 years	4.2	5.7	3.4	1.7
35 to 44 years	3.1	4.4	2.4	1.8
45 to 54 years	2.8	3.5	2.4	1.5
55 to 64 years	2.7	2.7	2.8	1.0
65 years and over	3.2	3.1	3.3	.9
Total, 16 years and over	4.9	5.9	4.4	1.3
1977				
16 and 17 years	19.9	20.4	19.5	1.0
18 and 19 years	16.2	16.8	15.6	1.1
20 to 24 years	10.9	11.2	10.7	1.0
25 to 34 years	6.4	7.7	5.6	1.4
35 to 44 years	4.4	5.8	3.5	1.7
45 to 54 years	4.0	5.1	3.2	1.6
55 to 64 years	3.9	4.5	3.5	1.3
65 years and over	5.1	4.7	5.2	.9
Total, 16 years and over	7.0	8.2	6.2	1.3

Source: *Employment and Training Report of the President*, 1978.

than men. The propensity of many reentrants to exit from the work force if they are unable to obtain a job within a reasonable time is probably responsible for much of this sex differential.

Marital Status

The changes in the size of the total female labor force are principally due to the increased participation of married women with husbands present. Since these women predominate among the adult female population, alterations in their work behavior have had a major influence upon the aggregate female labor force. Between 1950 and 1977, the number of wives increased by 12 million but the number in the labor force rose by 14.7 million, representing a gain of 117 percent in their participation rate (Table 6.3).

The percentage of never-married women in their early twenties rose by more than one-half between 1960 and 1977, alone, along with a 38 percent increase in the proportion aged 25 to 34 years. In addition, between 1950 and 1978, the annual divorce rate per 1,000 persons rose from 2.6 to 5.1, most of the increase having occurred in the last decade. In 1950, about three percent of all ever-married 25- to 64-year-old females were divorced; in 1977, almost nine percent of this group were divorced. In the past, widows aged 35 to 54 years outnumbered divorcees, but this trend has been reversed recently due to both improved male longevity and the higher incidence of divorce.

Since middle-aged women whose marriages have been terminated by death or divorce are less likely to remarry than men of similar ages, and wives have higher survival rates than husbands, the older age groups within the prime working population contain a surplus of women without spouses. These women are prominent among reentrants to the labor force, either because they are without other means of support or because of the impact of inflation upon the fixed incomes of those who have been subsisting on survivors' benefits, pensions, social security or alimony.

Between 1950 and 1977, a 38 percent increase in husband-wife families was overshadowed by an 110 percent increase in families with female heads who represented 13.6 percent of all families in the latter year. In 1977, 65 percent of women family heads were between 30 and 64 years of age, and 40 percent were 35 to 54 years old. Two million black families, one of every three, were headed by a woman in 1977, compared with five million, or one of nine, white families.

Although the participation rate of female family heads tends to be higher than the rate for married women with husbands present, the labor force participation of all mothers of children under the age of 18 years, regardless of family status, increased almost sixfold between 1940 and 1977 in an unanticipated and remarkable break with tradition. By 1977, more than

Table 6.3 Female Labor Force Participation Rates by Marital Status and Age, Selected Years, 1950 to 1977

Year and Marital Status	Total Number[a] (000)	Percent of Total Females							
		Total	Under 20 Years[a]	20–24 Years	25–34 Years	35–44 Years	45–54 Years	55–64 Years	65 Years and Over
1950									
Single	5,258	46.2	22.8	73.0	78.7	75.3	70.6	57.0	19.7
Married, spouse present	7,686	21.5	16.4	26.0	22.3	26.5	23.0	13.1	4.5
Married, spouse absent	936	46.7	33.7	48.0	52.6	57.5	50.3	34.5	10.1
Widowed or divorced	2,641	32.6	45.0	65.5	69.0	70.3	57.7	35.8	7.7
Total	16,522	28.9	22.6	42.8	31.7	34.9	32.8	23.4	7.8
1960									
Single	5,263	42.7	23.2	72.8	78.9	77.9	75.9	64.8	23.1
Married, spouse present	12,354	30.7	26.0	31.1	28.0	36.5	39.3	25.2	6.8
Married, spouse absent	1,245	48.5	32.7	49.1	57.4	59.4	59.2	44.3	12.6
Widowed	2,195	27.9	38.9	47.1	53.2	64.7	65.6	45.4	10.0
Divorced	1,312	70.6	56.6	73.3	77.2	80.9	78.9	64.9	23.8
Total	22,369	34.5	23.9	44.9	35.2	42.6	46.7	35.0	10.4
1970									
Single	6,896	50.7	34.6	69.8	78.5	74.5	73.3	64.9	18.7
Married, spouse present	17,418	39.2	35.6	46.3	38.0	45.6	47.3	34.6	8.0
Married, spouse absent	1,602	50.2	39.5	54.6	52.9	58.4	60.0	47.7	13.6
Widowed	2,551	26.4	36.8	55.6	57.0	62.0	65.4	51.0	9.1
Divorced	2,081	69.5	57.1	73.9	76.5	80.3	79.4	67.5	22.2
Total	30,547	41.4	34.9	56.1	44.9	50.3	52.5	42.1	10.0
1977									
Single	9,470	58.9	47.2	70.9	83.8	73.2	74.7	64.4	15.8
Married, spouse present	22,377	46.6	47.5	59.4	52.2	56.0	56.0	36.1	7.0
Married, spouse absent	1,715	55.1	47.7	55.9	67.3	57.9	58.1	46.5	11.3
Widowed	2,251	22.5	(b)	(b)	59.9	68.9	62.9	45.3	8.0
Divorced	3,561	73.2	(b)	(b)	82.3	81.2	79.3	62.5	17.9
Total	39,374	48.0	47.5	65.0	59.3	59.6	56.1	41.1	8.4

[a] 14 years and over for 1950 and 1960; 16 years and over, 1970 and 1976. [b] Percent not shown where base is less than 75,000 in 1977.

Sources: U.S. Department of Commerce, Bureau of the Census, U.S. Census of Population, 1955, and U.S. Department of Labor, Bureau of Labor Statistics, Special Labor Force Report, no. 216 (1978).

half of these mothers were in the work force and their participation rate (50.7 percent) surpassed that for all women (48 percent).

⌐What was especially remarkable was that the rise in the work rate of mothers in husband-wife families with children under 18 almost tripled between 1950 and 1977. Even more notable was the increase in the work activity of wives with children under six; and most dramatic was the heightened participation of those with children under three years of age whose rate of increase was 70 percent greater than that of women household heads with children of similar ages (Table 6.4).

Closely associated with mothers' propensity to work is family size as well as children's ages, and the fact that in 1976 the fertility of American women reached an historic low of 65.8 births per 1,000 women aged 15 to 44 has important implications for women's future work behavior. A 1977 reversal of the downward trend was interpreted by some as the start of an era of rising births, but this now appears to have been a premature inference, since provisional data for 1978 show a slight downturn in the birth rate. While there is still quite a while to go before the last of the women born during the postwar baby boom will no longer be of childbearing age, the low-birth pattern of this group is now entering its second decade. In 1977, the average number of children in families with any children was about two; just seven years earlier, the average was 2.29. Black women's birth rates have always been considerably higher than those for white women, but these also have been exhibiting a decline.

Education

Most Americans under the age of 65 in 1977 had completed at least four years of high school which is equivalent to 12 years of total schooling to about age 18. In 1950, this had been the case for only age groups under 35 years. Before 1977, more women than men terminated their schooling at high school completion; in 1977 women college students below the age of 22 outnumbered males. At the graduate level (five or more years of college) men are disproportionately represented.

In general, increases in the years of schooling of American women have been associated with rises in their labor force participation. However, in no age group has the proportion of women in the workforce with the highest educational attainment yet matched the participation rate of men with the least schooling, although the gap between the sexes at the peak school level has been rapidly shrinking (Table 6.5).

Nevertheless, even women with the least amount of education (eight years or less of elementary school) increased their labor force activity between 1967 and 1977, but their gain was much less than that of women with more schooling who are better able to qualify for available jobs.

While female educational achievement at the highest academic and professional levels has not caught up to that of males, the gap is closing.

Table 6.4   Labor Force Participation Rates for Ever-Married Women[a] by Presence and Age of Children, Selected Years, 1950 to 1977

Marital Status, Presence and Age of Children	Labor Force Participation Rates (percent)			
	1977	1970	1960	1950
Married women, husband present	46.6	40.8	39.0	23.8
No children under 18 years	44.9	42.2	34.7	30.3
With children under 18 years	48.2	39.7	27.6	18.4
Children 6 to 17 years only	55.6	49.2	39.0	28.3
Children under 6 years	39.3	30.3	18.6	11.9
Children 3 to 5 years, none under 3 years	46.4	37.0	25.1	(NA)
Children under 3 years	34.3	25.8	15.3	(NA)
Other ever-married women[b]	41.8	39.1	40.0	37.8
No children under 18 years	36.7	33.4	35.7	33.7
With children under 18 years	65.3	60.6	55.5	54.9
Children 6 to 17 years only	70.4	67.3	66.2	63.6
Children under 6 years	55.0	50.7	39.8	41.4
Children 3 to 5 years, none under 3 years	63.8	58.8	51.7	(NA)
Children under 3 years	44.0	43.6	32.4	(NA)

NA: Not available.
[a] Civilian noninstitutional population 16 years and over in 1977 and 1970, 14 years and over in 1960 and 1950.
[b] Includes widowed, divorced, and married, husband absent.
Sources: U.S. Department of Commerce, Bureau of the Census, "A Statistical Portrait of Women in the U.S.," *Current Population Reports, Special Studies* Series No. 58 (April 1976) p. 23; and U.S. Department of Labor, Bureau of Labor Statistics, "Marital and Family Characteristics of Workers: March 1977," *Special Labor Force Report* No. 216 (1978).

Still women's career choices as evidenced by field of study remain concentrated in traditional areas, despite substantial inroads to some nontraditional fields, particularly medicine and law.

Place of Residence

In 1950, about 15 percent of the population was living on farms, but less than four percent were doing so in 1976. An outward movement to more remote areas, oriented to recreation, energy supply, retirement or small manufacturing, has recently occurred. This migration has stimulated demand for new or expanded services in nonmetropolitan locales and may have opened up opportunities for female rural residents who have been experiencing difficulty in obtaining nonfarm entry and reentry employ-

Table 6.5 Labor Force Participation Rates of Men and Women 25 to 64 Years Old, by Age and Educational Attainment, March 1967 and 1977

Educational Attainment	25 to 34 years		35 to 44 years		45 to 54 years		55 to 64 years	
	1967	1977	1967	1977	1967	1977	1967	1977
Men								
Total	97.3	95.2	97.4	95.6	95.4	90.9	83.6	74.4
Less than 4 years of high school	94.7	92.2	97.6	90.2	93.1	85.9	79.9	65.9
Elementary: 8 years or less[a]	93.3	87.5	94.4	85.5	91.9	83.9	78.0	63.6
Hish school: 1 to 3 years	97.8	94.6	96.3	93.8	94.9	88.4	85.0	70.1
High school: 4 years	98.9	96.4	98.4	97.3	97.7	92.4	89.1	78.4
College: 1 year or more	96.3	95.3	99.1	97.9	97.4	95.4	90.4	85.1
College: 1 to 3 years	95.6	94.2	98.6	97.8	96.9	93.4	88.2	82.4
College: 4 years or more	96.8	96.2	99.5	97.9	97.7	96.9	92.1	87.6
Women								
Total	41.4	59.3	47.8	59.6	50.9	56.1	41.7	41.1
Less than 4 years of high school	37.9	45.2	45.2	50.4	44.9	46.8	37.5	33.4
Elementary: 8 years or less[a]	35.2	36.7	42.2	42.7	43.4	44.2	35.2	31.1
High school: 1 to 3 years	39.4	48.7	47.7	54.8	46.8	49.1	42.5	36.9
High school: 4 years	41.4	57.8	48.8	61.4	54.8	59.1	45.1	45.1
College: 1 year or more	45.9	67.6	50.3	66.1	59.2	64.6	54.6	51.2
College: 1 to 3 years	40.2	62.3	45.9	63.3	52.9	58.9	47.7	49.1
College: 4 years or more	52.6	72.4	55.8	69.0	67.2	71.1	63.0	53.5

[a] Includes persons reporting no school years completed.

Source: U.S. Department of Labor, Bureau of Labor Statistics, "Educational Attainment of Workers: March 1977," *Special Labor Force Report* No. 209 (1978).

ment. While women's work rate increased in all types of communities between 1970 and 1977, the sharpest growth in the participation rates of middle-aged women took place in nonmetropolitan areas. Female unemployment rates in agricultural communities tend to be lower than in nonfarm locations, but this is principally because the absence of work opportunities for women in these areas discourages them from ever entering the labor force.

Employment Characteristics

Despite changes in women's work participation in recent decades, there has been no major modification in the sex composition of industrial employment. Women still predominate in the same industries in which they were concentrated in 1950 (Table 6.6). In the '70s, as in the '50s, the service industry was the leading employer of women, and with government, wholesale and retail trade, and manufacturing provided most of the employment for the female additions to the labor force in that period.

Female white-collar employment increased at the expense of other occupational categories between 1960 and 1978 (Table 6.7). Currently, women aged 25 to 34 years are the most likely females to have white-collar jobs, particularly professional and technical employment, which is indicative of improved educational attainment and of some inroads into nontraditional fields, although most women professionals, like other women workers, remain clustered in predominantly female occupations.

Sex differentials in earnings are facts of economic life in the United States. Despite rapid advances in women's educational attainment, labor force participation and lifetime work attachment, there remains a considerable gap between the full-time earnings of female and male workers in similar occupations and industry groups. The 1976 median full-time weekly earnings of women workers ranged from 88 percent of those of males among farm workers and 73 percent among both professional-technical and nonfarm laborers to 45 percent of male earnings among sales workers. The span of industry differences was from 88 percent in agriculture to 53 percent in finance, insurance and real estate. Overall, the median annual earnings of year-round full-time women workers dropped from 64 percent of male earnings in 1955 to 59 percent in 1975. The widest gap between the median incomes of women and men is presently in the 45 to 54 year age range. A drop in the female median after age 34 and the maximal sex differential in the late middle years may be due in part to the depressive effect of low reentry wages.

Despite comparatively low earnings, wives make substantial contributions to their total family income. In 1977, in over 17 million families where both husbands and wives were wage earners, the median family income was $17,741 or 23 percent higher than in the 13.5 million husband-wife families where only the husband worked. In black families, there was a 60 percent

Table 6.6   Women Employed as Wage and Salary Workers in Nonagricultural Industries, Selected Years, 1950 to 1970

Industry	1950 Number of Women (000)	1950 Percent of Total Employed	1960 Number of Women (000)	1960 Percent of Total Employed	1970 Number of Women (000)	1970 Percent of Total Employed
Total Nonagricultural Industries	14,113	32	19,449	36	27,496	40
Mining	22	2	30	5	50	8
Construction	86	3	130	4	244	6
Manufacturing (total)	3,594	26	4,354	25	5,623	29
Durable goods	1,219	16	1,707	18	2,483	21
Nondurable	2,337	36	2,627	35	3,140	39
Knitting mills	119	63	132	68	445	46
Apparel, etc.	754	73	858	76	939	78
Leather & leather products	167	45	173	50	160	57
Food & kindred products	311	23	417	24	356	26
Meat products	55	21	76	24	(a)	(a)
Canned & preserved food & seafood	57	41	85	42	(a)	(a)
Confectionary & related products	37	51	38	51	(a)	(a)
Chemicals & allied products	129	20	163	19	222	23
Transportation & public utilities	666	16	757	18	1,106	22
Telecommunications	389	61	426	52	522	49
Radio and TV	(a)	(a)	22	25	33	25
Trucking & warehouse	42	8	61	8	106	11
Wholesale & retail trade (total)	3,013	37	3,835	40	5,871	43
Wholesale	362	21	422	22	699	24
Retail	2,651	41	3,413	44	5,172	47
General merchandise	595	68	821	68	1,392	69
Eating & drinking	719	57	912	69	1,271	62
Apparel & accessory stores	266	65	317	72	437	66
Finance, insurance & real estate	739	44	1,181	49	1,870	52
Services (total)	5,007	58	7,241	62	11,436	63
Personal, including private household and hotels	2,097	72	2,464	76	2,256	75
Private households	1,405	88	1,701	90	(1,124)	(a)
Business & repair	155	16	287	24	624	31
Medical & health	1,006	74	1,710	77	3,096	79
Except hospitals	302	77	448	82	1,039	83
Hospitals	704	82	1,262	75	2,057	77
Education (total)	1,283	75	2,062	63	3,788	62
Private	281	63	464	61	957	62
Government	1,002	61	1,598	63	2,831	62
Legal	81	63	109	76	178	46
Other services, including recreational & amusement	131	76	138	32	204	36
Public administration	648	32	909	28	1,297	31
Federal	391	27	509	28	690	31
State and local	258	25	400	29	557	31
State	100	38	152	38	202	38
Local	158	21	248	25	355	28

[a] Data not available. [b] Includes post office.

Note: Because some industries are not included in this table, subgroups do not always add to total for major industrial division.

Source: U.S. Department of Labor, U.S. Bureau of Labor Statistics, *Monthly Labor Review*, 97, no. 7 (May 1974).

**Table 6.7   Occupational Distribution of Employed Women, 20 Years and Over,
Annual Averages 1960–1977**

Occupational Group	Percent of Employed Women, 20 Years and Over			Women as Percent of all Workers in Occupation Group		
	1960	1970	1977	1960	1970	1977
Total: thousands	18,397	26,627	33,198			
percent	100.0	100.0	100.0	31.9	37.3	40.0
Total white-collar	57.3	61.8	64.6	42.1	47.2	50.1
Professional, technical etc.	14.5	16.8	15.5	37.7	40.0	42.5
Managers, except farm	4.2	3.9	6.4	14.4	16.5	22.1
Sales	8.0	7.0	6.3	35.7	37.6	41.1
Clerical	30.6	34.1	34.6	66.7	73.1	78.6
Total blue-collar	18.9	17.7	14.9	15.4	18.3	18.0
Craft	1.3	1.9	1.7	2.9	4.9	4.9
Operatives[a]	17.0	14.4	11.6	27.7	39.2	40.7
Transportation equipment[a]		0.5	0.7		4.5	6.8
Nonfarm laborers	0.5	0.9	1.0	3.6	9.0	9.8
Total service workers	22.1	19.8	19.2	62.7	61.4	62.7
Private household	7.9	3.9	2.7	96.7	97.0	97.7
Service except private household	14.2	15.9	16.5	52.5	56.3	59.3
Total farm workers	1.8	0.8	1.3	18.2	15.4	17.4
Farmers & farm managers	0.6	0.3	0.3	3.9	4.9	6.4
Farm laborers & supervisors	1.2	0.5	1.0	28.2	29.2	33.7

Not all totals equal the sum of the parts, due to rounding.
[a]Operatives in 1960 include transportation equipment.
Sources: U.S. Census, *Occupational Characteristics of the Population*, PC(2)7A, 1960 and
1970. U.S. Department of Labor, unpublished data, 1977.

difference between the median income of all families with wage-earning
female heads, $8,901, was less than half that of families with male heads.

DIMENSIONS OF REENTRY

Time Out from Work

Child rearing has been the long-established basis for American women's
abstention from gainful employment in the United States. Character-
istically, the birth of the first child marked the setting for a new life stage
that placed the performance of maternal duties in the spotlight. While a
dearth of community child care services and of acceptable inexpensive
mother substitutes has generally necessitated a mother's constant presence
in the home, this rarely has been contrary to her inclinations, since social
expectations that mothers would devote most of their time to the upbring-

ing of their children have been incorporated within women's own value system, as exemplified by the following remarks.

After working fo a year I got married and started on a new career as a homemaker. I had always planned to leave work to raise my family.

The idea of a working mother was totally foreign to me. When I became pregnant I resigned from my job. I never thought of anything else.

We were raised to think that when we got married our husbands would do the work and we'd stay home with the children. So I dropped out of school when I was 15, after 9th grade, because I didn't see the need for an education.

Child Care

The tendency of American women to leave the labor force to care for their children is partially caused by a lack of alternative sources of child care. The extended family where relatives assumed child care tasks is practically extinct, and there is no large-scale systematic approach to the public provision of day care, preschool services, or before-and-after school programs.

There are three basic models for child care outside the home: family day care, day care centers and preschool. Programs are either under public, voluntary, or proprietary auspices. School-age children (all-day schooling generally starts at age six) sometimes have access to before- and after-school care, but this type of program is relatively infrequent.

In 1974-75, less than two percent of children age three to 13 with working mothers were cared for in organized day care centers; the majority were cared for in their homes. There is evidence that this was a preferential rather than a forced decision by mothers. Researchers have found that simple subsidization of child care is not sufficient to produce substantial increases in mothers' labor force participation because it is the lack of adequate job opportunities rather than of adequate day care that limits their entrance to the labor market.[2]

There is no strong evidence that substantial numbers of women who are out of the labor force for reasons of child care would enter or reenter the workforce—or would never have exited—if day care services were more generally available. A 1975 survey found that only three percent of wives and 11 percent of female family heads were not seeking work solely because of their inability to make adequate child care arrangements. The vast majority of the latter had family incomes under $5,000, but they represented only five percent of all female heads at this income level.[3]

In the United States the government has been unwilling to usurp what are deemed to be parental prerogatives, unless parents are manifestly unable to provide their chldren with the basic necessities of life. There is no consensus in support of facilitating mothers' employment—except mothers whose families are a charge upon the public treasury. Most women have been flowing into the labor force *despite* the lack of public attention to their child care requirements, not *because* of any special encouragement by the government. Since many mothers appear to be satisfied with makeshift inexpensive child care arrangements that enable them to work, the government has thus far evaded serious consideration of the social implications of haphazard day care largely because of the high expenditures that would be involved combined with the lack of pressure from would-be users.

Some relevant remarks from mothers about child care problems follow:

I never found decent babysitters, and that was a real problem. Plus I found that I worked all day, came home and took care of the house and the baby—there was no help, zero help. So I decided it wasn't worth working and I quit.

We have tremendous family support. A sick child to me means a call to my mother or aunt. That's a very unique and special thing, I think, for a working mother.

I did not work during the summer because they could only afford to pay me to work part time and I could not arrange child care for my own children (aged 6, 8 and 12) on that basis. The Welfare Department pays for their care only while I work full time.

A woman in my neighborhood takes my children. They go to her house before school for breakfast and lunch. At 5:30 I pick them up and take them home for dinner. She also lives in the neighborhood so they go to the same schools. Everything is the same routine. That's what I needed. If I had that before, I could possibly have continued on. It makes me very relaxed and they are comfortable and secure.

In the past there were relatively few middle-class mothers with both the means and the will to add paid work to the unpaid family-centered tasks that were delegated to them, irrespective of other responsibilities. Moreover, the pervasiveness of the middle-class mystique that considers a working wife to be presumptive evidence of a husband's inability to provide sufficient family support influenced many men to discourage their spouses from staying in the work force.

My husband was always against women working. Their position was in the home. He wanted me in the house with the door shut and to never go out.

I didn't really care about building a career or getting ahead. I just wanted to do difficult exciting things. When I got married I gave up almost all of that. My husband made it clear that he didn't want me to work but I got bored quickly at home.

Attitudinal factors may be either reinforced or countered by economic considerations. Women who can command a high market wage have been more liable to remain in the labor force or to reenter after a brief hiatus than those whose earning potential is too low to warrant the cost of replacing their home-based services.

Since women's work is largely confined to segregated clusters of jobs that provide low returns, there has been little personal motivation and even less economic rationale for most mothers to remain in the labor force. The lack of a statutory requirement providing maternity leave has had two kinds of effect: women in current or potential high wage jobs try to make arrangements for child care that will enable them to work, and mothers in less-favorable positions in the labor market have no incentive toward a rapid return to work. In addition, employment discontinuity and intermittency are salient features of female occupations, and many young women who anticipate taking time off to raise children prepare for these fields in the knowledge that they offer flexibility in scheduling and ease of reentry.

Occasionally, women who may have every intention of returning to work after a maternity leave—which, although not legally required, is now provided routinely by some employers—eventually decide that they wish to remain at home. A few large corporations have estimated that between 40 and 50 percent of employees who take maternity leaves each year do not return within the prescribed period of unpaid leave and job protection, whose length varies according to individual employer policy.

The move toward continuous work commitment is still recent enough to stimulate constant soul searching. An assistant vice president of a bank who resumed her career four months after giving birth to her first child acknowledged that she was not free of doubts: "It really is a decision I virtually remake every day, a question I have to ask every day. And today for me the answer is yes. And tomorrow I'll re-ask the question."[4]

Trends in Reentry

Cross-sectional trends indicate secular changes in the age pattern of American women's labor force participation which portray a reversal in the previous work behavior of married women. No longer do most mothers leave the labor force at the birth of their first child, never to return; nor do as many wait until their youngest child graduates from high school before resuming work as in the past. Instead, increasing numbers of mothers return to work permanently when their last offspring enters kindergarten at the age of five or six, or nursery school at the age of three or four. Nevertheless, the reentry decision is still being made at practically every stage of adult life.

A more accurate picture of lifetime labor force participation than through cross-sectional trends is gained from the behavior of women of similar age cohorts over the course of time which demonstrates increasing work attachment, a rising incidence of labor force accessions, and progressively curtailed periods of withdrawal form the labor market (Table 6.8). Declines in age-specific participation that appear in cross-sectional patterns are either less steep or do not occur at all in this cohort view. Instead, each birth group shows greater continuity of labor force activity.

While withdrawal from the labor force at the birth of the first child continues to be dominant, it is less frequent and of shorter duration than

Table 6.8 Labor Force Participation Rates[a] of Women 20 Years and Over by Year of Birth and Age, Selected Years, 1955–1976

Year of Birth	1955 Age	1955 Rate	1960 Age	1960 Rate	1965 Age	1965 Rate	1970 Age	1970 Rate	1975 Age	1975 Rate	1976 Age	1976 Rate
1951–55									20–24	64.1	20–24	65.0
1946–50							20–24	57.8	25–29	57.0	25–29	59.2
1941–45					20–24	50.0	25–29	45.2	30–34	51.7	30–34	54.6
1936–40			20–24	46.2	25–29	38.9	30–34	44.7	35–39	54.9	35–39	57.2
1931–35	20–24	46.0	25–29	35.7	30–34	38.2	35–39	49.2	40–44	56.8	40–44	58.5
1926–30	25–29	35.3	30–34	36.3	35–39	43.6	40–44	52.9	45–49	55.9	45–49	57.0
1921–25	30–34	34.7	35–39	40.8	40–44	48.5	45–49	55.0	50–54	53.3	50–54	53.1
1916–20	35–39	39.2	40–44	46.8	45–49	51.7	50–54	53.8	55–59	47.9	55–59	48.1
1911–15	40–44	44.1	45–49	50.7	50–54	50.1	55–59	49.0	60–64	33.3	60–64	33.1
1906–10	45–49	45.9	50–54	48.8	55–59	47.1	60–64	36.1	65–69	14.5	65–69	14.9
1901–05	50–54	41.5	55–59	42.2	60–64	34.0	65–69	17.3	70 and over	4.8	70 and over	4.6
1896–1900	55–59	35.6	60–64	31.4	65–69	17.4	70 and over	5.7				
Before 1895	60–64	29.0	65–69	17.6	70 and over	6.1						
	65–69	17.8	70 and over	6.8								
	70 and over	6.4										

[a] Percent of population in labor force.

Source: U.S. Department of Labor, Bureau of Labor Statistics, *U.S. Working Women: A Data-book*, Bulletin 1977 (1977).

formerly. "The average woman now stays in the labor force until three or four months before the birth, and in many instances returns soon after the birth."[5]

The recent reduction in the tendency of young employed women to leave the labor force has been concentrated in the upper half of the earnings distribution, however, thereby precluding the equalizing effect on family income distribution that would have resulted had this trend also been found among low earners who are more likely to be married to low-earning men.[6]

Influences on Reentry Decisions

The following comments from interviews illustrate some of the pressures for and against reentry:

I tried to work when the baby was 5 or 6 but it was a chore for me because I had no babysitter. How much could I pay and who could care for all my 10 children? So I ended up watching them myself.

Once your kids are in first grade, Welfare says you have to find a job.

I do not like staying home, I hate housework. Finally it hit me that my daughter is growing up and she's not going to be home much longer. What will I do then? This is what led me to think about paid employment.

It is not always a simple matter to pinpoint a particular influence as paramount; multiple causation is more likely to be the rule. One investigator noted some of the problems associated with attempts to classify reentrants by specific reasons for returning to the labor force by listing the explanations given by 355 women who reentered the labor force between 1968 and 1969. Forty percent attributed their decision to the need for money; nine percent to the aging of their children; eight percent to boredom; six percent to a job opportunity for which they were qualified; and 37 percent to other causes. It was suggested that: "Those needing the money might have been able to take a job because their children were older and they therefore would not have to spend as much of what they would earn on child care. Those who were 'bored' or just heard about the job might include those with 'empty nests.' 'Other' reasons might also be related to changes in family responsibilities. In other words, responses to these and similar questions do not make clear how many women return to the labor market because of decreasing responsibility within the home."[7]

Remarks of reentrants, themselves, are pertinent in regard to multiple influences on their decisions. A 45-year-old woman commented:

A couple of years ago it was possible that my husband might lose his job so he suggested that it might be a good idea for me to get my insurance broker's license. The children were older and I felt it would be a relief for him to feel that there was some forward motion going on lest something drastic happened to his career.

A woman, aged 41, reported that:

Until four years ago I stayed at home, and then I came back to work since the children don't need me just to be there. My primary reason was just to get out of the house.

Another combination of boredom and children's maturation was described by the following mothers:

I worked for any volunteer group that needed anybody to do something since I was bored to death. I had been known to put both kids in the same bedroom for naps so that I could paint the other room—I was that bored. I dyed my hair red one year—those kinds of things. But by 1959, when both kids were in school full time, I started college again.

My husband was traveling a lot at that time, the children were in high school, and I felt the void during the day. I needed a change and wanted to do something different to occupy my time.

The following remarks of a 32-year-old women indicate how divorce and consequent financial need served to dispel doubts.

If it hadn't been for the economic necessity of going back to work I never could have adjusted to the guilt for leaving my children so young. To a certain degree my divorce released me from ambivalence. I *had* to go to work, but that was what I wanted to do all along.

Intermingled in the observations of a 48-year-old woman are financial stringency plus what appears to be the even more powerful force of a need for self-respect.

I decided a couple of years ago that I needed to try to go back to work because of the fact that welfare makes you paralyzed in some way. You're really looked down on all the time. You have to try to get work; otherwise you perish.

Education, training and prior work experience. The relationship between educational attainment and female labor force participation has already been demonstrated, and this association also applies to reentry. Since high educational status raises a woman's potential market wage, a woman with above-average schooling is more likely to find it economically beneficial to return to the labor force than one with less education. The relatively low wages available to less-educated women are generally insufficient to make it worthwhile for them to work under ordinary circumstances.

An analysis of a poll of housewives and working women concluded that housewives who had no intention of entering or reentering the labor force had the lowest educational level of all women surveyed. Housewives who planned to work were the youngest women and they had high educational attainment. Over time, this well-educated "plan to work" segment was found to have put its work intentions into practice.[8]

The acquisition or upgrading of skills through nonmarket work during absences from the labor force and their transferability to market work can be both an incentive and aid toward reentry. The United States has a large voluntary sector which engages much of the time of many nonworking women as well as that of many workers. To a large extent, volunteer activities parallel market functions but they have not generally been seriously considered as valid job qualifications for use in reentry job search, although there recently have been changed perceptions of the value of the contribution of volunteer work to employability.

One report about the positive effect of substantial volunteer work on reentry job search came from a 37-year-old woman who was in the process of obtaining a divorce.

I think I have been very lucky in having the level of volunteer things that I have been able to do. That's been an immense help to me. If I was now at the point where I was seven years ago, I would be a totally different kind of person in terms of my confidence in myself and my belief in my ability to do a good job and having up-to-date credentials. There wasn't a huge gap in my experience. I think that's a very difficult problem for someone going back to work who has been out of the labor force for ten years while raising children.

A more negative note was sounded by another woman:

I became board president for the YWCA and at that point I gave up all my other volunteer activities. It was about a 30-hour week job involving coordination of virtually every committee, fundraising and public relations. I held that position for three years. When it came time to find a paying job, however, I went to several employment agencies who told me that they could not do anything for me since I could not type. I figured at this point, if I had quit high school when I was 16 instead of getting a B.A., I would be just as well off. Most agencies returned my resume. Several suggested that I take a job as a file clerk and hope for a promotion.

The possession of prior specialized training tends to have effects similar to education on a woman's decision to return to work. In fact, it may even rank higher if it has been vocationally oriented. A woman with a credential in nursing, for example, may find it easier to obtain a satisfactory position upon reentry than one with more years of schooling but with no specific career-related skills. Another relevant example is a woman with steno-graphic training whose employability may be far greater than that of a baccalaureate in the humanities.

Some amount of past work experience is an advantage over a lack of any familiarity with the workplace. The labor force status of women at any time is strongly related to the intensity of previous work experience; prior market work tends to develop a taste for more of the same among women out of the labor force.[9] "The greatest barriers to entry may be experienced by older women who have never worked since they suffer from lack of experience, inadequate training and potential age discrimination."[10]

Interviews with employers revealed that it is to reentrants' advantage to produce evidence of prior employment, no matter how distant, nor how different from the job at issue. Knowledge of the work setting and its requirements is a plus, and it is in this respect that middle-aged reentrants sometimes have a definite advantage over younger entrants.

Maternal responsibilities. Although there has been a sharp step-up in the employment of wives with young children, it is not until their youngest is between six and 17 years that the majority of mothers are now in the labor force. As Kreps and Clark note:

> Once children are age 6, the school system begins to provide virtually free child care for most of the day. At this stage, the mother is 'freed' from daily babysitting duties and the family can reconsider the allocation of her time. . . . As the child matures, he or she is able to help in performing household tasks; the time of the older chldren thus can be substituted for the mother's time in home activities.[11]

Not only children's ages but family size can be a constraint upon mothers' work participation. The probability of a middle-aged mother's being in the labor force tends to be not only a function of the presence or absence of preschool children but of the number of children under 18 years of age. The proportion of white women with one child who remained in the labor force throughout a five-year period was 43 percent, but only 25 percent of women with three or more children had a similar work pattern. For blacks, the respective percentages were 62 and 41.[12]

Family income. A family's economic circumstances can be crucial to the reentry decision. A 45-year-old reentrant provided such an instance.

> My husband's family business was just sold. He had been making $20-$30,000 and had wanted his own auto dealership but that is absolutely out of the question. He just bought a distributorship for automotive tools and is one month into it. So right now his salary is zero. If I had my druthers, I'd like to go back to school full time, but there are still three in school and for monetary reasons I must keep working.

A 41-year-old mother of two teen-age daughters employed as a keypunch operator remarked:

> At first I don't think my husband cared for my job that much because he was used to me being home and running errands. But he likes it now. I don't think we got into a big discussion about it. But now that college is coming up, with the way college costs are going, two people working would be a big help.

Female family heads in or near poverty or whose husbands cannot provide sufficient family support have no alternative but to seek work or public assistance. Other women, whose families may not need their earnings for subsistance, wish to provide extra funds to maintain or improve their living standards. In these cases, need is often more of a subjective determination than in instances where total family income cannot cover all the necessities of life. In other words, beyond some point on the income scale, one woman's need is another woman's luxury.

Rising inflation, however, has served to increase the number of families who can only maintain their customary living style with contributions from an additional earner. The Consumer Price Index increased by 184 percent between 1950 and 1979 and the rising costs of good and services was a prime stimulus toward reentry.

The growth of two-income families has masked the effects of inflation to a certain extent, since wives' contributions to family income often are more than sufficient to compensate for decreases in husbands' real earnings. As a consequence, not only have consumer expenditures risen despite rising inflation but, as families have become accustomed to the higher incomes generated by wives' earnings, their tastes change accordingly. This in turn results in even greater reliance on the money wives bring in, so that what may have started out as a woman's temporary reentry to compensate for a presumed short-term decrease in real family income or to provide funds to meet a temporary obligation evolves into a permanent work involvement to finance a higher living standard.

Tax structure. The tax treatment of two-earner families in the United States is discriminatory in that it imposes a marriage penalty which may substantially increase their total federal income tax. The incomes of husbands and wives are aggregated for income tax purposes so that the second earner's first taxable dollar is taxed at the first earner's highest tax rate. This policy can serve as a disincentive to a wife's reentry to the work force since a wife's net earned income may be relatively small and the tax may greatly diminish the increment she provides. Nevertheless, the rise in the labor force participation of wives at all family income levels indicates that the income tax is not much of a deterrent to reentry. One possible explanation is that family work decisions are "sufficiently planned and integrated over the span of married life so that the wife's earnings are not, in fact, considered marginal earnings."[13] What is also possible is that tax considerations did play an important role in the past when wives were more likely to be transient secondary workers; and the few dollars they brought in, minus the costs of working, were not warranted by the extra taxes that might be incurred. Today, women workers are less likely to be peripheral workers and their actual earnings may be sufficient to supply an after-tax bonus, and/or their fringe benefits may provide nonpecuniary advantages that outweigh any tax deterrence. Nevertheless, wives whose potential market wage is low and who are unable to upgrade their skills in order to improve their job opportunities may be deflected from reentry because of negative tax implications.

Employment-related child care expenses can now be credited against tax obligations. Taxpayers are allowed a 20 percent tax credit, up to $400 for one child and $800 for two or more children, with a maximum claimable expense of $2000 and $4000, respectively. The application of the maximum credit to a two-child family demonstrates a use of tax policy to embody population policy.

There are also inequities in the social security system that discriminate against working wives and two-earner families. Of particular relevance to reentrants are provisions that penalize women workers who have spent part of their lives as full-time homemakers, since gaps in social security coverage during the homemaking period may result in a disproportionately low replacement of income.

Income transfers. The United States does not have universal family allowances. Instead, it has a means-tested system of social assistance, Aid to Families with Dependent Chldren (AFDC), administered by the states with federal cost-sharing.

There is a growing number of women in the United States who must rely on government assistance for family support. In 1977, AFDC payments were provided to 3.6 million families and totaled about $10 billion. In that year, women headed four-fifths of AFDC households; seven in ten of these women were over the age of 25.

While welfare dependency has been accused of destroying women's incentives to work, the realities of the situation are more complex. These women tend to be from the poorest backgrounds and to have had inferior schooling. Most of them despair of ever being able to live in comfort or security. Moreover, the nation itself despairs of them and has been unable to fashion a consensus regarding the most practical and fruitful means of bringing them to self-sufficiency. Entry to the work force for this group requires much more intensive social reform than most Americans are willing to countenance at this time. Yet, for every one of these women, the time arrives when she is no longer eligible for AFDC which is premised on her role as a parent of needy children, not as a needy individual. At that point, reentry is an imminent possibility and, at that point, these women may be well into middle age.

The displaced homemaker. Marital disruptions and consequent loss of income are major mainsprings to reentry or delayed entry whenever they occur.

I could see that my marriage was not as good a relationship as it once had been. I was beginning to feel my husband was drawing away from me and that I was becoming too involved in his life and in his work. I think that's what made me think about going back to work and to school. It was a very good thing for my ego. It helped me to separate myself to the extent that I was not an appendage any longer.

I have some alimony which will be severely reduced when my children graduate from college. That gives me $21,600 a year and roughly a third of that has to be paid in taxes. I've sold the house and moved into an inexpensive apartment, and now I'm job hunting.

In 1975, the term "displaced homemaker" was coined to describe a middle-aged woman who, as a result of widowhood, divorce or separation, had lost the sole source of income upon which she had been dependent during many years of fulfilling family and household responsibilities. Charging that such women comprise a rapidly growing but seriously neglected group with an assortment of needs, the Alliance for Displaced Homemakers was organized to act as a collective voice to call their plight to the attention of policy makers and the community.

In essence, the situation of the displaced homemaker reflects the inconsistency between the way the American homemaker is regarded and the way she is treated. Millions of women marry after having had little or no gainful employment and devote many years to the performance of unpaid home and family services, depending upon the largesse of their spouses to provide for their personal needs. After spending a substantial portion of their adult lives as voluntary homemakers, many middle-aged women become single again and find themselves without adequate resources to support themselves and any dependents because they have "fallen through the cracks of every income security system devised, and are left to fend for themselves in the market place."[14]

In cases of severe income loss as a result of "displacement," middle-aged long-term homemakers are ineligible for unemployment insurance, yet they are not qualified to receive categorical welfare assistance unless they have children under age 18 or are physically disabled. Widows cannot receive social security benefits on their deceased husbands' earnings record if they are below 60 years of age, unless they have dependent children; divorcees qualify only for one-third of total benefits (wives for one-half) but only if divorced after a minimum of ten consecutive years of marriage and only if their ex-husbands are retired. Similar problems exist for dependent separated women. The lack of fluid assets often results in the loss of a woman's one remaining holding, a home, due to inability to make tax payments or defray the costs of upkeep and because eligibility for public relief, as a last resort, usually requires the surrender of all assets. According to the Census Bureau, of 4.5 million divorced or separated women in 1975, only four percent received alimony.

A 53-year-old divorced unemployed reentrant provides one example of a displaced homemaker.

When I gave up my job 18 years ago, I just said good-bye. If I had it to do all over again, I would have kept in touch. But I bought the permanency of the mother-wife role, the promise of forever. Now I feel as if I'm living on borrowed time. If my ex-husband suddenly decides not to send the money then I won't get it. As somebody's wife I was operating from a safe inside world. I had no connection with what was really going on out there. I was protected.

About 30 percent of divorced mothers from families with predivorce incomes over $11,000 were found to have received no child support or alimony over a period of six years. When such payments were made they averaged approximately $2000 per year, an amount which went typically to support several children. Only two percent of these families received over $5,000 per year.[15] The Census Bureau reports that the poverty rate for mothers receiving child support in 1975 (12 percent) was less than half that for those who did not (32 percent).

Rural women who have been "displaced" have been found to be especially disadvantaged because of their lack of access to resources that might provide them with the types of assistance they need:

It's very difficult to ask a woman to drive 120 miles when she has no money to buy gasoline, to pay for childcare, and her car needs $300 worth of repairs before it will even run at all. These are the kinds of problems we face in a rural area. Being rural also means being isolated. There is no peer support. Next-door neighbors, if they're still married, do not identify with the problems that these women have.[16]

Bureau of Labor Statistics data indicate that, in 1976, 2.4 million widows and divorcees between the ages of 35 and 64, as well as 642,000 women with spouses absent, were either unemployed or out of the labor force; but the number of these women who properly may be classified as displaced homemakers because of their financial situation cannot be determined. There were 1.6 million widowed, divorced or separated women of the same ages who were reported by the Census Bureau to have had incomes below the poverty level, but the poverty threshold is a statistical yardstick that does not necessarily represent the amount of money required to satisfy all reasonable needs. Hence, this is probably a minimal estimate of the displaced homemaker population.*

Whereas many reentrants can afford the luxury of delay while they engage in extended preparation for a return to the labor force, large numbers of past and present wives, not to mention single mothers, have an imminent need for help. Regrettably, immediacy of need can often lead to less-desirable jobs than those available to women who can take things slowly. While some reentrants are the hard-to-employ entrant grown old, more of them are women who were acceptable employees when young but who, because of age and presumptive loss of skills, are belatedly hard-to-employ.

Attitudinal factors. Financial considerations aside, there is little doubt that a husband's attitudes can make or break a woman's resolve to enter or reenter the paid work force.

The following remarks by a 55-year-old woman provide an example of the former impact:

One night my husband brought home the Journal of Accountancy and showed me an ad. He said, 'Hey, Myrna, here's a program just for you.' It was a special

---

*The poverty level is an adjusted income cutoff based on changes in the Consumer Price Index. In 1976, the income threshold for a nonfarm female under 65 years living alone was $2,840, and rose with increased family size and number of children under 18 years old.

bachelor's degree program for adults at a local college—a pilot project funded by the Ford Foundation. You had to be over 35 and at the time I was 41. I said, 'I don't know. I've been out of school for so long and I'd have to take a test.' And he said, 'Try it! If you don't make it, you don't make it, but this seems as if it's for you.' He challenged me and was a great support for me. I took the exam and passed.

A more grudging reaction to a wife's reentry is depicted in this report:

My husband [a construction worker] is not entirely happy about my para-legal job, nor about my ambitions or salary. He makes $125 a week and I make $160. He likes the fact that I bring money home but he doesn't like the work I do. He doesn't like me having a job with any kind of 'position.' He would prefer that I was a waitress or did factory work. I deal with that the best I can. This is something that I want.

Research has shown that a woman's perception of her husband's attitude toward her working is a major determinant of the degree of time she devotes to market work. Married white women aged 30 to 44 years whose husbands had favorable views toward working wives were in the labor force nearly four times as long as those who reported that their husbands had negative attitudes in this respect. Black wives with supportive husbands averaged 50 percent more time at work.[17]

Attitudes toward the proper division of household labor are changing in the United States and serve to encourage the gainful employment of wives. A greater tendency toward task sharing than in the past lightens the customary dual burdens of working wives. Husbands are also learning that working wives can provide them with greater career flexibility by enabling them to take risks that otherwise might not be feasible. They can follow the example of their spouses by making mid-career changes with the assurance that whatever income loss may be involved will be at least partially offset by their wives' contributions to family support.

Discrimination. Outside the family there is the negative factor of discrimination in the labor market, as the following remarks of a 35-year-old reentrant after seven years at home indicates:

I feel very angry that my time away from work is held against me, because I feel that time does have experience attached to it. When you raise children, you're working like hell, putting in many more hours a day than you would in an office and doing something extremely valuable. I feel I've learned an enormous amount by raising them—about human nature, about children. It makes me angry that it's very difficult to put that on a resume because it's not considered to be 'real.'

Nevertheless, the pervasive tenor of the times is one in which outright employer discrimination is no longer considered a standard modus operandi or accepted as one of the rules of the game. A revived feminism commencing in the mid-1960s has been a major catalyst for changing the attitudes of American women and men toward women's economic and social roles. The egalitarian thrust of the women's movement has influenced widespread modifications in views and in behavior. The aspirational changes that these goals have evoked within the female population in tandem with affirmative responses within the larger community have undoubtedly been a major factor in the altered relationship to gainful employment of women of all ages.

In addition, strong pressures by women were instrumental in the passage of measures prohibiting sex discrimination in employment.

The Equal Pay Act of 1963 prohibits employers from discriminating on the basis of sex in paying wages. Title VII of the Civil Rights Act of 1964, as amended, prohibits discrimination in all aspects of employment, including hiring, firing, promotions, training, fringe benefits, seniority, and retirement, on the basis of race, color, religion, sex, or national origin. A 1967 Executive Order requires that federal contractors, who include the largest business firms in the nation, undertake affirmative action to improve the employment opportunities of women. Title IX of the Education Amendments of 1972 prohibits discrimination on the basis of sex in educational programs or activities receiving federal assistance.

In addition to action against sex bias, the Age Discrimination in Employment Act bars job discrimination against persons between the ages of 40 and 70. This law provides for exceptions where age is "a bona fide occupational qualification reasonably necessary to the normal operation of the particular business," a provision currently being challenged as serving to undermine much of the Act's force.

An unemployed reentrant, age 51, remarked:

> I *know* that I am being discriminated against because of my age. You can't really catch anybody at it because they always have some perfectly plausible reason why they don't hire you, but age makes a great deal of difference. I am interviewed but there is always some young girl looking too who will get the job even though my qualifications may be just as good. After my interview with one employer, I called up the woman at the employment agency who said that she thought that I was terrific but he asked her to send in a few more applicants who were a little younger.

Enforcement of anti-discrimination statutes has been far from rigorous, and much of the behavior that gave rise to these measures is so deeply entrenched in employment practices that it can be dislodged only by the most forceful efforts. Reentrants and delayed entrants may find it particularly difficult to bring charges of sex or age discrimination since lack of experience and recent employment relative to that of other job applicants are legally acceptable grounds for differential treatment.

Older women, however, can sometimes benefit when employers who are making good faith efforts to comply with affirmative action regulations expand their area of search for new hires or widen in-house opportunities. There is little question that governmental recognition of women's right to equal opportunity has persuaded many women to reenter the labor market in the expectation that they will be treated with more consideration than in the past. On the other hand, this right applies to women who have already made the decision to work. Equal treatment in the labor force does not extend to equal work expectations for women and men. In fact, a proposed equal rights amendment to the federal constitution has encountered strong opposition and may not be able to obtain the support of the required number of state legislatures, to some extent because of fears that it will promote social policies that would encourage women with family responsibilities to work.

The Pool of Current Reentrants

The actual number of women who annually enter or reenter the labor force after an extended period of nonmarket activity cannot be determined, nor is there any way of arriving at an estimate of those women who require or desire assistance to facilitate employment. An idea of the size of the pool of reentrants and delayed entrants is provided by the following data concerning unemployed persons and those out of the labor force.

Among 621,000 unemployed women aged 25 to 64 years who were reentrants to the labor force in 1977, one-quarter had not been employed full time within the past ten years (Table 6.9). More than three-fifths of the latter were 35 years of age or older, and almost one-third were over the age of 44. There were an additional 23,000 unemployed women between the ages of 25 and 64 years who had never worked full time and 29,000 who had never worked at all. Almost half of the latter were 35 years of age or older. The 673,000 reentrants and new entrants comprised two out of five of all unemployed women aged 25 to 64 years in that year.

There were more than 23 million women between the ages of 25 and 64 years who were not in the labor force in 1977, of whom nearly 15 million or 64 percent had no work experience within the past five years. More than one million of the latter women expressed the intention of seeking work within the year; two-thirds with prior work experience and more than half with no work history were 35 years of age or older.

More than two million of the 23 million women between ages 25 and 64 who were not in the labor force said they wanted a job "now" although the foregoing data indicate that only about half this number were contemplating early job search. The length of absence of those wanting jobs "now" is not known, but most of these women were not seeking employment because of home responsibilities. One woman in five, however, was out of the labor force because she did not think she could find a job, three-quarters citing market conditions rather than personal inadequacies. There is no way of knowing how many of these and other women would undertake active job search if labor market conditions were more favorable.

Fewer than four percent of all women aged 25 to 64 years who were out of the labor force expressed no desire to work at any time. This suggests a total of 22 million potential reentrants. While about eight million of the total

Table 6.9 Unemployed Persons, Age 25 to 64 Years, by Reasons for Unemployment, Sex and Age, 1977 (percent distribution)

Sex and Age	Total Unemployment	Job Losers	Job Leavers	Reentrants Total	Reentrants Last Full-time Work Since 1967	Reentrants Last Full-time Work Before 1967	New Entrants Total	New Entrants Never Worked Full-Time	New Entrants Never Worked
Female									
Number (000)	1,703	766	265	621	464	157	52	23	29
Percent 25 to 64 yrs.	100.0	100.0	100.0	100.0	100.0	100.0	100.0	100.0	100.0
25 to 34	44.5	36.8	54.0	49.1	52.8	38.2	51.9	50.0	51.7
35 to 44	24.3	23.8	22.3	25.9	24.1	31.2	21.2	27.3	17.3
45 to 54	19.9	23.8	16.6	16.7	15.1	21.7	17.3	13.6	24.1
55 to 64	11.4	15.7	7.2	8.2	8.0	8.9	9.6	9.1	6.9
Male									
Number (000)	1,785	1,270	199	285	260	25	31	18	13
Percent 25 to 64 yrs.	100.0	100.0	100.0	100.0	100.0	100.0	100.0	100.0	100.0
25 to 34	47.0	44.7	55.8	48.1	48.1	7.6	71.0	72.2	69.2
35 to 44	20.6	21.3	20.1	17.9	18.1	2.5	22.6	16.7	30.8
45 to 54	18.4	19.4	15.1	17.5	16.9	3.8	3.2	5.6	—
55 to 64	14.0	14.6	9.0	16.5	16.9	1.9	3.2	5.6	—

Not all totals are equal to the sum of the parts, due to rounding.

Source: U.S. Department of Labor, Bureau of Labor Statistics, unpublished data.

had worked within the past five years, many will undoubtedly have chalked up longer periods of absence by the time they are ready to return to work.

Future Trends

The growth in the female labor participation rate through the remainder of the decade will depend on the availability of job opportunities, the quality of those jobs, and the availability of other income from husband's earnings or transfer payments. It will also depend on the extent to which recent trends in marriage, divorce, number and ages of children, and sex role attitudes and expectations continue.[18]

The views of a woman on the propriety of labor force participation of mothers in general have a substantial causal effect on her own employment, and attitudes can continue to alter in such a way as to speed the trend toward women's increased work commitment. As older cohorts of women age and retire from the labor force, acceptance of nonfamilial roles by women in the prime work years are expected to increase, and it has been estimated that a continued trend toward such acceptance should result in a rise of 19 to 22 points in the 1975 female labor force participation rate of 46.3 percent by 1990, in the absence of severe economic downturns. Even in the presence of a loose labor market, it is suggested that just as a decreased supply of young, single female workers forced employers to hire older married mothers during the 1950s, a diminished supply of young male workers in the 1980s may pressure bosses to hire women for positions traditionally filled by men.[19]

Investigators have cautioned against reliance upon attitudinal changes among younger women only, since they are also relevant among older contingents. This would mean not only a flattening of the participation rates of women in their twenties and thirties in the near future, but less of a reduction after the age of 50.[20]

In 1978, for the first time, the Bureau of Labor Statistics developed three significantly different projections of future labor growth instead of only one projection. These were based on different assumptions about participation rates for various population groups. All three scenarios anticipate declining rates of total growth but a rise in female participation ranging from a total rate of 60 percent under high growth assumptions to 54 percent at the lowest growth level. In the past, BLS projections have tended to understate actual growth largely because of the unforeseen rise of women in the labor force, and this threefold set of projections was attempted as an alternative technique.

One problem encountered in projecting participation trends was that linear extrapolation of rates of women aged 25 to 29 from their 1970 trends would result in this group surpassing the rates of their male counterparts before the end of the 1980s. Since this possibility was not visualized as plausible, "it seemed logical to apply the constraint that these rates not be allowed to cross the participation rates for men of comparable age."[21] But, while this may not be "plausible," it is not unthinkable that male and female rates will be closer than projected ones under high growth conditions. The aforementioned prediction of a 19- to 22-point rise in women's participation rate by 1990, for example, is between seven and ten points higher than the BLS high growth prediction for that year. Nevertheless, even the most conservative BLS estimate predicts an average of about one million women added to the labor market each year between 1977 and 1990.

If the battle against rising inflation results in a severe job shortage, all bets are off with respect to the likelihood of a drastic change in women's work patterns. Instead, women will be forced to revert to their traditional life styles, even if this means forced rather than free choice.

The rate of inflation was about nine percent in 1978, and predictions for double digit inflation during 1979 were common. If this turns out to be the case, or even if inflation remains at current levels, more families will need the extra earnings of wives, and employed female family heads may be unable to provide adequately for their dependents. Policies and programs to upgrade reentrants' job potential have been developed in the United States but, at the same time, there has been no assurance of acceptable outcomes in the form of a demand for their labor. Hence, those who support these efforts are too often in the anomalous position of lending a hand to an unknown destination.

POLICIES AND PROGRAMS

Reentry programs in the United States were initially designed in the early 1960s for middle-class housewives who had no urgent need for paid work and who could afford to spend time and money investigating occupational alternatives. These programs were primarily established in the nonprofit sector, not as instrumentalities of government. More recently, government policy has directed attention to specific groups of reentrants, although some earlier public programs dealt with them indirectly.

The evolution from nonprofit assistance, supplemented to some extent by self-employed and profit-making providers, to government involvement, although not expropriation, has been a recurrent pattern in the development of social services in the United States. Nonprofit agencies have considerable freedom to experiment, and one of their principal *raisons d'être* has been to identify community needs and to introduce interventions that often lead to replication on a wider scale. When it became apparent that public resources were not responding to the expressed needs of many reentrants, voluntary agencies, as was their wont, were the first to devise means of assistance. Existing organizations like the Young Women's Christian Association and newly established community groups throughout the country initiated services designed to deal with various needs of long-term homemakers who, for one reason or another, were seeking to broaden their horizons.

At about the same time at many colleges and universities, continuing education programs were established with the principal aim of preparing housewives for formal schooling, with work as a probable but not necessarily inevitable outcome. Later, many of these institutions began to organize their own women's centers; by 1975, there were over 600 women's centers linked with institutions of higher education, although not all of them deal with the problems of reentrants.

Large-scale governmental training and employment efforts which were initiated in 1962 and 1973 were only related to reentry insofar as some homemakers qualified for enrollment because they met criteria other than discontinuity of labor force participation. Only in the late '70s have certain reentrants been specifically identified in legislation as targets for special types of assistance.

Today, manifold programs throughout the country provide some kind of aid to reentrants. Broadly, they tend to fall into the following categories: women's centers; employment and training programs; educational offerings; and placement services. Program sponsorship is primarily public or nonprofit, but in many instances, services are funded by a combination of sources. Relatively few current projects that deal with the needs of reentrants cater to them exclusively. Far more common are programs that are open to all persons with specified problems. Some programs have income restrictions, others do not; some are free, others charge fees, often on a sliding scale.

The rapid proliferation of efforts to improve the status of women, including reentrants, testifies to the American propensity to invent a multitude of corrective mechanisms as soon as a social problem is identified, or to appropriate, in full or in part, established machinery designed for other purposes. Since there is no archetypical American reentry program, in the discussion that follows, typical offerings will have to symbolize the many.

Services to Reentrants

Broadly speaking, the major services available to reentrants consist of counseling and guidance, skill training and education, placement, and job creation, each of which comprises a variety of components.

Counseling and guidance. The United States is the progenitor and nurturer of counseling. There is probably no life situation, from the cradle to the grave, that has not spawned counseling specialists. Since public school systems, which were among the first employers of guidance counselors on a large scale, have been curtailing support services due to financial stringency and have been closing down schools because of a declining pupil population, services to reentrants represent a new counseling focus.

The counseling available to many women who have been out of the labor force for extended periods, or who have never been gainfully employed, often consists of guidance with respect to vocational choice and any training implications, and job search. Often, occupational information as well as details about the local labor market are also provided. Sometimes encounters with peers and with successful reentrant models are facilitated to relieve women of anxieties attendant upon reentry, and occasionally postplacement counseling is available to counter any problems arising in the workplace.

Aside from specific job-related guidance, many programs offer counseling of a nonspecific psychologically oriented nature, with the professed aim of improving clients' "self-esteem," "assertiveness," "self-awareness," and the like. This is often supposed to establish defenses against presumptive discriminatory treatment in the workplace, but it sometimes appears to be counterproductive and may postpone job search unnecessarily.

A reentrant who consulted a counselor in a feminist organization reported:

I later realized that I'd gotten very negative feelings from it. The counselor had given me a lot of ideas about how to go out and look for a job, how to present myself in a resume, and suggested various areas I might try, but at the same time she gave me the feeling that I was going to run into enormous discrimination because I was a woman. Maybe that's true but I think there's less now than there used to be. Anyway, emphasizing it just made me say to myself, 'Oh, what's the use! It's a huge obstacle in my life. I'm just not going to make it so why put out the effort?'

Training and education. There are two types of training that are most commonly pursued by adult women as a prelude to reentry or belated entry to the labor force. The first involves basic preparation for those whose earlier formal schooling was deficient in providing the minimum competencies necessary to compete for decent jobs. This form of training is supplied in adult education programs sponsored by public school systems, and in government and nonprofit programs which usually utilize the classroom to provide teaching of fundamental skills and other sites to provide specific skill training. Mature women who participate in these programs tend to have had minimal prior work experience, if any, and to be at the lowest educational and income levels of all reentrants.

Reentrants above minimum competency levels who wish to obtain educational credentials for use in the labor market customarily receive this type of training in institutions of higher learning or trade and vocational schools.

A study of a sample of middle-aged women not employed in 1967 but employed in 1972 found that over 36 percent had pursued occupational training prior to entering the job market, often in order to complete their general education at the high school or college level. Their training was usually a brief encounter and was rarely for the purpose of preparing for a new career. Most of the reentrants had returned to traditional fields where they were able to use their prior training and work experience as credentials. The two groups found to be the most likely candidates for retraining were women planning to complete interrupted professional training or professionals interested in preparing for less-crowded occupations; and women who had never acquired any job skills.[22]

A divorced reentrant who had incomplete teacher training said:

If I had the six credits I need for my license I could be going for interviews. So that really is a stumbling block. Right now my education is useless—not worthless, but useless until I get those six credits.

Another reentrant currently taking courses after seven years at home remarked:

At first I went back to the greeting card company where I had worked for nine years. I had a portfolio of my work but had done just a few things through the years. They told me that competition was very stiff. I had always thought that I needed to go back to school because I had never had any formal art training.

A 34-year-old AFDC high school dropout with no work experience was enrolled in a government training program:

It was always in the back of my head to do something, but I think when I read the article about this one woman who was out there working, I said, 'that's what I need to push me out of the dumps.'

Apprenticeship training in the United States has rarely been available to women. In 1976, less than two percent of all registered apprentices were female. Although an Apprenticeship Outreach program sponsored jointly by trade unions, government and employers has been stepping up the recruitment of women, in most cases applicants must be below the age of 30, which effectively prevents the majority of reentrants from availing themselves of these new possibilities. Without an apprenticeship, opportunities for good jobs in the skilled trades are minimal in most areas of the country.

One of the recommendations of a survey in the early 1970s of women in apprenticeships in the State of Wisconsin was that age limitations be waived for qualified females candidates, since most women turn to apprenticeship opportunities after marriage and childbearing. A further recommendation was expansion of apprenticeable occupations to more trades where women have been traditionally employed, such as child care and health-related occupations.[23]

Placement. Placement is usually obtained either by the job seeker herself or through informal or formal intermediaries. The latter include public, private and nonprofit employment agencies, as well as training institutions and counseling centers.

Table 6.10 Unemployed Jobseekers by the Jobsearch Methods Used, Sex and Reason for Unemployment, 1978

Sex and Reason	Thousands of Persons		Methods Used as a Percent of Total Jobseekers						Average Number of Methods Used
	Total Unemployed	Total Jobseekers	Public Employment Agency	Private Employment Agency	Employer Directly	Placed or Answered Ads	Friends or Relatives	Other	
Total, 16 years and over	6,047	5,200	26.3	5.9	71.5	29.2	13.8	6.3	1.53
Job losers	2,514	1,809	35.3	7.2	69.9	30.5	15.9	7.4	1.66
Job leavers	851	837	26.4	6.5	74.1	33.8	12.7	4.3	1.58
Reentrants	1,814	1,704	21.5	5.6	69.4	28.3	13.0	7.0	1.45
New entrants	867	851	16.7	3.3	76.4	23.5	12.3	4.6	1.37
Males, 16 years and over	3,051	2,550	28.4	5.9	72.2	26.6	16.2	8.2	1.57
Job losers	1,572	1,137	35.4	7.1	70.6	27.4	16.8	9.2	1.67
Job leavers	406	398	28.1	6.0	74.1	31.2	14.6	5.0	1.59
Reentrants	687	637	22.6	5.2	71.3	24.6	16.3	9.9	1.50
New entrants	385	378	17.2	3.2	76.7	22.5	15.9	5.3	1.41
Females, 16 years and over	2,996	2,651	24.3	6.0	70.7	31.6	11.5	4.6	1.49
Job losers	942	672	35.1	7.4	68.6	35.6	14.3	4.2	1.65
Job leavers	445	439	24.8	6.8	74.0	36.2	11.2	3.6	1.57
Reentrants	1,127	1,066	20.7	5.8	68.4	30.6	10.9	5.4	1.42
New entrants	482	473	16.5	3.4	76.3	24.3	9.5	4.0	1.34

Source: U.S. Department of Labor, Bureau of Labor Statistics, *Employment and Earnings* 26, no. 1 (January 1979).

In 1978 unemployed female reentrants to the workforce utilized a variety of job search methods. More than two-thirds of these women said they had applied directly to employers. Next in order of frequency was the placement of or response to newspaper want ads (31 percent). The public employment agency was utilized by 21 percent of all women reentrants; private employment agencies were used by six percent (Table 6.10).

Employer application was the most succesful method by which women who had been keeping house obtained jobs, according to a 1973 survey which found that 40 percent of them had obtained their jobs in this manner, compared to 35 percent of all jobseekers. Answering want ads was also more productive for homemakers (19 percent) than for all job aspirants (12 percent). Employment agencies were quite low in the overall ranking and even lower as successful reentry intermediaries, 4.6 percent of reentrants having found jobs through the public employment service and 5.5 percent through private agencies.[24]

The fact that informal search methods were more fruitful means of securing reentry jobs than the use of formal intermediaries does not imply a lack of need for assistance to reentrants, since participation in various types of preparatory programs frequently provides these women with the knowhow to proceed on their own. Moreover, women in the greatest need of assistance have the least access to contacts who can facilitate introductions to prospective employers.

Job creation. Public and nonprofit efforts at creating jobs in the government and private sectors have been underway in recent years. However, public service jobs or government-sponsored work experience or on-the-job training in the private sector have had little applicability to the average reentrant since they have been largely designed for the unemployed or for persons receiving public assistance.

Some programs which have been especially designed for displaced homemakers have given a good deal of attention to developing new jobs, often building on competencies gained in housekeeping and child rearing. These are, of course, traditional jobs almost exclusively, and therefore are likely to have all the disadvantages attached to such employment—low wages, insecurity, poor potential. Yet they can be helpful to women of late middle age and older who are close to qualifying for social security and to those in dire need of rapid placement who may use them to qualify for better jobs subsequently.

Public Policy

Generally speaking, the policy of the United States government with respect to the provision of aid in negotiating the labor market has been to make placement services freely available to everyone but to limit programs designed to enhance employability to population groups who are considered incapable of fending for themselves, at least financially.

As far as reentrants or delayed entrants to the labor force are concerned, this means that most wives of employed husbands, and female household heads with adequate income, must look elsewhere if they want or need concrete assistance, other than aid in placement, during the process of reentry. In other words, there is a means test for eligibility for government-sponsored employment and training programs, and the mere desire for assistance in entering or reentering the labor force, absent defined need, has not been acknowledged as sufficient reason for the expenditure of public funds.

The Employment Service. The public employment service (ES) is a nationwide federal-state placement system which provides counseling and placement services in 2,500 local offices. While its primary function is that of a labor exchange, the ES also has been assigned various responsibilities in connection with specific government employment and training programs. Although most offices provide such services as counseling, testing, training referral, and job development, the bulk of attention is given to matching applicants and jobs.

In general, the public employment service is used only by a minority of all unemployed persons and, as noted earlier, reentrants are no exception to this rule. The extent to which reentrants are represented among the population that is assisted by the ES is unknown because of the absence of requirements to provide data delineating clients' age, sex *and* date of last employment. although women have been identified as one of eight target groups for special services, there is no way to pinpoint services to homemakers seeking to enter the labor force.

A disadvantage in the job search of reentrants to the work force, as well as that of new entrants, arises from the requirement that recipients of unemployment insurance must register for placement at ES offices. Since eligibility for unemployment insurance is limited to individuals with recent work experience, this segment of ES applicants is viewed as a more desirable labor supply by employers than reentrants without recent employment. IN 1973, for example, 7.8 percent of female job leavers compared to 4.6 percent of reentrants found their current job through the ES.[25] Moreover, links with employers are often strengthened when they can rely on ES referral of experienced personnel.

While the state network of public employment agencies has been encouraged to pay attention to the needs of women, personnel frequently complain of insufficient staff to handle both traditional placement services and new duties assigned in relation to special employment programs. The broad age span of the population to be served, from 18 to 65 years, and the wide range of problems presented, makes it extremely difficult to pursue selective efforts to serve particular groups that may need intensive help.

Even where efforts are made to provide specific aid to reentrants, they sometimes seem misplaced. A booklet prepared by the New York State

Employment Service for reentrants, for example, describes means of self-assessment of skills and suggests methods of pursuing job search, including whom to approach and how to prepare for a job interview. One page, entitled "Have You Thought Seriously About the Problems Which Having a Job May Make For You" brings up the following issues:

If money is your major concern:
    There's daily carfare
    And lunch—will you carry it?
    —tip at counter?
    —line up at a cafeteria?

And the cost of maintaining personal appearance
    —for beauty parlors
    —dry cleaners
    —laundries

And the cost of clothes; "house dresses" won't do on most jobs.
Family food costs may go up as you have less time to shop and prepare.
And don't overlook the cost of collections for charity drives and gifts.

There are personal "costs" too:
    —day after day you must be at work and on time.
    —there may be rush-hour travel, even standing all the way.
    —you will have little time to "call your own."

How does your family feel about your getting a job?
Can you keep your home the way you like it and work too?
Have you thought about any change in income tax rates which another income in the family might bring?

While it is reasonable to alert reentrants to some of the costs and problems of working, the foregoing list can hardly be described as supportive or encouraging. Note how many of these concerns are equally applicable to men, yet it is hardly likely that such questions would be posed to male job seekers. While this booklet presumably was designed to be helpful, one cannot help but conjecture about the number of reentrants who may have abandoned the idea of returning to work as the result of this series of caveats. Perhaps that was its underlying purpose!

A 1974 survey in 20 representative cities from 100,000 to 250,000 in population found that seekers of clerical and sales jobs were most likely to use the public employment service, although a disproportionately small percentage of employers listed such jobs with the ES. Since this group includes a large component of reentrants, the discrepancy between supply and demand prevented many women from finding jobs through the public agency. An additional finding was that only 20 percent of all ES applicants were counseled, 15 percent tested, and six percent referred to other programs, a significant departure from practices in the 1960s when employability development was stressed. Consequently, many reentrants probably could not rely on the ES for help in occupational choice but had to know beforehand what kind of job to seek.[26]

A 32-year-old divorcee with a B.A. but no work experience reported:

I got one suggestion from a man at the State Employment Agency that really knocked me out. I had gone to him, about getting a job in the art field, and he said, 'Here's one. This is a great job. You could make five or six dollars an hour. Weighing noodles at the airport. And it's not taxing at all.' I said, 'You don't understand. I want to be taxed. I want to do something that's hard. I don't want to sit there like I've had a lobotomy and make six dollars an hour.' That was the low point, especially when I considered doing it.

On the other hand, a woman who went to an ES professional office right after receiving a delayed bachelor's degree was quite satisfied:

It was a very nice experience. I had a woman who spent two hours with me. I had sent a resume to them and made an appointment and she went over the resume with me. Things I had forgotten or thought were inconsequential she pulled out of me which really made my resume look like something. It took her two or three months to come up with two suitable jobs—one as a hospital unit coordinator, the other as assistant registrar at a community college. I chose the job in education.

The Work Incentive Program. Some American women reenter the labor force through force of circumstance; some through force of law. The law in question is the Work Incentive Program, known as WIN, an acronym which has proven to be far from apt over the course of time. WIN was established by a 1967 amendment to the Social Security Act as a means of providing job training and placement services for employable AFDC recipients. In essence, WIN is a quid pro quo which obligates certain individuals who receive public support to accept the offer of jobs or job training with the goal of removing them from the welfare rolls.

Strictly speaking, WIN is not a program aimed at facilitating reentry or delayed entry of women to the labor force. In effect, however, it can serve this purpose for many women because the preponderance of persons eligible for the services it provides are female family heads, many of whom are nearing or have reached middle age with, at best, marginal experience in the labor force.

The initial legislation (WIN I) emphasized highly individualized services including training, counseling and other means of developing employability, with participants spending as long as a year in the program. Amendments in 1971 (WIN II) mandated a shift in priorities with a reduction of institutional training in favor of immediate job referral, in order to accelerate the entry of larger numbers to the labor force. In 1977, the federal obligation for WIN came to $245 million; enrollment totaled about 570,000 persons; and placements amounted to 272,000 jobs, more than three out of five of which were filled by women. In that year, there were about 3.6 million AFDC families, four-fifths headed by women.

All AFDC applicants and recipients 16 years of age or older are required to register for WIN as a condition of eligibility for assistance, unless legally exempt for such reasons as the presence of a child under the age of six, ill health, home responsibilities, advanced age, student status, etc. Welfare agencies determine exemptions, and nonexempt persons must register at the local ES office where their employability is appraised. Those who are considered readily employable are generally counseled in a day-long session of training in job-finding skills through role playing and are provided with labor market information and access to job listings. Only registrants for whom immediate placement is not considered feasible but who are judged to have employment potential may be provided with institutional training or other job preparation. One-third of all work and training funds is required to be expended for on-the-job training or public service employment. Day care and other supportive services are also provided, when necessary and if possible, to insure participation. In 1976, over one-third of total WIN funding was used for these purposes.

There are no data that would permit a definitive determination of the use of WIN as a vehicle for reentry or delayed entry to the labor force. Movement to and fro between welfare and employment is a common phenomenon, as is supplementation of welfare grants by some paid employment. Research has shown that selection for WIN is a creaming process which favors persons with recent work experience who are interested in improving their job status and who have participated in a previous job-training program.[27] Long time welfare clients who have shown little or no interest in labor force participation prior to WIN eligibility are unlikely to be considered favorable prospects for participation, especially in view of program limitations.

In fact, relatively few AFDC mothers are judged ready to participate in WIN. Analysis of 1975 data pertaining to WIN exemptions, registrations, and certifications indicates that only about one-third of all women with no child under the age of six years were certified for WIN training or placement.

A WIN counselor estimated that only about ten percent of welfare mothers really want to work. "Most see nothing but hassle from going to work. Being a mother is *the* thing. The only self-image they have is mother, not person, not worker." This perception, which appears to be fairly widespread among welfare workers, often leads to broad application of exemptions. Whether it is a correct inference or an example of "benign neglect" is unclear, but it has been found that there are distinct differences among AFDC mothers with respect to their orientation toward work and that women who prefer to be home rather than working are able to negotiate their way out of WIN. Adaptations of eligibility requirements have resulted in the selection of young, single and better-educated "modernizers" into the program rather than the traditionally oriented.[28] WIN, however, appears to have a poor reputation as an employment facilitator among many job aspirants.

When my daughter began school full-time in the fall of 1977, the Welfare Department required that I get a job. They would have enrolled me in their Work Incentive Program (WIN) but a housing problem delayed my entry. In the meantime I looked around for alternatives to WIN which I saw as a dead-end.

A 30-year old AFDC mother said:

Welfare tried to discourage me from going to college. They wanted me to go into the Work Incentive Program, but I told them I didn't want to because I didn't like what they offered. They wouldn't help me get into college, and I said, 'Fine. I'll do it on my own." When I got scholarship money for community college, they told me I was allowed only two years to finish.

WIN has failed to help large numbers of welfare recipients obtain the type of work in the regular job market that provides sufficient earnings to leave the welfare rolls. Although WIN women without recent work experience have been shown to benefit in terms of net earnings gains when exposed to assistance beyond mere job referral (such as vocational training, job search assistance and, most significantly, subsidized employment), very few of them are able to obtain long-term unsubsidized employment that permits them to achieve complete independence of welfare.[29] Where positive results have been achieved, the specific aspects of WIN services that are responsible for successful job retention have not been established. "The formal categories of help, such as 'education,' 'vocational training,' or 'on-the-job training' do not seem to signify the important events that help certain trainees improve their work effort over the longer run."[30]

The WIN program has been a tranquilizer for public anxiety about the rising costs of welfare rather than a practical approach to solving the employment problems of the welfare population. Yet even if welfare mothers who have had little or no work experience prior to becoming eligible for WIN were provided with the extraordinary assistance they need, there is no guarantee that the effort would be successful in the absence of sufficient job opportunities. Without a dual focus upon employment services *and* job development, the current WIN focus upon the employable is probably realistic, but it means abandoning any expectation of a massive reduction in the number of women on welfare.

A government-funded demonstration of supported work was initiated in 1976 to determine the effects of employment experience on individuals with special and persistent difficulties in the job market, AFDC mothers being one of four target groups. The aim of the program is to prepare participants for successful employment in regular unsubsidized jobs by providing a broad range of jobs at public, private and nonprofit work sites, where a number of specific supportive techniques are utilized that include peer support, graduated stress and close supervision. The average age of the AFDC demonstration group was 35 years, and about nine out of ten of the women were black. Only 30 percent had completed high school, and only six percent were married.

An analysis of experiences during the project found that these women perform very well when closely supervised and provided with a variety of supports during the training period. In comparison with the other groups (ex-offenders, ex-addicts and teen-age school dropouts), their rate of program completion has been superior, although they eventually found permanent placement in jobs with low hourly earnings relative to the male groups.[31] This finding suggests the pervasiveness of sex as an employment handicap regardless of performance.

The following remarks of a local program director about AFDC mothers in one supported work program suggest that the "protective" attitudes of welfare workers may arise from incorrect inferences.

> They come in on time, they don't miss work, they don't fight on the job. They're terrific. But I went over to the welfare office on some business or other and the people there looked at me with pity, saying 'You poor thing, you had to hire all those people who will never hold a job.'[32]

CETA. The Comprehensive Employment and Training Act of 1973 (CETA) has been the major vehicle for planning and delivery of manpower services to the economically disadvantaged, the unemployed and the underemployed. The CETA legislation makes provision for the funding of a diversity of programs including such services as outreach, counseling, institutional and on-the-job training, employer subsidies, training allowances, supportive services, job referrals, and public service employment. The authority for planning, implementing, operating, monitoring and assessing the programs is in the hands of states and units of local government, who design the services and the service mix to meet local needs. In some cases, private community-based organizations serving special target groups or delivering special services have been recipients of CETA funding. The 1977 federal obligation for CETA amounted to more than $9 billion and total enrollment to over 3.6 million persons.

Until 1978 when CETA was restructured, it contained no specific reference to female reentrants to the labor force per se as a target for employment-related services. Some reentrants, however, were eligible for participation in projects established under the terms of this legislation, primarily welfare recipients and members of families with incomes below the poverty standard. In many instances, these women were WIN registrants who were referred for CETA training or other assistance. Women who had already embarked on job search but had not obtained jobs, who had acquired jobs paying less than the poverty wage, or who were working part-time but seeking full-time work also were eligible. A small number of programs enrolled middle-aged entrants or reentrants who were out of the labor force and who were not economically disadvantaged, but these were exceptional.

CETA is not an entitlement program, and since resources have been limited, only a small proportion of the eligible population has participated. It has been estimated that there were more than ten times as many eligibles as people who received services. Data describing the characteristics of CETA participants are not available in a form that permits an estimate of the participation of female reentrants or delayed entrants to the labor force. They do indicate, however, that recipients of services were primarily under the age of 30 years and that, although women predominated among the eligible population, they comprised a minority of participants. Older women have not been considered a prime target for services, even when economically disadvantaged. Minimal or remote work experience coupled with relatively advanced age may have discouraged reentrants' acceptance in CETA programs, especially since applicants are often screened to obtain the best qualified.

Reauthorization of CETA in 1978 amounted to a major restructuring of the law and included new target groups for employment and training programs, among whom are displaced homemakers, women, and single parents. To those who question why it was necessary to include displaced homemakers as a separate target if women, themselves, were expressly cited as eligible for CETA assistance, the response was that special mention is warranted on the basis of specificity. Other groups of women may have to compete for funding but the displaced homemaker, as an explicit narrowly defined group of eligibles, has firmer ground for assistance.

The draft CETA regulations define a displaced homemaker as

an individual who has not worked in the labor force for a substantial number of years but has, during those years, worked in the home providing unpaid services for family members; *and* has been dependent on public assistance or on the income of another family member but is no longer supported by that income; or is receiving public assistance on account of dependent children in the home; especially where such assistance will soon be terminated; *and* is unemployed or underemployed and is experiencing difficulty in obtaining or upgrading employment.

New eligibility requirements specify both low income *and* a spell of unemployment. This will tend to restrict the number of eligibles since many low-income women who might benefit from CETA aid are out of the labor force. In fact, one analysis has shown that more displaced home-makers and single parents were eligible for assistance under the old than under the new rules. "An eligibility regulation that requires a long spell of unemployment prior to entry into the program may screen out precisely the most needy, and thus most discouraged, workers."[33] The use of the unemployment criterion together with a requirement that family income be 70 percent of the lower living standard narrowly circumscribes the number of women qualified to participate in CETA programs, not only because they are not counted among the unemployed, but also because many have incomes above the allowable maximum, although often not far above, and frequently only temporarily above.

While no age criterion or definition of the meaning of "substantial number of years" out of the labor force were included in the new Act, priority as displaced homemakers will be given to individuals out of the labor force for ten years or more "and/or" over 40 years of age. In effect, this means that length of absence alone is sufficient for priority consideration and, therefore, that the emphasis of the displaced homemaker movement on women of relatively late age will be diluted. On the other hand, this could be a boon to younger reentrants who meet the eligibility standards.

The type of projects that might be eligible for funding under the CETA displaced homemaker provision are described as programs

> to provide employment opportunities and appropriate training and support services (through multipurpose projects or otherwise) . . . Such training and support services shall include but not be limited to—
>
> (1) job training, job readiness services, job counseling, job search and job placement services;
> (2) outreach and information services, including information on available educational opportunities; and
> (3) referrals (through cooperative arrangements, to the maximum extent feasible) to health, financial management, legal, public assistance and other appropriate support services in the community being served.

The above activities are expected, as far as possible, to be coordinated with and supplement activities supported under other parts of the law and to emphasize training and other services designed to enhance employability and earnings, as well as concentrate on creating new jobs in the private sector for displaced homemakers. Additionally, the statute provides that supervisory, technical, and administrative positions within the program shall be filled, where feasible, by displaced homemakers and that enrollees should be selected on a priority basis by virtue of age, education, training, household support obligations, and employability.

This would appear to be a massive shopping list from which a prospective grantee can take what seems most choice—if the Secretary of Labor will allocate the money. Since the Department of Labor has committed "up to" $5 million for this section (out of an $11 billion CETA authorization), there will either be a few centers with sufficient funds or many who will get some funding but will have to look elsewhere for supplemental monies. Receipt of a CETA grant does not prevent application for other funds from other governmental sources, national, state, or local, as well as from private donors. Moreover, centers can raise money by charging fees to women who are not economically disadvantaged for services freely given to the disadvantaged. The inclusion of women and single parents as target groups may, of course, enlarge training opportunities for disadvantaged reentrants other than displaced homemakers.

Prior to the reauthorization, some number of reentrants were served under various titles of the act, primarily Title I which provided services to the "disadvantaged" (on welfare or with a family income below the poverty level or 70 percent of the BLS lower level living standard), and Title III which authorized services to "segments of the population that are in particular need." Several programs were organized by both public and private community-based organizations for which reentrants were eligible.

The single most common goal of special CETA programs for women was nontraditional training. Of 102 such programs in 1977, 80 were wholly or partially devoted to this purpose. Eight programs were designed to serve "displaced homemakers," four of which included nontraditional training among their offerings. Five programs were partly or solely directed to aiding "mature women," and twelve were established to serve female heads-of-household. These, too, often had a nontraditional job-training component. Nine programs were described as resource centers and generally were directed to assisting a diversity of female clients in different ways.

Because of the wide variations in approach and purpose, no single description can encompass all components of CETA programs that have provided services to reentrants. Therefore, the following account of CETA programs is a broad view obtained from onsite inspection and written reports.

Projects ranged from preorientation, designed to prepare women to enter training programs, to comprehensive services including testing, counseling, skills training and/or work experience. Most programs operated under contracts with public agencies or with private organizations such as women's centers, YWCA's and community colleges, which provided some or all of the services. Most work experience slots were arranged on public or nonprofit sites with stipends paid to participants, although some nontraditional programs have been able to secure on-the-job training in the private sector.

Eligibility criteria varied. Some programs had specific income requirements, while others used unemployment as the sole standard for acceptance. Assistance was occasionally provided to women without regard to their financial status but simply in response to perceived need for services. Recruitment was handled in a number of ways including referral by ES offices, social agencies and women's centers, and through various types of publicity.

Work experience and training usually stressed office skills. While most nontraditional programs provided training in apprenticeable trades, some programs avoided these areas as unrealistic in view of sex discrimination and limited job opportunities. Instead, they provided training in such areas as commission sales, computer repair and management. Attempts to encourage older women to consider nontraditional occupations were often reported to encounter strong resistance. White-collar employment is viewed as more prestigious despite its inferior returns. This viewpoint was said to be particularly prevalent among the poorest women for whom traditional female employment represented upward social mobility as long as it was not domestic employment.

Where placement was the goal, it was accomplished for a high proportion of those who completed programs and was often in subsidized employment. No estimate of the placement record of reentrants alone is available, because most programs served a diverse clientele. Moreover, there was considerable diversity among reentrants, themselves, in terms of job readiness. There were indications, however, that prolonged absence from the labor force in combination with poor educational background required intensive services that were often unavailable. In many cases, participant selection suggested considerable creaming of the most employable in terms of education, work experience or, quite simply, motivation to work. While this sometimes implied that services were redundant, where acceptance was principally based on the incentive to work the use of this criterion seems rational in view of time and service limitations. There was no indication that reentrants derived greater benefit from programs exclusively directed to them than from those serving women of all ages and backgrounds, as long as sufficient individualized attention was provided. Educational attainment and receptivity to program offerings appeared to have a more significant impact on employability than age, and maturity in combination with homemaking and other nonmarket experience was often a plus.

Excerpts from interviews with participants in CETA programs provide some indication of reentrants' experiences.

A 30-year-old high school dropout recalled:

For a brief period after we moved, my husband was out of work. He finally got a job but we couldn't make it on his money. I was ready to go to work so I looked through the newspapers for jobs but I really didn't think I was qualified for many things. In March I applied for a CETA job thinking that they could place me in a job because I'd been out of work so long, and I was accepted in the program.

A 26-year old welfare mother declared:

Where I come from if you work you're not cool. To work is a drag. Your mama worked all her life and she has nothing. But I knew I'm not going to work all my life and not have something. I don't have to be like my mother and my aunt and all the other women I see—factory work, keypunch, secretarial. Look at what *Women Working* [a CETA program] did for me. I swore to never work a day in my life. Really, I swore that and I meant that. It just changed me completely around.

A 40-year-old high school dropout with no work experience said:

Welfare didn't have any job for me. It's a shame. They make you stay on it because you're afraid to get off it. It really is a crutch. I didn't like it when I had to wonder when my check was coming. The CETA program gave me initiative and made me realize I could do something with my brain.

A 29-year-old reentrant in a nontraditional CETA program remarked:

I love it. I really didn't know this kind of opportunity was open to women. There is counseling available and there isn't any way that they don't back you up. They make everything very easy.

The Vocational Education Act. 1976 amendments to the Vocational Education Act marked the first time that federal legislation has specifically addressed the need of women for equal access to vocational education and job training. The Act consolidates most vocational education categorical grants into a single block grant for states who, in turn, distribute the funds to local education agencies and private groups.

The states must use some funds to provide vocational education programs for displaced homemakers, single heads of households, and homemakers seeking employment. Those programs must include organized education and training to prepare these individuals for employment, courses in job search techniques, and placement services. Although these programs are mandatory, the level of funding is left to the discretion of the state.

The requirement for funding programs for displaced homemakers has been the most difficult to fulfill because of the difficulty of identifying them, encouraging them to seek help and placing them. The other target adults are seen as younger and readier to seek training.

One Voc Ed project provides for a new credentialing method that will produce a standardized system to translate the life experience of women into formal credentials. The Educational Testing Service will develop a skill inventory to be submitted to employers for determination of the relevance of each experience to occupational skills. Test groups of women will then be placed in employment or vocational training on the basis of the results. Finally, a national standardized accreditation system will be established that can be utilized by reentrants to provide job credentials.

Part-Time Career Employment Act of 1978. The massive movement of adult women into the American labor force would not have occurred if part-time jobs had not been available on a large scale, since reduced work schedules make it possible for married women to combine home and family responsibilities. As desirable as part-time employment may be under these circumstances, however, it rarely provides the security or fringe benefits offered to full-time employees, and often does not serve as a bridge to full-time employment at the time when a woman's home duties have lightened. Nevertheless, serious doubt about the ability of the American economy to provide sufficient future full-time opportunities for all job seekers has led to considerable pressure to encourage alternative work patterns.

The Part-Time Career Opportunities Act authorizes three-year experimental programs of flexible and compressed work schedules in federal agencies for people who need variable hours as long as they carry the primary responsibility for child rearing and homemaking. This is a three-year experimental program which supplements other initiatives in the public and private sectors.

Educational Programs

Formal education.

I went to social work school really because I had absolutely no confidence in my ability to go out and get a job without having some sort of professional degree or training. Now that I'm in school I have become aware of what kinds of things are available and have some idea of where to look. It's a very tortuous way of going about it. Yet this is the way I felt most comfortable doing it.

When I got my masters in theatre arts in 1970, I found that there were tons of people with masters and Ph.D.s and I did not compete well in the metropolitan area. I could not get a college teaching job. I was competing with out-of-work Broadway actors and with my limited professional experience I was not successful.

I do want to be a doctor. There are times that I like what I'm doing and times that I hate it but on the whole I'm glad that I did it.

In October 1976, 958,000 women, 35 years and over, were enrolled in school at a variety of levels, representing more than three out of five of all students of these ages. These students were working to obtain diplomas or degrees or to acquire or upgrade vocational skills and do not include thousands of persons enrolled in noncredit continuing education courses, which are not generally vocationally oriented.

Of these women, 332,000, or 35 percent, were not in the labor force: about two-fifths of those in vocational and high schools, and one-third of the college undergraduate or graduate students. Graduate students were the most likely to be employed. One may infer that most women out of the work force were prospective reentrants, although it is probable that some did not intend to put their credentials to use in the labor market and others had temporarily left the labor force in order to prepare for new careers or to upgrade their qualifications.

Almost three-quarters of women college students in the 35 plus age group were married with husbands present; below the college level and in vocational and trade schools, the majority were not currently married. The preponderance of wives at the college level would appear to be associated with their ability to tap their husbands' incomes for tuition, since women with a taste for higher education tend to be from middle- and upper-income families. If such women plan to reenter the labor force, they are more likely not only to have the wherewithal to finance higher education than women from lower income households, but also to aspire to occupations requiring college and graduate degrees.

The eagerness with which institutions of higher education have embraced potential reentrants to the labor force is a testimonial to the ingenuity of American educational administrators. Aware that demographic projections presaged trouble ahead if they continued to devote most of their attention to a narrow youthful age group, they have expanded their focus to take in other groups while, at the same time, encouraging the development of a range of support services as extra added attractions. They have also persuaded arms of the government to aid them in these endeavors by funding adult programs or by assisting adult students to finance courses of study.

New 'clientele' had to be found. Women over age 22 seemed the most likely applicant pool—especially women who could afford to pay for their education. And so the administrators seized upon the rhetoric of the [women's] movement and urged women to explore new life options through their colleges. 'Special' programs for women reentering or entering college for the first time were inaugurated. Some were old programs with new titles; a few actually attempted to address special needs of adult women.[34]

Continuing education. Until quite recently attempts of mature women to gain entrance to regular programs of instruction at the undergraduate or graduate college levels were usually thwarted, due to combined age and sex discrimination that was rationalized by administrators as recognition of the facts of worklife. In an attempt to skirt the mainstream, programs of continuing education for women were organized in colleges and universities primarily to serve adult females who had not completed college and wished to determine the feasibility of starting from the beginning or from where they had left off. The initial focus of programs of continuing education for women was academic rather than occupational, although the linkage between these two arenas was not ignored. Most participants were viewed, however, not as imminent reentrants to the work force but as housewives who wished to initiate or renew contact with higher education, but only in a manner that meshed with home responsibilities.

Programs of continuing education for women have taken many shapes and forms. Although most offer noncredit courses, many programs now grant credit as well as academic degrees, and some permit older women to participate in classes with regular students. Furthermore, increasing numbers of these programs are directly oriented to the job market, providing occupational training, alone or in conjunction with schooling in the liberal arts.

In June 1976, 2,225 colleges and universities reported 8.8 million registrations in adult and continuing education programs, an increase of 3.2 million or 57 percent over the 1967-68 academic year. Enrollment continued to rise in 1977, with women increasing their percentages in both full- and part-time study.

Publications listing the locations of continuing education programs and their offerings are distributed by government and other agencies, and a great deal of outreach is accomplished through advertisements in newspapers and magazines, radio and television. Some courses are also provided on regular or closed-circuit television channels. In addition, some scholarships and loans are available to middle-aged women who wish to undertake higher education but cannot finance these studies themselves.

Federal support for the development of model programs of continuing education was provided under the Women's Educational Equity Act with an allocation of $7 million in 1977-78 to develop programs for various groups of women, including reentrants. Many of the projects funded are addressed to the job training and counseling needs of low-income female residents of rural and urban communities.

Community colleges. Continuing higher education for women is provided at two- and four-year colleges and at universities. The two-year institutions, in particular, are a major vehicle for adult training, hence for reentry.

The public two-year college began to establish itself as a significant fixture on the American educational scene after World War II. Between 1960 and 1977, the number of two-year institutions rose from 678 to 1,235, and enrollment increased from about 660,000 to more than 4.3 million students.

A major rationale for the development of these institutions was the need to provide occupationally oriented education that would address the specific labor requirements of local employers that were not being met in high school programs, especially training for emerging or expanding occupations in technical areas and human services leading to certificates, diplomas or the associate degree. Entrance standards are lower than in four-year colleges and universities, and offerings are directed to a diverse student body. Advanced age and inferior prior educational performance is rarely a barrier to acceptance by community colleges. Therefore, they represent second-chance institutions for large numbers of individuals who wish to reorient their lives.

Over 300 community colleges have established reentry programs since 1970, and they expect to continue their growth by serving increased proportions of women, minorities, and older students. Enrollment by persons 35 years of age or older in two-year colleges increased 30 percent from 1974 to 1976 alone. In the latter year, about 418,000 persons or 58 percent of all undergraduates in the 35 and over age group were enrolled in two-year colleges. While no data are available by both age and sex, women of all ages comprise half of the full-time student population and over half of part-time students in these institutions.

An inquiry into the offerings of over 800 two-year institutions indicated three types of recruitment efforts for women: noncredit continuing education workshops; specialized one-time events focusing on prelabor force entry needs; and credit or noncredit short-term career planning courses spotlighting specific college curricula, most of which were in such traditional fields as allied health, human services or secretarial science (the last, a euphemistic substitute for the type of training ordinarily provided on the high school level or in private vocational courses).[35]

Most of the women who attend such programs are middle-class housewives, some with baccalaureate degrees. Working class women are rarely in these programs because college is not within their purview. Some women are said to attend these sessions, not because they are eager to enter the labor market, but because of guilt about being at home, inspired by the new accent on women at work. Consequently, they use recruitment programs to seek reinforcement of their homemaking role, rather than to aid in assuming a work role. They want to be shown why work should be more attractive than homemaking. The counseling available to them, as well as to more committed reentrants, is variable in quality and often does nothing to alleviate their anxieties. The most productive community college reentry programs have an orientation period which provides extensive exposure to models in nontraditional areas, and labor market information indicating local demand occupations. They offer job search assistance for women deemed ready for employment and, for those who are not job ready, encourage enrollment in programs of occupational training directed toward meeting job requirements in well-paid fields where local opportunities are plentiful. Some programs maintain close ties with employers who commit themselves to employ qualified graduates.

Many community colleges provide special training for women enrolled in federally funded programs such as CETA and also are prime vehicles for realizing the equal opportunity goals of the Vocational Education Act.

Four-year colleges and universities. Four-year colleges and universities have also moved to broaden their student base and are increasingly acting to provide aid that has specific employment implications, although their stress continues to be placed on return to education rather than work. Few of these institutions provide places in regular undergraduate programs of instruction. Instead, separate entities have been organized on campuses to cater to adult students, and these are proliferating. At the graduate and professional levels, it is less difficult than formerly for older students to obtain admission although relatively advanced age is still a handicap. Another problem is costs, since government support is usually confined to full-time students; and this effectively restricts the access of many reentrants.

Special programs also have been developed to assist long-time homemakers to complete interrupted college careers; to provide short-term career training to women baccalaureates lacking employment-related skills; to translate volunteer experience into saleable job skills; and to refresh skills that have been unutilized or underutilized while out of the labor force.

The Science Career Facilitation Project of the National Science Foundation, for example, is aimed at working and nonworking women who received bachelor's or master's degrees in science between two and fifteen years ago and who are not presently employed in their fields of training. The purpose of the project is to increase participants' level of knowledge to that expected of a current recipient of a similar degree in order to enable them to enter directly into employment in their field of study, or into graduate training. The fields of training include engineering, chemistry, mathematics, computer science and such inter-disciplinary areas as polymer science and energy-related physical sciences. Funding was originally provided for educational costs only, but 1978 grants provided for some participant support. Eleven projects were funded in 1976 and another ten in 1977 with an annual expenditure of approximately $700,000 in each year.

A 1978 assessment of the program concluded that program offerings had to be tailored to meet personal needs: Women wishing to return to work gradually are best provided with updating on a part-time basis in order to test their motivation; those willing to make a full-time reentry commitment are best provided with a combination of updating and career preparation if these can be covered in a reasonable time and hold promise of eventual job placement. Financial support is often critical for these women who, unlike the gradual reentrants, would otherwise be unable to afford additional training.[36]

The Women's Management Development Project program at Goucher College, a four-year college for women in Maryland, is a government-financed experimental project with the dual aim of determining whether volunteer leadership experience is transferable to managerial employment and of evaluating the effectiveness of time-sharing at high job levels. The project consists of a six-month training program organized within the college, followed by a three-month time-sharing internship in the offices of major area private employers.

Internship development proved extremely difficult primarily because of the time-sharing aspect of the experiment—two women sharing one job, either part-day or part-week. In the end, eleven firms made a commitment to provide internships; some employers were converted to the idea of time-sharing by the directors of the program, who made a special point of its value as a means of retaining young female employees. The internships include jobs in sales, personnel, systems engineering, auditing, market analysis, etc. Among the employers are utilities, banking and insurance firms, large manufacturers and a health insurance organization.

In 1978-79, the initial year, participants comprised 22 women with bachelor's or master's degrees who ranged in age from 31 to 56 years and who had filled leadership volunteer positions. Some had never worked for pay; others had minimal work experience. The women were primarily white, suburban, upper-middle-class wives. Two were separated; one widowed. None had young children who required special attention.

Each woman will be paid by her employer for a 20-hour work-week (her half of total time on the job). While interning, the women will meet one evening a week with a support group and the projects' directors will have a liaison with each company. The women are not guaranteed a job after they complete their internships, nor are the employers guaranteed employees. If the women perform well, however, they may be offered jobs or use this experience as a reference for other placement possibilities.

The Fund for the Improvement of Postsecondary Education, which was established by the Education Amendments of 1972, provides support to colleges and universities "to reform their policies and practices to support new and returning learners." Although the fund is not exclusively involved with women's programs, one-half of the proposals submitted have sought funds to provide some form of counseling for older women, and the largest single category of awarded grants went to projects designed to help older women determine and attain their educational goals. The fund is authorized to award grants to accredited and nonaccredited institutions and has provided financing for a number of newly established community groups as well as assistance to educational institutions.

In the three years between 1973 and 1976, the Fund committed nearly $1.3 million for projects designed to help older women determine and attain their educational goals. While this commitment is to education not work, the decision of mature persons to consider further education is almost always career-related, and many of these projects take this fact into consideration. These include educational "brokerages," unaffiliated with particular institutions, whose purpose is to assist "nontraditional" college populations, including older women, in choosing among available educational options, as well as alternatives to formal education. One such program, Regional Learning Service in central New York State, was reported to have served 900 persons, almost 70 percent of whom were women.

In Boston, Massachusetts, WINNERS, an inner-city initiative which served over 1,000 women in three years, utilizes the concept of self-help. A staff of women from a predominately black community assists local women to select educational and/or career options and continues to offer personal and family supportive services after they have acted upon their choice. Its primary purpose is to serve as an advocate for women who do not have the access to information and assistance in career planning and preparation that is available to middle-class women. Similar programs have been established in other urban areas; many of them work with local colleges to develop programs to serve the needs of new populations of women students and to sensitize them to these women's needs.

External degree programs. Nontraditional projects that enable students to pursue education away from the campus are attracting growing interest, since they appeal to such people as homemakers who cannot accommodate their time to the hours of attendance required by academic institutions or who do not live near such institutions.

Some of these programs provide external degrees, which can be obtained entirely on the basis of credits earned through proficiency examinations or through acknowledgment of nonscholastic experience. Others require occasional attendance on campus, but some projects have neither campus nor permanent faculty.

These programs offer more flexibility, variety and opportunity for off-campus learning than do most adult education and correspondence programs. They also sometimes permit persons like reentrants to capitalize on the nonmarket activities they engaged in during their breaks from work.

The growth of external degree programs has been accompanied by some dissent, however, on the grounds that they devalue academic degrees and are simply devices for evaluating the scholastic value of life experiences with considerable lack of uniformity in the provision of credits for this type of learning. On the other hand, colleges and universities also use varying criteria for admission to regular programs of instruction and, at the least, an external degree can provide older persons with useful credentials for employment even if they do not make the same academic demands as traditional courses of instruction.

A recent publication aims to help women who are thinking about entering or returning to college after spending several years in home-making pursuits; it demonstrates how nonmarket experiences can be used to obtain college credits and how women can undertake self-assessments in order to aid in curriculum and career choice.[37]

Women's Centers

The problems of reentrants are dealt with, in one way or another, in most women's centers, although in many cases, college affiliation results in a stress on education rather than on direct job-related services. Too close an association with a college or university may result in the neglect of the needs of women who seek assistance in obtaining jobs as soon as possible. Many women's centers have been established independent of any adjunct relationship with an educational institution, although several have been established within other types of organization. Foremost among the latter have been the centers developed by units of the Young Women's Christian Association which has continued to provide reentry services at an increasing number of locations while experimenting with new modes of delivery and broadening the range of beneficiaries.

In 1978, more than 150 YWCAs were conducting some type of program designed to aid women who were contemplating reentry to the work force. Of these programs, 119 were entitled "Women's Resource Centers" and were not exclusively directed toward reentrants. About 40 were projects limited to displaced homemakers, occasionally specifically designed to serve separated and divorced women, widows, "women reentering the job market," and those suffering from the "empty nest syndrome."

Some program titles are especially provocative. A Nashville, Tennessee, program for women aged 25 to 50 is called, "What are You Doing with the Rest of Your Life?" In Hastings, Nebraska, the YWCA reentry project is entitled, "Out of the Supermarket into the Job Market" and undertakes to demonstrate "How to get a job when your husband's against it, your children are too young, or you can't do anything anyway!" Several YWCA programs, as well as other women's centers, have received funding as providers of specified services under various governmental programs. The utilization of many of these centers by local authorities who are empowered to contract for employment-related assistance has been often based on the high community repute of the nonprofit services, and has also obviated the need for creating new entities which would simply duplicate available services.

Independent women's centers have also expanded rapidly. Although there is a great deal of diversity in services provided, clientele, and funding sources, the following description gives some idea of how a typical community-based women's center functions.

The center is usually organized by a coalition of local women, and initial funding is provided by community drives, foundation grants, and/or the local or state government. Many free-standing organizations have received funding from CETA for various purposes, as well as from WIN. Initial clientele has tended to consist of educated women looking for "more meaningful lives," but women of lower socioeconomic status have become a growing segment of center users, either through special outreach strategies, word-of-mouth, or referral.

Many centers which originally were designed to provide counseling and referral to higher education or vocational training eventually found it necessary to engage in job development as more and more clients sought prompt placement rather than training. Most of them, however, depend on referrals to other institutions for employment, training, schooling or other resources. In certain instances, women are expected to proceed on their own following counseling.

Employers increasingly have been interested in supplying job listings as an aid in compliance with affirmative action regulations. Workshops for employers are conducted by some centers to describe their talent pool and the availability of women for nontraditional jobs.

One conclusion from a study of a center in Grand Rapids, Michigan, by an outside evaluator was that:

So many of the . . . clients are seeking employment and come to the . . . center expecting to find otherwise unpublished job openings and instead are referred elsewhere (i.e., to employment agencies, newspaper advertisements and other sources of job information). Although this is a legitimate and valuable service, apparently it is not what many clients expect.[38]

A report of the experiences of another women's center described a common problem encountered in dealing with reentrants.

Women are so accustomed to thinking of their worth in terms of paid jobs that they often overlook or underrate their skills. We try to help them see that they may have considerable experience even if they've worked for the PTA, run a fund-raising campaign, or been active in a church, or community group. One woman who thought she really couldn't do anything had actually been supervising her husband's busy medical office—but without pay. She was astonished when we pointed out that she had been handling the tasks of bookkeeper, secretary, receptionist and office manager all at once.[39]

Centers for displaced homemakers. Many displaced homemaker centers were in operation prior to the 1978 CETA reauthorization. These centers are usually multipurpose organizations which offer a range of services to improve the employability of long-term homemakers who range in age from 35 to 60 years and over, and who have moved from a condition of secure dependence to insecure self-reliance. In addition to job counseling, most centers are designed to provide training, placement, job development and often job creation, as well as assistance in utilizing resources within the community for improving clients' qualifications for employment. In addition, services usually include assistance in resolving financial, legal, health, and other problems arising from displaced homemakers' changed status that may interfere with their ability to fully profit from employment-related aid.

At present, 19 states have passed displaced homemaker legislation, although not all of them have funded centers since several were waiting to see whether federal legislation would provide matching funds for such a purpose. Also, as noted earlier, some CETA and YWCA programs have focused on this client constituency, as do vocational education and other types of scholastic programs.

The aim of these centers is to prepare displaced homemakers to enter the labor market with sufficient confidence and qualifications to obtain and maintain employment that will provide them with an adequate level of support. Among the means utilized to achieve this aim is the conversion into marketable skills of proficiencies developed as homemakers and volunteers. Peer support is considered to be an important element in the transition from home to work, and most centers employ displaced homemakers in various capacities.

Clients range from welfare mothers nearing loss of AFDC eligibility to women who are middle class but no longer middle income. Educational attainment runs the gamut from noncompletion of high school to the Ph.D. In large numbers of cases, work experience has been peripheral and in the distant past. Some clients have attempted to return to the labor force but have failed to secure satisfactory employment, if any. Many still have children at home, although mostly of school age.

Apart from their distinctive clientele, displaced homemaker centers are far more likely to provide skill training and work experience than women's centers that serve all segments of the female population. Skill evaluation is also a major function that helps determine the necessity of training, although it is claimed that many of these women need the confidence provided by real training. If training is indicated, it is sometimes provided through internships at the centers, on-the-job, or at local non-profit or government agencies, vocational schools or community colleges. Centers with government support provide training stipends, usually on a sliding scale according to income.

Job creation is a central concern of many displaced homemaker centers. Its rationale is based on the difficulty experienced by many of these women in entering the existing job market, and the consequent desirability of recycling homemaker experiences into paid work. Paraprofessional jobs have turned out to be an especially promising arena for job creation for middle-aged reentrants, since many of these jobs are extensions of home or volunteer activity. Examples are paralegal and paramedical jobs, as well as jobs in half-way houses, community mental health programs, hospices, and home health care.

Additionally, displaced homemakers have been encouraged and assisted to establish their own businesses, sometimes through special arms of the centers. These efforts at self-employment include home and office cleaning contractors, dressmaking, handicrafts instruction, messenger services, etc. Preparation for these ventures includes counseling in assertiveness and stress management as well as instruction in insurance, tax and contract requirements, credit management and bookkeeping. Seed capital is often provided through loans from the Federal Small Business Administration.

The New Orleans, Louisiana, Center for Displace Homemakers provided the following client profite for April 17 to October 1, 1978, which gives some idea of the women who tend to be served by these organizations.

One client of a Center for Displaced Homemakers declared:

I believe Displaced Homemakers can help you think positively in order to accomplish anything. I was almost down to zero, feeling ill-at-ease because I was such a homebody for a long, long time. This program has helped my personality— it got me to open up and talk to people.

Another client, a 48-year-old high school dropout on welfare with only menial work experience reported:

I didn't know what steps to take so I began to watch T.V. and go to the state employment office. But it seemed like every step was the wrong one. Everything seems to have blocked me. The first concrete step was coming to the Displaced Homemakers Program. It was a handicap not knowing what to do.

A woman in her early thirties, who had been at home seven years said:

My husband and I are divorced; it became final last summer. We had rather a bitter battle and he won, so I get visitation rights to our son. I tried to get a job and

Table 6.11 Client Profile, New Orleans Center for Displaced Homemakers, April 17—October 1, 1978

Number of Enrollees: 96

	Percentage of Total Enrollees
Economic status	
Economically disadvantaged	89
Not Economically disadvantaged	11
Marital status	
Separated	34
Married	11
Divorced	30
Widowed	25
Ethnic background	
Black	50
White	48
Other	2
Education	
Grade school (1-8)	11
Some high school (9-11)	19
High school diploma	45
Some college (1-3 years)	19
College degree	5
Masters degree	1
Age	
Under 40	22
40—49	41
50—59	34
Over 60	3
Length of marriage	
1—9 years	15
10—19 years	24
20—29 years	40
30—39 years	19
Over 40 years	2
Children	
Living at home	67
Adolescent (ages 14—18)	44
Under 18 years	50

couldn't find anything. I went to every place I could think of for a job, even if I knew I didn't want it, but if I had to I would do it. I was really down when I finally went to Women's Employable, a federally funded program for women who are out on their own again. I really don't have much of an income; the settlement from my divorce I can barely live on will stop in January, 1979. Many of the woman didn't have that.

Rural centers for displaced homemakers have been established in some states, although staff members find it much more difficult to assist these women than those in cities, not only because of their isolation but because of their traditionalism which prevents them from seeking help. "When they come to us," said one rural counselor, "it is pretty desperate, because they have used all the resources they have."[40]

The estimated cost of placement at the first center to be established in Oakland, California, was $2,063 per woman, "a figure far below placement costs for the traditional manpower programs." Every woman who applies to a Displaced Homemakers Centers has been described as a potential relief recipient: "They are all in the 'spendown' process prior to becoming eligible for general assistance. Any help that these women get at this point in time is a preventative measure which in the long-run will be a potential large saving to the State."[41]

Catalyst

In the same way that increasing numbers of entrepreneurs have been able to create and expand producers' services in the United States by selling specialized expertise (advertising, legal, accounting, pension, computer, etc.) to business firms who thereby avoid the necessity of establishing auxiliaries of their own, so too have nonprofit agencies led to the introduction of providers' services. In the case of women's centers, the leading organization of this type is Catalyst, which is essentially an informational resource for a network of approximately 185 autonomous local women's resource centers. Its principal service is the production of a variety of publications about women's career options and other relevant topics. It also assists in training and supervising the staffs of centers and aids employers in recruiting high-level female personnel, including members of corporate boards of directors. A nonprofit undertaking, it is supported by private foundations and a number of corporations. It offers its services to many projects with a reentrant constituency so that its publications and other services are designed to appeal to a broad range of female job seekers. Essentially, it obviates the need of individual centers to prepare their own guidance materials and, through a quarterly newsletter, it provides information about new ventures and services.

In terms of the job search, it cannot, by virtue of its national membership, provide any help with respect to local job opportunities. Moreover, its publications tend to be geared to middle-income, college-educated women and considerable effort is expended upon upgrading corporate women. Although it undoubtedly serves a worthwhile purpose, its primary attention is focused on the most socially or economically advantaged women.

Temporary Help Firms

Reentrants frequently turn to private temporary help firms (THF) as either the first step in returning to the labor market or as a means of making a partial recommitment to work. For reentrants, the THF may serve four major needs: flexibility in the allocation of time devoted to paid work, homemaking and/or leisure pursuits; opportunities for testing skills in the workplace; information about work settings and employers to guide an eventual search for permanent employment; and a sufficient taste of market work to judge whether it is palatable. A survey in the mid 1970s estimated that of 1.5 million THF employees at that time, temporary work provided reentry or entry for at least 300,000 (37.2 percent).

About 70 percent of the persons employed by one THF surburban office are reentrants, ranging in age from 35 to 55, but principally women in their forties, a growing proportion of whom are reentrants. Age discrimination was said to be no problem, not only because customers are not permitted to specify age requirements, but also because many of them prefer "mature" women.

Most reentrants who seek temporary jobs through this office have had earlier employment experience, usually in white-collar jobs, and most of their reentry jobs are in the same occupational area. The firm tries to place workers as soon as possible after they have been interviewed and tested, and they often do so on the same day, especially if they have skills in high demand. The temporary help firm sets pay rates according to the complexity of the job, but hourly wages of their employees are usually lower than those received by full-time employees working in the same firm.

The temporary jobs are for full days but may be for part-week. Many women deliberately seek the opportunity to work for as many different employers as possible, presumably as a means of assessing potential permanent work sites. It was estimated that from 50 to 60 percent of the reentrants remain as employees of the temporary service for only four months and sever connections because they have been hired on a permanent basis by their temporary employer or have decided to seek permanent employment, or because they have decided not to continue working.

Employers

Reentrants with acceptable job qualifications often are a preferred source of labor supply for many employers, particularly in clerical, retail sales and service jobs. Their main competitors are young female entrants who, while having the advantage of recency of training, still suffer from employer presumptions about eventual exit from the labor force as well as about the higher rate of turnover during job market exploration.

Adult women are increasingly being recognized as a stable and reliable work force, although precise age matters. There is a distinct difference in employer acceptance of reentrants in their thirties when they are seen as having long work lives ahead, and those in their forties and fifties who, regardless of qualifications, continue to face age discrimination. Thus, reentrants may not only have to compete with young entrants but with younger reentrants.

A 38-year-old reentrant to employment after a 12-year absence said:

More is accepted now. There is more freedom. It seems that there are so many women in the workforce that if you have a family and obligations, they're much more understanding. At least they have been here to me.

A chemist who returned to her last employer after a long absence told the following tale:

When I went back to the personnel office and filled out an application, I didn't mention that I had actually spoken to the department head—I just applied through the normal channels. My application was lost and they did not respond. Then the department head's office called me back and said to come in and apply again. I don't know if I would have gotten the job if I had gone just to the employment office, because I think my age was against me and 14 years away from the field.

A few comments from contented reentrants are in order. A 34-year-old secretary absent from work for eleven years said:

At last I'm free to be out and working. That's what I've been wanting to do for a long time. I think working gives a woman a lot more freedom to be herself. It's a matter of being independent. It's a good feeling.

A 32-year-old divorcee working as a technical assistant for a repertory theatre:

I genuinely love this job. People think I'm off the wall because sometimes I work all night. When I say I have to work, friends say, 'That's too bad,'' but I say, "No, I love it!'

Finally, from a 50-year-old teacher's aide:

Yes you get tired but we are so determined that we are going to do this that we get up the next morning bright-eyed and bushytailed, where a younger person might not do that . . . I think the business world is really missing the boat if they don't hire older people. We have so much to give.

FINDINGS AND RECOMMENDATIONS

Summary of Findings

A conglomeration of separate and intermingled public, voluntary and private services provides various types of assistance to women reentrants and delayed entrants to the American labor force, usually conjointly with other population groups. While some programs appear promising, in the absence of data distinguishing program participants, no estimates can be made about utilization, outcomes or costs, as these apply to reentrants alone. Hence, neither benefits nor beneficiaries can be clearly distinguished.

It is clear, however, that reentrants have a low position in the hierarchy of targets for public employment and training. Most public programs have been largely directed toward unemployed and underemployed persons in the labor force and not toward individuals out of the labor force who include large numbers of those reentrants most in need of assistance before attempting to negotiate the labor market.

In addition, the practice of creaming the most employable women for program admission, and self-selection by more sophisticated middle-class reentrants, results in both superfluous assistance for certain women and neglect of the hardest-to-employ. In effect, the receipt of reentry aid is fortuitous rather than meaningfully related to need.

The creation of employable women out of the most socioeconomically disadvantaged is no easy task, and it is not surprising that little success has been achieved in programs that demand rapid placement. Supported work holds promise, although here and elsewhere occupational sex segregation limits job opportunities and earnings sufficiency. Nevertheless, reentrants are hesitant about entering nontraditional fields despite their economic advantages. Attempts to press middle-aged women to eschew traditional occupations may be better directed to upgrading employment opportunities within these occupations.

Although withdrawal from the labor force is becoming less frequent than in the past and, where exits occur, the relative brevity of the period of absence may obviate the need for special employment aid, for some time to come there probably will be large numbers of women who will wait for many years to enter or reenter the work force. A more coordinated and selective approach to reentry assistance than currently exists should prove socially and personally rewarding.

Recommendations

The majority of adult women who enter or reenter the labor force in the United States appears to be able to make the transition from home to workplace without resorting to formal assistance, but those who need and want help in facilitating placement are often at a loss how to proceed.

One agency should be designated as the place of first resort for reentrants and delayed entrants. Its primary function would be to enable these women to assess their job skills in light of local job opportunities, and to devise individual plans or procedures for job search or job preparation. The obvious agency for this purpose is the State Employment Service since it is in place, it is free, and its offices are fairly generally accessible. What would be required of the ES is the assignment of expert reentry counselors at all offices, who would be thoroughly conversant with the types of problems that confront reentrants and with the range of possible solutions.

In order to attract reentrants, more emphasis must be placed on outreach of all types. The institution of specialized service of this type should be of significant benefit to women who flounder because they have no guides for action and to those who incur unnecessary training or educational costs because of misapprehensions about their employability.

There is no way of determining the extent to which reentrants are receiving beneficial job-related assistance, because agencies that deal with them do not provide relevant data. Such providers of employment and training assistance as the Employment Service, CETA, WIN, apprenticeship programs, educational institutions etc. should be required to collect and disseminate data that provide detailed descriptions of participants and outcomes in place of the disaggregated statistics currently available. This would facilitate evaluations of program processes and performances with respect to reentrants and would be generally helpful in programmatic assessments. In addition the Current Population Survey should introduce questions designed to clarify various aspects of the reentry process, including fulfillment of entry intentions after periods of lengthy absence from the labor force, not simply absence from full-time employment.

Legislative recognition of the displaced homemaker as a target for employment assistance has been achieved but this is only one solution to the problems faced by these women. The financial gap confronting many displaced homemakers could be mitigated by means other than reentry. While services to women who wish to enter the labor market and are young enough to be able to envision a substantial future worklife are desirable, consideration should be given to alternatives for others. Measures that would qualify homemakers for unemployment insurance, or that would provide earlier eligibility for social security payments under the same conditions, can have particular value for women of preretirement age whose job prospects may be poor. Training costs may not always be warranted in cases where such women are in late middle age and would rather not work. A reorientation toward the recognition of the economic contribution of homemaking would permit these women to avail themselves of the worker option of early retirement.

There is no evidence that the problems of reentrants are sufficiently different from those of other work aspirants to require the establishment of special employment and training programs.

Access to education and training should be available on the basis of requirements rather than on age or previous labor force status. Distinctive reentry counseling needs must be addressed, but this can be done without establishing separate programs that have similar informational, training and experience components. The problem of age discrimination is an issue unrelated to employment preparation per se and must be dealt with through the proper legal channels.

Mandatory labor force entry or reentry of welfare mothers has not led to any appreciable increase in self-sufficiency largely because of inadequate attention to improving their employability and to the development of suitable jobs. If adult female AFDC recipients are to become self-sustaining members of the regular labor force, they require intensive preparatory and supportive services that are not generally available through the WIN program. Job development should be undertaken in conjunction with training efforts to insure that preparation is meaningfully related to adequate employment opportunities. Schooling in basic educational competencies should be provided prior to eligibility for WIN at sites with child care facilities so that WIN can concentrate on specific job-related training and work experience. Research is needed to determine the precise aspects of various services that lead to the most successful long-run outcomes.

Screening of WIN eligibles should distinguish among women with recent experience who may need only facilitation of acceptable placement; those with little or no experience who can be encouraged to enter the work force if assured of training and promising jobs; and those who are not likely to benefit from services because they are predisposed to concentrate exclusively upon their maternal responsibilities. There is no social or economic rationale for investing in job-related services when an unsuccessful outcome is foreordained because of a woman's disinclination to work while her children are young.

Although low-income nonwelfare reentrants comprise a significant segment of discouraged workers who need jobs but who refrain from seeking employment because of the lack of marketable skills, many are now excluded from eligibility for CETA programs. A spell of unemployment should not be a sine qua non for CETA. A family income at or near the poverty level in conjunction with discouragement due to lack of skill and/or work experience should be sufficient to qualify a woman for reentry assistance. It is unrealistic to disqualify women for services that might enable them to improve their income position particularly when the alternative is likely to be public transfer payments.

There is insufficient information about the process of reentry to permit a determination of the variables that lead to long-run success and failure. Longitudinal data and in-depth research should be utilized to analyze more fully the personal and market factors that influence favorable reentry outcomes, including the contribution of assistance of various types, and the impact of age upon employment opportunities.

The absence of quality child care services and of mandatory maternity leave exacerbates the reentry problem because many women are forced to leave the labor force as a consequence and to prolong their absences. The costs of reentry relative to the cost of improved day care services of various types should be investigated in order to determine the impact of improved child care services upon their work plans.

Studies should also be initiated to compare the experiences of firms which do and do not provide maternity leaves with a view to discovering any differential effects influenced by the right to return.

The success of reentry ultimately depends upon the ability of the economy to provide sufficient good jobs. Apart from the question of inter-group job competition which has yet to be answered fully, the growth in the total female labor force must be addressed in positive ways, instead of through attempts to discourage the labor force participation of married women. Explorations of work-sharing and other kinds of restructured scheduling should be intensified as part of a total strategy that recognizes the regenerative effects of job creation.

NOTES

1. Center for Human Resources Research, The Ohio State University, *Dual Careers*, R&D Monograph 21 (Washington, D.C.: U.S. vols. 1–4. Department of Labor, 1970–76). Vol. 4, p. 18.

2. Congressional Budget Office, *Child Care and Preschool: Options for Federal Support* (Washington, D.C.: U.S. Government Printing Office, 1978), p. xi.

3. Ibid., p. 24.

4. Sue Mittenthal, "After Baby, Whither the Career?," *the New York Times*, February 4, 1979, p. C1.

5. Frank L. Mott and David Shapiro, "Pregnancy, Motherhood and Work Activity," in *Women, Work and Family*, ed. Frank L. Mott (Lexington, Mass.: Lexington Books, 1976), p. 29.

6. Edward I. Steinberg, "Labor Mobility in 1960–65 and 1970–75," *Survey of Current Business* (January 1979), p. 25.

7. Rachel A. Rosenfeld, "Breaks in Women's Employment and Labor Market Re-entry." Paper presented at annual meeting of Canadian Sociology and Anthropology Association, Fredericton, N.B., June 1977.

8. Rena Bartos, "What Every Marketer Should Know About Women," *Harvard Business Review* (May–June 1978), p. 81.

9. Francine d. Blau, "Longitudinal Patterns of Female Labor Force Participation" in *Dual Careers*, Vol. 4, op. cit.

10. Carol Jusenius and Steven H. Sandell, "Barriers to Entry and Re-entry Into the Labor Force." Paper presented at Workshop on Research Needed to Improve the Employment and Employability of Women, U.S. Department of Labor, Women's Bureau, June 1, 1974.

11. Juanita Kreps and Robert Clark, *Sex, Age, and Work* (Baltimore: Johns Hopkins University Press, 1975), pp. 17–18.

12. *Dual Careers*, vol. 3, 1975. op. cit., pp. 8–9.

13. Glen G. Cain, *Married Women in the Labor Force* (Chicago: University of Chicago Press, 1966), p. 19.

14. U.S. Congress, House of Representatives, Committee on Education and Labor. *Displaced Homemaker, Hearings*, Statement of Hon. Yvonne Brathwaite Burke before the Subcommittee on Employment Opportunities, 95th Congress, 1977. p. 17.

15. Sheila S. Keeny, Urban Institute, letter to *The New York Times*, September 24, 1977.

16. Proceedings, Displaced Homemakers Conference, Baltimore, MD., October 1978.

17. *Dual Careers*, vol. 1, 1970. Op. cit.

18. Ralph E. Smith, "The Impact of Macroeconomic Conditions on Employment Opportunities for Women." A Study Prepared for the Joint Economic Committee, Congress of the United States (Washington, D.C.: U.S. Government Printing Office, 1977), p. 24.

19. Linda J. Waite, "Projecting Female Labor Force Participation from Sex-Role Attitudes," University of Illinois, September 1978.

20. Anne Statham Macke, Paula M. Hudis and Don Larrick, "Sex-Role Attitudes and Employment Among Women: A Dynamic Model of Change and Continuity." Paper Presented at the Secretary of Labor's Invitational Conference on the National Longitudinal Surveys of Mature Women, January 26, 1977.

21. Paul O. Flaim and Howard N. Fullerton, Jr., "Labor Force Projections to 1990: Three Possible Paths," *Monthly Labor Review* December 1978.

22. Joan M. McCrea, "Retraining Older Women: Needs and Programs," University of Texas at Arlington, 1978.

23. Charles Nye and Patricia Mapp, *Women in Apprenticeship—Why Not?*, Manpower Resource Monograph No. 33 (Washington, D.C.: U.S. Department of Labor, Manpower Administration, 1974).

24. Carl Rosenfeld, "Jobseeking Methods Used by American Workers," *Monthly Labor Review*, August 1975.

25. Ibid.

26. Camil Associates, *Recruitment, Job Search, and the United States Employment Service*, R&D Monograph 43 (Washington, D.C.: U.S. Department of Labor, Employment and Training Administration, 1976).

27. Samuel Z. Klausner, *Six Years in the Lives of the Impoverished: An Examination of the WIN Thesis* (Philadelphia: Center for Research on the Acts of Man, 1978), p. 16.

28. Ibid.

29. Bradley R. Schiller, "Lessons from WIN: A Manpower Evaluation," *The Journal of Human Resources*, 13, no. 4 (Fall 1978).

30. Employment and Training Administration, *The Work Incentive (WIN) Program and Related Experiences*, R&D Monograph 49 (Washington, D.C.: Department of Labor, 1977), p. 2.

31. Rebecca Maynard with Irwin Garfinkel and Valerie Leach, *Analysis of Nine-Month Interviews for Supported Work: Results of An Early AFDC Sample* (New York: Manpower Demonstration and Research Corporation, 1977).

32. *Supported Work* 5 (Fall 1976–Winter 1977), p. 13.

33. Marilyn Manser and Myles Maxfield, *Targeting CETA and Single Heads of Families*, preliminary draft (Washington, D.C.: Mathematica Policy Research, 1979), p. 128.

34. The Fund for the Improvement of Postsecondary Education, *Reports from the Fund— Projects/Women* (Washington, D.C.: U.S. Department of Health, Education, and Welfare, Education Division, 1977) p. 1.

35. Carol Eliason, *Women in Community and Junior Colleges* (Washington, D.C.: American Association of Community and Junior Colleges, 1977).

36. Conrad Katzenmeyer and Frances Lawrence, *On-Site Assessment of the Women in Science Career Facilities Program*, National Science Foundation, February 1978, p. 5.

37. Ruth B. Ekstrom, Abigail M. Harris, and Marlaine E. Lockheed, *How to Get College Credit For What You Have Learned As a Homemaker And Volunteer* (Princeton, N.J.: Educational Testing Service, 1977).

38. Women's Resource Center, *A Case Study* (Grand Rapids, Mich.: Women's Resource Center, 1976), p. 24.

39. Ruth Glick and Nancy Baggett, "Free Help for Women Who Are Looking for Work," *Baltimore Sunday Sun*, March 1977.

40. Displaced Homemakers Conference, op. cit.

41. Testimony of Jean Dixon, Hearing on H. R. 28, The Displaced Homemaker Act, op. cit., p. 85.

BIBLIOGRAPHY

Astin, Helen S. *Some Action of Her Own*. Lexington, MA: Lexington Books, 1976.

Center for Women's Opportunities. *The Status of Women in Two-Year Colleges*. Washington: American Association of Community and Junior Colleges (n.d.).

Congressional Budget Office. *CETA Reauthorization Issues*. Washington: U.S. Government Printing Office, August 1978.

———. *Postsecondary Education: The Current Federal Role in Alternative Approaches*. Washington: U.S. Government Printing Office, 1977.

Congress of the United States, Joint Economic Committee, Sub-committee in Economic Growth and Stabilization, *American Women Workers in a Full Employment Economy*. Washington: U.S. Government Printing Office, 1977.

Jaffe, A. J., and Ridley, Jeanne Clare. *Employment of Women and Fertility*. Washington: U.S. Department of Health, Education and Welfare, 1976.

Jones, Ethel B., and Long, James E. *Women in Part-Week Work*. Washington: U.S. Department of Labor, Employment and Training Administration, 1978.

Kreps, Juanita M., ed. *Women in the American Economy: A Look to the 1980s*. Englewood, N.J.: Prentice-Hall, 1976.

Lloyd, Cynthia, ed. *Sex Discrimination and the Division of Labor*. New York: Columbia University Press, 1975.

Mathematica Policy Research. *The National Supported Work Demonstration: Effects During the First 18 Months*. New York: Manpower Demonstration Research Corporation, April 1979.

National Advisory Council on Extension and Continuing Education. *Continuing Need, Continuing Response, Continuing Education*. Annual Report 1977. Washington: U.S. Government Printing Office, 1977.

National Commission for Manpower Policy. *CETA: An Analysis of the Issues*. Special Report No. 23. Washington: U.S. Government Printing Office.

―――. *Labor Market Intermediaries*. Special Report No. 22. Washington: U.S. Government Printing Office, 1978.

―――. *Women's Changing Roles at Home and on the Job*. Special Report No. 26; Washington: U.S. Government Printing Office, 1978.

Oppenheimer, Valerie Kincade. *The Female Labor Force in the United States*. Population Monograph Series No. 5 Berkeley, CA: University of California, 1970.

Ross, Heather L., and Sawhill, Isabel V. *Time of Transition*. Washington: The Urban Institute, 1975.

Stromberg, Ann H., and Harkess, Shirley, eds. *Women Working*. Palo Alto, CA: Mayfield Publishing Co., 1978.

Survey Research Center. *Five Thousand American Families—Patterns of Economic Progress*, vol. 5. Eds. Greg J. Duncan and James N. Morgan. Ann Arbor, MI: Institute for Social Research, 1977.

U.S. Department of Commerce, Bureau of the Census. *A Statistical Portrait of Women in the United States*. Washington: U.S. Government Printing Office, 1976.

U.S. Department of Health, Education and Welfare. *Participation in Adult Education*. Final Report, 1972. Washington: U.S. Government Printing Office, 1976.

U.S. Department of Labor. *Years for Decision*. Manpower Research Monograph No. 24. Vols. 1-4. Washington: U.S. Government Printing Office, 1971-1978.

U.S. Department of Labor, Employment and Training Administration. *Women and Work*. R&D Monograph 46. Washington: U.S. Government Printing Office, 1977.

U.S. Department of Labor, Women's Bureau, 1975 *Handbook on Women Workers*. Bulletin 297, 1975.

U.S. House of Representatives, *Comprehensive Employment and Training Amendments of 1978*. Report No. 95-1124, May 10, 1978.

U.S. House of Representatives. Select Committee on Aging and The Subcommittee on Retirement Income and Employment. *Women in Midlife—Security and Fulfillment*. Washington: U.S. Government Printing Office, 1978.

U.S. Senate. Hearings Before the Subcommittee on Employment, Poverty, and Migratory Labor of the Committee on Human Resources on S. 418, *Displaced Homemakers Act, 1977*. Washington: U.S. Government Printing Office, 1975.

―――. Special Committee on Aging. *Women and Social Security: Adapting to a New Era*. Washington: U.S. Government Printing Office, 1975.

Valley, John R., *Career Education of Adults*. Princeton, N.J.: Educational Testing Service, 1977.

Wolf, Wendy C., and Rosenfeld, Rachel. *Sex Structure of Occupations and Job Mobility*. Reprint 293. Madison, WI: Institute on Research on Poverty, University of Wisconsin, 1978.

Yohalem, Alice M. *The Careers of Professional Women: Commitment and Conflict*. Montclair, N.J.: Allanheld, Osmun & Co., 1979.

Index

Agricultural employment, 3; in France, 65, 69, 102-3; in Germany, 23, 27-30

Birth rate: decline in, 8, 18; in Germany, 18, 21-22; in United Kingdom, 162; in United States, 227
Blacks (see United States: minorities, non-whites)
Britain (see United Kingdom)

Carter, Jimmy, 10
Child care, 3-5, 15 (see also France; Germany; Sweden; United Kingdom; United States)
Clark, Robert, 240

Education of women, 3, 15 (see also France; Germany; Sweden; United Kingdom; United States)
Equal employment opportunities, 5, 6, 11-12

Family allowances, 11
France, 59-106; AFPA (Association for the Professional Training of Adults), 82-83, 85, 86, 97, 99; agricultural employment, 65, 69, 102-3; ANFOPAR (National Association for the Training and Occupational Improvement of Rural Adults), 103; A.N.P.E. (National Employment Agency), 84, 85, 89, 91-92, 94-100, 104; Associations under the Law of 1901, 90; Caen, 72, 73, 90, 93; Calvados, 61, 93; C.E.S.I. (Center of Higher Industrial Studies), 95; Chambers of Commerce, 96; child care, 11, 75-76, 87-88, 101, table, 88; children / as reasons

for work interruption, 72-76 / and women's return to work, 74-82/; C.I.F. (Women's Information Center), 91, 98, 100; civil servants, 65, 88-89; C.N.D.P. (National Center for Pedagogical Documentation), 83; C.N.T.E. (National Center of Education by Correspondence), 83; commercial sector of employment, 65, 67, 69; D.A.F.C.O. (Continuing Training Delegation), 97-98; dependent children, 74-75, 85-87, 89; divorcees, widows, and single women, 74-77, 85, 86, 89, 91, 101; education, government agencies and associations, 82-83; employment of women / aid in job placement, 89-92/ institutions and agencies for, 84-86, 90-100/; employment policies, 9, 82-90; executives, employment of, 67, 69; family allowances, 75, 77-78, 86-87, 89, 91, 102; G.R.E.T.A. (Groups of Establishments), training programs, 83, 93, 96, 103; I.F.O.C.O.P., 96-97; industrial employment, 65-67, 69; labor force / active population, 61, 65-67, 69, tables, 63, 68 / men and women, occupational distribution, 67, 69, table, 68 /; legislation on employment and training, 82-90; Lyon, 61, 72, 73, 90, 93-96; maternity leave, 60, 88; Ministry of Education, 82-83; Ministry of Labor, 82-85; National Association for Widows of Civilians, 91; National Health Insurance, 75; National Pact for the Employment of Youth, Second, 60, 85-86, 100; parental leave, 11, 60, 72-73, 88-89; Parisian Center of Management, 95; Paris